Migration and Marriage in Asian Contexts

This book analyses how Asian migrants adapt and assimilate into their host societies, and how this assimilation differs across their sociodemographic backgrounds, ethnic profiles, and political contexts. The diversities in Asian migrants' assimilation trajectories challenge the assumption that given time, migrants will eventually integrate holistically into their host societies.

This book captures the diverse patterns and trajectories of assimilation by going beyond marriage migration to look at how family formation processes are shaped by migration driven by reasons other than marriage. Using quantitative, qualitative, and mixed-method analyses, not only does this book uncover the nuances of the link between marriage and migration, but it also widens methodological repertoires in research on marriage and migration. It also captures various social outcomes that may have been influenced by migration, including migrants' economic well-being, cultural assimilation, subjective well-being, and gender inequality vis-à-vis marriages. This book further embeds the studies in the Asian contexts by drawing on individual countries' unique policies relevant to cross-cultural marriages, the persistent impacts of extended families, the patriarchal traditions, and systems of religion and caste.

The chapters in this book were originally published as a special issue of the *Journal of Ethnic and Migration Studies*.

Zheng Mu is Assistant Professor of Sociology at the National University of Singapore. Her research interests include trends, social determinants, and consequences of marriage and family behaviours, with focus on how marriage and family serve as major inequality-generating mechanisms.

Wei-Jun Jean Yeung is Provost-Chair Professor of Sociology at the National University of Singapore. She is the founding Director of the Centre for Family and Population Research and the Cluster Leader of the Changing Family in Asia research cluster in the Asia Research Institute at NUS.

Research in Ethnic and Migration Studies

Series editor: **Paul Statham**, *Director, Sussex Centre for Migration Research (SCMR), University of Sussex, UK*

The *Research in Ethnic and Migration Studies* series publishes the results of high-quality, cutting-edge research that addresses key questions relating to ethnic relations, diversity and migration. The series is open to a range of disciplines and brings together research collaborations on specifically defined topics on all aspects of migration and its consequences, including migration processes, migrants and their experiences, ethnic relations, discrimination, integration, racism, transnationalism, citizenship, identity and cultural diversity. Contributions are especially welcome when they are the result of comparative research, either across countries, cities or groups. All articles have previously been published in the *Journal of Ethnic and Migration Studies (JEMS)*, which has a rigorous peer review system. Collective volumes in this series are either the product of Special Issues published in the journal or published articles that the Editor has selected from individual submissions.

Migration and Marriage in Asian Contexts
Edited by Zheng Mu and Wei-Jun Jean Yeung

Thai-Western Mobilities and Migration
Intimacy within Cross-Border Connections
Edited by Paul Statham, Sarah Scuzzarello, Sirijit Sunanta and Alexander Trupp

Undocumented and Unaccompanied
Children of Migration in the European Union and the United States
Edited by Cecilia Menjívar and Krista M. Perreira

Children of the Crisis
Ethnographic Perspectives on Unaccompanied Refugee Youth in and En Route to Europe
Edited by Annika Lems, Kathrin Oester and Sabine Strasser

Diaspora Governance and Transnational Entrepreneurship
The Rise of an Emerging Global Social Pattern in Migration Studies
Edited by Ricard Zapata-Barrero and Shahamak Rezaei

The Microfoundations of Diaspora Politics
Edited by Alexandra Délano Alonso and Harris Mylonas

Aspiration, Desire and the Drivers of Migration
Edited by Francis Collins and Jørgen Carling

For more information about this series, please visit: www.routledge.com/Research-in-Ethnic-and-Migration-Studies/book-series/REMS

Migration and Marriage in Asian Contexts

Edited by
Zheng Mu and Wei-Jun Jean Yeung

LONDON AND NEW YORK

First published 2022
by Routledge
2 Park Square, Milton Park, Abingdon, Oxon OX14 4RN

and by Routledge
605 Third Avenue, New York, NY 10158

Routledge is an imprint of the Taylor & Francis Group, an informa business

© 2022 Taylor & Francis

All rights reserved. No part of this book may be reprinted or reproduced or utilised in any form or by any electronic, mechanical, or other means, now known or hereafter invented, including photocopying and recording, or in any information storage or retrieval system, without permission in writing from the publishers.

Trademark notice: Product or corporate names may be trademarks or registered trademarks, and are used only for identification and explanation without intent to infringe.

British Library Cataloguing in Publication Data
A catalogue record for this book is available from the British Library

ISBN: 978-1-032-14659-1 (hbk)
ISBN: 978-1-032-14660-7 (pbk)
ISBN: 978-1-003-24040-2 (ebk)

DOI: 10.4324/9781003240402

Typeset in Minion Pro
by Newgen Publishing UK

Publisher's Note
The publisher accepts responsibility for any inconsistencies that may have arisen during the conversion of this book from journal articles to book chapters, namely the inclusion of journal terminology.

Disclaimer
Every effort has been made to contact copyright holders for their permission to reprint material in this book. The publishers would be grateful to hear from any copyright holder who is not here acknowledged and will undertake to rectify any errors or omissions in future editions of this book.

Contents

Citation Information		vii
Notes on Contributors		ix
1	Introduction Wei-Jun Jean Yeung and Zheng Mu	1
2	Generation, education, and intermarriage of Asian Americans Zhenchao Qian and Yue Qian	18
3	Love in the melting pot: ethnic intermarriage in Jakarta Ariane J. Utomo	34
4	Internal migration, marriage timing and assortative mating: a mixed-method study in China Zheng Mu and Wei-Jun Jean Yeung	52
5	Do gender systems in the origin and destination societies affect immigrant integration? Vietnamese marriage migrants in Taiwan and South Korea Hsin-Chieh Chang	75
6	Happiness of female immigrants in cross-border marriages in Taiwan Chun-Hao Li and Wenshan Yang	94
7	Physical versus imagined communities: migration and women's autonomy in India Esha Chatterjee and Sonalde Desai	115
8	The decoupling of legal and spatial migration of female marriage migrants Tuen Yi Chiu and Susanne Y. P. Choi	135
9	Marital dissolution of transnational couples in South Korea Yool Choi, Doo-Sub Kim and Jungkyun Ryu	152

10 Transnational divorces in Singapore: experiences of low-income divorced marriage migrant women 178
Sharon Ee Ling Quah

11 Remarriages and transnational marriages in Hong Kong: implications and challenges 197
Mengni Chen and Paul Yip

Index 216

Citation Information

The chapters in this book were originally published in the *Journal of Ethnic and Migration Studies*, volume 46, issue 14 (2020). When citing this material, please use the original page numbering for each article, as follows:

Chapter 1
Migration and marriage in Asian contexts
Wei-Jun Jean Yeung and Zheng Mu
Journal of Ethnic and Migration Studies, volume 46, issue 14 (2020), pp. 2863–2879

Chapter 2
Generation, education, and intermarriage of Asian Americans
Zhenchao Qian and Yue Qian
Journal of Ethnic and Migration Studies, volume 46, issue 14 (2020), pp. 2880–2895

Chapter 3
Love in the melting pot: ethnic intermarriage in Jakarta
Ariane J. Utomo
Journal of Ethnic and Migration Studies, volume 46, issue 14 (2020), pp. 2896–2913

Chapter 4
Internal migration, marriage timing and assortative mating: a mixed-method study in China
Zheng Mu and Wei-Jun Jean Yeung
Journal of Ethnic and Migration Studies, volume 46, issue 14 (2020), pp. 2914–2936

Chapter 5
Do gender systems in the origin and destination societies affect immigrant integration? Vietnamese marriage migrants in Taiwan and South Korea
Hsin-Chieh Chang
Journal of Ethnic and Migration Studies, volume 46, issue 14 (2020), pp. 2937–2955

Chapter 6
Happiness of female immigrants in cross-border marriages in Taiwan
Chun-Hao Li and Wenshan Yang
Journal of Ethnic and Migration Studies, volume 46, issue 14 (2020), pp. 2956–2976

Chapter 7
Physical versus imagined communities: migration and women's autonomy in India
Esha Chatterjee and Sonalde Desai
Journal of Ethnic and Migration Studies, volume 46, issue 14 (2020), pp. 2977–2996

Chapter 8
The decoupling of legal and spatial migration of female marriage migrants
Tuen Yi Chiu and Susanne Y. P. Choi
Journal of Ethnic and Migration Studies, volume 46, issue 14 (2020), pp. 2997–3013

Chapter 9
Marital dissolution of transnational couples in South Korea
Yool Choi, Doo-Sub Kim and Jungkyun Ryu
Journal of Ethnic and Migration Studies, volume 46, issue 14 (2020), pp. 3014–3039

Chapter 10
Transnational divorces in Singapore: experiences of low-income divorced marriage migrant women
Sharon Ee Ling Quah
Journal of Ethnic and Migration Studies, volume 46, issue 14 (2020), pp. 3040–3058

Chapter 11
Remarriages and transnational marriages in Hong Kong: implications and challenges
Mengni Chen and Paul Yip
Journal of Ethnic and Migration Studies, volume 46, issue 14 (2020), pp. 3059–3077

For any permission-related enquiries please visit:
www.tandfonline.com/page/help/permissions

Notes on Contributors

Hsin-Chieh Chang, Department of Sociology, School of Social Development and Public Policy, Fudan University, Shanghai, China.

Esha Chatterjee, Department of Humanities and Social Sciences, Indian Institute of Technology Kanpur, Uttar Pradesh 208016, India.

Mengni Chen, Department of Sociology, University of Copenhagen, Nørregade 10, 1165 København, Denmark.

Tuen Yi Chiu, Department of Sociology and Social Policy, Lingnan University, Tuen Mun, Hong Kong.

Susanne Y. P. Choi, Department of Sociology, The Chinese University of Hong Kong, Hong Kong.

Yool Choi, Department of Sociology, Chung-Ang University, Seoul, South Korea.

Sonalde Desai, Department of Sociology, University of Maryland College Park, College Park, MD, USA.

Doo-Sub Kim, Department of Sociology, Hanyang University, Seoul, South Korea.

Chun-Hao Li, Department of Social and Policy Sciences, Yuan Ze University, Taoyuan City, Taiwan; Research Center for Humanities and Social Sciences, Academia Sinica, Taipei, Taiwan.

Zheng Mu, Department of Sociology, National University of Singapore, Singapore; Asia Research Institute, National University of Singapore, Singapore; Centre for Family and Population Research, National University of Singapore, Singapore.

Yue Qian, Department of Sociology, University of British Columbia, Vancouver, BC, Canada.

Zhenchao Qian, Department of Sociology, Brown University, Providence, RI, USA.

Sharon Ee Ling Quah, University of Wollongong, Wollongong, Australia.

Jungkyun Ryu, Department of Issues & Strategy Analysis, Gyeonggi Research Institute, Gyeonggido, South Korea.

Ariane J. Utomo, School of Geography, The University of Melbourne, Carlton, Australia.

Wenshan Yang, Institute of Sociology, Academia Sinica, Taipei, Taiwan.

Wei-Jun Jean Yeung, Department of Sociology, National University of Singapore, Singapore; Asia Research Institute, National University of Singapore, Singapore; Centre for Family and Population Research, National University of Singapore, Singapore.

Paul Yip, Department of Social Work and Social Administration, The University of Hong Kong, Pokfulam, Hong Kong.

Introduction

Wei-Jun Jean Yeung and Zheng Mu

ABSTRACT
This article reviews literature on migration and marriage and highlights contributions of the papers in this special issue. The papers show that Asian marriage migrants' experience of integration and assimilation are complex, nuanced, and heterogeneous across migrants' sociodemographic backgrounds, ethnic profiles, and political contexts. The heterogeneities in Asian marriage migrants' assimilation trajectories challenge the classic assimilation theory which assumes an unilinear integration trajectory in all relevant aspects. This issue diversifies the academic discourses on migration and marriage by going beyond marriage migration to include how other types of migration shape family formation processes including divorce and remarriage. It also examines the mechanisms underlying the migration-marriage link. Finally, this special issue widens methodological repertoires in the field of marriage and migration by using quantitative, qualitative, and mixed-method analyses to divulge the complexity of the relationships. Topics examined in these papers include variations in economic well-being, cultural assimilation, gender inequality vis-à-vis marriages, migrants' subjective well-being, and how policies pertinent to cross-cultural marriages affect migrants. Unlike in the western societies where race/ethnic integration is a dominant concern, in Asia, the extended families of marriage migrants and their spouses, patriarchy, religion, and caste also play a big role in Asian migrants' family formation behaviours.

Introduction

Although most migration is motivated by better economic opportunities in the receiving communities, migrants' social lives are also greatly shaped by their migration experience because migration often occurs around the life stage of emerging adulthood and could last for an extended period of time (Juárez et al. 2013; Lee and Pol 1993; Liang 2001; Zenteno, Giorguli, and Gutiérrez 2013). An important but under-investigated aspect is how migration affects marriage, one of the major markers of transitioning to adulthood (Choi and Peng 2016; Kulu and Milewski 2008). Migrants' family formation behaviour has profound implications for their emotional well-being, lifestyle choices, as well as their socioeconomic prospects (Mu and Yeung 2018). This special issue aims to gain a better understanding of the relationship between migration and marriage through both qualitative and quantitative studies.

Asia has witnessed tremendous increase and change in both international and internal migration in recent decades. In 2017, of the 258 million international migrants worldwide, 106 million (41%) were born in Asia and 80 million (31%) currently live there (United Nations 2017). An increasing number of Asians have moved to other continents, most notably to North America and Europe, as well as across Asia.

With the surge in transnational marriages in Asia, countries such as Singapore, South Korea (hereafter, Korea), and Taiwan have seen a rise in local men tying the knot with women from countries such as Vietnam, Indonesia, and China (Jongwilaiwan and Thompson 2013). Constable (2005) uses the term 'global imagination' to suggest that in a transnational marriage, people imagine themselves as being in a different social geographical location. This imagined social geographical location facilitates the emergence of transnational 'marriage-scapes' which are driven by one's social imagination of gender, sexuality, and modernity. This is particularly true for women (Hondagneu-Sotelo 2011; Kim 2010). Studies have shown that migrant women negotiate their gender roles in both the sending and receiving communities (Jones and Shen 2008; Toyota 2008). They choose to enter an international marriage and marry up in order to improve their economic status back home, and to attain greater social status and increased autonomy in decision making, although research has documented both negative and positive impacts for those involved in cross-border marriages (Ehrenreich and Hochschild 2003; Huang, Yeoh, and Lam 2008). While they are motivated to pursue upward mobilities and productively contribute to both the sending and the receiving societies, they are often vulnerable and face economic, cultural, and legal constraints (Constable 2009; Yeoh et al. 2013). As a result, they are often in a continuum between being a 'victim' and 'agent', negotiating and strategising between the constraints and opportunities they face (Constable 2009; Ehrenreich and Hochschild 2003; Huang and Yeoh 2003; Lutz 2010; Quah 2020).

In addition to cross-border marriages, many countries experience rapid urbanisation during which large numbers of rural migrants move to urban areas (Jacka 2005; Lee and Pol 1993; Liang 2001). Disparities between the sending and receiving cities uniquely influence marital choices and lifestyles (Kulu and Milewski 2008; Mu and Yeung 2018). Such massive internal migration takes place in countries such as China, India, Indonesia, Vietnam, and Thailand (Dang, Goldstein, and McNally 1997; Desai and Banerji 2008; Liang 2001; Lucas 1997).

Migrants across Asia encounter a wide array of institutional, policy, and cultural contexts that shape their marriage behaviours, and the contextual heterogeneities have added nuances beyond the 'victim versus agent' binary (Constable 2009; Quah 2020). Not only has migration in Asia involved more ethnicities and countries of origin, it has also occurred in more diverse political and socioeconomic contexts with complex trajectories. As characterised by Vertovec (2007), this can be described as a situation of 'super-diversity.' For example, Singapore has a very high proportion of cross-national marriages with about 40% of all marriages per year involving a foreigner (Yeung and Hu 2018), and the foreign spouses often face substantial cultural and policy challenges (Huang, Yeoh, and Lam 2008; Quah 2020; Yeoh et al. 2013); in China, the residential registration system (*Hukou* system) greatly constrains internal migrants' family formation behaviours

(Fan 2008; Mu and Yeung 2018, 2020); Mainland China's unique administrative relationship and economic interactions with Hong Kong has added complications to the marriage markets in both regions (Chen and Yip 2020; Chiu and Choi 2020); in India, cultural norms of marriage in different regions and for different castes largely shape one's marital choices and behaviours expected after marriage (Bloch, Rao, and Desai 2004; Chatterjee and Desai 2020); in Indonesia, its diverse ethnic background has made patterns of assortative mating particularly complex across migration status and ethnicity (Utomo and McDonald 2016; Utomo 2020); in Korea and Taiwan, the diverse countries of origin of foreign brides create potential sources of tension and challenges for integration in an originally homogeneous society (Chang 2020; Choi, Kim, and Ryu 2020; Li and Yang 2020).

More recently, the changing distribution of Asian migrants' skills qualifications have led to more heterogeneous motivations for migration and more dynamic assimilation processes. Compared to earlier migrants who were predominantly low- or semi-skilled, more recent migrants have relatively higher level of skills and are more likely to stay longer in the receiving communities and assimilate there (Ishii 2016; Mu and Yeung 2018). They tend to seek new lifestyles beyond economic improvement, which include finding a spouse, starting a family and settling permanently in the receiving communities (Fan and Li 2002; Gaetano and Jacka 2013; Palriwala and Uberoi 2008). Consequently, migrants' marriage patterns are more diverse in terms of marriage timing, assortative mating choices, integration, and power relations between genders (Ishii 2016; Choi and Peng 2016). Particularly, given the rising transnational marriages and multiculturalism in many Asian countries, migration has profoundly shaped patterns of interethnic marriages (Utomo 2020). Some Asian migrants have also crossed continental boundaries to settle in countries with very different social and cultural backgrounds, such as North America (Qian and Qian 2020). This migration experience uniquely shapes their marriage patterns (Choi and Tienda 2018; Qian, Lichter, and Tumin 2018).

Earlier research on migration and marriage in Asia is largely qualitative in nature (Constable 2005, 2009; Yeoh et al. 2013; Fan 2003, 2008). Exceptions include articles in Kim (2008, 2012). This special collection includes articles based on quantitative (Chatterjee and Desai 2020; Chen and Yip 2020; Choi, Kim, and Ryu 2020; Qian and Qian 2020; Li and Yang 2020), qualitative (Chiu and Choi 2020; Quah 2020), and mixed-method analysis (Chang 2020; Mu and Yeung 2020; Utomo 2020). The papers systematically examine how the experience of migration has influenced individuals' family formation behaviours and related outcomes in assimilation and well-being, under diverse policy and cultural contexts across Asia. Collectively, this special issue seeks to better understand the patterns, mechanisms and issues underlying the migration-marriage link. Topics examined in the papers include variations in economic well-being, cultural assimilation, subjective well-being, gender inequality vis-à-vis marriages, marriage trajectories, and individuals' adaptation to policies pertinent to cross-cultural marriages.

Most of these papers were first presented in an international conference 'Migration and Marriage in Asia' on July 26-27, 2016, at the Asia Research Institute of the National University of Singapore convened by the guest editors. It is our hope that this collection will stimulate new theoretical development on migration and marriage and that scholars of migration, family studies, social demography, population studies, social work, and policy researchers, particularly those interested in Asian contexts, will find new insights from them.

Contextualising the migration and marriage experience in Asia

Each article in this issue contextualises the marriage migration experience in a particular society. Research on the link between marriage and migration often focuses on the assimilation, adaptation, and integration experiences of marriage migrants, particularly those who move across national boundaries (Constable 2005, 2009). It has been established in the literature that marriage migration is often driven by migrant women's motivations to alleviate their economic status back home and to attain greater socioeconomic status and an increased authority in decision-making (Ishii 2016). They tend to migrate from the Global South to the Global North to enter into an international marriage. Within the developmental hierarchies between the sending and the receiving countries, these marriages are often hypergamous in which the wives marry up in socioeconomic status (Jones and Shen 2008; Mu and Hu 2018). Constable (2005) uses the term 'global marriage-scapes' to describe this unique migration flow. This notion is consistent with the classic assimilation theory, which portrays the decision of migration as a rational process of the migrant to maximise their own and their families' well-being (Massey et al. 1993; Yinger 1981).

As a result, marriage migrants have often been portrayed within the continuum between 'victim' and 'agent' in recent literature. At one end, some studies have established that female marriage migrants, moving from less developed countries, are vulnerable and powerless in fully integrating into the receiving societies and achieving equality within the public and the domestic spheres with their local counterparts (Charsley 2005, 2006; Stephnitz 2009; Kim 2011). At the other end of the spectrum, other studies have argued that due to the hypergamous nature of cross-border marriages, marriage migrants have often managed to manoeuvre agency, realise upward mobility, and make contributions to both the sending and the receiving societies, which makes the portrayal of them as victims inaccurate (Brennan 2004; Cheng 2005; Chong 2014; Kempadoo 2005; Parker 2005; Yeoh et al. 2013). In reality, most marriage migrants move between the two extremes of 'victim' and 'agent', manoeuvring their lives through complex trajectories toward integration, empowerment, and achievements (Faier 2007; Constable 2009; Ehrenreich and Hochschild 2003; Quah 2020). As summarised by Portes (2007), the actual pattern and level of assimilation can be highly 'segmented,' depending on the specific mode of migration and the contexts in which they occur. Marriage migrants are faced with both constraints and opportunities. They resort to various resources and channels available to them in the political, economic, and cultural contexts to cope strategically and creatively with the problems they encounter in the hope of achieving survival, and even mobility and success.

Even though global hypergamy has been common, there are other patterns beyond the 'marriage-scapes' perspective in marriage migration that have started to receive academic attention (Ishii 2016). Some researchers reveal the heterogeneous directions of marriage migration (Kudo 2016; Sakai 2016; Lumayag 2016). That is, aside from the conventional move from the Global South to the Global North, increasingly more marriage migrants move from wealthier countries to poorer ones or move within the two regions, which add to the diversity in migrants' socioeconomic status, cultural assimilation and legal issues.

Aside from the direction of migration, trajectories of marriage migration have also become increasingly diverse, involving a combination of reversed, return and circular migration, due to the dynamic interactions between the migrants, the spouses, the receiving society and the sending societies (Tokoro 2016; Dealwis 2016). These migration trajectories have increased uncertainties in migrants' economic, legal, and cultural experiences, which makes it increasingly important for the migrants to resort to more dynamic and flexible coping strategies.

While cross-border marriages are influenced by differences in countries' economic development, legal systems, and cultural backgrounds (Constable 2005), complexities and unique patterns of social inequalities within a country also influence marital choices and lifestyles of internal migrants (Fan and Huang 1998).

Findings in this issue show that heterogeneities in Asian marriage migrants' life trajectories and contextual factors challenge the applicability of the classic assimilation theory. The classic assimilation theory often assumes a unilineal integration trajectory when marriage migrants assimilate to receiving societies in all relevant aspects – socially, culturally, legally and so on (Massey et al. 1993). However, in reality, the migration experience can be highly complex, and the nature of migration may change contingent on specific contexts. Migrants may strategically arrange the sequence and aspects of assimilation. Several papers in this special issue jointly show that marriage migrants both struggle and strategise under the diverse and unequal legal, economic, and cultural landscapes between the sending and the receiving societies, both across and within national boundaries.

Chiu and Choi (2020) show that legal and spatial migration may not always go hand in hand. Rather, female marriage migrants from mainland China to Hong Kong have creatively decoupled the two types of migration into various combinations so as to strike a balance between their marriage life, social adaptation, and career development. Chang (2020) finds that Vietnamese marriage migrants in Taiwan and Korea have responsively adjusted their social and cultural integration in both the private and domestic spheres based on the perceived differences of gender systems in the sending and the receiving societies. Chatterjee and Desai's research (2020) demonstrate how India's internal female marriage migrants pursue autonomy in the public sphere through proactively constructing their sense of community based on both the geographical community where they reside and the imagined communities, that is, the mindset of the communities where their natal families belong. In Quah's (2020) study, she finds that divorced low-income marriage migrant women in Singapore use diverse approaches and strategies to cope with difficulties and problems both during and after divorce.

Diversifying the academic discourses in migration and marriage

Research on the link between migration and marriage has mainly focused on the adaption and upward mobility patterns of marriage migrants (Constable 2005, 2009; Yeoh et al. 2013). That is, most of the previous literature has looked at how marriage, as the main cause of migration, has shaped migrants' well-being and life choices. Studies that have examined the impact of migration often focus on outcomes such as socioeconomic profiles (Liang and Ma 2004; Massey et al. 1993; Portes 2007; Zhang and Ye 2018) and intergenerational relations (Dreby 2007; Huang and Yeoh 2005; Huang, Yeoh, and Lam 2008; Zhou 2009). However, given the rising prevalence of migration, the heterogeneous migration trajectories and motivations, and the elongated migration spells, the literature on migration and marriage should focus more on how different types of migration (e.g. labour migration) shape individuals' marriage formation process. The literature should also examine other phases of family formation such as marriage dissolution and remarriages (Mazzucato and Schans 2011).

In this special issue, three articles examine how migration, intertwined with other mechanisms such as citizenship, ethnicity, and urban/rural divide, shape individuals' marriage timing and assortative mating patterns. Specifically, Qian and Qian (2020) investigate how different generations of Asian immigrants in the United States marry across generations of immigration and across racial groups. Utomo (2020) discusses how internal migration has added to the complexities in the patterns of ethnic intermarriages in Jakarta, a main destination for internal migrants across the ethnically diverse Indonesia. Mu and Yeung (2020) demonstrate how migration, interacts with gender, the urban/rural origin, and parental and individual socioeconomic status, to influence individuals' marriage timing and their likelihood of marrying someone of different social origins.

This collection also expands on the existing literature on migration and marriage by examining the various phases related to family formation, including to marital dissolution (Choi, Kim, and Ryu 2020; Quah 2020) and reformation (Chen and Yip 2020) as Mazzucato and Schans (2011) suggest family scholarship on transnational families should explore. This helps deepen our understanding of the dynamic relationships between migration experiences and family formation trajectories.

Widening methodological repertoires in the field of migration and marriage

Previous literature on migration and marriage tends to be ethnographic and narrative-oriented, lacking quantitative documentation and systematic explanations. While qualitative findings help detail motivations, attitudes and feelings of the migrants, quantitative estimates of distributions and relationships among multiple factors help capture trends and patterns more accurately and disentangle complex causal relationships. Articles in this special collection use multiple methods, including quantitative, qualitative, and mixed-method analyses to examine the complex and nuanced experiences of migrants in their marital choices, social integration, and mobility trajectories. For example, based on statistical models including measures of female marriage migrants' life satisfaction and its potential determinants in Taiwan (Li and Yang 2020), we gain a more accurate understanding about how the experiences of marriage migration have shaped individuals' subjective well-being, and what the most relevant and significant determinants of marriage migrants' integration process in the receiving societies are. Relying on representative and longitudinal marriage and divorce registration data in Korea (Choi, Kim, and Ryu 2020) and Hong Kong (Chen and Yip 2020), the authors disentangle the mechanisms of how and why marriage migrants are subject to martial instabilities, and when divorce happens, how they make decisions about remarriage in the receiving societies.

Contributions of articles in this special issue

In addition to the joint contributions discussed above, each paper in this collection is a valuable addition to studies on the relationship between migration and marriage. They are all theoretically informed empirical studies investigating Asian migrants' marriage patterns in China, Hong Kong, India, Indonesia, Korea, Singapore, Taiwan, as well as in the United States. The papers touch on how migration influences Asian migrants' marriage timing and assortative mating patterns, how heterogeneous migration experiences shape Asian migrants' social integration process and subjective well-being, and how migration, legally and spatially, has introduced instabilities in Asian migrants' marital lives. The papers are broadly grouped under three themes: (1) Migration, Marriage Partners and Timing, (2) Migration, Gender, and Subjective Well-being, and (3) Law, Identity, and Marital Instabilities.

Migration, marriage partners and timing

There has been an increasing number of Asians migrating and settling in other countries, particularly North America. A substantial number of these migrants are in interracial marriages which has implications for Asian migrants' integration in America. Qian and Qian (2020) use data from the Current Population Survey to examine how different generations of Asian immigrants in the United States marry across generations of immigration and across racial groups. They apply the new assimilation theory (Alba and Nee 2009) that posits that assimilation may take diverse paths for different subpopulations. The authors hypothesise that educational attainment may play an important role in shaping marriage behaviour among different generations of Asian migrants. They first examine whether a larger marriage pool of Asian immigrants reinforces cultural identities and strengthens intergroup boundaries. Second, the authors examine how educational attainment plays a role in patterns of intergenerational marriage and interracial marriage. Finally, they examine whether there is retreat from intermarriage among Asian Americans of the second generation.

They find that generational endogamy became stronger between 1994–2004 and 2005–2015 among second generation men and third-plus generation men. Over time, the proportion of Asian immigrants marrying whites declined for all three generations. Meanwhile, there has been an increase in first-generation Asian men marrying second-generation Asian women, and a declining number of third-plus-generation Asian men marrying first-generation Asian women. Education indeed shapes race/generation assortative mating, seen in the divergent paths of integration between highly educated and less educated second-generation Asians. These results provide support for the new assimilation theory and offer new insights on migrants' integration process through marriage.

In Asia, some countries are very ethnically diverse. One such example is Indonesia where interethnic marriages occur at a high rate, especially in the metropolitan areas. With a mixed-method approach, Utomo (2020) investigates how migration has shaped patterns of ethnic intermarriages in Jakarta, which has long been a prime destination for internal migrants across the ethnically diverse country. Based on the 2010 Census data, she examines intermarriage patterns across 1,340 ethnic sub-groups, such as the Betawi, Sundanese, Batak, Minang, Chinese, Malays, and Bugis. She then supplements these analyses with insights from qualitative data from sources such as newspapers, online media (e.g. blogs), online dating sites, magazines, books and movies about norms for ethnic assortative mating among major ethnic groups particularly among young adults aged 20-39.

The census data show that about one-third of co-residing married couples in Jakarta were in an interethnic marriage in 2010. The Chinese, Madurese, and Batak sub-groups have high rates of endogamy despite their small relative size in Jakarta. Those with higher education are more likely to marry someone from other ethnic groups, and the youngest group are most likely to be in an interethnic marriage. Migration status is an important factor, in that more recent migrants are less likely to marry someone from other ethnic groups than those who had migrated earlier. The author also conducted in-depth interviews with 14 respondents in 2014 and 2015. Data from both popular media and in-depth interviews indicate that although crossing ethnic boundaries is not as challenging as it used to be, crossing the religious boundary is largely shunned by both parents and families, and by the respondents themselves. Educational homogamy was important for all the female respondents interviewed, but did not come through as such for the male respondents.

The qualitative data suggest that increased migration has changed the norm and behaviour in family formation in Indonesia. Although arranged marriage has declined, parents and kinship network continue to play an important role in migrants' choice of spouse. In addition, in Indonesia, religious authorities and states also have an interest in shaping norms in the marriage market. Identifying the role of these third parties contributes to ethnic assortative mating theories. These results shed nuanced insights on ethnic assortative mating perspectives that are often based on western or developed countries. The author challenges Kalmijn's framework (1998) by arguing that it is difficult to disentangle migrants' own preferences from that of the third party, be it their parents' wishes, the broader cultural networks, or religious communities in considering one's decisions and attitudes towards interethnic marriages.

Mu and Yeung (2020) examine how internal migration of both high-skilled and low- and semi-skilled migrants in China influences their family formation behaviours, including when and whom they marry, and how gender, education, and family background moderate the relationship. A mixed-method approach, based on data from the 2012 Chinese Family Panel Studies (CFPS) and 127 in-depth interviews conducted in Beijing in 2015, helps to triangulate findings about the relationship between migration, marriage timing, and assortative mating by family origins.

Findings show that both female and male rural migrants tend to enter first marriage later than local residents, though the 'delaying' effect of migration is stronger for men, suggesting that men bear greater economic pressures of household establishment in China where housing prices are skyrocketing in many cities. A further look into individual and parental education shows that only rural migrant women who did not attend college or whose parents did not attend college marry earlier. The authors suggest that these patterns likely reflect the gendered impact of education and family background on the timing of marriage. Whereas having lower education indicates higher acceptance of early marriage for women, it means lower financial ability for men, which makes them less attractive in the marriage market. Regarding patterns of assortative mating by family origins, rural migrants with higher education and better family SES background are less likely to marry someone from the same province, and more likely to marry an urban spouse or a rural migrant than a rural local. These results highlight the significance of structural and financial barriers as well as the strong role of parents and patriarchy in shaping marriage behaviours of the rural-to-urban migrants in China.

Migration, gender, and subjective well-being

Chang (2020) examines how the perceived gaps of the gender system between the sending and receiving societies affect female Vietnamese marriage migrants' (VMM) integration experiences in Taiwan and Korea. She uses qualitative interviews with VMMs during two waves of multi-sited fieldwork in Taiwan and Korea between 2011 and 2017, and survey data that capture relevant gender-related attitudes in Vietnam, Taiwan, and Korea. Overall, Chang observes that the gender system in Taiwan is relatively more equitable than that in Vietnam in two aspects: married women are protected by domestic violence laws in Taiwan but not in Vietnam, and married women in Taiwan have more autonomy and power although women from abroad are treated less equally than local women. In contrast, the gender system in Korea is more rigid than that in Vietnam, especially due to the 'mother-in-law' culture. Marriage migrant women's participation in the public sphere often improves their social status at home. This study adds to the literature on gender and immigrant integration by showing the heterogeneity in intra-Asia marriage migrants' integration experiences and the importance of gender system in the destination country in mediating the relationship between migration and gender relations within a marriage.

Marriage immigrants currently account for more than 2% of the national population in Taiwan with many having children. Their well-being is crucial for themselves, their children and to society as a whole. Li and Yang (2020) use a valuable national database to examine the under-studied area of the psychological well-being of foreign brides in cross-border marriages in Taiwan from the economic and acculturative perspectives. In Taiwan, marriage immigration has been overwhelmingly female, with women accounting for 92.0% of marriage migrants, mainly Chinese (67.1%) from China, Hong Kong and Macau and one third from mostly Southeast Asian countries. The authors use data from a national survey on marriage immigrants conducted by the National Immigration Agency in 2013 to examine factors of the acculturative process, including the length of stay in host society, access to social networks, perceived discrimination, and acculturative difficulties associated with migrants' psychological well-being.

Results show that a majority of the marriage immigrants (92%) feel happy about their lives in Taiwan, and two thirds of them feel unwelcome. Data reveal that family income is the most influential factor in the happiness of female marriage immigrants, being positively associated with it. The families of immigrant brides in Taiwan have on average a lower family income than the general population. About 60% of the immigrant brides are employed, and they earn significantly lower income than locals. Those employed are less happy because they often encounter discrimination and feel burdened with a second shift at home after work. More than half of the immigrant brides have stayed for more than 10 years. Those with longer residency report lower psychological well-being than the newcomers who had arrived in Taiwan within the past two years. The authors argue that this may be due to unexpected hardships and barriers from the system later into marriage. Compared to those who access professional organisations, such as legal institutions, governmental agents, and religious organisations, immigrant brides who mainly access primary social networks in Taiwan are happier. Data also show that when immigrant brides perceive local residents around them as friendly, they are more likely to feel accepted, and such perceived friendliness mediates the impacts of some covariates on their happiness. Most of the findings support the acculturation and emotional stress theories when controlling for economic resources. However, some findings such as those regarding the length of stay and employment status of the immigrant brides challenge extant literature and underscore the value of accounting for the unique Asian gender norms and institutional barriers.

An Asian country that has the largest and an increasing group of marriage migrants is India, although most of these are internal migrants within India. It has been estimated that 48% of women in rural India in 2008 were internal migrants, a majority of them marriage migrants. However, systematic research on marriage migrants in India is rare thus far. Chatterjee and Desai (2020) seek to understand whether Indian marriage migrant women's sense of belonging to the sending and receiving communities shape their autonomy in the public sphere with respect to physical autonomy, economic autonomy and civic participation.

Using data from the 2012 India Human Development Survey (IHDS), a nationally representative dataset, the authors note that while marriage migration is part of the accepted kinship system in India, there is a complex set of social norms and structures that defines the relationship of a woman with her marital family and community. They argue that these norms need to be distinguished from the physical environment. They show that being a migrant in a community or growing up in one's own community of residence are both positively associated with women's participation in wage labour, but they have no impact on women's physical autonomy in terms of going out of the house alone or participating in civic activities. Women who belong to communities which allow for marriage within their natal villages are far more likely to have autonomy in all three aspects. Moreover, being a long-time resident in a community offers women greater knowledge about the community and the available infrastructure, and such knowledge helps them improve their social networks, although it is not sufficient to improve their autonomy. In contrast, marriage patterns that are oriented towards village endogamy develop norms and ideologies that permit far greater autonomy than those that are oriented towards village exogamy. The findings also suggest that belonging to a caste that allows endogamous marriages increases women's participation in civic activities. These results help reconcile some of the existing literature that find divergent results in different areas in India. The authors conclude that norms of marriage migration in a woman's caste are more important than the physical community she migrates to. The study is a valuable contribution that demonstrates that culture and geography are closely linked and that distinguishing their various impacts can provide a more nuanced understanding of the demographic process of migration.

Law, identity, and marital instabilities

The legal systems in the destination have strong implications for cross-border marriage migrants. Most research assumes that migrants undergo legal and spatial migration simultaneously. However, in Hong Kong, marriage migrants' legal and spatial migration often do not coincide. Chiu and Choi (2020) use ethnographic data to illustrate the complications and instabilities introduced by the decoupling of legal migration and the actual spatial migration in cross-border marriages between Mainland Chinese and Hong Kongers. The authors posit that such inconsistency underscores the gendered power relations of marriage migration and propose a conceptual framework that decouples marriage migrants' legal and spatial migration to untangle the intricate nexus of relations between gender, power, and space. They examine the causes and consequences of two forms of decoupling of legal and spatial migration among female marriage migrants – (1) wife migrates spatially before her legal status changes and (2) wife's change in legal status is not accompanied by spatial migration. They argue that these two forms of decoupling have their origin in state policies, economic constraints and personal choices, and that their impact on the intimate and household dynamics of cross-border families is gendered.

The main reason for the first type of decoupling is the proliferation of government restrictions on migration and granting of residency and citizenship, and the second form relates to the economic and family circumstances of cross-border families and the personal preferences of female marriage migrants. Some women would like to migrate spatially in order to benefit from spatial hypergamy but end up being trapped in their region of origin because of financial and familial constraints. On the other hand, legal migration that happens without spatial migration reveals the formidable structural obstacles faced by female marriage migrants when striving to create a normative family, which force some of them to be in a long-term split household arrangement. In some cases, it can represent marriage migrants' agency to strive for autonomy or to achieve personal goals. The social effects of the decoupling of legal and spatial migration that are regularised by the state have implications for similar situations in neighbouring societies such as Taiwan, Macau and Singapore.

The number of transnational marriages in Korea, mostly between a Korean husband and a foreign wife, has increased rapidly. This trend has caused concerns over the quality of marriage, how multi-ethnic children fare, and citizenship status of marriage immigrants. Choi, Kim, and Ryu (2020), drawing on marriage and divorce registration data, examine the risk of transnational divorce in Korea, and the socio-demographic factors influencing the risk. This study provides the most complete description of transnational marital dissolution to date. The authors raise questions about whether transnational marriages are at a higher risk of marital dissolution and how the socio-demographic characteristics of a transnational couple affect the probability of a marital dissolution.

They find that transnational marriages have an extremely high risk of divorce within the first 48 months of marriage, when controlling for spouses' socio-demographic characteristics and spousal dissimilarities. About 19% of marriages between a Korean husband and a foreign wife were dissolved and 6% of marriages between Korean nationals ended within 48 months. Both Chinese husbands and wives have the highest risk of divorce, and foreign wives from Southeast Asian countries also have a high risk of divorce. In addition, they find that foreign wives who have a lower education have a significantly higher probability of divorce than those with a higher education. Lastly, foreign wives who have acquired citizenship status have lower risks of divorce. These patterns do not fully support the heterogamy hypothesis as spouses' compositional traits such as their unique socioeconomic and demographic characteristics, as hypothesised by the selectivity perspective, partly explain the high divorce rates. The authors argue that the different motivations for transnational marriage and its processes in Western and Korean contexts explain these differences.

Given the higher divorce rates for transnational marriages, it is important to examine how marriage migrants cope after a divorce. To date, this topic has been rarely investigated. Quah (2020) provides a detailed depiction of the lives of low-income marriage migrant women in Singapore who had dissolved their marriages with their Singaporean citizen ex-husbands. Through in-depth interviews with 47 transnational divorcees, Quah finds that, first, to cope with divorce proceedings and to obtain legal representation, the foreign spouse builds the savvy to turn to local community organisations for information and support such as legal aid from non-profit organisations for migrants in Singapore. Second, Quah shows that gendered asymmetric relations persist through the divorce proceedings and into the women's post-divorce interactions with their ex-spouses. Marriage migrant women are often immediately thrust into 'visa limbo' after divorce, and burdened with visa issues and the uncertainty of remaining in Singapore. Singaporean ex-husbands, for instance, have the power to exclude non-resident mothers from claiming child custody and making other divorce claims by withdrawing sponsorship of their ex-wives' visit pass. Some marriage migrant women obtain joint child custody with their Singaporean ex-husbands and get to care for and control their children, but those who lack the permit to remain in the country could be coerced into giving up custody of their children. Third, marriage migrants often find themselves with little bargaining power during divorce proceedings. They struggle to find means to remain in Singapore and to juggle other livelihood challenges and strategically negotiate with their ex-husbands over post-divorce co-parenting arrangements.

Quah's paper challenges the literature that conceptualises female marriage migrants from low-income countries in a 'victim versus agent' binary and shows that they struggle as well as strategise under the conditions of asymmetric global economic restructuring. From a transnational, intersectional feminist perspective, Quah argues that these foreign brides' life trajectories are non-linear and non-standardised.

Beyond migrants' marital instability and divorce experience, Chen and Yip (2020) examine the likelihood and assortative mating patterns of remarriage among marriage migrants in Hong Kong and their policy implications. Based on data from the Hong Kong Marriage Registry during the period of 1995-2012, they find that the age difference between partners is smaller in first marriages than in remarriages. However, for educational selection between marriage partners, homogamy is dominant in both first marriages and remarriages, but with notable differences between local marriages and transnational marriages. Multivariate analysis further shows that both Hong Kong men and women with low education and in low-skilled occupations are more likely to remarry Mainland Chinese as choice of spouse is limited for them due to their low SES, and Hong Kongers of high socioeconomic status are more likely to remarry spouses from western countries. There are also gender differences. For Hong Kong men, remarriage with Mainland brides tends to be more age and education hypergamous, while remarriage with western brides are more age and education hypogamous. In contrast, hypogamy is more likely to be practised by Hong Kong women who remarry Mainland men, while hypergamy is more likely to be practised by Hong Kong women who remarry western men.

Conclusion

Marriage migration has become an increasingly prevalent phenomenon in Asia. Migrants mainly from China and a few Southeast Asian countries such as Vietnam, the Philippines, and Indonesia migrate to destinations such as Hong Kong, Korea, Singapore, and Taiwan. Thus, marriage migrants comprise an increasing share of the population in Asia. In addition, the trajectories of such migration have become more diverse, and the duration has become longer, spanning over multiple life stages. Compared to labour migration, marriage migration can potentially have a wider and longer-term impact on the well-being of individuals and the society as it involves marriage partners and potentially children and other family members.

Aside from marriage migration, other types of migration in Asia have also become more diverse in terms of migrants' socio-demographic characteristics and motivations. In particular, labour migrants with higher skills are more likely to stay longer and to seek new lives beyond economic improvement, including finding a spouse, starting a family, and settling permanently in the receiving communities. There is a need to diversify academic discourses in the field of migration and marriage beyond marriage migrants. In addition to intra-Asia migration, immigration from Asia to the West also continues to increase. Hence, migrants' marriage patterns are more heterogeneous in terms of assortative mating choices, marriage timing, integration, and power relations between genders. Given the rapid globalisation and urbanisation occurring in Asia, these trends will only be on the rise and their implications for society will become more vital.

The studies in this special issue use good quality data and methodologies to advance our knowledge about the motivations, patterns, and consequences of these new demographic and social trends in Asia. We have moved beyond the 'marriage-scapes' perspective and the classic assimilation theory to enrich understanding by showing migrants' complex strategising processes between difficulties and opportunities in specific social, legal, and cultural contexts in Asia. We have also broadened the understanding of the relationship between migration and marriage by examining how different types of migration influence the family formation process, from entry into marriage, to marital dissolution and remarriages. The multi-methods used in this issue, including qualitative, quantitative, and mixed-method approaches, have enabled both systematic overview of the patterns and determinants of migrants' well-being and marital outcomes, and an in-depth understanding of the underlying decision-making mechanisms.

The unique Asian contexts push the boundaries of many existing theories. The studies in this special issue provide nuanced evidence that shows how the integration process of Asian migrants is fraught with formal and informal inequalities in legal systems, labour markets, social networks, and private spheres that are different from patterns more frequently seen in western literature. Consistent with the neo-assimilation models developed in the Western context, assimilation takes place within racially and economically heterogeneous Asian contexts. Social barriers created across national boundaries and sometimes within a country make marriages of migrants unstable and vulnerable, which is detrimental to the migrants and to the society. Lingering discrimination and institutional barriers to citizenship, employment and other opportunities often block complete assimilation for some migrants while those more advantaged migrants assimilate more easily. It is important to consider both the political and cultural contexts in the origin and destination countries, in particular the gender norms, developmental policies, and socioeconomic and demographic contexts when examining migrants' subjective well-being, the assimilation and integration process, and their implications for their families and society at large.

The papers in this special issue show how migration modifies ethnic homogeneity and the socioeconomic mix in the receiving communities. Unlike literature in the western contexts where race/ethnic integration is a key concern, the papers show that, in Asia, spouses and the extended families of migrants, patriarchy, institutional and socioeconomic backgrounds, religion, caste, and ethnicity all play a big role in Asian migrants' marriage behaviours and marital relations. Taken together, this special issue makes valuable empirical and theoretical contributions to the fields of migration, race/ethnicity, family, and gender studies. Future studies should investigate in greater detail the well-being and identity of marriage migrants and the long-term consequences of these geographic moves to the family system, the social fabric, and a wide range of institutions in both the origin and destination.

Acknowledgements

We are grateful to the Asia Research Institute at the National University of Singapore for the financial support of the international conference 'Migration and Marriage in Asia' on July 26–27, 2016. Most papers in this special issue were first presented in that conference. We also thank Saharah Abubakar for her capable editorial help.

Disclosure statement

No potential conflict of interest was reported by the authors.

ORCID

Wei-Jun Jean Yeung http://orcid.org/0000-0001-7519-5576
Zheng Mu http://orcid.org/0000-0003-2664-4106

References

Alba, Richard, and Victor Nee. 2009. *Remaking the American Mainstream: Assimilation and Contemporary Immigration*. Cambridge: Harvard University Press.

Bloch, Francis, Vijayendra Rao, and Sonale Desai. 2004. "Wedding Celebrations as Conspicuous Consumption: Signaling Social Status in Rural India." *The Journal of Human Resources* 39 (3): 675–695.

Brennan, Denise. 2004. *What's Love Got to Do With It? Transnational Desires and Sex Tourism in the Dominican Republic*. Durham, NC: Duke University Press.

Chang, Hsin-Chieh. 2020. "Do Gender Systems in the Origin and Destination Societies Affect Immigrant Integration? Vietnamese Marriage Migrants in Taiwan and South Korea." *Journal of Ethnic and Migration Studies* 46 (14): 2937–2955. doi:10.1080/1369183X.2019.1585014.

Charsley, Katharine. 2005. "Vulnerable Brides and Transnational Ghar Damads: Gender, Risk and 'Adjustment' among Pakistani Marriage Migrants to Britain." *Indian Journal of Gender Studies* 12 (2 & 3): 381–406.

Charsley, Katharine. 2006. "Risk and Ritual: The Protection of British Pakistani Women in Transnational Marriage." *Journal of Ethnic and Migration Studies* 32 (7): 1169–1187.

Chatterjee, Esha, and Sonalde Desai. 2020. "Physical versus Imagined Communities: Migration and Women's Autonomy in India." *Journal of Ethnic and Migration Studies* 46 (14): 2977–2996. doi:10.1080/1369183X.2019.1585016.

Chen, Mengni, and Paul Yip. 2020. "Remarriages and Transnational Marriages in Hong Kong: Implications and Challenges." *Journal of Ethnic and Migration Studies* 46 (14): 3059–3077. doi:10.1080/1369183X.2019.1585026.

Cheng, Sealing. 2005. "The 'Success' of Anti-trafficking Policy: Women's Human Rights and Women's Sexuality in South Korea." Paper presented at Ethnography and Policy: What Do We Know About Trafficking? School for Advanced Research, Santa Fe, New Mexico, April 17–21.

Chiu, Tuen Yi, and Susanne Y. P. Choi. 2020. "The Decoupling of Legal and Spatial Migration of Female Marriage Migrants." *Journal of Ethnic and Migration Studies* 46 (14): 2997–3013. doi:10.1080/1369183X.2019.1585018.

Choi, Yool, Doo-Sub Kim, and Jungkyun Ryu. 2020. "Marital Dissolution of Transnational Couples in South Korea." *Journal of Ethnic and Migration Studies* 46 (14): 3014–3039. doi:10.1080/1369183X.2019.1585021.

Choi, Susanne Yuk-Ping, and Yinni Peng. 2016. *Masculine Compromise: Migration, Family, and Gender in China*. Oakland: University of California Press.

Choi, Kate H., and Marta Tienda. 2018. "Intermarriage and the Lifecycle Timing of Migration." *International Migration Review*. doi:10.1111/imre.12326.

Chong, Amanda W. 2014. "Migrant Brides in Singapore: Women Strategizing Within Family, Market and State." *Harvard Journal of Law and Gender* 37 (332): 331–405.

Constable, Nicole. 2005. *Cross Border Marriages: Gender and Mobility in Transnational Asia*. Philadelphia: University of Pennsylvania.

Constable, Nicole. 2009. "The Commodification of Intimacy: Marriage, Sex and Reproductive Labour." *Annual Review Anthropology* 38: 49–64.

Dang, Anh, Sidney Goldstein, and James McNally. 1997. "Internal Migration and Development in Vietnam." *International Migration Review* 31 (2): 312–337.

Dealwis, Caesar. 2016. "Assimilation of the Descendants of Caucasian Muslims in Sarawak, Malaysia." In *Marriage Migration in Asia: Emerging Minorities at the Frontiers of Nation-States*, edited by Sari K. Ishii, 135–152. Singapore: NUS Press.

Desai, Sonalde, and Manjistha Banerji. 2008. "Negotiated Identities: Male Migration and Left-Behind Wives in India." *Journal of Population Research* 25 (3): 337–355.

Dreby, Joanna. 2007. "Children and Power in Mexican Transnational Families." *Journal of Marriage and Family* 69 (4): 1050–1064.

Ehrenreich, Barbara, and Arlie Russell Hochschild, eds. 2003. *Global Woman: Nannies, Maids, and Sex Workers in the New Economy*. New York: Metropolitan Books.

Faier, Lieba. 2007. "Filipina Migrants in Rural Japan and Their Professions of Love." *American Ethnologist* 34 (1): 148–162.

Fan, C. Cindy. 2003. "Rural-urban Migration and Gender Division of Labor in Transitional China." *International Journal of Urban and Regional Research* 27 (1): 24–47.

Fan, C. Cindy. 2008. "China on the Move: Migration, the State, and the Household." *The China Quarterly* 196: 924–956.

Fan, C. Cindy, and Youqin Huang. 1998. "Waves of Rural Brides: Female Marriage Migration in China." *Annals of the Association of American Geographers* 88 (2): 227–251.

Fan, C. Cindy, and Ling Li. 2002. "Marriage and Migration in Transitional China: A Field Study of Gaozhou, Western Guangdong." *Environment and Planning A: Economy and Space* 34 (4): 619–638.

Gaetano, Arianne M., and Tamara Jacka. 2013. *On the Move: Women and Rural-to-Urban Migration in Contemporary China*. New York: Columbia University Press.

Hondagneu-Sotelo, Pierrette. 2011. "Gender and Migration Scholarship: An Overview From a 21st Century Perspective." *Migraciones Internacionales* 6 (1): 219–233.

Huang, Shirlena, and Brenda S. A. Yeoh. 2003. "The Difference Gender Makes: State Policy and Contract Migrant Workers in Singapore." *Asian and Pacific Migration Journal* 12 (1–2): 75–97.

Huang, Shirlena, and Brenda S. A. Yeoh. 2005. "Transnational Families and Their Children's Education: China's 'Study Mothers' in Singapore." *Global Networks* 5 (4): 379–400.

Huang, Shirlena, Brenda S. A. Yeoh, and Theodora Lam. 2008. "Asian Transnational Families in Transition: The Liminality of Simultaneity." *International Migration* 46 (4): 3–13.

Ishii, Sari K. 2016. *Marriage Migration in Asia: Emerging Minorities at the Frontiers of Nation-States*. Singapore: NUS Press.

Jacka, Tamara. 2005. *Rural Women in Urban China: Gender, Migration, and Social Change*. Armonk, NY: M.E. Sharpe.

Jones, Gavins, and Hsiu-hua Shen. 2008. "International Marriage in East and Southeast Asia: Trends and Research Emphases." *Citizenship Studies* 12 (1): 9–25.

Jongwilaiwan, Rattana, and Eric C. Thompson. 2013. "Thai Wives in Singapore and Transnational Patriarchy." *Gender, Place & Culture* 20 (3): 363–381.

Juárez, Fatima, Thomas LeGrand, Cynthia B. Lloyd, Susheela Singh, and Véronique Hertrich. 2013. "Youth Migration and Transitions to Adulthood in Developing Countries." *The Annals of the American Academy of Political and Social Science* 648 (1): 6–15.

Kalmijn, Matthijs. 1998. "Intermarriage and Homogamy: Causes, Patterns, Trends." *Annual Review of Sociology* 24 (1): 395–421.

Kempadoo, Kamala, ed. 2005. *Trafficking and Prostitution Reconsidered: New Perspectives on Migration, Sex Work and Human Rights*. Boulder, CO: Paradigm.

Kim, Doo-Sub, ed. 2008. *Cross-Border Marriage: Process and Dynamics*. Seoul: The Institute of Population and Aging Research, Hanyang University.

Kim, Minjeong. 2010. "Gender and International Marriage Migration." *Sociology Compass* 4 (9): 718–731.

Kim, Jane. 2011. "Trafficked: Domestic Violence, Exploitation in Marriage and the Foreign-Bride Industry." *Virginia Journal of International Law* 51 (2): 443–506.

Kim, Doo-Sub, ed. 2012. *Cross-Border Marriage: Global Trends and Diversity*. Seoul: Korean Institute for Health and Social Affairs.

Kudo, Masako. 2016. "Forging Intimate Ties in Transnational Spaces: The Life Trajectories of Japanese Women Married to Pakistani Migrants." In *Marriage Migration in Asia: Emerging Minorities at the Frontiers of Nation-States*, edited by Sari K. Ishii, 27–42. Singapore: NUS Press.

Kulu, Hill, and Nadja Milewski. 2008. "Family Change and Migration in the Life Course: An Introduction." *Demographic Research* 17 (19): 567–590.

Lee, Bun Song, and Louis G. Pol. 1993. "The Influence of Rural-Urban Migration on Migrants' Fertility in Korea, Mexico and Cameroon." *Population Research and Policy Review* 12 (1): 3–26.

Li, Chun-Hao, and Wen-Shan Yang. 2020. "Happiness of Female Immigrants in Cross-Border Marriages in Taiwan." *Journal of Ethnic and Migration Studies* 46 (14): 2956–2976. doi:10.1080/1369183X.2019.1585015.

Liang, Zai. 2001. "The Age of Migration in China." *Population and Development Review* 27 (3): 499–524.

Liang, Zai, and Zhongdong Ma. 2004. "China's Floating Population: New Evidence From the 2000 Census." *Population and Development Review* 30 (3): 467–488.

Lucas, Robert E. B. 1997. "Internal Migration in Developing Countries." *Handbook of Population and Family Economics* 1: 721–798.

Lumayag, Linda A. 2016. "Marriage 'During' Work Migration: Lived Experiences of Filipinos Marriage Migrants in Malaysia." In *Marriage Migration in Asia: Emerging Minorities at the Frontiers of Nation-States*, edited by Sari K. Ishii, 73–104. Singapore: NUS Press.

Lutz, Helma. 2010. "Gender in the Migratory Process." *Journal of Ethnic and Migration Studies* 36 (10): 1647–1663.

Massey, Douglas S., Joaquin Arango, Graeme Hugo, Ali Kouaouci, Adela Pellegrino, and J. Edward Taylor. 1993. "Theories of International Migration: A Review and Appraisal." *Population and Development Review* 19 (3): 431–466.

Mazzucato, Valentina, and Djamila Schans. 2011. "Transnational Families and the Well-Being of Children: Conceptual and Methodological Challenges." *Journal of Marriage and Family* 73 (4): 704–712.

Mu, Zheng, and Shu Hu. 2018. "Origin and Transition of Singapore Families." In *Family and Population Changes in Singapore: A Unique Case in the Global Family Change*, edited by Wei-Jun Jean Yeung and Shu Hu, 27–52. New York: Routledge.

Mu, Zheng, and Wei-Jun Jean Yeung. 2018. "For Money or for a Life: A Mixed-Method Study on Migration and Time Use in China." *Social Indicators Research* 139 (1): 347–379.

Mu, Zheng, and Wei-Jun Jean Yeung. 2020. "Internal Migration, Marriage Timing and Assortative Mating: A Mixed-Method Study in China." *Journal of Ethnic and Migration Studies* 46 (14): 2914–2936. doi:10.1080/1369183X.2019.1585009.
Palriwala, Rajni, and Patricia Uberoi. 2008. *Marriage, Migration and Gender*. Vol. 5. Thousand Oaks, CA: SAGE Publications.
Parker, Lyn, ed. 2005. *The Agency of Women in Asia*. Singapore: Marshall Cavendish.
Portes, Alejandro. 2007. "Migration, Development, and Segmented Assimilation: A Conceptual Review of the Evidence." *The ANNALS of the American Academy of Political and Social Science* 610 (1): 73–97.
Qian, Zhenchao, Daniel T. Lichter, and Dmitry Tumin. 2018. "Divergent Pathways to Assimilation? Local Marriage Markets and Intermarriage among US Hispanics." *Journal of Marriage and Family* 80 (1): 271–288.
Qian, Zhenchao, and Yue Qian. 2020. "Generation, Education, and Intermarriage of Asian Americans." *Journal of Ethnic and Migration Studies* 46 (14): 2880–2895. doi:10.1080/1369183X.2019.1585006.
Quah, Sharon Ee Ling. 2020. "Transnational Divorces in Singapore: Experiences of Low-income Divorced Marriage Migrant Women." *Journal of Ethnic and Migration Studies* 46 (14): 3040–3058. doi:10.1080/1369183X.2019.1585023.
Sakai, Chie. 2016. "Unintentional Cross-Cultural Families: The Diverse Community of Japanese Wives in Shanghai." In *Marriage Migration in Asia: Emerging Minorities at the Frontiers of Nation-States*, edited by Sari K. Ishii, 43–72. Singapore: NUS Press.
Stephnitz, Abigail. 2009. "Male-ordered: The Mail-order Bride Industry and Trafficking in Women for Sexual and Labor Exploitation." The Poppy Project Report. Eaves Housing for Women, London, UK.
Tokoro, Ikuya. 2016. "'Centre/Periphery' Flow Reversed? Twenty Years of Cross-Border Marriages Between Philippine Women and Japanese Men." In *Marriage Migration in Asia: Emerging Minorities at the Frontiers of Nation-States*, edited by Sari K. Ishii, 105–117. Singapore: NUS Press.
Toyota, Mika. 2008. "Editorial Introduction: International Marriage, Rights and the State in East and Southeast Asia." *Citizenship Studies* 12 (1): 1–7.
United Nations. 2017. *International Migration Report 2017*. New York: UN.
Utomo, Ariane J. 2020. "Love in the Melting Pot: Ethnic Intermarriage in Jakarta." *Journal of Ethnic and Migration Studies* 46 (14): 2896–2913. doi:10.1080/1369183X.2019.1585008.
Utomo, Ariane, and Peter McDonald. 2016. "Who Marries Whom?: Ethnicity and Marriage Pairing Patterns in Indonesia." *Asian Population Studies* 12 (1): 28–49.
Vertovec, Steven. 2007. "Super-diversity and Its Implications." *Ethnic and Racial Studies* 30 (6): 1024–1054.
Yeoh, Brenda S. A., Heng Leng Chee, Thi Kieu Dung Vu, and Cheng Yi'En. 2013. "Between Two Families: The Social Meaning of Remittances for Vietnamese Marriage Migrants in Singapore." *Global Networks* 13 (4): 441–458.
Yeung, Wei-Jun Jean, and Shu Hu. 2018. *Family and Population Changes in Singapore: A Unique Case in Global Family Change*. London: Routledge.
Yinger, J. Milton. 1981. "Toward a Theory of Assimilation and Dissimilation." *Ethnic and Racial Studies* 4 (3): 249–264.
Zenteno, René, Silvia E. Giorguli, and Edith Gutiérrez. 2013. "Mexican Adolescent Migration to the United States and Transitions to Adulthood." *The Annals of the American Academy of Political and Social Science* 648 (1): 18–37.
Zhang, Zhuoni, and Hua Ye. 2018. "Mode of Migration, Age at Arrival, and Occupational Attainment of Immigrants From Mainland China to Hong Kong." *Chinese Sociological Review* 50 (1): 83–112.
Zhou, Min. 2009. "Conflict, Coping, and Reconciliation: Intergenerational Relations in Chinese Immigrant Families." In *Across Generations*, edited by Nancy Foner, 21–46. New York: New York University Press.

Generation, education, and intermarriage of Asian Americans

Zhenchao Qian and Yue Qian

ABSTRACT
The influx of immigrants from Asia to the United States (U.S.) has expanded the pool of co-ethnic marriageable partners, strengthened racial identity, and contributed to the decline in interracial marriage with whites among Asian Americans. Yet, retreat from interracial marriage with whites may well vary by immigrant generation, an important factor in marital assimilation. Using data from the March Current Population Survey (1994–2015), we examine generational differences in intergenerational marriage and interracial marriage with whites among Asian Americans. The results reveal that over time third-plus-generation Asians show no significant change in interracial marriage with whites but declines in intergenerational marriage with first- or second-generation Asians. Second-generation Asians, on the other hand, have become more likely to marry first-generation Asians and less likely to marry whites. In addition, education provides different opportunities for intermarriage, with highly-educated Asian Americans more likely than their less-educated counterparts to marry whites and less likely to marry other Asians. Notably, highly-educated second-generation Asians tend to marry third-plus-generation Asians and whites while their less-educated counterparts marry first-generation Asians. These findings highlight the importance of generation and education in integration of Asian Americans.

Asians in the U.S. are fast growing. The share of the Asian population increased from less than 1% in 1965, the year when Congress passed the Immigration and Nationality Act, to nearly 6% in the early 2010s (Pew Research Center 2013). Continuous waves of immigrants from Asia are the engine that drives this growth. According to the Pew Report (2013), new arrivals from Asia have outnumbered those from Latin America since 2009; in 2010, about 36% of new immigrants were Asian and 31% were Hispanic; and today, three quarters of Asians in the U.S. are immigrants. The large influx of immigrants from Asia has contributed to the decline in intermarriage with whites among Asian Americans (Qian and Lichter 2007). Asian immigrants, diverse in migration history, socioeconomic status, culture, language, and religion, are less likely to intermarry than their U.S.-born counterparts. At the same time, Asian immigrants provide a large pool of marriageable partners, which may increase marriages between U.S.-born and foreign-born Asians.

Asian Americans exhibited high levels of interracial marriage with whites in the past. In 1990, nearly half of U.S.-born Asians married whites (Qian, Blair and Ruf 2001). The high level of intermarriage was related to population size. Population size influences social interactions between groups (Blau 1977). When a population group is small, contact opportunities are low within the group and high outside the group. Thus, Asian Americans had limited opportunities to interact among themselves in schools, workplaces, or residential neighbourhoods. In recent decades, a growing Asian immigrant population has not only replenished the marriage pool for their native-born counterparts, but also increased cultural awareness, promoted ethnic solidarity, and developed in-group contact opportunities (Massey 1995; Okamoto 2014).

Indeed, the past few decades brought significant declines in intermarriage with whites among Asian Americans (including Asian immigrants, thereafter) (Qian and Lichter 2007, 2011). Yet, it is unclear to what extent foreign-born Asians marry their U.S.-born counterparts; whether each generation, especially the second generation – children of many immigrants who arrived after the congressional passage of the Immigration Reform and Control Act in 1986 – married whites or other Asians; and whether educational attainment played a role in marriage with whites or other Asians. Our paper examines patterns of intergenerational marriage (i.e. marriage across first, second, and third-plus generations) and interracial marriage with whites among Asian Americans, by pooling annual data from the March Annual Demographic Supplements of the Current Population Survey (1994–2015). Specifically, we explore: 1) whether there has been an increase in intergenerational marriage and a decline in marriage with whites among Asians over time; 2) whether educational attainment plays a role in intergenerational marriage or interracial marriage; and 3) whether second-generation Asians are more likely to marry first-generation Asians or third-plus-generation Asians or whites. Our results reveal the role generation plays in Asian Americans' integration in the U.S. and shed light on how differences in marriage with co-ethnics and whites by educational attainment or generation shape the future of American society. This article contributes to our understanding of how marriage and assortative mating play a role in assimilation among Asian immigrants and Asian Americans (Yeung and Mu 2020).

Assimilation and intermarriage

Gordon (1964) formulated classical assimilation theory based on the experiences of European immigrants who came to the U.S. around the turn of the twentieth century. The immigrants were diverse in language, religion, socioeconomic status, and national origin at the time of arrival. Yet it did not take long that they and their descendants became culturally integrated and achieved parity with their native-born counterparts in education and socioeconomic status. Cultural and structural assimilation fostered marital assimilation as intermarriage with U.S.-born whites became commonplace.

Classical assimilation theory views marital assimilation of immigrants into middle class white America as an inevitable outcome after cultural and structural assimilation. This theory explains well the experiences of European immigrants and their descendants at the turn of the twentieth century (Gordon 1964). Asian immigrants today are different. Immigrants from Asia are positively selected and Asian Americans in general have achieved high levels of educational attainment and socioeconomic status (Lee 2015;

Pew Research Center 2013). Yet, as one of the racial minority groups, Asian Americans face low returns to education and high glass ceilings (Sakamoto, Goyette, and Kim 2009). Asian Americans, regardless of whether they are first, second, or third-plus generation, are perceived forever foreign and experience routine prejudice and discrimination (Okamoto 2014). As a result, their racial minority status and their U.S. experiences suggest that they are unlikely to follow a single path of marital assimilation stipulated by classical assimilation theory.

Alba and Nee (2003) reformulate the assimilation theory, taking into account that American society is racially diverse and immigration continues in the U.S. This new assimilation theory does not assume a universal outcome and posits that assimilation may be segmented and take diverse paths. Asian Americans who have achieved success in education, employment, and residential location may be more likely than other Asians to marry whites. For them, cultural and ethnic differences pale in comparison to their social and economic standing. Yet, other Asian Americans, especially first-generation immigrants, are at the other end of the spectrum. They have low levels of education, do not speak English well, work in segregated workplaces, and reside in ethnic enclaves (Zhou 1992). They may seek to marry their U.S.-born counterparts as a way of getting connected with the communities and becoming eligible for naturalisation (Bean and Stevens 2003; Stevens, Ishizawa, and Escandell 2012).

Clearly the growing number of Asian Americans, to say the least, increases the number of potential partners of the same race. Yet, opportunities to meet and marry an Asian are unequal and depend on an individual Asian American's position in American society. The generation mix of Asians, that is, the shares of the Asian American population that comprise the first, second, and third-plus generations, may play an important role.

Generation and education

Asian Americans have had a long history in the U.S., dating back to the 1850s when Chinese immigrants came to work in gold mines and on railroads (Hirschman and Wong 1981). For a long time, Asian Americans, mostly Chinese and Japanese Americans, suffered from exclusion, discrimination, prejudice, and even internment in the case of Japanese Americans during World War Two. They were considered 'unassimilable,' banned from intermarriage, and unfit for citizenship until 1952 with the passage of the McCarren-Walter Immigration and Naturalisation Act (Lee 2015). The third-plus generations of Asian Americans are descendants of earlier Asian immigrants who lived and worked in ethnic enclaves with limited outside contact.

The 1965 passage of the Immigration and Nationality Act finally opened doors for immigrants from Asia. Asian immigrants who arrived after 1965 were more socioeconomically selective than those who came in the nineteenth- and early-twentieth-century. They were more ethnically diverse than in the past, originating from China, the Philippines, Korea, India, and Southeast Asia (Hirschman and Wong 1986; Xie and Goyette 2004). Although ethnic enclaves still exist, immigrant selectivity puts many in integrated or predominantly white neighbourhoods (White, Biddlecom, and Guo 1993). These immigrants' children have come of age and become today's second generations.

With the continuous influx of immigrants from Asia, we would expect that intermarriage with whites is least likely among new immigrants. First, this is due to their socioeconomic position. Despite their selectivity in socioeconomic status relative to the peers in their countries of origin, they do not speak English well, are less familiar with American culture, and have lower educational attainment than their U.S.-born counterparts (Lee and Edmonston 2005). The second reason is the population size. The structural theory of intergroup relationships argues that in-marriage necessarily increases as the relative population size increases (Blau, Blum, and Schwartz 1982). These two factors indicate that the changing generational mix of Asian Americans, especially given that today three quarters of Asians are immigrants, will give demographic impetus to a retreat from intermarriage with whites among Asian Americans, also seen among Hispanics (Qian, Lichter, and Tumin 2018).

Previous studies on Asian Americans' intermarriage with whites focus on a comparison between foreign-born and U.S.-born Asians (Qian and Lichter 2011). The retreat from intermarriage with whites among the U.S. born does not distinguish between the second and third-plus generations. While third-plus-generation Asians may not be well versed in ethnic culture, second-generation Asians grew up in immigrant families. Arguably, the second generation is the cornerstone in the assimilation process. Second generations often juggle through both worlds, the one of foreign-born parents, their cultures, and social networks versus the one where they interact with their peers, schools, work places, and community organisations (Zhou 2009). It is conceivable that marriage patterns of second-generation Asians, whether they are more likely to marry whites or other Asians (especially first-generation Asians), help understand the assimilation process of Asians in the U.S.

Studying generational differences in intermarriage among Hispanics, Lichter, Carmalt, and Qian (2011) highlight the role of second-generation Hispanics. Second generations span boundaries that often separate the foreign born and the U.S. born. Intermarriage patterns of second-generation Hispanics indicate how quickly or slowly Hispanics integrate in American society (Lichter, Carmalt, and Qian 2011). They find that second-generation Hispanics are more likely to marry first- rather than third-plus-generation Hispanics or whites, which suggests a retreat from intermarriage with whites among second-generation Hispanics. They offer two hypotheses that are highly relevant and can also be tested for Asian Americans. One is that enormous growth of immigration reinforces racial identity and increases demographic opportunities for their U.S.-born peers. As a result, U.S.-born Asians, especially the second generation, are increasingly more likely to marry their immigrant counterparts and less likely to marry whites over time. The second hypothesis states that rather than retreating from interracial marriage with whites, second-generation and third-plus-generation Asians may continue to marry whites at the same level as in the past and do not show much increase in marriage with their immigrant peers. Under this scenario, they move culturally and economically toward the mainstream society, and social distance between U.S.-born and foreign-born Asians increases. Third-plus-generation Asians, in particular, are at least one generation removed from ethnic cultures and identities and may share little in common with contemporary Asian immigrants because the countries their ancestors came from have changed dramatically or no longer sent many immigrants to the U.S. (Japan for example). As a result, social distance between first and second generations may be smaller than that between second and third-plus generations. We expect second-generation Asians to have higher rates of marriage with first-generation Asians than with third-plus-generation Asians.

How generation influences intermarriage may also be associated with educational attainment. Although Asians have the highest percent among all racial groups to have earned a college degree, disproportionately more have less than a high school degree (Pew Research Center 2013; Sakamoto, Goyette, and Kim 2009). For Asian Americans, educational attainment is positively associated with intermarriage with whites (Qian and Lichter 2011). College-educated Asians, for example, have greater opportunities of meeting whites on campus, in the workplace, and in residential areas. These opportunities separate college-educated Asians culturally and socially away from their less-educated counterparts and reduce social distance with whites. In contrast, U.S.-born Asians with low levels of education lack such opportunities and tend to live and work in segregated ethnic enclaves (Zhou and Logan 1991). They may instead have more opportunities to meet and marry co-ethnic newcomers from Asia in ethnic enclaves. Consequently, second-generation Asians with low levels of education are more likely to marry first-generation Asians and less likely to marry whites than their highly-educated counterparts. It is likely that less-educated second-generation Asians may marry highly-educated first-generation Asians as an exchange for higher educational attainment with 'higher' generation status (Merton 1941).

Current study

Selectivity of first-generation Asians with high socioeconomic status increases the likelihood of success in socioeconomic integration and Asian Americans are considered at the vanguard of rising intermarriage in the U.S. (Lee 2015). Previous studies of Asian intermarriage have focused on marriages with non-Hispanic whites (Qian and Lichter 2007, 2011). Little is known about how generational mix of Asian Americans shapes intergenerational marriage and interracial marriage with whites. This paper fills the void. In this paper, we first examine whether a larger marriage pool of Asian immigrants reinforces cultural identities and strengthens intergroup boundaries. We hypothesise that over time there is an increase in intergenerational marriage among Asians and a decline in interracial marriage with whites.

Second, we examine how educational attainment plays a role in intergenerational marriage and interracial marriage. We hypothesise that less-educated Asian Americans are more likely to marry across generations and less likely to marry whites than their highly-educated peers. Third, we examine whether there is retreat from intermarriage among Asian Americans by focusing on the second generation. Given that the second-generation is tied to their immigrant parents and cultures, we hypothesise that second-generation Asians are more likely to marry first-generation Asians than third-plus-generation Asians.

Data and methods

Data for this study come from the Integrated Public Use Microdata Series March Current Population Survey (IPUMS-CPS) for the years 1994–2015 (https://cps.ipums.org/cps/). In 1994, the IPUMS-CPS began including information about each household member's birthplace and the birthplace of the household members' parents. This information, coupled with information about household members' race and ethnicity, allows us to examine detailed racial and ethnic patterns of intermarriage among the first, second, and third-plus generations of Asians over the 1994–2015 period.

Before 2003, the CPS did not distinguish Asians from Hawaiians/Pacific Islanders, whereas from 2003 onwards, Asian only, Hawaiian/Pacific Islander only, and Asian-Hawaiian/Pacific Islander biracial individuals are coded into three different categories. To maintain consistency through the survey years, Asians in this study refer to Asians or Hawaiians/Pacific Islanders. We believe, however, including Hawaiians/Pacific Islanders and Asian-Hawaiian/Pacific Islander biracial individuals does not change our results because they only comprise about 6% of the Asian population based on data from 2003–2015.

We consider the comparative intermarriage patterns of: (1) foreign-born Asians (first-generation Asians) who arrived in the U.S. roughly prior to age 20.[1] This will increase the chance that they had not married before immigration and had been exposed to the U.S. marriage market conditions before marriage; (2) native-born Asians with at least one foreign-born parent (second-generation Asians); (3) native-born Asians with two native-born parents (third-plus generation Asians); and (4) non-Hispanic whites (of any generation). Intermarriages between Asians and all other races are excluded due to extremely small sample sizes. To reduce zero cells in contingency tables and highlight the central role of college education in shaping marriage patterns (Cherlin 2010), we dichotomise educational attainment into two categories: no bachelor's degree and at least a bachelor's degree.

Our data consist of information on married heads of households who are then linked to similar information on their co-resident spouses. Following Lichter and his colleagues (2011), we restrict the sample to household heads and their spouses who were aged 18–34 at the time of interview. Marriages among young adults are more likely to have been formed recently and thus, this age restriction helps minimise potential selection bias caused by marital disruption and remarriage (Qian and Lichter 2007). Our sample consists of 61,993 heterosexual married couples. To examine changes over time and ensure enough cases for each time period, we divide the data into two time periods: 1994–2004 and 2005–2015.

To examine changes in assortative mating between 1994–2004 and 2005–2015, we fit log-linear models that identify the associations between spouses' race/generation and educational attainment independent of the marginal distributions of these characteristics. When studying race/generation assortative mating, we employ crossings models (e.g. Mare 1991; Qian and Qian 2014; Schwartz and Mare 2005).

Table 1 presents the crossings parameters in detail. Supposing that intermarriage is a process of crossing barriers of different levels, under crossings models, each barrier is

Table 1. Parameters for crossings effects on race-generation assortative marriage.

Husbands' race/generation	Wives' race/generation			
	First-generation Asian	Second-generation Asian	Third-plus-generation Asian	White
First-generation Asian	1	v1	v1 + v2	v1 + v2 + v3
Second-generation Asian	v1	1	v2	v2 + v3
Third-plus-generation Asian	v1 + v2	v2	1	v3
White	v1 + v2 + v3	v2 + v3	v3	1

Note: Table is adapted from Schwartz and Mare (2005).

determined by which two adjacent levels it separates. For instance, the barrier between first- and second-generation Asians is v1, the barrier between second- and third-plus-generation Asians is v2, and the barrier between third-plus-generation Asians and whites is v3 (Hout 1983). Thus, crossings models can reveal the barrier to intermarriage between two race/generation groups (Mare 1991). Parameters in Table 1 indicate the log odds of intermarriage across two adjacent race/generation groups relative to the log odds of endogamy, controlling for marginal distributions of husband's and wife's race/generation. Prospective spouses with a greater distance in race/generation must cross more barriers to get married. In other words, the log odds of marriage for couples across several race/generation boundaries are the sum of the crossings parameters separating husbands' and wives' race/generation (Schwartz and Mare 2005).

In order to examine gender differences in marriage patterns, we add a race/generation hypergamy parameter in the model to explore gender asymmetries (Mare 1991; Qian 2017). Specifically, we constrain the cells in which Asian husbands are in later generations than their Asian wives or white husbands are married to Asian wives into one parameter (i.e. the bottom half below the main diagonal of the four-by-four contingency table of husbands' and wives' race/generation). To measure the tendency for college graduates to marry each other (Schwartz and Mare 2005), we create a variable which indicates that both spouses are college graduates (=1; otherwise = 0). When exploring how race/generation assortative mating varies by spouses' education, we add interactions between the crossings parameters and the variable indicating that both spouses are college graduates. Furthermore, we add three-way interactions of the crossings parameters, the variable indicating that both spouses are college graduates, and the time period indicator to examine change over time.

Results

We first present descriptive results of the spousal distributions by race/generation and time period for men and women, respectively, in Table 2. In 1994–2004, generational endogamy (i.e. marriage in which two spouses belong to the same generational status group) was most common among first-generation Asian men: 70% of them married first-generation Asian women, followed by third-plus-generation Asians (52%); second-generation Asian men were spread out in their marriage patterns with nearly one quarter married to first-generation Asian women, one third married to second-generation Asian women, and 9% married to third-plus-generation Asian women. Notably, generational endogamy became stronger between 1994–2004 and 2005–2015, from 32% to 49% among second-generation men and from 52% to 69% among third-plus-generation men. Among Asian men over the 1994–2004 period, 23% of the first generation, 35% of the second generation, and 28% of the third-plus generation married whites. Over time, percent marrying whites declined for all three generations, to 19%, 22%, and 22%, respectively. Meanwhile, there was an increase among first-generation Asian men marrying second-generation Asian women, from 5% in 1994–2004 to 15% in 2005–2015, and there was a decline among third-plus-generation Asian men marrying first-generation Asian women, from 13% in 1994–2004 to 3% in 2005–2015.

Now we examine intermarriage patterns from women's perspectives, as shown in the lower panel of Table 2. As expected, there was a noticeable decline in marriage with

Table 2. Percentage distribution of marriages by spouses' race-generation, by men's and women's generation and time period.

	Spouses				
	First-generation Asian	Second-generation Asian	Third-plus-generation Asian	White	N
Men					
1994–2004					
First-generation Asian	70.2	5.0	1.9	22.9	423
Second-generation Asian	23.4	32.4	9.0	35.1	111
Third-plus-generation Asian	12.9	7.5	51.7	27.9	147
2005–2015					
First-generation Asian	65.6	14.9	0.8	18.7	369
Second-generation Asian	22.8	48.5	7.1	21.6	268
Third-plus-generation Asian	3.4	5.2	69.0	22.4	116
Women					
1994–2004					
First-generation Asian	62.9	5.5	4.0	27.5	472
Second-generation Asian	14.5	24.8	7.6	53.1	145
Third-plus-generation Asian	5.4	6.8	51.4	36.5	148
2005–2015					
First-generation Asian	54.4	13.7	0.9	31.0	445
Second-generation Asian	18.3	43.3	2.0	36.3	300
Third-plus-generation Asian	2.1	13.2	55.6	29.2	144

whites from 53% in 1994–2004 to 36% in 2005–2015 among second-generation Asian women and from 37% to 29% among third-plus-generation Asian women. One exception is that percent marrying whites actually increased somewhat for first-generation Asian women, from 28% to 31%, possibly due to the improved socioeconomic profile of more recent immigrants. Meanwhile, from women's perspectives, there was an increase in percent of marriages between first- and second-generation Asians (6% and 14% of first-generation Asian women were married to second-generation men in 1994–2004 and 2005–2015 respectively, and 15% and 18% of second-generation Asian women were married to first-generation men, respectively). There was also an increase in marriages between third-plus-generation Asian women and second-generation men, from 7% in 1994–2004 to 13% in 2005–2015.

The descriptive results reveal a decline in interracial marriage with whites and an increase in intergenerational marriage among both Asian men and women. Yet, these results are confounded by men's and women's generational differences and shifts in marginal distributions. We now introduce log-linear models to control for changes and differences in marginal distributions. In addition, we include educational attainment of men and women in the models to examine how couples' generational statuses interact with their educational pairings. Table 3 reports the goodness-of-fit statistics – the deviance and the Bayesian information criterion (BIC) statistics – for the log-linear models examined in this study. The goal of log-linear modelling is to reveal the association among the variables in consideration of finding a parsimonious model with acceptable goodness of fit, using the Likelihood Ratio Test (L^2) and the BIC (Hout 1983). The BIC statistic is equal to $L^2 - (df) \log(N)$, which adjusts L^2 based on degrees of freedom (df) and sample size (N). A smaller value of BIC indicates a better-fitting model (Raftery 1986). We mainly focus on the BIC statistic due to our large sample size (Gullickson and Torche 2014).

Model 1 includes only the time period indicator, marginal distributions of men's and women's race/generation and education, and associations between race/generation and

Table 3. Fit statistics for log-linear models of race-generation and educational assortative marriage.

Model		df	Deviance	BIC
1	Marginals (HR + HE + WR + WE + P) + HR × HE + WR × WE	112	29,597.95	28,362.06
2	Model 1 + C	109	21,397.36	20,194.57
3	Model 2 + RHyper	108	21,397.36	20,205.60
4	Model 2 + EduCol	108	1,362.63	170.87
5	Model 4 + HR × P + WR × P	102	1,175.88	50.33
6	Model 5 + C × P	99	1,164.61	72.17
7	Model 5 + HE × P + WE × P	100	328.55	−774.93
8	Model 7 + EduCol × P	99	325.10	−767.34
9	Model 7 + C × EduCol	97	250.70	−819.68
10	Model 9 + C × EduCol × P	90	225.60	−767.53

Notes: N = 61,993; cells = 128. df = degrees of freedom.
HR = husbands' race/generation; HE = husbands' education; WR = wives' race/generation; WE = wives' education; C = race/generation crossings parameters; RHyper = race/generation hypergamy (marriages in which Asian husbands are in later generations than their Asian wives or white husbands marry Asian wives = 1, otherwise = 0); EduCol = parameter indicating both spouses are college graduates (both spouses are college graduates = 1, otherwise = 0); P = time period (2005–2015 = 1; 1994–2004 = 0).

education of both husbands and wives. In other words, Model 1 assumes no association between husband's and wife's attributes. Not surprisingly, the BIC for Model 1 is much larger than zero, indicating a poor model fit.

From Models 2 through 4, we investigate time-invariant patterns of assortative mating on race/generation and education. In Model 2, we examine barriers to race/generation intermarriage by adding the crossings parameters. The great reduction in the BIC statistic, relative to Model 1, indicates that assortative mating on race/generation is far from random. Instead, there are severe barriers to cross before individuals marry spouses from other generational or racial groups. In Model 3, adding a uniform race/generation hypergamy parameter does not further decrease the BIC relative to Model 2, indicating that once we control for marginal distributions of spouses' race/generation, race/generation assortative mating patterns are symmetric with respect to gender. In other words, the probability of a marriage between two persons from different race/generation groups is unaffected by whether the husband or the wife is white or later-generation Asian. Building on Model 2 (a better-fitting model than Model 3), we examine the tendency for college graduates to marry each other in Model 4. After we add this term, the BIC decreases considerably relative to Model 2, indicating a strong tendency for college graduates to marry each other.

In models 5 through 8, we examine how marginal distributions of spouses' race/generation and educational attainment as well as assortative mating on race/generation and education have changed over the two time periods. In Model 5, we add interaction terms to investigate whether or not the marginal distributions of husbands' and wives' race/generation vary by time period (1994–2004 or 2005–2015). Based on the BIC, Model 5 fits more closely to the data than Model 4, which is not surprising due to the large, sustained influx of Asian immigrants in recent decades. Building on Model 5, further adding the interactions between the crossings parameters and time period (Model 6) does not significantly improve the model fit, as the BIC statistic becomes more positive with the loss of 3 degrees of freedom. This result suggests that percentage changes in marriage we see in Table 2 were largely due to shifts in marginal distributions of spouses' race/generation; once shifts in marginal distributions are controlled for, the likelihood of forming intermarriage between two race/generation groups relative to forming racial/generation endogamy did not change much between 1994–2004 and 2005–2015. Building on Model 5 (the best-fitting model thus far), we add the interaction terms between spouses' educational attainment and time period in Model 7. Model 7's BIC drops substantially relative to Model 5's BIC, indicating that husbands' and wives' educational distributions have changed significantly over the two time periods. Model 8 includes the interaction term between the parameter indicating both couples are college graduates and the parameter for time period. Model 8 does not improve relative to Model 7, indicating that among couples under examination, the tendency for college graduates to marry each other did not change over time after shifts in spouses' educational attainment are taken into account.

Do patterns of race/generation assortative mating differ by spouses' educational attainment? Building on Model 7 (the best-fitting model thus far), we include the interactions between the crossings parameters and the parameter indicating both couples are college graduates in Model 9. According to the BIC statistics, Model 9 fit more closely to the data than Model 7, suggesting that education indeed shapes race/generation assortative mating. Has the interaction between educational and race/generation assortative mating changed over time? We include three-way interactions of the crossings parameters, the variable indicating both spouses are college graduates, and the time period indicator in Model 10, but the model is not the most parsimonious. In the end, we focus on the parameter estimates based on the three better-fitting models (Models 7, 9 and 10, all with BICs much smaller than zero) to examine intergenerational marriage and interracial marriage by couples' educational attainment and time period.

Table 4 presents the parameter estimates based on the three better-fitting models for married couples involving Asians Americans of different generations and whites. Model 7 includes the crossings parameter estimates. All three parameters were negative, suggesting strong endogamy (Asian Americans married within their own generational group and whites married whites). Boundaries were the easiest to cross between first- and second-generation Asians ($\beta = -1.33$, $p < .001$) and hardest to cross between third-plus-generation Asians and whites ($\beta = -3.31$, $p < .001$).

In addition, barriers to intergenerational and interracial marriage vary by couples' educational pairing. Model 9, which includes the interactions between the crossings parameters and the educational pairing parameter, reveals that compared with their less-educated counterparts, Asian American couples who were both college graduates were less likely to form intergenerational marriages between first and second generations, more likely to form intergenerational marriages between second and third-plus generations, and to a lesser extent, more likely to form marriages between third-plus-generation Asians and whites.

Model 10 includes the three-way interactions between time period, the crossings parameters, and the educational pairing of spouses. For ease of presentation, we graph the predicted odds ratio in Figure 1 based on the parameter estimates of Model 10. Among couples who had both completed college education, the odds of marriage between second- and third-plus-generation Asians declined from .25 in 1994–2004 to .12 in 2005–2015 ($p = .03$). This decline may be due to increasing opportunities of generationally endogamous marriages among the U.S. born. Meanwhile, there was a small but insignificant increase in interracial marriage with whites (from .05 to .06, $p = .14$) among the college-educated couples. In contrast, among couples at least one of whom had not

Table 4. Select parameters from Models 7, 9, and 10, married sample.

Select Parameters	Model 7 β	Model 7 Std. Err.	Model 9 β	Model 9 Std. Err.	Model 10 β	Model 10 Std. Err.
Race/generation crossings						
(1)First- / second-generation Asian	−1.33***	0.09	−1.21***	0.11	−1.67***	0.19
(2)Second- / third-plus-generation Asian	−2.35***	0.12	−2.74***	0.17	−2.55***	0.21
(3)Third-plus-generation Asian / white	−3.31***	0.04	−3.51***	0.05	−3.46***	0.07
Both spouses are college graduates	2.67***	0.02	2.66***	0.02	2.69***	0.03
Crossings × Both spouses are college graduates						
Crossings(1) × Both spouses are college graduates			−0.33+	0.19	0.13	0.32
Crossings(2) × Both spouses are college graduates			1.00***	0.24	1.17***	0.30
Crossings(3) × Both spouses are college graduates			0.59***	0.08	0.44***	0.11
Crossings × Period						
Crossings(1) × 2005–2015					0.68**	0.23
Crossings(2) × 2005–2015					−0.46	0.34
Crossings(3) × 2005–2015					−0.12	0.10
Both spouses are college graduates × Period						
Both spouses are college graduates × 2005–2015					−0.08+	0.04
Crossings × Both spouses are college graduates × Period						
Crossings(1) × Both spouses are college graduates × 2005–2015					−0.70+	0.37
Crossings(2) × Both spouses are college graduates × 2005–2015					−0.27	0.46
Crossings(3) × Both spouses are college graduates × 2005–2015					0.29*	0.14

Notes: Std. Err. = Standard Errors.
***$p < 0.001$; **$p < 0.01$; *$p < 0.05$; +$p < 0.1$

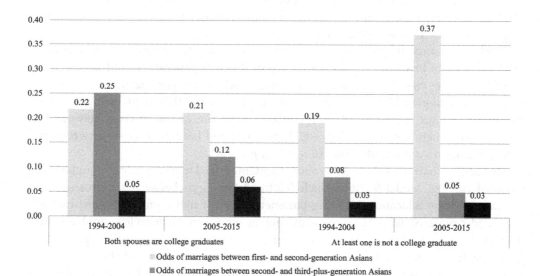

Figure 1. Odds of intergenerational marriage or intermarriage with whites, relative to odds of race-generation endogamy, by time period and educational pairing.

completed college education, the odds of intergenerational marriage between first and second generations doubled, from .19 in 1994–2004 to .37 in 2005–2015 ($p = .003$). This is accompanied by a small and insignificant decline in intergenerational marriage between second and third-plus generations, from .08 to .05 ($p = .18$). The results suggest that second-generation Asians move closer to their first-generation Asians in partnering, possibly due to increasing contact opportunities between first- and second-

Table 5. Select parameters from Models 7, 9, and 10, including all unions (marriage and cohabitation).

Select Parameters	Model 7 β	Model 7 Std. Err.	Model 9 β	Model 9 Std. Err.	Model 10 β	Model 10 Std. Err.
Race/generation crossings						
(1) First- / second-generation Asian	−1.28***	0.08	−1.19***	0.09	−1.56***	0.17
(2) Second- / third-plus-generation Asian	−2.25***	0.10	−2.57***	0.14	−2.45***	0.19
(3) Third-plus-generation Asian / white	−3.21***	0.03	−3.39***	0.04	−3.33***	0.06
Both spouses are college graduates	2.69***	0.02	2.68***	0.02	2.70***	0.03
Crossings × Both spouses are college graduates						
Crossings(1) × Both spouses are college graduates			−0.29+	0.17	0.05	0.29
Crossings(2) × Both spouses are college graduates			0.93***	0.21	1.13***	0.28
Crossings(3) × Both spouses are college graduates			0.56***	0.07	0.39***	0.10
Crossings × Period						
Crossings(1) × 2005–2015					0.55**	0.20
Crossings(2) × 2005–2015					−0.23	0.27
Crossings(3) × 2005–2015					−0.12	0.08
Both spouses are college graduates × Period						
Both spouses are college graduates × 2005–2015					−0.04	0.04
Crossings × Both spouses are college graduates × Period						
Crossings(1) × Both spouses are college graduates × 2005–2015					−0.50	0.34
Crossings(2) × Both spouses are college graduates × 2005–2015					−0.35	0.38
Crossings(3) × Both spouses are college graduates × 2005–2015					0.30*	0.12

Notes: Std. Err. = Standard Errors.
***$p < 0.001$; **$p < 0.01$; *$p < 0.05$; +$p < 0.1$.

generation Asians. Yet, the beneficiaries were selective of second-generation Asians without bachelor's degrees. Second-generation Asians' integration in American society very much depends on their educational attainment. Highly-educated individuals are far more likely to work in integrated workplaces, live in integrated neighbourhoods, and have greater opportunities for intergroup contact than their less-educated counterparts (Zhou and Logan 1991).

The results discussed above are limited to married couples. An emerging living arrangement is cohabitation. Cohabitation is short lived, but it has played an important role in the decline of marriage rates (Bumpass, Sweet, and Cherlin 1991). Cohabitation is more likely than marriage to involve couples who are interracial or exogamous (Blackwell and Lichter 2000). To examine how cohabitation may influence intergenerational or interracial marriages among Asian Americans, we replicate the analyses by including cohabiting couples in the models. Table 5 presents the results for the expanded sample (married and cohabiting couples). For Model 7, the crossings parameter between the first- and second-generation Asians was −1.28, slightly less negative than −1.33 as in Table 4 when only the married sample was considered. The other two crossings parameter estimates moved to similar positions (−2.25 versus −2.35 and −3.21 versus −3.31, respectively). These results along with those from the other two models confirm that cohabitation was more likely than marriage to be intergenerational or interracial. Overall, the conclusion remains the same when we consider both marital and cohabiting unions.

Discussion and conclusion

For Asian Americans, intermarriage rates with whites have declined in recent decades (Qian and Lichter 2007). This decline is in large part due to the continuous influx of immigrants originating from Asia. The rapid growth of the Asian population in the U.S. has increased the number of Asian ethnic neighbourhoods, stores, restaurants, and religious institutions, which has strengthened and heightened Asian ethnic identities. The growing population and reinforced cultural boundaries may redefine marriage markets where Asian Americans have more opportunities to meet, date, and marry among themselves. This raises the questions about how Asian Americans integrate in the U.S. and how increases of first-generation Asians influence intermarriage patterns of second- and third-plus-generation Asians.

Applying new assimilation theory (Alba and Nee 2003), we posit that Asian Americans' integration does not follow a single path. Specifically, growing Asian immigrants and changing generation mix of Asian Americans may lead to different intermarriage patterns among Asian Americans, depending on generation and socioeconomic position. Following Lichter, Carmalt, and Qian (2011) and using data from the March Current Population Survey for the years 1994–2015, we focus on generational differences in intergenerational marriage among Asian Americans and interracial marriage with whites. Descriptive statistics shows that marriage rates with whites declined for Asians of all generations (with the exception of first-generation Asian women) and marriage rates between first- and second-generation Asians increased between 1994–2004 and 2005–2015 (with the exception of second-generation Asian men who married first-generation Asian women).

Our statistical analyses yield several important findings. First, generational endogamy and white endogamy are much stronger than intergenerational and interracial marriages. Barriers between second- and third-plus-generation Asians are lower among couples both with college education than among couples with at least one non-college educated spouse. This suggests divergent paths of integration between highly-educated and less-educated second-generation Asians. Highly-educated second- and third-plus-generation Asians may have greater contact opportunities and thus a higher likelihood of intergenerational marriage than their less educated counterparts.

Second, over time, there is no strong retreat from intermarriage with whites among third-plus-generation Asians. This suggests that third-plus-generation Asians are assimilating, via intermarriage with whites, albeit not at a faster pace. They appear to have moved away from their cultural and immigrant roots due to their residential and workplace integration in the U.S. (Hirschman and Wong 1981; Hirschman and Wong 1986; Xie and Goyette 2004).

Third, differences in intergenerational and interracial marriages between second- and third-plus-generation Asians have grown stronger over time. The retreat from intermarriage with whites for the second generation is evident, as odds of intergenerational marriage between first- and second-generation Asians have increased especially among couples with at least one non-college graduated spouse. The population growth of first-generation Asians and their positive selectivity in terms of socioeconomic status have increased contact opportunities and narrowed social distance between the two generations (Lee 2015). The shared immigrant roots and national origins may have reinforced ethnic identities and fostered marriages across first and second generations (Qian, Blair and Ruf 2001; Shinagawa and Pang 1996).

The annual March demographic supplements of the Current Population Survey provide a great source of data for understanding generational differences in intergenerational marriage among Asians and interracial marriage with whites. These data, however, are not without limitations. We have pooled twenty-two years of CPS supplements from 1994 to 2015, yet the sample size of Asians is still small. A more severe limitation is that we are unable to further classify Asians into different ethnic or national origin groups (Chinese, Filipinos, or Asian Indians, for example). This limitation could confound findings as residential patterns may vary by national origin. Furthermore, ethnic or national origin compositions may vary by generation due to different immigration histories over time. For example, first-generation Asians consist of more national origin groups than ancestors of third-plus-generation Asians. The compositional differences in national origin may play a role in lowering levels of intergenerational marriage between the two generations.

Intermarriage helps understand paths of integration in American society. Patterns of intergenerational marriage and generational differences in interracial marriage among Asian Americans shed light on how generational and racial boundaries are shaped and reinforced. Third-plus-generation Asians have been integrated or assimilated as measured by interracial marriage with whites, despite a rapid increase in the share of the Asian population. Second-generation Asians on the other hand experienced a pause and had much greater likelihoods of marrying their first-generation counterparts, especially among those with less education. In the end, education has become a strong divider and leads to diverse paths of integration.

Note

1. The IPUMS-CPS classifies the time when an immigrant came to the U.S. into several year intervals. We take the median value of each interval and estimate age at immigration based on age, survey year, and median year at arrival.

Acknowledgement

An earlier version of this paper was presented at the Conference of Migration and Marriage in Asia, July 26–27, 2016.

Disclosure Statement

No potential conflict of interest was reported by the authors.

Funding

The authors acknowledge centre grant support from the National Institute of Child Health and Human Development (NIH) to Brown University (P2C HD041020).

References

Alba, Richard D., and Victor Nee. 2003. *Remaking the American Mainstream: Assimilation and Contemporary Immigration*. Cambridge: Harvard University Press.

Bean, Frank D., and Gillian Stevens. 2003. *America's Newcomers and the Dynamics of Diversity*. New York: Russell Sage Foundation.

Blackwell, D. L., and D. T. Lichter. 2000. "Mate Selection Among Married and Cohabiting Couples." *Journal of Family Issues* 21 (3): 275–302.

Blau, Peter M. 1977. *Inequality and Heterogeneity: A Primitive Theory of Social Structure.* New York: Free Press.
Blau, Peter M., Terry C. Blum, and Joseph E. Schwartz. 1982. "Heterogeneity and Intermarriage." *American Sociological Review* 47: 45–62.
Bumpass, L. L., J. A. Sweet, and A. Cherlin. 1991. "The Role of Cohabitation in Declining Rates of Marriage." *Journal of Marriage and the Family* 53: 913–927.
Cherlin, Andrew J. 2010. "Demographic Trends in the United States: A Review of Research in the 2000s." *Journal of Marriage and Family* 72: 403–19.
Gordon, Milton M. 1964. *Assimilation in American Life.* New York: Oxford University Press.
Gullickson, Aaron, and Florencia Torche. 2014. "Patterns of Racial and Educational Assortative Mating in Brazil." *Demography* 51 (3): 835–56. doi:10.1007/s13524-014-0300-2.
Hirschman, Charles, and Morrison G. Wong. 1981. "Trends in Socioeconomic Achievement among Immigrant and Native-Born Asian-Americans, 1960-1976." *The Sociological Quarterly* 22 (Autumn): 495–514.
Hirschman, Charles, and Morrison G. Wong. 1986. "The Extraordinary Educational Attainment of Asian-Americans: A Search for Historical Evidence and Explanations." *Social Forces* 65: 1–27.
Hout, Michael. 1983. *Mobility Tables.* Newbury Park, CA: Sage.
Lee, Jennifer. 2015. "From Undesirable to Marriageable: Hyper-Selectivity and the Racial Mobility of Asian Americans." *The ANNALS of the American Academy of Political and Social Science* 662 (1): 79–93. doi:10.1177/0002716215594626.
Lee, Sharon M., and Barry Edmonston. 2005. *New Marriages, New Families: U.S. Racial and Hispanic Intermarriage, Vol. 60.* Washington, DC: Population Reference Bureau.
Lichter, Daniel T., Julie H. Carmalt, and Zhenchao Qian. 2011. "Immigration and Intermarriage among Hispanics: Crossing Racial and Generational Boundaries." *Sociological Forum* 26: 241–64.
Mare, Robert D. 1991. "Five Decades of Educational Assortative Mating." *American Sociological Review* 56: 15–32.
Massey, Douglas S. 1995. "The New Immigration and Ethnicity in the United States." *Population and Development Review* 21: 631–52.
Merton, Robert K. 1941. "Intermarriage and the Social Structure: Fact and Theory." *Psychiatry* 4: 361–74.
Okamoto, Dina. 2014. *Redefining Race: Asian American Panethnicity and Shifting Ethnic Boundaries.* New York: Russell Sage Foundation.
Pew Research Center. 2013. *The Rise of Asian Americans.* Vol. Washington, DC: Pew Research Center.
Qian, Yue. 2017. "Gender Asymmetry in Educational and Income Assortative Marriage." *Journal of Marriage and Family* 79 (2): 318–336.
Qian, Zhenchao, Sampson Lee Blair, and Stacey Ruf. 2001. "Asian American Interracial and Interethnic Marriages: Differences by Education and Nativity." *International Migration Review* 35: 557–86.
Qian, Zhenchao, and Daniel T. Lichter. 2007. "Social Boundaries and Marital Assimilation: Interpreting Trends in Racial and Ethnic Intermarriage." *American Sociological Review* 72: 68–94. doi:10.1177/000312240707200104.
Qian, Zhenchao, and Daniel T. Lichter. 2011. "Changing Patterns of Interracial Marriage in a Multiracial Society." *Journal of Marriage and Family* 73: 1065–84. doi:10.1111/j.1741-3737.2011.00866.x.
Qian, Zhenchao, Daniel T. Lichter, and Dmitry Tumin. 2018. "Divergent Pathways to Assimilation? Local Marriage Markets and Intermarriage among U.S. Hispanics." *Journal of Marriage and Family* 80: 271–88. doi:10.1111/jomf.12423.
Qian, Yue, and Zhenchao Qian. 2014. "The Gender Divide in Urban China: Singlehood and Assortative Mating by Age and Education." *Demographic Research* 31: 1337–64.
Raftery, Adrian E. 1986. "Choosing Models for Cross-Classifications." *American Sociological Review* 51: 145–46.
Sakamoto, Arthur, Kimberly A. Goyette, and Chang Hwan Kim. 2009. "Socioeconomic Attainments of Asian Americans." *Annual Review of Sociology* 35: 255–76.

Schwartz, Christine R., and Robert D. Mare. 2005. "Trends in Educational Assortative Marriage From 1940 to 2003." *Demography* 42: 621–46.
Shinagawa, Larry Hajime, and Gin Young Pang. 1996. "Asian American Panethnicity and Intermarriage." *Amerasian Journal* 22 (2): 127–52.
Stevens, Gillian, Hiromi Ishizawa, and Xavier Escandell. 2012. "Marrying Into the American Population: Pathways Into Cross-Nativity Marraiges." *International Migration Review* 46: 740–59.
White, Michael J., Ann E. Biddlecom, and Shenyang Guo. 1993. "Immigration, Naturalization, and Residential Assimilation among Asian Americans in 1980." *Social Forces* 72: 93–117.
Xie, Yu, and Kimberly A. Goyette. 2004. *A Demographic Portrait of Asian Americans*. New York and Washington, DC: Russell Sage Foundation and Population Reference Bureau.
Yeung, Wei-Jun Jean, and Zheng Mu. 2020. "Migration and Marriage in Asian Contexts." *Journal of Ethnic and Migration Studies* 46 (14): 2863–2879. doi:10.1080/1369183X.2019.1585005.
Zhou, Min. 1992. *Chinatown: The Socioeconomic Potential of an Urban Enclave*. Philadelphia: Temple University Press.
Zhou, Min. 2009. *Contemporary Chinese America: Immigration, Ethnicity, and Community Transformation*. Philadelphia: Temple University Press.
Zhou, Min, and John R. Logan. 1991. "In and out of Chinatown: Residential Mobility and Segregation of New York City's Chinese." *Social Forces* 70: 387–407.

Love in the melting pot: ethnic intermarriage in Jakarta

Ariane J. Utomo

ABSTRACT
Jakarta has long been a prime destination for migrants across the ethnically diverse Indonesian archipelago. Using qualitative insights from fieldwork and data from the 2010 Census, this paper examines patterns and drivers of ethnic intermarriage in Jakarta. Jakarta has the highest rate of interethnic marriage in Indonesia (33%). Among married adults aged 20–39, recent migrants have a notably lower likelihood of intermarriage than non-migrants and non-recent migrants. Fieldwork findings suggest that despite the decline in the practice of arranged marriage, third party influence and broader social structures continue to influence individuals' preferences on *who* they should and should not marry. The popular notion that marriage signifies the union of two families reflects the unrelenting influence of parents and kinship networks in family formation decisions, and in contributing to a norm of ethnic assortative mating. Studying ethnic intermarriage in one of the world's largest metropolises contributes to two growing strands of scholarship in social demography: the literature on assortative mating in multi-ethnic developing societies, and the literature on marriage transitions in Asia.

Introduction

Social boundaries and identity are frequently amplified in marriage markets. This is especially the case in plural societies, where intergroup marriage – or the lack thereof – becomes a telling indicator of openness and social mobility. In a particular community, two different ethnic groups may live side-by-side in harmony, but this does not necessarily mean marriages between individuals from the two groups are welcomed. An inquiry into assortative mating – the tendency for individuals with the same group characteristics to marry one another – thus offers a unique window to study the nature of social stratification in these societies.

In the diverse Indonesian archipelago, education, social class, ethnicity, geographic origin and religion are concepts of identities with important bearings on assortative mating and family formation decisions (Yeung and Mu 2020). Following an earlier Census-based studies on ethnic assortative mating in Indonesia (Utomo and McDonald 2016), this paper draws on both the 2010 Population Census and qualitative insights from fieldwork to study prevailing patterns and attitudes to ethnic assortative mating in the capital region of Jakarta.

Across the many intricate layers of social boundaries and identities in marriage pairing decisions that one could delve into, studying the role of ethnicity is timely, at least, for two reasons. First, there is a long history of population movements and ethnic intermixing within Indonesia. But, following the end, after 32 years, of Suharto's rule in 1998 (the New Order period, Ind: *Orde Baru*), ethnicity has been an increasingly politicised social category. Since the Chinese-targeted violence that preceded the fall of Suharto, there has been a growing scholarship on identities, belonging and representation of the Indonesian Chinese (Hoon 2006; Setijadi 2016). Beyond the Chinese – *pribumi* (natives/sons of the soil) dichotomy, the study of ethnicity has also taken centre stage in studies on communal conflicts and identity politics in the context of political decentralisation following *Reformasi* (Bertrand 2004; Davidson 2008; Toha 2015).

A second, and related reason, is that this renewed attention to ethnicity in the *Reformasi* period is complemented by newly available data sources. Despite being one of the most ethnically diverse regions in the world, ethno-demographic studies on Indonesia have been few and far between owing to a long absence of population data on ethnicity.

Population data containing information on ethnicity was first collected by the Dutch in 1930. After Indonesian independence in 1945, data on ethnicity was not collected in the four population censuses that took place between 1960 and 1990. The deliberate exclusion of ethnicity from the Census was part of a bigger nation-building agenda (Hugo 2015). Following calls for a more democratic State, the political taboo surrounding data collection on ethnicity eventually subsided.[1] The resumption of data collection on ethnicity in the Census is one example of how new political regimes in Southeast Asia have begun adopting more inclusive forms in managing minority assertions since the late 1990s (see Miller 2011). Data on ethnicity was collected in the 2000 Census, from which Suryadinata, Ananta and Arifin (2003) pioneered a bourgeoning literature on Indonesian ethno-demography (see Ananta et al. 2015). For demographers, the post-*Reformasi* period is important in that data on ethnicity came about after decades of attempts to stifle it from the national narrative on population composition. It is following this junction along the census timeline that I seek to inquire into the extent to which ethnicity matters in the Indonesian marriage markets.

My discussion of ethnicity and marriage pairing patterns in Jakarta is informed by two major theoretical underpinnings. First, I refer to well-developed sociological literature on ethnic and/or racial-based assortative mating. Many theoretical constructs in this scholarship have been largely based on the experience of marriage patterns in the West. Earlier studies in this field had taken an interest in intermarriage from an assimilation perspective (see Qian and Lichter 2001). Research concerning forms of ethnic assortative mating that emerged in the context of rising internal migration within developing countries is relatively sparse. At the heart of theoretical themes in the ethnic assortative mating literature is research that tries to distinguish between opportunity (demographic factors such as group size) and preference. Included in the latter is what is theoretically conceptualised as *third party influence*: how parents and kinship networks affect individuals' marriage decisions. It is here that I introduce the second strand of demographic literature on marriage transitions in Asia.

A number of scholars have highlighted the steadfast nature of the Asian family, and have challenged the binary categorisation between arranged and self-choice marriage (Malhotra and Tsui 1996; Tsutsui 2013). They have argued that parents have continued to play an important role in the family formation processes of their children, including in timing, spousal choice, and post-marital residence. Extending this a little further, I shall argue that not only parents, but wider kinship networks, religious authorities, and the State in Indonesia all have interests in shaping norms and attitudes in the marriage market. My paper thereby uses the social category of 'ethnicity' as a case study to tease out the strength of the role of third parties in family formation processes in Indonesia's capital, Jakarta.

The paper is organised as follows. First, I outline the theoretical framework above in greater details. To provide further contexts on ethnic assortative mating, I then provide a brief overview on the notion of ethnicity in Indonesia, particularly on what it means as a demographic category, and how it matters in marriage decisions in Jakarta. Here, I compare and contrast concepts of ethnic assortative mating in Indonesia, with concepts around racial assortative mating as commonly understood in Western contexts. The Data and Methods, and the Results sections are both structured to outline Census-based analysis first, with qualitative insights to follow.

Theoretical framework: ethnicity and the in-between marriage

I use the term endogamy to mean marriage between individuals of the same ethnic group, and exogamy or interethnic marriage to indicate marriages between couples from different ethnic groups. Ethnic assortative mating is often contextualised as a study of intra- and interracial marriage in migrant-receiving nations of the West. In this context, intermarriage is used as a proxy for integration of a particular migrant group (minorities) to the host/dominant group. A number of key theoretical concepts have emerged from this scholarship (see Kalmijn 1998).

The first of these is that group size matters. Individuals from large ethnic groups are more likely to marry in. Assuming there is no preference for any ethnicity over another, the probability of meeting someone from the same ethnic group is higher due to sheer numbers. Second, a preference for endogamy reflects broader societal practices and norms in family formation. In groups where third parties such as parents and kinship networks hold a central role in deciding who and when an individual shall marry, the rate of endogamy for the group will be high. Third, minority-majority exogamy may embody processes of status exchange. This is exemplified when an educated migrant 'marries down' to a *native*.

There has been emerging interest in testing the applicability of theories on assortative mating in the context of other non-Western multi-ethnic societies, especially in the context of rising volumes of internal migration within these societies (Mu and Yeung 2020; Song 2009). The underlying tenet in the study of ethnic assortative mating in these societies is modernisation theory. The practice of endogamy is theorised to decline alongside the broader processes of modernisation, including urbanisation, increased schooling, and declining arranged marriages. In Mauritius, where ethnic endogamy has been the norm, the preference for same ethnic marriage was found to override the preference for class-based similarities (Nave 2000). In urban China, it was common to find ethnic minorities marrying out to the Han majority. In this minority-majority type intermarriage, there was little evidence to suggest that ethnicity-related status exchange is taking place. Rather, status exchanges in marriage were based on gender as opposed to ethnicity (Xing 2007). In rural China, ethnic intermarriage is much less common, but there are indications that marriage practices are changing due to development and increased population mobility (Wu 2013).

In Indonesia, although ethnic endogamy remains the norm, there are notable variations in rates of endogamy across the provinces and across population groups. Utomo and McDonald (2016) found that the likelihood of endogamy is lower among younger age cohorts, those with higher levels of education, and those residing in urban areas. Such findings are supported by another smaller scale survey. In the district of Banyuwangi in East Java, intermarriages of couples from different origins are more likely to happen among younger generations (Feirizza and Artaria 2008).

In examining why ethnic assortative mating remains the norm in Indonesia, this paper aims to take a closer look at the role of third parties. Identifying the role of the third party in ethnic assortative mating has theoretical implications for marriage transitions in Asia. In examining the influence of economic and social change on family structure across the West, South Asia, and China, Thornton and Fricke's seminal work outlined a number of common features in marriage transitions in these regions:

> the separation of the workplace from the home, increased training of children in non-familial institutions, the development of living arrangements outside the family household, increased access of children to financial and other productive resources, and increased participation by children in the selection of a mate. (1987, 746)

These features in marriage transitions are occurring gradually and at varying speeds across Asia. Rather than conceptualising marriage forms in Asia as binary, between arranged marriage and self-choice marriage, previous studies have documented varied forms of what could be conceptualised as the *in-between marriage* (Tsutsui 2013). This could be in the form of young adults actively choosing their own marriage partners but still needing to obtain consent from their parents and extended families. Or, the arrangement commonly found among the Indian middle class where parents and children together select partners for the so-called endogamous companionate marriage (Fuller and Narasimhan 2008). These various forms of marriage along the continuum of arranged versus purely self-choice love marriages are broadly in line with modernisation theory on family change.

Others have documented this continued influence of parents and other kin networks in marriage choice across Asia (Abeyasekera 2013; Allendorf 2013; Allendorf and Pandian 2016; Nilan 2008; Raymo et al. 2015). Although the causal link has not been fully ascertained, in theory, a primary factor for this is a norm of continued reliance of children and young adults on parents for education costs, and for economic welfare and housing security. For example, in East Asia, Raymo et al. (2015) identified that the duration of pre-marital co-residence of young adults with their parents is becoming longer. Apart from cultural factors that place little emphasis on familial independence, other issues such as weak welfare systems and increasingly high costs of living are cited as contributing factors. Such patterns in intergenerational transfers and living arrangements are also noted for young adults in Indonesia. I argue that similar forces are at work in marriage pairing decisions. In practice, most contemporary marriages in Indonesia would have a notable degree of parental influence in spousal choice.

The way young people seek parental approval for their marriage partners, or the way in which they take account of parental expectations when making judgements in this regard, places certain constraints on the narrative of *agency* in the so-called self-choice marriage. As an example, a common milestone in a young adult's romantic relationship is the introduction of a 'serious' boyfriend or girlfriend to his or her parents. The foreboding question of *'Orang Mana?'* – loosely translated as what ethnicity is she/he or where does she/he belong – would be among the first question that parents ask of a child's prospective spouse. Nilan (2008) demonstrated how parents play a central part in the way urban middle-class young people in Indonesia consider serious suitors for marriage. This idea is supported by survey data indicating that over half of married young adults in Greater Jakarta reported parental roles in spouse selection (Utomo et al. 2016).

It remains unclear, however, which aspects parents are involved in during the spouse selection process – or whether they attach particular importance to the ethnic characteristics of their children's prospective spouses. It is plausible to expect that the extent to which ethnicity matters in marriage decisions would tend to dissipate over generations of migrants. This is in line with sociological studies in the West showing that distinct ethnic identities are likely to dissipate among later generation migrants (Glazer & Moynihan, 1963; Sanders 2002). Another recent study in the US suggests that when it comes to intercultural dating, third generation young adults perceived fewer conflicts with their parents than their first and second generation migrant peers (Shenhav, Campos, and Goldberg 2016).

But considerations over ethnic marriage pairings often go beyond the parent–child realm, involving other actors including kinship networks, and – in an indirect but overbearing manner – the State and religious authorities. In certain ethnic groups in Indonesia, kinship alliances and boundary maintenance are among primary motivations for ethnic endogamy (Kipp 1996; Saenong 2012). Long-held attitudes and stereotypes about certain unfavourable ethnic pairings have circulated in communities. In many cases ethnicity and religion are conterminous. Anxieties about ethnic differences in romantic relationships are first and foremost tied to religion (Connolly 2009). The Indonesian Marriage Law stipulates that a marriage is considered legal if it was carried out according to the norms and regulations of one of the country's six recognised religions. This makes it difficult for an interreligious marriage to have legal grounds. In response to this Law, religious conversions prior to marriage are common (Aini 2008).

Research context

What is ethnicity?

The geographic boundary of present-day Indonesia traces back to territorial borders around a vast archipelago defined during Dutch colonial rule (circa 1800s–1945). For millennia before the Dutch came, the archipelago had been a crossroads of human contacts and migration. Studies into the genetic diversity of people from different parts of present-day Indonesia suggest that the area had been an 'ancient genetic highway' linking Greater Asia and the Pacific (Marzuki et al. 2003; Tumonggor et al. 2013).

The idea that the archipelagic Dutch East Indies were made up of people of diverse linguistic and cultural characteristics was documented in the colony's first population Census in 1930 (Van Der Eng 2002). Under the 1930 Census, major native ethnic groups in the archipelago were classified into seven major groups: the Javanese (47%), the Sunda

(14.5%), the Madura (7.3%), the Minang of Sumatra (3.4%), the Bugis of Sulawesi (2.6%), the Batak of Sumatra (2%), and the Balinese (1.9%). The remaining 21.3% of the population were classified as belonging to 'Others' (Van Klinken 2003).

In the post-colonial context, ethnicity has evolved to become a complex and contested social category in Indonesia. Unlike the case in many Western contexts, ethnic categories in Indonesia are less to do with racial distinctions. Of course, there are some exceptions such as the ethnic Chinese, Arabs, and groups of Melanesian origins from Eastern Indonesia. The concepts and definitions of ethnicity in contemporary Indonesia are often contradictory to one another. In this manner, the notion of ethnicity in Indonesia shares many parallels with concepts associated with racial identities as theorised by Western sociologists (see Lamont and Molnár 2002; Sanders 2002).

Ethnicity in Indonesia is relational and socially constructed, but it hinges on geographical objectivity. It is both a symbolic and a social category: which ethnic group one belongs to is widely agreed upon, not only by members of your group but by those outside of the group. It is non-static but implies a sense of permanence. It is fluid but the extent to which it becomes optional is largely situational. For the most part, however, every Indonesian is an Indonesian, and something else. Along with the formal ethnic categories, there are prevailing beliefs of cultural traits and norms distinct to each group (Ind: *adat dan budaya*). Examples of distinct cultural traits broadly include food and diet, language, dominant religion, and customs. There are also popularised ethnic stereotypes associated with temperaments, habits, and work ethics (Warnaen 2002).

Ethnicity in the city

Among the vast regions of Indonesia, I focus my attention on Jakarta. Jakarta, the capital of Indonesia, is the epicentre of economic and political power in Indonesia. Jakarta has a population of around 10.2 million in its core (BPS-Statistics Indonesia 2016).[2] Combined with the population in bordering districts, the total population of Greater Jakarta is estimated to be close to 30 million people.

About 42% of Jakarta's population was born outside the province (BPS-Statistics Indonesia 2011). The province of Jakarta is ranked second after Riau Islands as the province with the greatest proportion of recent migrants among its total population.[3] But it is the top destination in terms of the volume of recent inter-provincial migrants received. In Jakarta, later generation migrants may not be able to speak their ancestral ethnic languages, but in general, they would be able to easily answer the question of 'what are you?'; even when it means articulating multiple ancestries through their mother's and father's sides of the family.

Unlike other parts of Indonesia, Jakarta is uniquely placed in its ethnic composition (Jones et al. 2016). There is no single demographically dominant ethnic group in the province and its surrounding areas. The *native* ethnic group, the Betawi – creolised descendants of various people living in the Dutch coastal colony of Batavia (Knörr 2014) – accounts for 25% of the population in the Greater Jakarta. The Sundanese make up the largest ethnic group within the capital (33%). The Javanese constitute about 25% of the population. Other key groups in Greater Jakarta are Batak, Minang, Chinese, Malays and Bugis. Although small remains of urban ethnic *kampungs* do exist, formal demarcation of residential patterns along ethnic lines within Greater Jakarta's residential areas is largely invisible today.[4]

With the highest concentration of the educated middle class in the country, and a long history of large volumes of in-migration, Jakarta would be the best contender if one were to seek the least ethnically stratified marriage market in Indonesia. A recent 2010 Census-based study on the patterns of ethnic assortative mating in Indonesia confirmed such expectations (Utomo and McDonald 2016). Among the 33 provinces in Indonesia, Jakarta has the lowest prevalence of endogamy, with about 33% of married couples in interethnic marriages.

The objective of this paper is to provide a region-specific context that outlines both patterns and qualitative insights of ethnic pairing outcomes in Jakarta, particularly among recent first marriage age cohorts (young adults aged 20–39). Employing a mixed methods research design, the paper poses three broad research questions: what is the norm of ethnic assortative mating among major ethnic groups in Jakarta?; what are the correlates of ethnic intermarriage among young adults aged 20–39?; how is 'ethnicity' expressed, and how and why does it matter in contemporary marriage markets in Jakarta?

Data and methods

First, data from the Census 2010 were analyzed and used to provide context for the fieldwork, particularly for both respondent selection and question formulation for the in-depth interviews. To obtain an overview of the prevailing patterns of ethnic assortative mating in Jakarta, I follow the work of Utomo and McDonald (2016) and make use of 2010 full count Indonesian Population Census data. The full data set allows me to identify over 1.7 million co-residing married couples residing in the province of Jakarta, whose status includes either the head or the spouse to the head of household ($N = 1,769,714$ couples).[5]

The 2010 Census provides a classification system for over 1340 ethnic sub-groups. The way ethnicity is recorded in the latest Population Census does not allow for multiple ethnic categories for one individual. In a household where the mother and father were enumerated under different ethnic categories, their children were usually recorded as having the same ethnic category as their father.

Given the many and complex classifications of ethnicity and sub-ethnic groups in Indonesia, what constitutes an endogamous, or conversely, exogamous marriage is context dependent. For example, does a marriage between a male from the Muslim majority Batak Mandailing of North Sumatra and a woman from the Protestant majority Batak Karo constitute an endogamous Batak marriage? In a case where all Batak sub-groups are classified as one ethnic category, their marriage would be categorised as endogamous. But in the case where distinct religion and group identity act as strong barriers in marriage markets, it makes more sense to classify such a marriage as exogamous. Thus, in the Census analyses, I refer to the 1340 item detailed ethnic classification provided by the Census bureau to define what makes an endogamous or exogamous marriage. A marriage between two people belonging to different Batak sub-groups would be considered exogamous.

My analytical strategies are summarised as follows. First, I calculate ethnic-specific rates of endogamy for the top ethnic groups. For each ethnic grouping, rates of endogamy are plotted against total group size (of all ages) in Jakarta for the 10 largest ethnic categories in the city.

Second, I use multivariate analysis to examine the variation in the likelihood of ethnic intermarriage by gender, education and migration status for married individuals aged

Table 1. Sample statistics: Co-resident married men and women aged 20–39.

	Male	Female
Exogamy (%)		
No	64.85	64.73
Yes	35.15	35.27
Mean ethnic size	2,349,892	2,373,990
Education (%)		
None/Less than PS	1.36	1.78
PS	12.35	17.11
JHS	20.84	25.13
SHS	50.07	41.94
Tertiary	15.38	14.04
Age group (%)		
20–24	4.54	12.29
25–29	22.71	27.96
30–34	35.31	30.94
35–39	37.44	28.81
Migration status (%)		
Born in Jakarta	40.57	41.95
Non-recent migrant	52.47	50.22
Recent migrant	6.96	7.83
N	765,110	981,797

Note: The total observations of married males and females are different because spouse age may fall outside of 20–39.

20–39. Table 1 outlines the sample statistics for this analysis. As data on marriage cohorts are not available in the Census, the multivariate analysis focuses on the 20–39 age cohort, who were selected as they provide the closest depiction of relatively recent marriages. Using logistic regression, the dependent variable ethnic intermarriage, or exogamy, takes the value of 1 if an individual is married to someone of a different ethnic category. Independent variables are log of ethnic size, a categorical variable for migration status (=0 if individual was born in Jakarta, =1 if individual was born outside of Jakarta and was in Jakarta 5 years preceding the Census date (non-recent migrants), =2 if individual was born outside of Jakarta and was not in Jakarta 5 years preceding the Census date (recent migrants)), highest level of completed education, and age group. Results are plotted to outline how the likelihood of ethnic intermarriage differs across gender, migration status and education levels.

Through a qualitative approach, the paper then sets out to explore why and how ethnicity matters in marriage pairing decisions among tertiary educated young adults in Jakarta. The tertiary educated sub-group is of particular interest for two seemingly conflicting reasons. On the one hand, tertiary educated individuals have the lowest likelihood of same ethnic marriage in Jakarta. But on the other hand, relative to others with lower educational attainment, they are in fact the sub-group who are most likely to report parental involvement in their marriage decisions (Utomo et al. 2016).

The qualitative research encompasses two elements. To address the first research question, I gather information from secondary sources, including newspapers, online media (e.g. blogs), online dating sites, magazines, books and movies. These sources are important to canvass the contemporary discourse on ethnicity in romantic relationships. To address the second research question, in-depth interviews took place in two visits across 2014 and 2015 with a total of 14 respondents. The in-depth interview sample is not designed to be representative. Respondents were recruited through a purposive and convenient sampling.

Three of the respondents are key informants: a wedding organiser, a relationship psychologist, and a founder of an online matchmaking/dating site. The other respondents are young people aged in their early 20s who were all enrolled in tertiary education.

Results

Census results: Norms of ethnic assortative mating

Using the most detailed ethnic classification, 33% of co-resident married couples in Jakarta were identified as being in an interethnic marriage in 2010. Changing the definition of exogamy/endogamy by using the 24 aggregated categories of ethnic groupings changed the marriage classification for 4,314 couples out of the total 1,748,147 in the analytical subset (0.24%).

There is considerable variation in the rate of endogamy among large ethnic groups in Jakarta (Figure 1). If we look at the pattern of endogamy for the 10 largest ethnic groups in Jakarta, what we tend to see is that group size does matter, but not always. Note how the Chinese, Madurese, and Batak sub-groups seem to have high rates of endogamy despite their small relative size in Jakarta. This suggests that, demographic size aside, there are other cultural-specific factors at play behind the assortative mating patterns for these 10 groups.

Census results: correlates of exogamy among young adults

Among married individuals aged 20–39, less than 40 percent are exogamous (Table 1). A series of logistic regressions looking at interethnic marriage correlates among married

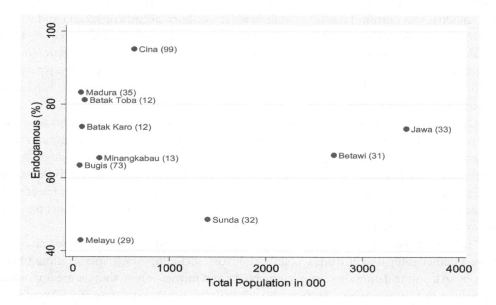

Figure 1. Endogamy and ethnic size: Jakarta, 2010. *Source*: Author's calculation using Population Census 2010. Number in brackets after each ethnic category corresponds to ethnic codes supplied by BPS-Statistics Indonesia.

Table 2. Logistic regression: Correlates of ethnic intermarriage in Jakarta, 20–39 year old married men and women.

	Male		Female	
	OR	SE	OR	SE
Log(ethnic size)	0.804***	0.001	0.871***	0.001
Education				
None/Less than PS	0.795***	0.018	0.846***	0.014
PS	0.786***	0.007	0.839***	0.006
JHS (ref)				
SHS	1.165***	0.008	1.072***	0.006
Tertiary	1.166***	0.010	1.081***	0.008
Age group				
20–24 (ref)				
25–29	0.939***	0.012	0.969***	0.007
30–34	0.903***	0.011	0.949***	0.007
35–39	0.873***	0.011	0.929***	0.007
Migration status				
Born in Jakarta (ref)				
Non-recent migrant	0.836***	0.004	0.919***	0.004
Recent migrant	0.564***	0.006	0.665***	0.006
Constant	13.825***	0.376	4.302***	0.099
N	765,110		981,797	

Note: The outcome of interest, exogamy, is a binary variable defined as 1 if the individual has a spouse of a different ethnic category, and zero otherwise.
***$p < .001$.

individuals aged 20–39 in Jakarta suggests the following (Table 2). As expected, holding everything else constant, an individual's likelihood of interethnic marriage decreases as their ethnic group size increases.

The other three independent variables in the model support the modernisation theory in assortative mating. Educational attainment is positively associated with interethnic marriage: an individual's increased *social mobility* resulting from attending or completing higher levels of education may encourage ethnic intermixing. The likelihood of intermarriage is highest among the youngest age group. Migration status drives variation in the likelihood of ethnic intermarriage, with recent migrants showing the lowest likelihood. Drawing from the results of the logistic regression, Figure 2 plots the variation in the likelihood of intermarriage by migration status and highest education for men and women. Across all levels of education, differences in the likelihood of intermarriage for Jakarta-born individuals and for non-recent migrants are relatively small. In the 20–39 age cohort, recent migrants have a notably lower likelihood of intermarriage compared with those in the other two categories.

Qualitative insights: popular discourse on interethnic relationships
Content from popular culture platforms consumed by young adults in Jakarta suggests that ethnicity continues to matter in contemporary marriage markets. Illicit relationships, heartbreaks, family conflicts and feuds resulting from interethnic romance were popular story plots in fictional novels, television dramas, and movies in the past, and have made countless returns in more recent periods.[6] Although narratives and stereotypes of interethnic pairings have long circulated, the Internet has made such narratives more visible in popular culture. In dating ads found in print newspapers and online forums, ethnicity is often specified for both the individual seeking

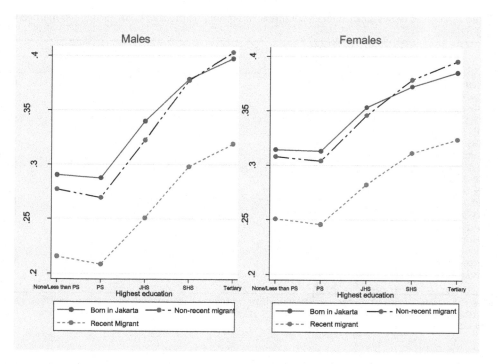

Figure 2. Likelihood of ethnic intermarriage by highest education and migration status. *Note*: Margins plotted from logistics regression detailed in Table 2.

romance and as a preference category for the kind of person that he/she is looking for. There are specialised online dating sites targeted for specific ethnic groups or religions: *KontakJodohBatak dot com, KontakJodohChinese dot com, Kontak JodohKatolik dot com* and so on. Numerous online articles providing romantic advice targeted to young adult readers tend to categorise interethnic relationships as *potentially problematic,* and offer solutions to readers in such situations.[7] User-generated content on the Internet – such as web logs – feature tales of interethnic pairings that are particularly unwelcomed by third parties.

The extent to which coming from a different ethnic group would prohibit a marital union varies from one case to another. I found cases in both print and online forums where young people experienced staunch opposition from their parents when dating someone of a different ethnicity. Though cautionary tales of interethnic relationships can be easily found in the popular media, so can happy endings to such romances. Among the Jakartan middle class, an interethnic marriage hardly seems to be controversial. The conflictual aspects of interethnic romance seem to have more to do with religious differences than with ethnic differences per se (Ind: *pasangan beda agama*). For example, such themes were regularly found in gossip columns on celebrity romance around the time of the fieldwork.[8] The general feeling seems to be that as long as a couple profess the same religion (Ind: *asal seiman*), ethnic differences become more of a complicating and/or preference issue than a prohibitive factor in the marriage market. As expressed during an interview with the founder of an online dating company whose clients are mostly young and educated urban middle class:

> A marriage is between two families not just between two individuals. Meaning, in that, if you have less barriers for success, meaning you don't have to deal with your parents or religion, because you are the same religion or you are the same ethnicity, then it will increase the likelihood of success. So we are not saying that you have to, but if we had an option, I always tell people this, if we have two exact people, like two potential suitors who are exactly the same, as if they were cloned, with identical life experiences, except one is of the same ethnicity and one is not, we'll give you the same ethnicity first; just because it's a little bit of an advantage. So our algorithm is based on identifying these advantages. (*Reza, founder of an online dating app*)

The interview highlights that despite the general impressions that an individual is free to decide who they should marry, the views of parents, extended families and other third parties are still taken into consideration in the spouse selection process. The fieldwork further suggests that although there are some exceptions, interethnic romances are generally accommodated by third parties. This is evident in the increasingly common practice of middle-class wedding parties of interethnic couples.

Across all ethnic groups, a wedding is a primary showcase of ethnic identity and social standing. In interethnic weddings, the ethnic heritage of both the bride and the groom are typically celebrated, either simultaneously, or one after another in different parts of the wedding celebration. In the latter, the couples would usually put on a particular ethnic outfit for the marriage ceremony (Ind: *Ijab Kabul/Akad Nikah*), and another outfit for the reception. Although common, interethnic weddings tend to incite certain complexities. For the couples involved, these anticipated setbacks are largely to do with the meddling of third parties. As stated by a key informant who co-owns a wedding organiser company in Jakarta:

> Forget about interethnic marriages. Joining two families, any families, are difficult. So, this is even more so when they grew up in different cultures. First, in terms of the (wedding) events that they want to have. For example, one is from Java, the other from Sumatra. They will say, we will wear Javanese costumes for the solemnization of our marriage (Ind: *akad),* but we will wear Sumatran for the reception, or vice versa. Next, they also think differently. The Javanese, for sure, tend to give in. They are more accepting of fate (*Javanese: Nrimo*). But the Sumatran, they are usually tougher (Ind: *lebih keras*). The bride will say (to me), please help me, my family is so difficult, so can you figure out a way to influence their minds so I can have the wedding that I want? Remember when we were about to get married? We did that too, arguing with our parents. Given that we argued with parents, imagine the extended families? And sometimes, one culture to another – even though we are all one nation of Indonesia, we have such different characters. ... The Javanese has many processions (in its wedding ritual): *Siraman, Midodareni, Akad, Panggih*, Reception. Then the Sumatrans have their own rituals. Like tomorrow, have to do a Bugis wedding. They have *siraman, Mappacci, malam pakai pacar,* then *akad*, then reception. All those, in terms of the decoration, the rituals, are different to the Javanese. So they (the interethnic bride and groom) ask me what should we do?

(Dewi, owner of a wedding organizer company)

Qualitative insights: interviews with young adults. The series of interviews identified variations in the ways young adults expressed their own attitudes, the perceptions of their families, and wider societal attitudes towards ethnic assortative mating.

Respondents who first came to Jakarta to study at a tertiary institution in their early twenties have adopted cosmopolitan identities in their day-to-day interaction with their peers. But at the same time, they remain most passionate in articulating their ethnic identities. They also tend to be actively engaged in ethnic and sub-ethnic student organisations on campus.

One such student – Salim, a male respondent from Madura – described that back home, his parents are particular not only about the ethnicity and religion of his wife-to-be. The allegiance of the girl's family to a particular brand of Islam – the modernist Muhamadiyah or a more traditional Nahdlatul Ulama – is also a decisive factor (see Schweizer 1983).

But having a strong sense of ethnic identity does not necessarily mean Salim would only engage in an endogamous relationship, in practice: the network of campuses around South Jakarta is a melting pot of potential dates. In general, young adults in Greater Jakarta have vast and varying social networks that go beyond the confine of their school/campus, neighbourhood, and workplace. These various networks are further augmented by the Internet and social media, such as Instagram, Facebook, WhatsApp, Twitter and Line.

In Salim's case, ethnicity plays out differently in dating and marrying contexts. At the time of the interview, Salim was dating a Malay girl from Jambi, Sumatra. When asked about his long-term intentions with his current girlfriend, Salim responded:

> Yes (I have intentions to be more serious), but to tell you the truth, I am a little pessimistic about it. Again, it's my family. My family has a very strong Madurese character (Ind: *keluarga saya kental ke- Maduraan-nya*), so (they prefer) a Madurese girl, or perhaps a Javanese girl at least ... For Madurese, a good woman is not one who is clever, can write a book and is highly educated. For my family, a good woman must be able to socialize with the Madurese community. For example, she should know what to do in a gathering with other Madurese, like she knows how to work in the kitchen, she knows how to communicate like a Madurese, she knows how to dress, and the way we sit cross-legged silently – we have our own ways. It does not matter whether she has a bachelor or master degree. (Salim, 28, male, post graduate student)

Salim's case is exemplary of a more definitive stance of third parties' roles in spouse selection. In contrast, other respondents did not describe their parents and/or extended families as being intrusive or authoritative when it came to ethnicity of their romantic partners. Some respondents described their parents as giving *soft nudges*, as opposed to giving clear instructions about who they should marry. A common phrase in such parental advice is something along the lines of '*it is better/easier if you were to marry someone of same ethnicity*'.

Third parties' influence aside, I often encountered expressed preferences related to ethnic stereotypes from the respondents themselves. Fitriany, a half Bugis half Javanese female student who grew up in a fishing village in Banyuwangi, identifies herself as being Bugis. She prefers to have a Bugis husband, because she sees them as being strong, decisive, and upfront and manly:

> Yes, we Bugis are tough, Javanese are soft. We are very upfront, if we don't like it, we say it; Javanese has their Blangkon (ed: Javanese hat). It looks good in the front, but there is a knot at the back. It means they act nice in front of you, but they 'hit you' from behind. (Fitriany, 23, female, undergraduate student)

Another mixed Betawi–Sundanese female respondent expressed a preference for a relationship with someone of a similar ethnic background:

Yes, I prefer (to date) someone of the same (ethnic background). If it's different, well, their ways are also different, like someone from Lampung, they tend to have harder characters, it doesn't suit me. (Ai, 19, female, undergraduate student)

In Ai's case, the preference for having someone who shares the same ethnic background comes out of her personal experience rather than through the influence of her parents. The only two criteria for her suitor espoused by her parents are that he must be a Muslim, and a tertiary graduate (Ind: *Sarjana*).

Importance attached to religious endogamy was a consistent finding throughout the interviews. Although respondents noted that crossing ethnic boundaries might not be as challenging as it used to be in the past, crossing the religious boundary is really shunned – by both parents and families, and by the respondents themselves. Educational homogamy was important for all the female respondents interviewed, but did not come through as such for the male respondents.

Discussion

This paper contributes to the emerging ethno-demography scholarship by highlighting the continued relevance of ethnicity in marriage pairings within the context of a cosmopolitan mega urban region in Southeast Asia.

Judging by Census estimates on the prevalence of interethnic marriages, Jakarta appears to have the least ethnically stratified marriage pairing landscape in Indonesia. Among married young adults aged 20–39, endogamous marriage remains the norm, but ethnic intermarriage is not atypical either. The Census results are supportive of the modernisation hypotheses in explaining assortative mating: being older, less educated, and recently migrating to Jakarta are associated with a lower likelihood of intermarriage. Using data from a full count Census may yield statistical power to canvass demographic trends, however the Census offers little in the way of identifying the underlying attitudes that drive marriage pairing patterns. This paper fills this gap by complementing results from the Census analysis with qualitative data gathered online and through fieldwork.

Jakarta's long-standing history as a prime destination for migrants and as a melting pot of cultures is an important backdrop to this study. I found that by and large, interethnic marriage is not a contentious issue, but ethnicity continues to matter in the spouse selection process in this Southeast Asian metropolis. On the one hand, Jakarta's melting pot of ethnicity offers a unique element of chance or opportunity for interethnic romantic encounters. This is especially the case in higher education settings where students from all over Indonesia are coming to study in Jakarta's many tertiary institutions. Yet, qualitative data suggest that the way individuals pair up for marriage is far from being a random process of interethnic encounters and matches.

Data from various platforms of popular media and in-depth interviews indicated that the extent to which ethnicity becomes a salient factor in the dating and marriage markets varies from one case to another. Young adults interviewed expressed individual preferences, third parties' influence, and societal norms in characterising the way ethnicity and ethnic stereotypes matter in these markets. But it is difficult to disentangle whether respondents' attitudes to ethnic intermarriage are largely attributed to their own individual preferences, to adherence to their parents' wishes, to their broader cultural networks, to religious teachings, or to a combination of all these factors.

In most cases, the respondents' nominated preference of marriage partner is situated within broader considerations of their family, class, ethnicity, religion and cultural networks. The interviews suggest that ethnic boundaries are relatively more permeable in the context of a spousal search. The conflictual aspect in interethnic marriage is largely to do with religion. It can be difficult to separate ethnicity and religion as these identities can be synonymous with one another.

These findings have a number of theoretical implications. Kalmijn (1998) distinguished individual preferences of marriage candidates, and third parties' roles, as two distinct but complementary social forces behind endogamy. In Kalmijn's framework, the manner in which third parties are theorised to promote endogamy is further divided into two categories: through promoting group identification, and through applying group sanctions against exogamy. In assessing the narratives of the in-depth interviews, I found that the respondents' descriptions of their ethnic identity, dating preferences and qualities of their ideal spouse were indicative of a long process of in-group and out-group identification. For example, the interviews highlight many preconceived ethnic stereotypes of potential suitors, and whether they would work with the respondents' inherent personalities and temperaments. Given that the family and kinship network plays a fundamental role in socialising group identities, boundaries, and ethnic stereotypes, it is difficult to explicate whether norms of assortative mating are largely driven by third party interference, or by individuals fully asserting their own preferences. In another example, the prevailing marriage law and religious doctrines that discourage interreligious marriage are examples of strong group sanctions against religious exogamy. Correspondingly, respondents expressed that the most important category for their ideal spouse is for him or her to have the same religion. This suggests that group sanctions – created by third parties – are internalised into individuals' preferences in marriage markets.

What transpires from the qualitative insights is that romantic relationships ending in marriage do not generally occur within a vacuum of total individual freedom to choose a partner. When assessing ideal spousal qualities, ethnicity is often framed together with other relational identities in the marriage markets. The way young adults account for parental and societal expectations of preferred spousal characteristics demands a more nuanced re-definition in the concept of self-choice marriage. These findings are supportive of previous work on so-called hybrid or in-between marriage models in other Asian societies (Allendorf 2013; Tsutsui 2013). Reflecting the nature of these societies at large, a marriage is more of a collective family affair than a private marker of transition to adulthood of the two individuals involved.

This study is not without its limitations. The Census analysis was intended to provide a general picture of the patterns and correlates of ethnic intermarriage, and not to identity causal relationships. On the one hand, certain aspects of the qualitative insights from the fieldwork are in line with the Census findings. For example, the multivariate analysis suggests that married recent migrants have a significantly lower likelihood of intermarriage than non-migrants and non-recent migrants. The interviews correspondingly identified that respondents who had recently arrived in Jakarta are more likely to express stronger ethnic identity and adherence to their parents' wish for endogamy. But, the small and unrepresentative nature of the interviews makes it difficult to draw general conclusions about drivers of ethnic intermarriage. Despite such limitations, the qualitative insights canvassed in this paper provide a number of useful directions for future research.

First, the fieldwork found that expressed preference and adherence to norms of endogamy do seem to vary with age at migration to Jakarta. Future studies can look into ways to test how these differences in migration-related characteristics drive variation in attitudes towards endogamy and exogamy. It would be fruitful to test whether patterns of living arrangements/co-residence vary among migrant categories, and have direct/indirect effects on parental influence in spouse selection. Second, the interviews identified differences in reported levels of individual and third party *tolerance* of different groups in the marital context. For example, a Betawi–Sunda respondent nominated a preference for men from a similar ethnic background but not a Sumatran. Such preconceived notions of ethnic distance in spousal preference warrant closer examination in future studies.

Notes

1. See https://www.bps.go.id/KegiatanLain/view/id/127.
2. Data for the province of Jakarta based on Intercensal Survey 2015. Data for the population of districts in Greater Jakarta based on 2010 Population Census.https://www.bps.go.id/website/pdf_publikasi/Penduduk-Indonesia-hasil-SUPAS-2015_rev.pdf.
3. A recent migrant here refers to an individual whose place of residence 5 years prior to census date was different to his/her current province of residence. About 7.3 per cent of Jakarta's population were recent migrants.
4. This is in contrast to Jakarta's colonial past. Jakarta evolved from the port city of Batavia – the trading capital of the Dutch East Indies Company. In the seventeenth and eighteenth century, ethnic Balinese, Bugis, Ambonese, Bandanese and the Moors were concentrated in their ethnic *kampungs* (urban settlements) outside the city centre. Central Batavia was occupied by the Dutch, the Chinese, and the Mardjikers (Asian Christians). This residential segregation along ethnic lines was commonly found across other colonial cities in Southeast Asia (Evers, 1975).
5. I have effectively excluded other married couples in the household whose household relationship status falls beyond these two categories (for example daughter to the head of household or child-in-law). As the census data is originally stored for each individual embedded within a household, it was hard to match the correct husband-wife pairs, such as in the case where there are multiple married couples living in the same household, and when they are not enumerated as the head or the spouse to head of the household. Co-resident polygamous individuals were also excluded from the analysis.
6. For example: the novel titled Raumanen by Marianne Katoppo (1977); the movie Ci(n)ta by Sammaria Simandjuntak 2009; the movie Cinta Tapi Beda by Hanung Brahmantyo (2012).
7. For example: https://life.idntimes.com/relationship/erwanto/11-hal-yang-kamu-pasti-rasakan-jika-punya-pasangan-beda-suku;
8. See for example: http://showbiz.liputan6.com/read/2163308/pacaran-beda-keyakinan-junior-liem-dan-putri-titian-jalani-saja.

Disclosure statement

No potential conflict of interest was reported by the author.

References

Abeyasekera, Asha L. 2013. The Choosing Person: Marriage, Middle-Class Identities, and Modernity in Contemporary Sri Lanka. UK: University of Bath. http://opus.bath.ac.uk/44943/

Aini, Noryamin. 2008. "Inter-religious Marriage from Socio-Historical Islamic Perspectives." *Brigham Young University Law Review* 2008 (3): 669–705.
Allendorf, Keera. 2013. "Schemas of Marital Change: From Arranged Marriages to Eloping for Love." *Journal of Marriage and Family* 75 (2): 453-469. doi:10.1111/jomf.12003
Allendorf, Keera, and Roshan K. Pandian. (2016). "The Decline of Arranged Marriage? Marital Change and Continuity in India." *Population and Development Review* 42 (3): 435-464. doi:10.1111/j.1728-4457.2016.00149.x
Ananta, Aris, Evi Nurvidya Arifin, M. Sairi Hasbullah, Nur Budi Handayani, and Agus Pramono. 2015. *Demography of Indonesia's Ethnicity*. Singapore: Institute of Southeast Asian Studies.
Bertrand, Jacques. 2004. *Nationalism and Ethnic Conflict in Indonesia*. Cambridge, UK: Cambridge University Press.
Connolly, Jennifer. 2009. "Forbidden Intimacies: Christian–Muslim Intermarriage in East Kalimantan, Indonesia." *American Ethnologist* 36 (3): 492-506.
Davidson, Jamie S. 2008. *From Rebellion to Riots: Collective Violence on Indonesian Borneo*. Madison: University of Wisconsin Press.
Evers, Hans-Dieter. 1975. "Urbanization and Urban Conflict in Southeast Asia." *Asian Survey* 15 (9): 775-785. doi:10.2307/2643173
Feirizza, and Myrtati D. Artaria. 2008. "Exogamy and Increased MMR (Mean Marital Radius) in Banyuwangi." Paper presented at the International Symposium Faculty of Humanity, Airlangga University, Surabaya, December 11.
Fuller, C. J., and Haripriya Narasimhan. 2008. "Companionate Marriage in India: The Changing Marriage System in a Middle-Class Brahman Subcaste." *Journal of the Royal Anthropological Institute* 14 (4): 736-754. doi:10.1111/j.1467-9655.2008.00528.x.
Glazer, Nathan, and Daniel Patrick Moynihan. 1963. Beyond the Melting Pot: The Negroes, Puerto Ricans, Jews, Italians and Irish of New York City. Cambridge, MA: MIT Press.
Hoon, Chang Yau. 2006. "Assimilation, Multiculturalism, Hybridity: The Dilemmas of the Ethnic Chinese in Post-Suharto Indonesia." *Asian Ethnicity* 7 (2): 149-166.
Hugo, Graeme. 2015. "Demography of Race and Ethnicity in Indonesia." In *The International Handbook of the Demography of Race and Ethnicity*, edited by Rogelio Sáenz, David G. Embrick, and Néstor P. Rodríguez, 259-280. Dordrecht: Springer Netherlands.
Jones, Gavin W., Hasnani Rangkuti, Ariane Utomo, and Peter McDonald. 2016. "Migration, Ethnicity, and the Educational Gradient in the Jakarta Mega-Urban Region: A Spatial Analysis." *Bulletin of Indonesian Economic Studies* 52 (1): 55-76. doi:10.1080/00074918.2015.1129050.
Kalmijn, Matthijs. 1998. "Intermarriage and Homogamy: Causes, Patterns, Trends." *Annual Review of Sociology* 24 (1): 395-421. doi:10.1146/annurev.soc.24.1.395.
Kipp, Rita S. 1996. Dissociated Identities: Ethnicity, Religion, and Class in an Indonesian Society. Ann Arbor: University of Michigan Press.
Knörr, Jacqueline. 2014. *Creole Identity in Postcolonial Indonesia*. Vol. 9. Oxford: Berghahn Books.
Lamont, Michèle, and Virág Molnár. (2002). "The Study of Boundaries in the Social Sciences." *Annual Review of Sociology* 28: 167-195.
Malhotra, Anju, and Amy Ong Tsui. 1996. "Marriage Timing in Sri Lanka: The Role of Modern Norms and Ideas." *Journal of Marriage and the Family* 58 (2): 476-490. doi:10.2307/353511.
Marzuki, Sangkot, Herawati Sudoyo, Helena Suryadi, Iswari Setianingsih, and Patcharin Pramoonjago. 2003. "Human Genome Diversity and Disease on the Island Southeast Asia." In *Tropical Diseases: From Molecule to Bedside. Advances in Experimental Medicine and Biology*, Vol. 531, edited by Sanglot Marzuki, Jan Verhoef, and Harme Snippe, 3–18. New York: Springer.
Miller, Michelle A. 2011. "Introduction – Ethnic Minorities in Asia: Inclusion or Exclusion?" *Ethnic and Racial Studies* 34 (5): 751-761. doi:10.1080/01419870.2010.537361.
Mu, Zheng, and Wei-Jun Jean Yeung. 2020. "Internal Migration, Marriage Timing and Assortative Mating: A Mixed-Method Study in China." *Journal of Ethnic and Migration Studies* 46 (14): 2914–2936. doi:10.1080/1369183X.2019.1585009.
Nave, Ari. 2000. "Marriage and the Maintenance of Ethnic Group Boundaries: The Case of Mauritius." *Ethnic and Racial Studies* 23 (2): 329-352. doi:10.1080/014198700329079.

Nilan, Pam. 2008. "Youth Transitions to Urban, Middle-Class Marriage in Indonesia: Faith, Family and Finances." *Journal of Youth Studies* 11 (1): 65-82. doi:10.1080/13676260701690402.

Qian, Zhenchao, and Daniel T. Lichter. 2001. "Measuring Marital Assimilation: Intermarriage among Natives and Immigrants." *Social Science Research* 30 (2): 289-312. doi:10.1006/ssre.2000.0699.

Raymo, James M., Hyunjoon Park, Yu Xie, and Wei-jun Jean Yeung. 2015. "Marriage and Family in East Asia: Continuity and Change." *Annual Review of Sociology* 41 (1): 471-492. doi:10.1146/annurev-soc-073014-112428.

Saenong, Faried F. 2012. "Kindred Endogamy in a Bugis Migrant Community." *Intersections: Gender and Sexuality in Asia and the Pacific* 30. http://intersections.anu.edu.au/issue30/saenong1.htm.

Sanders, Jimy M. 2002. "Ethnic Boundaries and Identity in Plural Societies." *Annual Review of Sociology* 28: 327-357.

Schweizer, Margarete. 1983. "Religion and Social Stratification in a Santri Village in Klaten, Central Java." *Indonesia Circle. School of Oriental & African Studies. Newsletter* 11 (32), 25-34. doi:10.1080/03062848308729563.

Setijadi, Charlotte. 2016. "Ethnic Chinese in Contemporary Indonesia: Changing Identity Politics and the Paradox of Sinification." *ISEAS Perspective* 12, 17 March.

Shenhav, Sharon, Belinda Campos, and Wendy A. Goldberg. 2016. "Dating out is Intercultural." *Journal of Social and Personal Relationships* 34: 397–422. doi:10.1177/0265407516640387.

Song, Miri. 2009. "Is Intermarriage a Good Indicator of Integration?" *Journal of Ethnic and Migration Studies* 35 (2): 331-348. doi:10.1080/13691830802586476.

Suryadinata, Leo, Evi Nurvidya Arifin, and Aris Ananta. 2003. *Indonesia's Population Ethnicity and Religion in a Changing Political Landscape*. Vol. 1. Singapore: Institute of Southeast Asian Studies.

Thornton, Arland, and Thomas E. Fricke. 1987. "Social Change and the Family: Comparative Perspectives from the West, China, and South Asia." Paper presented at the Sociological Forum.

Toha, Risa J. 2015. "Political Competition and Ethnic Riots in Democratic Transition: A Lesson From Indonesia." *British Journal of Political Science* 47 (3): 631-651. doi:10.1017/S0007123415000423.

Tsutsui, Junya. 2013. "The Transitional Phase of Mate Selection in East Asian Countries." *International Sociology* 28 (3): 257-276. doi:10.1177/0268580913484775.

Tumonggor, Meryanne, Tatiana M. Karafet, Brian Hallmark, J. Stephen Lansing, Herawati Sudoyo, Michael F. Hammer, and Murray P. Cox. 2013. "The Indonesian Archipelago: An Ancient Genetic Highway Linking Asia and the Pacific." *Journal of Human Genetics* 58 (3): 165-173. http://www.nature.com/jhg/journal/v58/n3/suppinfo/jhg2012154s1.html.

Utomo, Ariane, and Peter McDonald. 2016. "Who Marries Whom?: Ethnicity and Marriage Pairing Patterns in Indonesia." *Asian Population Studies* 12 (1): 28-49.

Utomo, Ariane, Anna Reimondos, Iwu Utomo, Peter F. McDonald, and Terence H. Hull. 2016. "Transition Into Marriage in Greater Jakarta." *South East Asia Research* 24: 492–509. doi:10.1177/0967828X16674134.

Van Der Eng, Pierre. 2002. "Bridging a Gap: A Reconstruction of Population Patterns in Indonesia, 1930-61." *Asian Studies Review* 26 (4): 487-509. doi:10.1111/1467-8403.00140.

Van Klinken, Gerry. 2003. "Ethnicity in Indonesia." In *Ethnicity in Asia*, edited by Colin Mackerras, 64-87. Curzon: Routledge.

Warnaen, Suwarsih. 2002. *Stereotip Etnis dalam Masyarakat Multietnis*. Jogjakarta: Matabangsa.

Wu, Hexian. 2013. "The Changing Xiangxi Miao Marriage Practices in Contemporary China." *Asian Ethnicity* 14 (2): 189-205. doi:10.1080/14631369.2012.745738.

Xing, Wei. 2007. "Prevalence of Ethnic Intermarriage in Kunming: Social Exchange or Insignificance of Ethnicity?" *Asian Ethnicity* 8 (2), 165-179. doi:10.1080/14631360701406296.

Yeung, Wei-Jun Jean, and Zheng Mu. 2020. "Migration and Marriage in Asian Contexts." *Journal of Ethnic and Migration Studies* 46 (14): 2863–2879. doi:10.1080/1369183X.2019.1585005.

Internal migration, marriage timing and assortative mating: a mixed-method study in China

Zheng Mu and Wei-Jun Jean Yeung

ABSTRACT
We examine how rural-to-urban migration influences marriage timing and assortative mating by family origins using data from the 2012 Chinese Family Panel Studies and in-depth interviews conducted in Beijing. To account for potential selection bias, we compare marriage timing across migration status by holding all other variables at group-specific averages based on event history analysis and propensity-score matching analysis. Results from both approaches show that compared with rural locals, rural migrants marry later, and the negative effects are more pronounced for men, which may be attributed to the greater burden placed on grooms and their families for establishing a household in China. The migration effects are moderated by education and family backgrounds. The in-depth interviews illuminate the mechanisms through pressure and aspiration for career and consumption, uncertainties in life, the timing of education completion, and more liberal attitudes toward marriage in the receiving communities. For assortative mating, we show that rural migrants who are better endowed in human, social, and cultural capital are more likely to marry across birth place, *hukou*, or migration status.

Introduction

China has witnessed a tremendous increase in internal migration, most of which from rural to urban areas, since the early 1980s, when the government relaxed geographic mobility restrictions. Specifically, China had a migrant population of 245 million at the end of 2016, registering as one of the largest human migration in the history. Earlier research on China's internal migration mainly focused on Chinese internal migrants' socioeconomic profiles and inter-generational relations, and low- or semi-skilled migrants (Fan 2008; Liang and Ma 2004; Zhang and Ye 2018). Little attention has been paid to the increasing high-skilled migrants resulted from educational advancement and industrial restructuring, or to internal migrants' marital outcomes (Chang 2009; Fan 2003; Liang and Chen 2004). Recent changes of China's internal migrants have made a systematic examination on their marital behaviours particularly important.

First, the changing distribution of migrants' skill qualifications has led to more heterogeneous migration motivations and experiences. Due to institutional constraints and the high living costs in the receiving communities, it is harder for low-skilled migrants to permanently settle down (Piotrowski and Tong 2013). Low-skilled migrants are concerned with financial gains which they can remit home or save for their lives after returning to their hometowns. Therefore, their daily schedules are usually occupied with multiple jobs, and leave limited time for leisure or social activities (Mu and Yeung 2018). In contrast, high-skilled migrants are better off economically. They are likely to have more active and integrated interactions with locals in the receiving communities and are more likely to stay longer (Fan and Li 2002). Thus, they may be interested in seeking new lifestyles beyond economic improvements, and desire to settle down and start a family in the receiving communities (Gaetano and Jacka 2013). That is, while low- or semi-skilled migrants tend to be more consumed by financial pressures and transient in nature, high-skilled migrants are more likely to pursue a 'package deal' in the receiving communities, embracing the liberal ideas and aspiring for a holistic lifestyle in their migrant lives (Mu and Yeung 2018). In terms of marriage formation, they are better equipped to marry locals and cross the rural/urban divide than low- or semi-skilled migrants (Palriwala and Uberoi 2008).

Second, migration often occurs at a relatively early life stage, lasts for an extended period, and plays an important role in migrants' transitioning to adulthood through shaping one's major life events, such as completion of education, initiation of employment, and entry into first marriage and parenthood (Choi and Peng 2016; Juárez et al. 2013; Kulu and Milewski 2008; Lee and Pol 1993; Qian and Qian 2020; Utomo 2020). However, previous studies focused predominantly on socioeconomic well-being, such as earnings and work, or intergenerational relations, such as child care, migrant children's education, and care for the elderly (Chang 2009; Liang and Ma 2004; Zhang and Ye 2018), while few systematic studies have paid attention to migrants' family formation behaviours. Moreover, family formation, as one of the major markers of transitioning into adulthood, profoundly influences one's emotional satisfaction, taste preference, lifestyle options, and socioeconomic prospects. Thus, examining migration's influences on one's family formation behaviours will shed light on migrants' life trajectories and social mobility pathways (Yeung and Mu 2020).

Third, extant studies on the migration-marriage link are mostly on western countries such as on Australia (Carlson 1985), Britain (Flowerdew and Al-Hamad 2004), the US (Jang, Casterline, and Snyder 2014), and Mexico (Zenteno, Giorguli, and Gutiérrez 2013). As a country with sizeable and increasing internal migrants, China warrants more attention.

In this paper, we include both high-skilled and low- and semi-skilled migrants in China. We aim to systematically examine how internal migration influences individuals' transitioning to adulthood through their family formation behaviours, including when and whom they marry, and investigate how gender, education, and family background moderate the relationship. We use a mixed-method approach, based on data from the 2012 Chinese Family Panel Studies (CFPS) and 127 in-depth interviews conducted in Beijing in 2015 to triangulate our findings.

Theoretical issues and the Chinese context

Emerging adulthood, specifically the life stage ranging from late teens to the mid-20s, has been characterised as 'the age of identity explorations, the age of instability, the self-focused age, the age of feeling in-between, and the age of possibilities' (Arnett 2000, 2007; Yeung and Alipio 2013). This is the stage in which young people launch into the world of work, romantic relationships and family formation, and start to make choices that will exert enduring impacts on their career and life trajectories. While this life stage offers a rich set of possibilities for young adults to experience and to choose from, the relatively limited means to actualise the high expectations and competitions between parallel goals may lead to many struggles and uncertainties.

Migration adds even more uncertainties to one's emerging adulthood (Zenteno, Giorguli, and Gutiérrez 2013). As migration is often motivated by the pursuit of more favourable opportunities for personal and family betterments in the receiving communities, it is closely related to one's pursuit of education, career developments, relationship, and marriage. Among these goals, entry into first marriage has particularly enduring and profound implications for young adults' lives. Marriage is not only related to one's emotional satisfaction, preference, and lifestyle options, but is also instrumental to young adults' prospects of socioeconomic attainment and mobility (Schwartz and Mare 2005). Thus, we aim to examine how migration shapes migrants' family formation behaviours.

China has a sizeable and fast-growing migrant population (Liang and Ma 2004). However, due to the restrictive residential registration system (*hukou*), it is very difficult for migrants to change their *hukou* status into that in the receiving cities. In China, *hukou* status is associated with various welfare benefits in the receiving communities, including education for children, medical care, and retirement insurance (Fan 2008). Thus, migrants without a local *hukou* often live with great instabilities and hardship. They are often referred to as the 'floating population', depicting their rootless and unstable situation (Liang and Ma 2004). Aside from *hukou*, cultural differences, hierarchical economic development across regions, and social exclusion experienced by migrants in the receiving communities further add to migrants' emotional strain (Chang 2009; Jacka 2005).

Economic reforms since the late 1970s have opened China up to foreign investment, and the market economy has since been in the ascendant. The progress of economic reforms has been accompanied by the overall economic growth, improved living conditions, rising costs of living and heightened inequality (Ji and Yeung 2014; Meisner 1999; Wu 2002). Particularly pronounced are the skyrocketing housing prices in cities with the most prosperous economic development such as Beijing and Shanghai, which are often major migrant-receiving cities (Chen, Guo, and Wu 2011). The instabilities and high living costs in the cities make it difficult for migrants to settle down permanently. Many migrants plan to return to the hometown or to settle down in places with lower living costs (Mu and Yeung 2018). Accordingly, many of them work as hard as possible in the receiving cities for their future. The uncertainties about their future destinations and the pressure to gain financial security may delay their first marriages.

Improvement in education is another crucial consequence of the rapid economic growth in China, and it may be particularly relevant to migration (Treiman 2013; Wu and Zhang 2010; Yeung 2013). Due to China's education expansion, young people have been extending time spent in schools (Yeung and Hu 2013). Given China's regional disparities in educational resources, pursuing better educational opportunities, especially at the post-secondary level, becomes a major motivator of rural-to-urban migration. Since the timing of education completion often coincides with that of courtship, this change in educational experience may contribute to migrants' timing of first marriages. Education may also be positively related to more liberal ideals about marriage, such as late marriage and assortative mating on achieved attributes such as education, rather than on ascribed attributes such as family origins (Piotrowski et al. 2016; Schwartz 2010). Education can also be indicative of socioeconomic status. Migrants with a higher education often have greater economic and social resources which make them more attractive candidates in the marriage markets and afford them to establish a household earlier, even in the receiving cities (Tian 2013; Xie et al. 2003).

The impact of migration may be different for men and women. Due to the entrenched patriarchy in China, women face less economic pressure to financially establish themselves (Mu and Xie 2014). Female migrants often assume roles as homemakers to accommodate their husbands or partners' migration decisions and work schedules (Choi and Peng 2016).

In addition, Chinese parents play an important role in their adult children's marriage (Davis 2014; Whyte 1992; Xu and Whyte 1990). Many parents, especially those in less developed regions and rural areas, shoulder the costs of household establishment for their children, especially for their sons. The list of preparations often includes a betrothal gift money, a wedding ceremony, and usually, a new house for the newly-weds. Thus, parents' socioeconomic background may also influence young people's ability to establish a household and thus, timing of marriage. Related to the aforementioned patriarchal tradition and parents' roles in helping adult children establishing households, individual and parental socioeconomic status may influence male migrants' attractiveness on the marriage market to a greater extent than for female migrants. Thus, higher individual and parental education may improve migrants' prospects in the marriage markets to the extent of enabling them to cross social boundaries related to place of birth, rural/urban divide and migrant/local distinctions.

Hypotheses

The discussions above show that there are multiple ongoing social processes that may influence Chinese migrants' family formation behaviours, and directions of the potential influences are complex. Based on the context reviewed above, we develop the following hypotheses:

H1a: Compared with locals, migrants marry at an older age.

H1b: Migration effects on marriage timing are stronger for male migrants than for female migrants.

Regarding the moderation effects of individual and parental education, we expect:

H2a: Rural migrants who are better educated or have better-educated parents are more likely to marry at a younger age.

H2b: The influence of individual and parental education is stronger for male rural migrants than for female rural migrants.

Migration may also influence patterns of assortative mating by family origins, specifically, we expect:

H3: Rural migrants who are better educated or have better-educated parents are more likely to marry those from other places of birth, urban *hukou* holders and locals.

Data and methods

We use a mix-method approach, based on national data and in-depth interviews, to understand the relationship between migration, marriage timing, and assortative mating by origins.

Quantitative study

Data

For quantitative analysis, we utilise data from the nationally representative 2012 CFPS. We restrict to those aged 21–50, an age range likely to cover trajectories of family formation and migration. We then restrict to those who have valid values on age, gender, migration status, education, income, and parental education, which leaves us with 8484 women and 7973 men, with proportions of missing values ranging from 5% to 7%. All the analyses are weighted to reflect the national patterns.

2012 CFPS was conducted using multistage probability proportional-to-size sampling with implicit stratification. It includes information on current migration status and migration history due to work, as well as respondents' demographic and socioeconomic characteristics, *hukou* status at younger ages, and parental information. The richness of the above information enables us to measure pre-migration status, and to provide rigorous estimates of the migration effects. We conduct analysis separately for men and women to capture the gendered economic and subjective pressures. Note that migration history is retrieved through current migration status and migration histories due to work. Therefore, respondents who were not currently a migrant or migrated only due to reasons other than work are excluded from the sample.

Table 1 exhibits the distribution of weighted sample characteristics by migration status. As shown, for both women and men, most are rural non-migrants, respectively at around 72% for women, and 62% for men. Urban non-migrants constitute another 15% to 16%. Moreover, percentages of rural migrants are higher for men than for women, with percentages of respectively 11% for women, and 19% for men. This is consistent with the male-dominant feature of China's internal migration (Fan 2000). That is, although female migrants have been on the rise, they are still smaller in size and proportion relative to men. Urban migrants are the smallest group, with 2% and 3% respectively for women and men. That is, most internal migration happens among rural residents who are mostly driven to pursue upward social mobility through opportunities for earning

Table 1. Distribution of migration status.

Migration status	CFPS: weighted % Female	CFPS: weighted % Male	Qualitative: frequency Female	Qualitative: frequency Male
Urban non-migrant	15.09	16.16	22	13
Urban migrant	2.48	3.01	13	9
Rural non-migrant	71.83	62.17	7	7
Rural migrant	10.61	18.66	24	32
Total	8484	7973	66	61

Source: Chinese Family Panel Studies 2012 and in-depth interviews conducted by the authors in summer 2015.
Notes: Migration status is measured by the combination of whether the respondent was rural or urban at age 12, and whether the respondent has ever migrated to other counties in the same province or to other provinces. The sample is based on respondents aged 21–50, and who have valid values on age, gender, migration status, education, income, and parental education.

money and for personal development in the receiving communities (Liang and Ma 2004). In the meantime, urban residents have weaker motivations to migrate.

Analytic strategy

We apply different modelling strategies for the two marital outcomes. For entry into first marriage, we use event history analysis to capture transitions from the status of never married to first married. To accurately capture the risk exposed to the first marriage, the sample is in the person-year format. Time is measured as years from the legal minimum marriage age to the age of first marriage. We cover marriages happening in and after 1980, when state started to relax internal migration in China. We restricted the sample to those who had valid values on all variables included in the models. These treatments and restrictions leave us with 47,055 person-years for females and 47,442 person-years for males. Furthermore, note that respondents of different migration status differ greatly in their various characteristics, especially their socioeconomic status, which shape marriage timing. Therefore, to more accurately capture the differential patterns of entry into first marriage by migration status, based on estimates from the event history analysis, we further project survival trajectories of entry into first marriage for different migration status by holding all other variables at the group-specific averages of each migration status. Finally, to further strengthen causal claims and to test the robustness of the quantitative results against potential selection biases, we conducted propensity-score matching to estimate the influence of migration on the timing of marriage. Specifically, we used the nearest neighbour and stratification matching methods with bootstrapped standard errors.

For assortative mating by family origins, we focus on rural migrants. We use binary logistic models to predict whether the spouse was born in the same province and of urban origin. We then use multinomial logistic models to predict the spouse's migration status. We restricted the sample to those who had valid values on all variables included in the models. These restrictions leave us with 338 female rural migrants and 409 male rural migrants.

Measures

Dependent variables. We use two sets of main dependent variables, namely, the timing of entry into first marriage and the pattern of assortative marriage. Entry into first marriage is a binary variable with 0 = no, and 1 = yes. Specifically, for those who got married in 1980, legal marriage age is set at 20 for males, and 18 for females, according to the Marriage Law of 1951. In 1981, the Marriage Law was revised, and the legal marriage at age was increased to 22 and 20 for males and females respectively. In the analysis, we set the starting points of exposure to entry into first marriage for males and females according to the respective legal marriage ages.

We use three variables to capture individuals' patterns in assortative mating by family origins, specifically, whether the spouse was born in the same province, whether the spouse had urban *hukou* status at the age of 12, and the migration status of the spouse. The first two variables are both binary, and the third variable is a four-category measure that captures both spousal *hukou* origin at age 12, and their migration experience. We constructed this variable in the same way as migration status. Details about the migration status are shown below.

Main independent variables. Our main independent variable is respondent's migration status. It is measured with a four-category variable based on whether the respondent has ever migrated and their residential registration status at age 12, which shows whether the respondent has a rural or urban origin. This measure is intended to show how migration and social origin jointly influence their marital trajectories. Specifically, this variable is coded as 1 = urban non-migrant, 2 = urban migrant, 3 = rural non-migrants, and 4 = rural migrants. For analysis on marriage timing, migration status is time-varying and refers to the status at the time of marriage. For analysis on assortative mating by family origins, it is based on the respondent's *hukou* origin and whether the respondent has ever been a migrant by the time of the survey.

Other independent variables. As noted above, gender, individual socioeconomic status, and family background may all moderate how migration influences marriage experiences. Thus, we include three moderators – gender, socioeconomic status and family background.

We conducted gender-specific analyses throughout the paper to capture the impact of China's entrenched patriarchal tradition on migrants' well-being and behaviour.

We measure the socioeconomic status by respondents' education, specifically, 1 = junior high or less, 2 = senior high, and 3 = associate college or above. This variable captures individuals' skill profiles and socioeconomic status.

Family background is measured by respondent's parental education, which is the highest number of years of schooling received by the respondent's parents. If one parent's education is missing, we use the other parent's education to impute. This variable is intended to indicate the respondent's parental socioeconomic status and family backgrounds.

We also control for several other individual characteristics and the temporal variations.

Age is measured in spline functions. People at different ages may face varying degrees of urgency to enter first marriages. To capture the heterogeneity, age was divided into five age splines, namely, 18–25, 26–30, 31–35, 36–40, and 41–50.

We also control for three contemporaneous characteristics, including whether the respondent was a migrant, whether the respondent was living in an urban community and annual income at the time of the survey. The first two are binary variables with 0 = no, and 1 = yes. Annual income includes salary, bonuses, subsidies, and all other sources of individual income, and we use natural logarithm of annual income to address the issue of positive skewness. These contemporaneous variables are used to control for an individuals' unobserved characteristics, such as personality traits and ability, which may influence their overall tendencies of migration, their earlier migration experience before marriage, and their decisions about when to get married. For example, some respondents may be more liberal-minded and entrepreneurial, who are more likely to migrate, live in an urban community, have higher income, and get married later.

Two other traits of the respondents that could affect individuals' 'marriageability' are also controlled for – physical appearance and manners. It is the average of four interviewer-rated indicators on the degree to which the respondent looked attractive, how tidy the respondent's clothes were, level of politeness and appropriateness the way the respondent deals with people, and how healthy they look. All the ratings range from 1 to 7 with a higher score indicating better manners and appearance.

We also include an indicator to proxy the respondent's cultural capital in the receiving communities – mastery of Mandarin. This is an interviewer-rated indicator of how well the respondent masters Mandarin, ranging from 0 to 7 with a higher score indicating better proficiency. Since Mandarin is the only official language in China, those with a good command of Mandarin often have a more cosmopolitan temperament and more sophisticated social skills, and hence are more likely to fare well in both labour and marriage markets. Migrants who mostly speak dialects in their hometown or speak poor Mandarin could suffer disadvantages in both the marriage market and the job market in the receiving cities.

As China has experienced tremendous social transitions in its recent past, it is important to control for temporal variation in the model. We include three year splines, namely, 1980–1991, 1992–1998, and 1999–2012 to characterise three policy changes in contemporary China. The first period captures the historical period beginning at the time when the Communist Chinese government started to relax its migration policies in the early 1980s, which allowed the rural population to temporarily move to cities for non-agricultural employment opportunities. The second period starts in 1992, when rapid development and maturation of the market economy provided more job opportunities in urban China, and the number of internal migrants increased tremendously afterward. The third period began in 1999, when the welfare housing allocation system was ended by the state, and the commercial housing prices soared swiftly. This policy change dramatically increased costs of household establishment, and reduced migrants' chances of settling down in the receiving cities. During this period, China also began its college expansion in 1999 and joined the World Trade Organization in 2001.

Qualitative study

We supplement quantitative analyses with 127 in-depth interviews conducted by authors in Beijing from May to July 2015 to better understand the underlying mechanisms. Informants include both men and women, and migrants and non-migrants aged 21–50. Moreover, to capture migrants' skill heterogeneities, we include informants with varying education.

Informants were recruited based on a quota sampling scheme through public internet forums, email listservs, and word of mouth. Interviews used semi-structured open-ended questions regarding informants' feelings, attitudes and experiences in lifestyles, relationships, jobs and careers, and migration experience. Interviews lasted one to two hours and were recorded and transcribed. The authors analysed the qualitative data following a dynamic coding process through inductive analysis (Reczek et al. 2016). We coded and developed themes around how migration experiences were perceived to matter for family formation. Then we established categories and subcategories conceptually connected to the relationship between migration and family formation to organise the data.

We over-sampled migrants with senior high school and above education, since they are diverse in migration motivations, return intentions, and socioeconomic backgrounds. We included all intended demographic groups except for urban-to-urban migrants with junior high school or below education. In all, we have 61 male informants, and 66 female informants.

Results

Entry into first marriage

Descriptive statistics for quantitative data
Table 2 shows characteristics of the analysis sample on entry into first marriage in person-years. As seen, the distribution of migration status is similar to that shown in Table 1, which demonstrates the representativeness of this analysis sample.

Multivariate analysis
Table 3 shows the odds ratios from the event history analysis predicting the probabilities of entering first marriages. Compared to rural non-migrants, urban non-migrants enter first marriage later. Nevertheless, both female urban and rural migrants enter first marriage at significantly earlier ages than their rural non-migrant counterparts. In comparison, both male urban and rural migrants enter first marriage at later ages, although only the coefficient for rural migrants is significant. However, we need to be cautious about these results as different migration groups have very diverse demographic profiles, for which we will explore subsequently.

Table 2. Descriptive statistics of sample for entry into first marriage, in person-years.

	Female Mean	Female S.D.	Male Mean	Male S.D.
Dependent variables				
Entry into first marriage	0.10	0.30	0.07	0.25
Independent variable: migration status				
Urban non-migrant	0.17	0.38	0.19	0.39
Urban migrant	0.03	0.17	0.03	0.18
Rural non-migrant	0.70	0.46	0.65	0.48
Rural migrant	0.10	0.30	0.13	0.34
Independent variable: control variables				
Education				
Junior high or less (ref. = no)	0.70	0.46	0.68	0.47
Senior high (ref. = no)	0.15	0.36	0.17	0.38
Associate college or above (ref. = no)	0.15	0.36	0.15	0.35
Parental SES (maximum parental schooling)	6.66	3.44	6.66	3.37
Age	37.77	8.20	39.09	7.33
Currently migrating (ref. = no)	0.08	0.27	0.07	0.26
Current community of residence is urban (ref. = no)	0.40	0.49	0.39	0.49
Annual income	10,145.3	19,487.8	20,957.2	62,194.4
Manner and apperance (1–7)	5.43	1.04	5.43	1.00
Mastery of mandarin (0–7)	3.48	2.49	3.59	2.40
Period splines				
1980–1991	0.18	0.38	0.12	0.32
1992–1998	0.24	0.43	0.24	0.43
1999–2012	0.60	0.49	0.67	0.47
Total	47,055		47,442	

Source: Chinese Family Panel Studies 2012.
Notes: Descriptive statistics for entry into first marriage were based on the person-year-level analysis sample. Aside from restrictions in Table 1, this sample is further excludes those who entered first marriage before 1980. Due to the change in marriage administration, for those who entered first marriage in 1980, we include them into the risk pool of first marriage from age 18 for women, and 20 for men; for those who entered first marriage after 1980, we include them into the risk pool of first marriage from age 20 for women, and 22 for men. We further restrict to those who have valid values on year of first marriage, year of first migration experience, current migration status, whether current community of residence is urban, manner and apperance, and mastery of mandarin. All statistics are weighted to be nationally representative.

Table 3. Event history models predicting entry into first marriage (in odds ratios).

Independent variables	Entry into first marriage (ref. = no) Female	Entry into first marriage (ref. = no) Male
Migration status (ref = .rural non-migrant)		
Urban non-migrant	0.817**	0.694***
	(0.062)	(0.057)
Urban migrant	1.416*	0.844
	(0.248)	(0.169)
Rural migrant	1.251*	0.788*
	(0.118)	(0.080)
Education (ref. = junior high or less)		
Senior high	0.848*	0.975
	(0.055)	(0.064)
Associate college or above	0.593***	0.916
	(0.051)	(0.081)
Parental SES (maximum parental schooling)	1.023**	0.998
	(0.007)	(0.008)
Age splines		
Ages 18–25	1.164***	1.172***
	(0.015)	−0.027
Ages 26–30	0.630***	0.791***
	(0.018)	−0.016
Ages 31–35	0.831**	0.816***
	(0.054)	−0.037
Ages 36–40	0.508***	0.826*
	(0.093)	(0.069)
Ages 41–50	0.837	0.857
	(0.128)	(0.127)
Currently migrating (ref. = no)	0.607***	0.660***
	(0.059)	(0.075)
Current community of residence is urban (ref. = no)	0.984	1.159*
	(0.053)	(0.071)
Ln(annual income)	0.997	0.999
	(0.003)	(0.003)
Manner and apperance (1–7)	1.026	1.066*
	(0.021)	(0.027)
Mastery of mandarin (0–7)	1.002	1.019+
	(0.009)	(0.011)
Period splines		
Years 1980–1991	0.941***	0.909***
	(0.011)	(0.017)
Years 1992–1998	1.026*	1.006
	(0.011)	(0.012)
Years 1999–2012	0.917***	0.926***
	(0.006)	(0.006)
Intercept	5.90E+50***	2.22E+80***
	(1.34E+52)	(8.04E+81)
Chi-squared	1017.55	874.84
DF consumed	19	19
N	47,055	47,442

Source: Chinese Family Panel Studies 2012.
†$p < 0.10$, *$p < 0.05$, **$p < 0.01$, ***$p < 0.001$.

Moreover, those better educated postpone entry into first marriage, although the coefficients are only significant for women. The gender difference may be because women are expected to be the primary homemakers, making juggling family life and education difficult.

One's family background also influences one's marriage timing. Having better educated parents is associated with earlier first marriage for women, possibly because women with better family background are more attractive marriage partners to men.

Age effects vary across the life course. For both men and women, from 18 to 25, getting older expedites entry into first marriages. However, after age 25, aging slows down the process of marriage formation.

As noted above, current migration status and community of residence may reflect their entrepreneurship and tendencies of migration. For both men and women, being a migrant at the time of the interview significantly delays their timing of first marriage, while men who live in an urban community enter marriage earlier.

Table 3 also shows that men who have better manners and appearance and a greater mastery of Mandarin tend to marry earlier.

The temporal changes are consistent with our expectations. From 1980 to 1991, the newly emerging economic opportunities led people to focus more on work and to postpone their first marriages. However, from 1992 to 1998, economic accumulations enabled earlier marriages. Then after the state called off the national welfare housing allocation system, the rising and prohibitively high housing prices made household establishment costly which is associated with a later age at marriage.

As the four groups differ greatly in their demographic and socioeconomic traits, it is necessary to account for group-specific characteristics across migration status in order to accurately capture the differential trajectories of entry into first marriage by migration status. For example, urban migrants are the most socioeconomically advantaged, having the highest education, income, and parental education. Figure 1a and b show the survival curves of entering first marriage for different migration groups. We divide the sample into eight groups by gender and migration status, and all other covariates are held at group-specific averages. As shown, after holding demographic characteristics at averages, patterns differ from those in Table 3. Patterns across migration groups are similar for men and women. Specifically, rural migrants tend to enter first marriage the latest, followed subsequently by urban migrants, urban non-migrants, and rural non-migrants. These patterns account for both the migration effects and that of the group-specific demographic characteristics, which may better approximate reality.

To further address the differential demographic and socioeconomic profiles across migration status and to test the validity of the causal claims, we conducted propensity-score matching for migration impacts on entry into first marriage. Table 4 shows migration postpones first marriage, regardless of urban/rural origin and gender. This supports patterns for men in Table 3, while indicating potential selection biases for women with differential education, family backgrounds, and migration status. Thus, it is consistent with patterns shown in Figure 1a and b. That is, after accounting for heterogeneities in demographic characteristics, migration's 'delaying' effects on entry into first marriage hold for both men and women.

How do the above results speak to our hypotheses? When we account for demographic and socioeconomic differences across migration status by holding other variables at group-specific averages, and estimate based on propensity score matching, both migrant men and women marry at older ages, which supports hypothesis *H1a*.

Still, as shown by Figure 1a and b and Table 4, the delaying effects of migration on marriage timing are smaller for female migrants than for male migrants, supporting *H1b* and suggesting the gender differences in economic pressures for household establishments. The gendered patterns may be because female migrants do not need to shoulder heavy burdens of household establishments at the time of wedding as their male counterparts

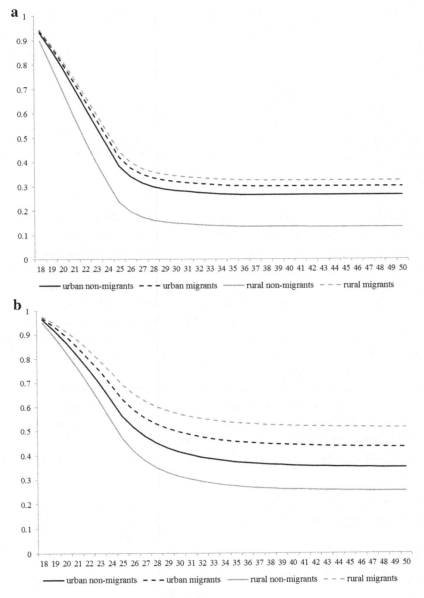

Figure 1. (a) Survival from entry into first marriage, female. (b) Survival from entry into first marriage, male.

do. Meanwhile, migration provides female migrants with more opportunities to meet potential spouses in the cities as women tend to 'marry up'. Male migrants, on the other hand, are faced with greater pressures of financial responsibility and career advancement and have more limited opportunities to find potential spouses in the cities as males tend to 'marry down'.

As noted earlier, migrants are highly heterogeneous in their migration motivations, intentions to return to the hometown, and demographic and socioeconomic backgrounds. While striving for a better life, migrants are endowed with varying capabilities to realise

Table 4. Propensity score estimation of migration effects on entry into first marriage.

Matching methods	Rural origin Female	Rural origin Male	Urban origin Female	Urban origin Male
Nearest neighbour	−0.010 (0.011)	−0.059*** (0.005)	0.016 (0.024)	−0.023* (0.011)
Stratification	−0.013* (0.006)	−0.062*** (0.007)	0.019 (0.008)	−0.015 (0.020)

Source: Chinese Family Panel Studies 2012.
Notes: The coefficients are effects of migration in linear probabilities respectively for rural- and urban-origin respondents, estimated using propensity score methods based on education, ethnicity, parental education, manner and apperance, province of birth, and mental health, with nearest neighbour and stratification matching. Numbers in the parentheses are bootstrapped standard errors.
†$p < 0.10$, *$p < 0.05$, **$p < 0.01$, ***$p < 0.001$.

social mobility. Thus, we further divide rural migrants into different subgroups based on individual and parental education. The results are shown in Table 5. Compared to rural non-migrant women, rural migrant women who did not attend college or whose parents did not attend college marry earlier. However, compared to rural non-migrant men, rural migrant men who attended college or whose parents did not attend college marry later. The gendered patterns may indicate that while highly-educated male migrants marry later due to lengthened schooling and more liberal attitudes, those from worse-off families bear heavier financial burdens of marriage. Thus, these results do not support hypothesis *H2a* that rural migrants who are better educated or have better-educated parents are more likely to marry at a younger age.

H2b proposes that the expediting effects of individual and parental education are stronger for male rural migrants than for female rural migrant. This is partly supported in that both lower individual and parental education expedite migrant women's entry into marriage, while rural migrant men with less-educated parents marry later. That is, for women, lower education indicates a lower opportunity cost for and perhaps a greater acceptance

Table 5. Event history models predicting entry into first marriage (in odds ratios), reference switched and rural migrants diversified.

Independent variables	Female	Male	Female	Male	Female	Male
Migration status (ref. = rural non-migrant)						
Urban non-migrant	0.817** (0.062)	0.694*** (0.057)	0.812** (0.062)	0.689*** (0.057)	0.818** (0.063)	0.694*** (0.057)
Urban migrant	1.416* (0.248)	0.844 (0.169)	1.406† (0.246)	0.836 (0.168)	1.418* (0.248)	0.844 (0.169)
Rural migrant	1.251* (0.118)	0.788* (0.080)				
Rural migrant: *non-college graduate*			1.299* (0.131)	0.840 (0.091)		
Rural migrant: *college graduate*			1.023 (0.240)	0.621* (0.141)		
Rural migrant: *no parents college graduate*					1.241* (0.118)	0.790* (0.081)
Rural migrant: *at least one parent college graduate*					1.697 (0.820)	0.646 (0.285)
Other coefficients are omitted.						

Source: Chinese Family Panel Studies 2012.
Note: Since coefficients on other variables are the same as those in Table 3, they are omitted in this table.
†$p < 0.10$, *$p < 0.05$, **$p < 0.01$, ***$p < 0.001$.

toward early marriage; while for men, lower education mainly reflects weaker financial abilities.

Qualitative results

In-depth interviews corroborate our main quantitative findings. Specifically, migration influences marriage timing through migrants' economic pressures, lifestyle, attitudes toward marriage, and timing of education completion.

Economic pressures. Male migrants sense great financial pressures when considering marriage. This is particularly true given the norms in rural areas for the strict financial requirements for men to provide a house upon marriage.

Han, a single male migrant, aged 36, with a junior high school education is of rural origin, with his father completed primary school, and his mother completed junior high school. He shares that his fiancée is waiting for him back in his hometown, and they plan to get married as soon as he has saved enough money for a decent betrothal gift, a grand wedding, a house and some start-up funds for a small business in the hometown. Currently, he has one primary job as a security guard in a public enterprise, and three part-time jobs. He insists that a 'financial foundation' is a must when a couple decides to get married:

> (I)n rural areas, a big banquet is necessary for a wedding. All relatives care about how elaborate the wedding is. After all, I am a man, even if it is not extravagant, I need to have the basics.

Some migrants mention financial pressures of establishing a household in the receiving communities. Yue is a single urban migrant man with a college education. When asked about his intention to settle down in Beijing, he smiles bitterly:

> Back home, most families have a house, so marriage is less of a problem. ... In Beijing, it is very difficult to buy a house. I have a colleague who bought a house in outskirts of Beijing. His financial burden is very heavy – mortgage 4000 per month, then childcare 3000 or 4000 a month. His monthly pay is only RMB8000.

The interviews reveal how family background could affect migrants' marriage timing, as Yue remarked, 'Some friends bought a house by using their parents' money; otherwise, it is difficult.'

Liang, a married male migrant aged 42, is a father who has been committed to be financially prepared for his son's marriage. Having worked in Beijing for more than 20 years, he gets relatively economically established, owning two small restaurants. He had started to make financial preparations for his son's potential marriage when his son was only 16. He has built and decorated a new house of 380 square metres back in hometown for his son, which cost him RMB600,000. Then, during the marriage proposal, based on conventions in his hometown, they also need to give the bride's parents some betrothal money, between RMB70,000 and 80,000. Nowadays, there is also a trendy demand for a car for the newlyweds, which, he estimates, will cost him another RMB50,000–60,000.

Monetary support significantly differs for sons and for daughters. When we asked about preparations for his daughter, Liang says, 'Not much actually. (For daughters), it more depends on the parents' economic conditions. For myself, I probably will open a savings account for her, with around RMB 100,000 or 200,000, or a car if she needs it.' That is, while it is widely considered as an obligation of the groom's side to financially support the newly-weds, financial support from the bride's side is often optional and depends on bride's family background.

Faced with the prohibitively high costs of household establishment, some migrants have chosen to put career development as their highest priority and postpone entry into first marriage. Xiangyang is a single 29-year-old migrant of rural origin. He has an associate college degree and owns a small business in Beijing. He feels that a romantic relationship in Beijing is a great waste of time, and he wants to focus on his career:

> (When I had a girlfriend,) my time was much more limited... After we broke up... I can focus on my work... I feel so much pressure right now... About girlfriend, even if you give me one this moment, I don't want to be with her. I don't have the energy.

Lifestyles. The interviews also show that migrant life is filled with uncertainties and pressures, which adds to the difficulty of mate selection in the receiving communities. Min is a married female rural migrant aged 33, with a college education. When asked about her marriage timing compared to her peers back in her hometown, she mentions that her friends who stay at home marry earlier. She attributes this to the unstable and busy lifestyle of migrants:

> It is easier to meet someone back home. Generally, if we come out to work, we want to marry later, though our family want us to get married earlier.... Many of my colleagues are like that, (their) families are rushing them to get married.... Also, out here, everyone is not stable. Even if both are in Beijing, both have their own place. It is too far and inconvenient to go visit each other. Even if someone introduces us, if there is little communication, not much will happen.

Some respondents also mentioned how the extended education completion in the receiving communities has postponed their entry into first marriage. Due to their pursuit of education, compared to their friends back in the hometown, they marry much later.

Attitudes toward marriage. Some attribute migrants' later marriages to the more liberal attitudes toward late marriage in the receiving communities, and to the lack of peer pressure when away from their hometowns. Lili is a female urban migrant aged 27 who is pursuing a PhD degree. She expresses anxiety and concerns about being single. However, living away from the hometown provides her with some relief:

> What I like most is that people are more tolerant (here)... You may meet someone very different, but there is nothing wrong about it. If you are back at home, especially if it is a small city... everyone knows what your family and other families' circumstances are. If things do not live up to others' expectations, there will be pressures... In this aspect, Beijing is better.

Assortative mating by family origins

Aside from marriage timing, migration experience may also expose individuals to varying 'pools of eligible', which may shape patterns of how they get matched in family origins. Diverse demographic profiles may endow them with different capabilities and mindsets to overcome group boundaries in family origins such as place of origin, the rural/urban divide, and migration status. This is particularly relevant to rural migrants, who are more likely to be motivated by the possibilities to realise upward mobility. We now focus on rural migrants' patterns in assortative mating by family origins.

Descriptive statistics for quantitative data

Figure 2a and b show patterns of assortative mating by migration status across gender for urban and rural migrants, using the sample as described in Table 1. As shown, although there are more urban migrants marrying other urbanites, migrants or locals, their marriages with rural residents are also sizeable. Overall, urban migrants' marital choices are very balanced across migration groups. However, for rural migrants, the distributions are highly skewed. More than 90% of both female and male rural migrants marry either rural migrants or locals. Specifically, most rural migrants married rural migrants, at 58% and 53% for women and men respectively; 34% of women and 38% of men married rural non-migrants; only 7% of women and 10% of men married urbanites, either migrants or non-migrants.

The comparison between urban migrants and rural migrants indicates the smoother assimilation processes experienced by urban migrants, while rural migrants struggle more with integration and upward mobility. These differential patterns corroborate our decision to focus on rural migrants for the analysis on assortative mating below.

Multivariate analysis

Next, we explore how assortative mating by family origins, namely, province of birth, *hukou* origin, and migration status, differ among rural migrants with varying individual and family characteristics.

Table 6 shows the odds ratios from logistic models predicting whether the spouse was from the same province of birth. For female rural migrants, attending college and having better-educated parents increase the probability for them to cross the regional boundaries. For men, completing senior high school and having a greater mastery of Mandarin increase the probability for them to marry spouses born in a different province.

Table 7 shows the odds ratios for marrying a spouse of urban origin. For both female and male rural migrants, attending college is associated with higher odds of marrying an urban spouse. Specifically for women, having better manners and appearance is also associated with a higher likelihood of marrying a husband with an urban origin.

Table 8 shows results from multinomial models predicting spouse's migration status. Overall, the results are consistent with those in Tables 6 and 7. Specifically, having better-educated parents increases the likelihood for women to marry urban migrants and marry among their peer rural migrants, relative to marrying rural non-migrants. Moreover, better mastery of Mandarin is related to a higher likelihood of marrying rural migrants than rural non-migrants. For men, having a college education increases the likelihood for them to marry either urban non-migrants or urban migrants. However, surprisingly, having better-educated parents is associated with a lower likelihood for men to marry a rural migrant rather than a rural non-migrant. This may be because rural parents with better education have greater say about their children's marriage partners and may prefer having children closer to them after marriage. For men,

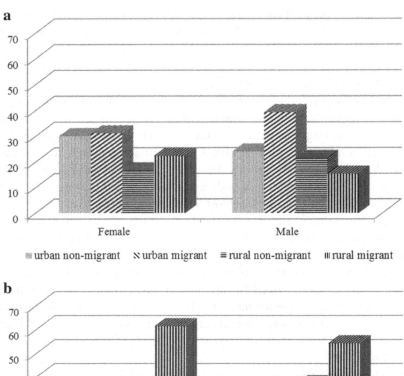

Figure 2. (a) Who marries whom? Urban migrants. (b). Who marries whom? Rural migrants.

having better manners and appearance increases their odds of marrying an urban non-migrant, and having a greater mastery of Mandarin is related to both a higher likelihood of marrying an urban migrant and a rural migrant, relative to a rural non-migrant.

The above quantitative results largely support H3. Specifically, better individual and parental education are related to a lower likelihood of marrying someone from the same province, a higher likelihood of marrying an urban spouse, and to an urban non-migrant spouse, an urban migrant spouse, or a rural migrant, compared to a rural non-migrant. The only exceptions are that having better-educated parents is related to a lower likelihood of migrant men marrying rural migrants relative to rural non-migrants, suggesting that men's better educated parents are often more financially established and are more likely to help with their sons' household establishment.

Table 6. Logistic models predicting whether spouse from the same province for rural migrants (in odds ratios).

Independent variables	Same province of birth (ref. = no)	
	Female	Male
Education (ref. = junior high or less)		
Senior high	0.906	0.378†
	(0.517)	(0.192)
Associate college or above	0.288*	0.468
	(0.171)	(0.263)
Parental SES (maximum parental schooling)	0.887*	1.040
	(0.053)	(0.062)
Age	1.028	1.063*
	(0.029)	(0.029)
Manner and apperance (1–7)	1.320	1.391
	(0.250)	(0.359)
Mastery of mandarin (0–7)	1.027	0.831+
	(0.089)	(0.081)
Intercept	0.962	0.208
	(1.419)	(0.386)
Chi-squared	14.69	13.30
DF consumed	6	6
N	338	409

Source: Chinese Family Panel Studies 2012.
Note: Whether spouse is from the same province was measure by whether spouse was born in the same province.
†$p < 0.10$, *$p < 0.05$, **$p < 0.01$, ***$p < 0.001$.

Qualitative results: the role of education

The qualitative data show stark educational differences in assortative mating by family origins. Specifically, a higher education is related to more liberal attitudes toward matching on achieved, rather than ascribed attributes. It also reflects class differences in migrants' ability to use migration as a pathway to assimilation and upward mobility.

Table 7. Logistic models predicting whether spouse with urban origin for rural migrants (in odds ratios).

Independent variables	Whether spouse with urban origin (ref. = no)	
	Female	Male
Education (ref. = junior high or less)		
Senior high	2.029	1.940
	(1.513)	(1.359)
Associate college or above	4.283*	7.407**
	(3.154)	(4.381)
Parental SES (maximum parental schooling)	1.081	1.070
	(0.100)	(0.089)
Age	1.020	0.939†
	(0.048)	(0.033)
Manner and apperance (1–7)	1.656†	1.255
	(0.448)	(0.301)
Mastery of mandarin (0–7)	1.097	1.199
	(0.154)	(0.153)
Intercept	0.001**	0.046
	(0.002)	(0.090)
Chi-squared	22.13	30.09
DF consumed	6	6
N	338	409

Source: Chinese Family Panel Studies 2012.
Note: Whether spouse is with urban origin was measured by whether spouse had urban hukou at age 12.
†$p < 0.10$, *$p < 0.05$, **$p < 0.01$, ***$p < 0.001$.

Table 8. Multinomial logistic models predicting spousal migration status for rural migrants (in relative risk ratios).

Independent Variables	Spouse is an urban non-migrant (ref. = rural non-migrant) Female	Male	Spouse is an urban migrant (ref. = rural non-migrant) Female	Male	Spouse is a rural migrant (ref. = rural non-migrant) Female	Male
Education (ref. = junior high or less)						
Senior high	2.567	4.336	0.033**	0.346	0.383†	0.661
	(2.454)	(4.114)	(0.043)	(0.338)	(0.193)	(0.302)
Associate college or above	4.715	10.037*	2.616	10.929**	0.728	1.635
	(5.607)	(9.010)	(2.911)	(8.455)	(0.537)	(0.960)
Parental SES (maximum parental schooling)	1.092	1.046	1.355*	0.988	1.168*	0.914*
	(0.157)	(0.120)	(0.179)	(0.110)	(0.071)	(0.040)
Age	1.000	0.892†	1.137	0.940	1.064*	0.974
	(0.067)	(0.054)	(0.095)	(0.042)	(0.026)	(0.020)
Manner and apperance (1–7)	1.721	1.905†	1.279	1.058	0.871	1.068
	(0.690)	(0.715)	(0.397)	(0.318)	(0.153)	(0.181)
Mastery of mandarin (0–7)	1.099	1.228	1.331	1.490*	1.135†	1.251***
	(0.225)	(0.219)	(0.272)	(0.262)	(0.083)	(0.075)
Intercept	0.001	0.019	8.16E-06**	0.149	0.116	2.096
	(0.006)	(0.063)	(0.00003)	(0.368)	(0.166)	(2.795)
Chi-squared	73.15	72.02	73.15	72.02	73.15	72.02
DF consumed	18	18	18	18	18	18
N	338	409	338	409	338	409

Source: Chinese Family Panel Studies 2012.
†$p < 0.10$, *$p < 0.05$, **$p < 0.01$, ***$p < 0.001$.

Overall, while those with lower education care more about potential spouses' financial and family backgrounds, highly-educated individuals tend to give greater consideration to non-monetary characteristics, such as personality and taste.

Kun is a 35-year-old male urban migrant with a senior high school education. When asked about main considerations in mate selection, he says, 'Basically, half or more than half (of the criteria for a potential partner) are about economic considerations, then less so about whether she should have similar ways of thinking as I do.'

Then Yao, a 37 year-old rural migrant woman with a primary school education, further emphasised the partner's financial ability in mate selection nowadays. When asked whether her son will look for a spouse in Beijing, she answers firmly, 'He cannot find any. Beijing girls won't possibly marry us migrants... unless your son is particularly capable of making money.'

In contrast, most college-educated informants prioritise non-monetary qualities in mate selection. The aforementioned informant Lili tells us, 'I am not picky about where my partner is from. I think as long as two persons can communicate and understand each other, it does not matter where the person comes from.'

When asked if she needs a house to get married, she says, 'It doesn't matter. As long as we have hope in the future. I don't need that now.'

Luyang, a male rural migrant aged 24 with college education, summarises the criteria for his potential spouse:

> First, she should know how to enjoy life. She cannot be like a housewife who only cares about tedious domestic matters. She should have something she is pursuing herself, which at a certain level matches my own, such as some common hobbies or career aspirations. We should match at this level, not only at a shallow level.

When asked whether he considers the family background of the spouse, he says decisively, 'No, I do not.'

The above narratives corroborate the positive coefficients on college education in Tables 6–8. Having a better education indicates greater economic prospects, which enable highly-educated rural migrants to cross boundaries of social origins and to select based on tastes and personalities. Education is also positively related to more liberal attitudes in mate selection, which promotes matching on achieved, rather than ascribed attributes.

Conclusions and discussion

Using a mixed-method approach, we systematically examine how migration affects marriage timing and assortative mating by family origins. We further investigate how gender, education, and family background moderate the relationship. Theoretically, we contribute by examining how transition to adulthood through marriage has been shaped by migration experience, and how gender and social class add to heterogeneities in migrants' family formation behaviours.

Based on the correlational analysis, we find that compared to rural non-migrants, while migration relates to earlier first marriage for female rural migrants, it leads to later marriage for male rural migrants. However, after accounting for differential distributions in various demographic characteristics and using propensity score matching analysis, the patterns for women and men converge. That is, both female and male rural migrants tend to enter first marriage later, though the 'delaying' effect is smaller among women. The original opposing migration effects across gender and the gendered migration effects after accounting for group differences may be attributed to the prohibitively high costs of household establishment, predominantly borne by the groom's family. Overall, this 'delaying' effect of migration is likely due to the impact of heavy economic pressures, extended time in education, unstable migrant lifestyles, and liberal attitudes in the receiving communities. These patterns show the importance of including high-skilled migrants and accounting for the gender differences in understanding migration experiences.

Moreover, the gendered migration effects are moderated by both migrants' own education and their family backgrounds. Specifically, the 'marriage-expediting' effects for female rural migrants are only significant among those who themselves or whose parents have not attended college. On the other hand, the 'delaying' effects for male rural migrants are only significant among those who have attended college themselves or whose parents have not attended college. The heterogeneities in the migration effects across individual and parental education indicate education delays first marriage through various pathways, including its influence on financial abilities, ideals of marriage, and the timing conflicts between education completion, career development, and entry into first marriage.

For patterns on assortative mating by family origins, among rural migrants, having a college degree and having better educated parents are associated with a higher likelihood of marrying across social boundaries, that is, to marry someone with a different birth place, *hukou*, or migration status. Again, education is both an economic and an ideational factor. Having a higher education not only indicates greater economic prospects, which could afford rural migrants to select mates based on tastes and personalities, but also relates to having more liberal attitudes toward mate selection, which promotes matching on achieved, rather than ascribed attributes.

We acknowledge some limitations in these analyses. First, it will be desirable to use panel data to directly address the causal relationship. Second, due to the nature of the available data, we only capture migration histories due to work, while migration exclusively for education and marriage may be left out in the analyses. This omission may mask some differences in how migration influences family formation. Finally, Beijing is only one of the major migrant-receiving cities in China. Given the regional differences, it would be crucial to extend the qualitative study to other migrant-receiving sites, such as Shanghai, Guangzhou, and Shenzhen. These limitations will serve as directions for further development on related topics.

Acknowledgments

We thank Man Yao and Zhengliang Song for their capable research assistance, and Professor Jingming Liu and Lipeng Zhao for helping us establish an interview site at an urban migrant enclave. Financial support for this research was provided by the Centre for Family and Population Research and Asia Research Institute at the National University of Singapore.

Disclosure statement

No potential conflict of interest was reported by the authors.

Funding

This work was supported by Centre for Family and Population Research, National University of Singapore [grant number N-101-000-177-001]; Asia Research Institute, National University of Singapore [grant number R-101-000-045-133].

ORCID

Zheng Mu http://orcid.org/0000-0003-2664-4106
Wei-Jun Jean Yeung http://orcid.org/0000-0001-7519-5576

References

Arnett, Jeffrey Jensen. 2000. "Emerging Adulthood: A Theory of Development from the Late Teens Through the Twenties." *American Psychologist* 55 (5): 469–480.
Arnett, Jeffrey Jensen. 2007. "Emerging Adulthood: What is It, and What is It Good For?" *Child Development Perspectives* 1 (2): 68–73.
Carlson, Elwood D. 1985. "The Impact of International Migration Upon the Timing of Marriage and Childbearing." *Demography* 22 (1): 61–72.
Chang, Leslie T. 2009. *Factory Girls: From Village to City in a Changing China*. New York: Random House LLC.
Chen, Junhua, Fei Guo, and Ying Wu. 2011. "One Decade of Urban Housing Reform in China: Urban Housing Price Dynamics and the Role of Migration and Urbanization, 1995-2005." *Habitat International* 35 (1): 1–8.
Choi, Susanne Yuk-Ping, and Yinni Peng. 2016. *Masculine Compromise: Migration, Family, and Gender in China*. Oakland, CA: University of California Press.

Davis, Deborah S. 2014. "Privatization of Marriage in Post-socialist China." *Modern China* 40 (6): 551–577.
Fan, C. Cindy. 2000. "Migration and Gender in China." *China Review*: 423–454.
Fan, C. Cindy. 2003. "Rural-Urban Migration and Gender Division of Labor in Transitional China." *International Journal of Urban and Regional Research* 27 (1): 24–47.
Fan, C. Cindy. 2008. "China on the Move: Migration, the State, and the Household." *The China Quarterly* 196: 924–956.
Fan, C. Cindy, and Ling Li. 2002. "Marriage and Migration in Transitional China: A Field Study of Gaozhou, Western Guangdong." *Environment and Planning A: Economy and Space* 34 (4): 619–638.
Flowerdew, Robin, and Alaa Al-Hamad. 2004. "The Relationship Between Marriage, Divorce and Migration in a British Data Set." *Journal of Ethnic and Migration Studies* 30 (2): 339–351.
Gaetano, Arianne M., and Tamara Jacka. 2013. *On the Move: Women and Rural-to-urban Migration in Contemporary China*. New York: Columbia University Press.
Jacka, Tamara. 2005. *Rural Women in Urban China: Gender, Migration, and Social Change*. Armonk, NY: M.E. Sharpe.
Jang, Bohyun Joy, John B. Casterline, and Anastasia R. Snyder. 2014. "Migration and Marriage: Modeling the Joint Process." *Demographic Research* 30: 1339–1366.
Ji, Yingchun, and Wei-Jun Jean Yeung. 2014. "Heterogeneity in Contemporary Chinese Marriage." *Journal of Family Issues* 35 (12): 1662–1682.
Juárez, Fatima, Thomas LeGrand, Cynthia B. Lloyd, Susheela Singh, and Véronique Hertrich. 2013. "Youth Migration and Transitions to Adulthood in Developing Countries." *The Annals of the American Academy of Political and Social Science* 648 (1): 6–15.
Kulu, Hill, and Nadja Milewski. 2008. "Family Change and Migration in the Life Course: An Introduction." *Demographic Research* 17: 567–590.
Lee, Bun Song, and Louis G. Pol. 1993. "The Influence of Rural-urban Migration on Migrants' Fertility in Korea, Mexico and Cameroon." *Population Research and Policy Review* 12 (1): 3–26.
Liang, Zai, and Yiu Por Chen. 2004. "Migration and Gender in China: An Origin-destination Linked Approach." *Economic Development and Cultural Change* 52 (2): 423–443.
Liang, Zai, and Zhongdong Ma. 2004. "China's Floating Population: New Evidence from the 2000 Census." *Population and Development Review* 30 (3): 467–488.
Meisner, Maurice. 1999. *Mao's China and After: A History of the People's Republic*. New York: The Free Press.
Mu, Zheng, and Yu Xie. 2014. "Marital Age Homogamy in China: A Reversal of Trend in the Reform Era?" *Social Science Research* 44 (2): 141–157.
Mu, Zheng, and Wei-Jun Jean Yeung. 2018. "For Money or For a Life: A Mixed-method Study on Migration and Time Use in China." *Social Indicators Research* 139 (1): 347–379.
Palriwala, Rajni, and Patricia Uberoi. 2008. *Marriage, Migration and Gender*, Vol. 5. New Delhi: SAGE Publications.
Piotrowski, Martin, and Yuying Tong. 2013. "Straddling Two Geographic Regions: The Impact of Place of Origin and Destination on Return Migration Intentions in China." *Population, Space and Place* 19 (3): 329–349.
Piotrowski, Martin, Yuying Tong, Yueyun Zhang, and Lu Chao. 2016. "The Transition to First Marriage in China, 1966–2008: An Examination of Gender Differences in Education and Hukou Status." *European Journal of Population* 32 (1): 129–154.
Qian, Zhenchao, and Yue Qian. 2020. "Generation, Education, and Intermarriage of Asian Americans." *Journal of Ethnic and Migration Studies* 46 (14): 2880–2895. doi:10.1080/1369183X.2019.1585006.
Reczek, Corinne, Tetyana Pudrovska, Deborah Carr, Debra Umberson, and Mieke Beth Thomeer. 2016. "Marital Histories and Heavy Alcohol Use among Older Adults." *Journal of Health and Social Behavior* 57 (1): 77–96.
Schwartz, Christine R. 2010. "Earnings Inequality and the Changing Association Between Spouses' Earnings." *American Journal of Sociology* 115 (5): 1524–1557.

Schwartz, Christine R., and Robert D. Mare. 2005. "Trends in Educational Assortative Marriage from 1940 to 2003." *Demography* 42 (4): 621–646.

Tian, Felicia Feng. 2013. "Transition to First Marriage in Reform-era Urban China: The Persistent Effect of Education in a Period of Rapid Social Change." *Population Research and Policy Review* 32 (4): 529–552.

Treiman, Donald J. 2013. "Trends in Educational Attainment in China." *Chinese Sociological Review* 45 (3): 3–25.

Utomo, Ariane J. 2020. "Love in the Melting Pot: Ethnic Intermarriage in Jakarta." *Journal of Ethnic and Migration Studies* 46 (14): 2896–2913. doi:10.1080/1369183X.2019.1585008.

Whyte, Martin King. 1992. *From Arranged Marriages to Love Matches in Urban China*. Hong Kong: Hong Kong Institute of Asia-Pacific Studies, Chinese University of Hong Kong.

Wu, Xiaogang. 2002. "Work Units and Income Inequality: The Effect of Market Transition in Urban China." *Social Forces* 80 (3): 1069–1099.

Wu, Xiaogang, and Zhuoni Zhang. 2010. "Changes in Educational Inequality in China, 1990–2005: Evidence from the Population Census Data." *Research in Sociology of Education* 17: 123–152.

Xie, Yu, James M. Raymo, Kimberl Goyette, and Arland Thornton. 2003. "Economic Potential and Entry into Marriage and Cohabitation." *Demography* 40 (2): 351–367.

Xu, Xiaohe, and Martin King Whyte. 1990. "Love Matches and Arranged Marriages: A Chinese Replication." *Journal of Marriage and the Family* 52 (3): 709–722.

Yeung, Wei-Jun J. 2013. "Higher Education Expansion and Social Stratification in China." *Chinese Sociological Review* 45 (4): 54–80.

Yeung, Wei-Jun J., and Cheryll Alipio. 2013. "Transitioning to Adulthood in Asia School, Work, and Family Life." *The Annals of the American Academy of Political and Social Science* 646 (1): 6–27.

Yeung, Wei-Jun J., and Shu Hu. 2013. "Coming of Age in Times of Change: The Transition to Adulthood in China." *The Annals of the American Academy of Political and Social Science* 646 (1): 149–171.

Yeung, Wei-Jun Jean, and Zheng Mu. 2020. "Migration and Marriage in Asian Contexts." *Journal of Ethnic and Migration Studies* 46 (14): 2863–2879. doi:10.1080/1369183X.2019.1585005.

Zenteno, René, Silvia E. Giorguli, and Edith Gutiérrez. 2013. "Mexican Adolescent Migration to the United States and Transitions to Adulthood." *The Annals of the American Academy of Political and Social Science* 648 (1): 18–37.

Zhang, Zhuoni, and Hua Ye. 2018. "Mode of Migration, Age at Arrival, and Occupational Attainment of Immigrants from Mainland China to Hong Kong." *Chinese Sociological Review* 50 (1): 83–112.

Do gender systems in the origin and destination societies affect immigrant integration? Vietnamese marriage migrants in Taiwan and South Korea

Hsin-Chieh Chang

ABSTRACT
This study engages with the literature on gender, migration, and integration through examining how gender systems in the origin and destination societies affect intra-Asia marriage migrants' integration experiences. Primary data were from over 100 interviews with Vietnamese marriage migrants (VMMs) in Taiwan or South Korea, including 44 migrant-serving civic organisation staff or volunteers. Patterns of gender ideology from large-scale surveys were used to depict the gendered social and family contexts. For some VMMs in Taiwan, they perceived that married women have more autonomy and social rights than in Vietnam, which at some point facilitated their integration processes. For some VMMs in South Korea, they struggled with the rigid gendered expectations of family roles as migrant wives and daughters-in-law, which were considered less flexible than in Vietnam. Through contrasting three patriarchal societies in Asia that may seem similar in the Western literature, this study provides insights into how gender systems affect marriage migrants' cultural integration in the private, the public, and the civic spheres. Despite that wealthier new migrant destination societies do not guarantee more equitable gender systems and may create additional integration challenges, civic engagement may facilitate female migrants' cultural integration through improved awareness of gender-based and ethnicised discrimination.

1. Introduction

The immigrant integration literature has considered gender equality as an aspect of social or cultural integration for immigrants (Su, Richardson, and Wang 2010; Röder and Mühlau 2014; Itzigsohn and Giorguli-Saucedo 2005; Maliepaard and Alba 2016). Some scholars are concerned about how post-migration gender role attitudes are conditioned by the origin societal context (Röder and Mühlau 2014); while others explored whether migrants' degree of embeddedness in the ethnic community explains patterns of post-migration gender ideology (Maliepaard and Alba 2016). Whether and how migrant women 'acculturate' to adapt more liberal gender ideology after migration may affect their social status, sense of self, and may further impact the gender ideology of their children (Maliepaard and Alba 2016).

This line of inquiry has a significant impact on migrant women's integration because typical Western immigrant societies have higher level of gender equality, which might not be the case in Asia. Researchers have emphasised gender as a central analytical focus in understanding intra-Asia marriage migration (Kim 2010; Kim 2012; Wang 2011) and in interpreting the patriarchal logic of immigration policy (Hsia 2009; Wang and Belanger 2008; Bélanger, Lee, and Wang 2010). To date, there lacks empirical studies that addresses how the origin-destination contrasts of gender norms, gender relations, and gendered expectations may affect the integration experiences of marriage migrants. Compared to migrant workers or migrant women who married co-ethnic husbands, inter-married marriage migrants are exposed to the gender logics through everyday interactions with family members in the marital families and citizens in the host societies after they migrate.

Based on multiple data sources, this study examines how gender systems of the origin and destination contexts affect Vietnamese marriage migrants (VMMs)'s integration experiences in Taiwan and South Korea (hereafter, Korea). Gender system generally refers to the social roles, social statuses, and the accompanied obligations and rights of men and women (Mason 1997). It is not migration that changes gender inequalities in the origin or destination societies. Instead, gender system plays a vital role in mediating how migration may potentially impact gender relations and gender equalities in the process of population movement (Giorguli and Angoa 2016; Donato et al. 2011). Taiwan and Korea are two new migrant societies hosting the majority of the region's marriage migrants. The VMMs represent the largest migrant group without ethnic ties to or shared languages in Taiwan or Korea. Their migration flows are influenced by the proliferation of profit-oriented transnational matchmaking agencies, socioeconomic inequalities within Asia, societal change including fertility declines and population aging in East Asia, and the Confucian traditions of patriarchy and *familism* which persist in Vietnam, Taiwan, and Korea (Croll 2001). As of 2016, there are 119,481 VMMs in Taiwan[1] and 87,025 of them in Korea.[2]

Examining how gender systems in the origin and destination contexts affect VMMs' integration experiences in Taiwan and Korea contributes to the gender, migration, and integration literature in three aspects. First, Asian migrant women typically migrate to destination societies with higher levels of gender equality in North America, Western Europe, or Australia. However, the contrast between the gender systems in the origin and destination societies may present different scenarios for intra-Asia migration, which remains under-addressed in the literature. Second, despite the persisting male–dominant social structures in Taiwan and Korea, women's movement, the LGBTQ movement, and other social movements that involve heated debates over minority rights have made some progress in Korea and more significantly in Taiwan since the turn of the century. It is important to investigate whether some VMMs have been exposed to the more equitable segments of the gender systems, and whether different migration destinations matter for marriage migrants' integration. Last, as a typical migrant-sending society, gender system in Vietnam and women's emigration have evolved since the government officially adopted a market-oriented economic system in 1986. Narratives' from VMMs on how they perceive gender system in Vietnam may illuminate some unknown facts that deserve further scholarly attention.

2. Gender and immigrant integration: the roles of origin and destination contexts

As prominent feminists scholar Hondagneu-Sotelo observes how the gender and migration scholarship has evolved over the past three decades, she noted a gradual paradigm shift from 'gender and development' towards 'gender and immigrant integration' (Hondagneu-Sotelo 2011). The immigrant integration scholarship recognises that the integration experiences of men and women differ, and such processes may be further complicated by social stratifications based on economic status and racial/ethnic lines (Hondagneu-Sotelo 2003; Itzigsohn and Giorguli-Saucedo 2005). Recent works have proposed new inquiries within and beyond the immigrant integration literature that involve gender. First, compared with some traditional dimensions of integration like education, housing, and labour market participation, Rodríguez-García (2015) proposed that immigrant integration should consider social, cultural, and political dimensions including gender equality, religion, and identity. Second, instead of integration policy measures, empirical work should address actual integration outcomes such as the acquisition of new gender values and norms (Rodríguez-García 2015).

Emprically, Bélanger and Linh (2011) identified that marriage migration from Vietnam to East Asia had made a gender impact to their sending communities, primarily because of the significant amount of remittances that VMMs sent back home. The remittance-sending behaviours improved their social status and power in the natal families and in the village, which also improved the overall status of women in Southern Vietnam (Bélanger and Linh 2011). Within European countries, country of origin plays an important role in shaping post-migration gender values among migrants (Röder and Mühlau 2014). Generally, migrants who come from societies with a higher level of gender inequality are less likely to support gender equality than members of destination society. However, migrants adapt to the more liberal gender ideology of the destination society over time. In terms of gender differences, first generation migrant women tend to embrace more liberal gender attitudes earlier than migrant men (Röder and Mühlau 2014).

The integration experiences of those who inter-marry are one emerging research focus within the immigrant integration literature (Törngren, Irastorza, and Song 2016; Rodríguez-García 2015). The major challenge of those who marry across racial or ethnic lines, and especially those who migrate to a new society at the same time, involves integrating into both the marriage as a spouse and to the host society as a new immigrant. Rather than applying the assimilation theory developed in North America, Chang proposed that the integration perspective better illustrates intra-Asia marriage migrants' post-migration experiences (2017).

In proposing the Two-Step Social Integration Model, Chang describes how VMMs who had a smooth integration process into the marital family tend to experience a somewhat flexible gender structure in the marital family. In other words, supportive husband and parents-in-law allowed them to exercise individual agency beyond the traditional images of filial daughter-in-law and obedient wife (Chang 2017). The model indicates that perception of gender is a key component that differentiates VMMs' integration trajectories, yet did not specifically contrast the perceived gender gaps between Vietnam and Taiwan, or between Vietnam and Korea.

3. Gender systems compared: Vietnam, Taiwan, and South Korea

Gender scholars have used various terms to illustrate the gendered aspects of our everyday social, cultural, and political environments. On a spectrum capturing the macro-level to the micro-level of gendered life, some relevant terms include gender cultures, gender regimes, gender systems and gender arrangements (Walby 1990; Aboim 2010; Pfau-Effinger 2004; Ridgeway and Smith-Lovin 1999). I adopt Mason's definition of gender system (1997) to capture VMMs' everyday gendered experiences both in the origin and destination societies. Mason's conceptualisation of gender system differentiates two levels of analysis. At the micro- or interactional level, gender system captures the socially constructed roles and expectations for men and women, such as the household division of labour within the family. At the macro-level, it measures the level of institutionalised inequality between men and women including gender segregation in the labour market and other aspects (Mason 1997).

In a similar fashion, Ridgeway and Correll (2004) considered gender as 'an institutionalised system of social practices' that organises the unequal social relations of men and women (Ridgeway and Correll 2004). They further illustrated that like other multilevel systems of difference and inequality, such as race and class, gender system at the individual level involves selves and identities; at the macro level, it involves cultural beliefs and how resources are being distributed (Ridgeway and Correll 2004). Importantly, what distinguishes gender system from other systems of difference and inequality, is the constant interaction between men and women: 'Gender's constitutive cultural beliefs and confirmatory experiences must be sustained in the context of constant interaction, often on familiar terms, between those advantaged and disadvantaged by the system (p. 192)' (Ridgeway and Smith-Lovin 1999). Consequently, at the interactional level, gender system involves patterns of social behaviours and practices sorted by gendered hierarchies across various institutions that organise the human society (Ridgeway and Correll 2004).

In contemporary Vietnam, scholars believe that the culture of gender and the kinship system are influenced by the Confucian style of patrilineality and patriarchy especially in the North, the historical practice of bilateral kinship system in the South, and the changes in terms of gender relations brought forth by the official adoption of a market-oriented economic system in 1986 (Wang 2019; Bélanger and Barbieri 2009; Werner and Belanger 2002). Scholars on Vietnam mostly consider market economy as detrimental for women (Werner and Belanger 2002). Some empirical observations include more precarious working conditions, increase in domestic violence, and the rising cost of education that may situate daughters in a rather disadvantaged position as opposed to sons (Werner and Belanger 2002; Bélanger and Barbieri 2009). Regarding gender division of household labour, an empirical study found that the more than 80 percent of respondents reported that wife take up a lot of house chore regardless of cohorts and regions. Compared to those who were born before the market reform, recent cohorts of Vietnamese men share more housework. Overall, men in the Northern region share more housework than men in the South. Yet significant cohort change was only observed in the South (Teerawichitchainan et al. 2010).

Despite Taiwan and Korea's economic progress over the past few decades, patriarchal values persist in their gender systems and family practices (Brinton 2001). Within such patriarchal systems, intra-Asia cross-border marriage decisions are not always made based on an individual's preference but involve consultation from one's family and community. Moreover, pressures from routine familial interaction in a traditional culture of *familism* has pushed men beyond a 'suitable age' to look for wives across national boundaries, in order to fulfil the obligations of the 'filial son' (Suzuki 2008). Women from less-developed countries with similar traditions and cultural backgrounds are ideal candidates to marry into families who seek someone with 'traditional virtues': a woman who is submissive, obedient, and follows the practice of filial piety (Wang 2007). Under such rigid gendered expectations, how VMMs observe and interpret their gender-related experiences before and after migration, as well as how the social systems are organised by gender in Vietnam, Taiwan, and Korea remain an interesting empirical puzzle.

3.1 Global gender-related indices: Marrying up, or marrying down?

Among the several ways to contrast these three societies' gender systems, gender-related indices released by International Organizations may provide some macro-level evidence. Table 1 shows the Global Gender Gap Index of year 2008, 2011, and 2015. This index was developed by the World Economic Forum in 2006 and measures the extent to which female citizens of each country are disadvantaged in four following areas: economic participation and opportunity, educational attainment, political empowerment, and health and survival (WEF 2015). Across these three time periods, Taiwan ranked the highest (or the narrowest gender gap) at 52, 40, and 43 respectively, followed by Vietnam (68, 79, and 83). Korea holds the image of a rising powerful economy, yet its GGI rankings were lower than more than 100 countries in 2008, 2011, and 2015. Based on these criteria, the gender system in Vietnam appeared to be less equal than Taiwan but more advanced than in Korea, meaning that some VMMs may experience the processes of 'marrying down' to a more rigid gender system, when they migrated to Korea and joined the marital family of the Korean husband.

4. Methods

I use multiple data sources – qualitative interviews with VMMs during two waves of multi-sited fieldwork in Taiwan and Korea, and social surveys that capture relevant gender-related attitudes in Vietnam, Taiwan, and Korea – for two purposes. The first is to facilitate the origin-destination and Taiwan-Korea comparison. The second purpose is for triangulation between VMMs' narratives and how social surveys capture relevant aspects of the gender norms, role expectations and practices in these three societies.

Table 1. Global gender gap index (GGI): Ranking of Vietnam, Taiwan, and South Korea (2008–2015).

GGI	Vietnam	Taiwan	South Korea
2008	68	52	108
2011	79	40	107
2015	83	43	115

4.1. Fieldwork, sample, and analytic strategy

In collaboration with local NGOs, migrant-serving organisations, and key informants from community centres in both rural and urban settings, I conducted two waves of multi-sited fieldwork in Taiwan and Korea. Between 2011 and 2013, I conducted participant observation, collected 55 interviews and held four focus groups. Wave 2 includes 47 interviews that took place between 2015 and 2017. I collaborated with non-profit media outlets, feminist organisations, faith-based organisations, marriage brokerage agency, and both government-funded and non-government-funded community centres. In Taiwan, I interviewed VMMs in Mandarin and Taiwanese. In Korea, I worked with Vietnamese interpreters who were international students and fluent English speakers for interviews.

To capture a wider range of VMMs' integration experiences, I intentionally sampled three specific groups: those who were involved in civic organisations, those who experienced adversity such as domestic violence or who had been divorced or widowed, and other VMMs. Among the interviews, forty-four were VMMs who were involved in civic organisations, broadly referred to migrant-serving organisations or community centres that provide integration assistance for migrants. These VMMs may work full-time, part-time on specific projects, or served as long-term volunteers. This group was unique for three reasons. First, they were exposed to a welcoming civic atmosphere that respects their contributions to the community, helping them to develop a sense of belonging as citizens. Second, they were exposed to a multicultural work environment and mediate across several cultures or social groups: with co-ethnics, migrants from other countries, community residents, and local officials. Third, they demonstrated a decent level of local language proficiency, some were quite knowledgeable about the spirits of civic participation. Consequently, each of them had served a large number of co-ethnics. Such experiences familiarised them with the integration challenges that marriage migrants might encounter at different life and family stages. During fieldwork in wave 2, I conducted some follow-up interviews to understand their integration trajectories and the unexpected consequences of civic participation.

All interviews were digitally recorded. Verbal informed consent was obtained from interviewees prior to interview. Tables 2 and 3 show the socio-demographic characteristics of the sample. All names used in this article are pseudo names.

Vietnamese to English interviews were transcribed by native Vietnamese speakers proficient in English. Interviews in Taiwan were transcribed by native Chinese Mandarin speakers. The transcripts were uploaded into Dedoose (www.dedoose.com), a web-based

Table 2. Backgrounds of VMMs interviewees: Fieldwork Wave 1, 2011–2013.

	Taiwan	Korea	All
N	38	17	55
Mean age (min–max)	33.3 (24–63)	29.6 (22–42)	32.1 (22–63)
High school education and above	61%	65%	62%
Married through brokers	32%	41%	35%
Length of stay (mean, min–max)	9.9 (1–20)	6.3 (2.5–18)	8.8 (1–20)
From urban Vietnam	39%	18%	33%
From Southern Vietnam	76%	71%	75%
Ethnic Chinese	18%	6%	15%
Divorced, widowed, or separated	21%	29%	24%

Table 3. Backgrounds of VMMs interviewees: Fieldwork Wave 2, 2015–2017.

	Taiwan	Korea	All
N	25	22	47
Mean age (min–max)	39.5 (30–65)	36 (24–48)	37.9 (24–65)
High school education and above	60%	77%	68%
Married through brokers	20%	32%	26%
Length of stay (mean, min–max)	15.1 (7–21)	10.4 (0.5–22)	12.9 (0.5–22)
From urban Vietnam	32%	27%	30%
From Southern Vietnam	84%	68%	77%
Ethnic Chinese	24%	0	13%
Divorced, widowed, or separated	28%	32%	32%

analytic programme. Overall, I developed the parent codes (main themes) and child codes (sub-themes) surrounding gender based on the principles of grounded theory (Charmaz and Belgrave 2003). To discover patterns and themes that emerged from VMMs' gender-related observations and its relevance to integration experiences, I applied thematic analysis (Patton 2002) as the main method of content analysis.

4.2. Selected questions from nationally-representative social surveys

To better contextualise the gender systems in Vietnam, Taiwan, and Korea, I identified questions that measure similar aspects of the gender system from nationally-representative surveys to supplement and triangulate the qualitative findings. The question from The AsiaBarometer (AB) Survey[3] examined whether there were gendered expectations toward sons and daughters. It asked: 'How would you like to see your son(s) and your daughter(s) grow up? Of the following accomplishments, please select two that you would wish for a daughter, and two that you would wish for a son. If you don't have a son/daughter, please imagine what you would feel if you do'. The respondents had ten accomplishments to choose from: (a) Become a great scholar; (b) Become a powerful political leader; (c) Become very wealthy; (d) Become a loving and charitable person; (e) Become a person respected by the general public; (f) Become more proficient in profession than I am; (g) Follow in my footsteps; (h) Become a person who cares about family; (i) Find a good marriage partner; and (j) Become fulfilled spiritually. Each respondent was required to choose exactly two wishes from the list, ending up with a total of 200% instead of 100%. The question from the East Asia Social Survey (EASS) 2006 (Kim et al. 2014)[4] measures attitudes towards the importance of having a son: To continue the family line, one must have at least one son. The answering categories ranged from strongly disagree, disagree, neither, agree, and strongly agree.

5. Results

The results section is organised as follows. First, I start with how VMMs perceived the differences between the gender systems of origin and destinations. Second, I present VMMs' common experiences in Taiwan. Third, regardless of the gaps across social and economic indicators across Vietnam, Taiwan, and Korea, I show how parents share similar expectations towards daughters across these three societies from a comparative social survey, echoing those migrants who perceived that their gendered encounters as rather similar in the origin and destination societies. The last part showcases observations from VMMs who were involved in civic organisations, who acculturate themselves with laws and ideologies that promote gender equality through assisting co-ethnics' integration.

5.1. Rigid gendered expectations and arrangements in the private sphere in Korea

5.1.1. In Vietnam, we are supposed to take care of family meals; in Korea, we are forced to do so even when we have to work

Several Confucian traditions in Korean families may create additional integration challenges for marriage migrants, such as division of household labour, and responsibilities of daughters-in-law in the marital families. Research has documented such persisting patriarchal beliefs among Korean husbands who migrated to the United States (Min 2001). If Korean men who migrated to the U.S. before the turn of the century maintain rigid gender attitudes, would those in Korea who married Vietnamese around the year of 2010 hold different gender ideology and household division of labour? Trịnh and Phi, one from the rural South and another from the urban North in Vietnam, illustrated how the household division of labour within couples differs even in subtle ways in Vietnam and Korea:

> In Vietnam, we are supposed to take care of family meals; here in Korea, we are forced to do so even when we have to work. That thought cannot be changed. In Vietnam, when the husbands sometimes stay at home, they would help us with cooking, but Korean husbands never do that. The mother spends so much time taking care of the children than the father. (26 years old, in Korea for 4½ years, married)

> In Korean family, men get more respect, women are considered to be inferior and should stay at home and do all the housework. In Vietnam, difficult housework would be assigned to men. But in Korea, all housework is assigned to women, husbands rarely do anything. Husbands only deal with issues related to household documents and land certificate. (30 years old, in Korea for 10 years, married)

Under certain circumstances, the presence of mother-in-law may deteriorate the already imbalanced power relations between the Korean husband and the Vietnamese wife. Based on a large-scale social survey in Korea, marriage migrants who live with in-laws significantly reported worse life satisfaction compared to those who do not live with in-laws or whose in-laws have passed away (Chang 2016). On average, the spousal age gap between Vietnamese wives and Korean husbands were 17 years. That is to say, the age of some Korean mother-in-law may be close to marriage migrants' grandmothers in Vietnam. Consequently, the mothers in-law and migrant wives may hold varied gender attitudes reflecting their own life experiences, cultures, and age cohorts.

5.1.2. If Korean men volunteers to help, the mother-in-law would give the daughter-in-law a hard time

> I feel women in Vietnam have more social rights than in Korea. Vietnamese men help their wives and other family members also share some housework. But here in Korea it is almost never the case, at least not for me. Of course I know some Korean men who help their wives but there are just few. Especially when the couple lives with the parents-in-law, there is no way for the son to help. If he volunteers to help, his mother gets angry and later they will give the daughter-in-law a hard time. (32 years old, in Korea for 5½ years, married)

At the time of interview, Tím had already migrated to Korea for 20 years. Born in Ho Chi Minh City, she was attracted to Korea's culture and promising image. Shortly after Vietnam established diplomatic relationships with Korea in 1992 when she was a college student in Vietnam, she went to Korea to study Korean language for three years. Tim was very enthusiastic about our discussion on gender, because she has witnessed similar struggles of marriage migrants who had to meet the rigid family expectations towards daughters-in-law, herself is no exception.

> The most difficult things for married migrants, not only to me, is like this. Mother-in-law only respects her son. It is different from Vietnam, the mother-in-law may not like the daughter-in-law, yet she would still stand for her. Here in Korea, the son is always the priority. The daughter-in-law must serve him and be dependent on him. That is the general difficulty for all migrant daughters-in-law here. I was so stressful. The wife is always the person who serves and gets back no respect. In addition, the husband always thinks that the mother-in-law has the right to interfere our marriage life. (45 years old, in Korea for 20 years, separated)

Sáu, who went to Korea to take language course and to visit her sister who had already married a Korean, described her husband as loyal and honest. She met her husband through her brother-in-law's introduction. When the friend who introduced them knew from her husband that the family expected Sáu to live with mother-in-law, the friend asked Sáu to consider other Korean men. Sáu decided to marry this guy after dating him for seven months and to take up the challenge to live with the mother-in-law. The couple had moved out after two years which was a great relief for Sáu. She recalled her struggle to communicate with her mother-in-law during the first year as a full-time housewife:

> Before I started working, I had stayed at home for 7 months. I cooked and asked my husband help me to prepare the table for dinner. My mother-in-law disagreed, she said that my husband goes to work and is very tired, preparing the table is my job. After we had dinner, we watched TV together and I said that 'we are members in a family, I think that we should help each other some housework. It is not a bid deal'. My mother-in-law replied to me: 'It only happens in Vietnam, not Korea.' (28 years old, in Korea for 6 years, married)

Miều, who is originally from Northern Vietnam, migrated to Korea in the mid-1990s as a migrant worker and later married a colleague in the same factory. Compared to other VMMs whose husbands may be ten years older or more, her husband is only one year older. She has been collaborating quite well with her husband over the past 20 years. However, the only issue that she would constantly argue with her husband is about the assumed unequal social status among men and women:

> Korean men have patriarchal thinking. My husband is just one year older than me but he still has that way of thinking. He did help me a lot, but he had no concept of 'sharing', but only the concept of 'helping'. Whenever he did the household chores, he considered that he was helping me, but not sharing the household chores with me. Therefore, we argued for that. For Vietnamese women, we thought of gender equality was a normal thing in daily life; however, Korean people think women locate at a lower position and men are at a higher position. We still argue about this now. (43 years old, in Korea for 22 years, married)

In a nutshell, VMMs in Korea shared common experiences on the challenging family role as daughter-in-law and the unreasonable gender division of labour between wife and husband. Both aspects of gender arrangement in the private sphere are considered 'worse' than in Vietnam, which have been the major obstacles during their integration processes.

5.2. A more equitable gender system in Taiwan but traditional values persist

Overall, VMMs perceived the gender system in Taiwan as more equitable than in Vietnam based on two aspects: married women are protected by domestic violence laws in Taiwan but not in Vietnam, and married women have more autonomy and power. However, one major exception was that son preference among the elder generations in Taiwan is considered quite similar, in some cases worse than in Vietnam. I use narratives and descriptive statistics on son preference for cross-country comparison ad triangulation.

5.2.1. In Taiwan, married women are ACTUALLY protected by the domestic violence law, this is not the case in Vietnam

The most common comparison that was raised, regardless of interviewees' education and whether they are from Northern or Southern Vietnam, was about the domestic violence laws in Taiwan. In Vietnam, relatives or neighbours often ask beaten wives to tolerate and forgive the husbands, 'the law is there, but it does not function':

> Domestic violence is considered normal in Vietnam, women should just tolerate, women are trained to tolerate men's behaviours when they were little girls; the situation could be really bad in rural Vietnam, when the husband gets angry, he would just slap his wife for no reason.. … .but in Taiwan, it is against the law to hit other people, we know that we could go to the lawyers, the wife should speak out if the husband beats her, (domestic violence is) not something to be tolerated. (30 years old, in Taiwan for 10 years, married)

Born in rural Southern Vietnam, Phương shared similar views with Anh, who is from the urban areas in Northern Vietnam. Both have arrived Taiwan for 10 years at the time of interview. San, who works full-time in a civic organisation that served migrants, specifically mentioned the rural-urban differences in Vietnam, so did Quyết, both were full-time staff.

> In rural areas, when you report to the police, the best case scenario was that the husband would need to take a class at the police office, some men would feel bad after that, but many would continue slapping their wives after taking that course.

Quyết described the situation that she knew about in Northern Vietnam.

In 1998, Taiwan became the first East Asian society to pass the 'Domestic Violence Prevention and Treatment Act (DVPTA)', just right before the migration flows from Vietnam arrived around 2000. After over a decade's hard work by feminist groups, the general public were aware of the DVPTA and that both central and local governments allocated a substantial amount of funds to establish a social system that provide support to abused women (Chao 2005). This major progress in women's movement became something novel for marriage migrants who come from other Asian countries without the implementation of relevant laws, including Vietnam. However, criminalisation of domestic violence does not reduce the incidence of violence all of a sudden. Ha, who is from a rather well-off family in Ho Chi Minh City, indicated such gaps between the law and everyday encounters:

In Vietnam, if my uncle beats my aunt-in-law, either my parents or the marital family of my aunt-in-law would ask her to tolerate, and would try to convince her that it is just a one-time thing, he did not mean it. Such situations would not happen in Taiwan, because women are protected by the law. But, still many women are beaten by their husbands, have you seen the news recently? (28 years old, in Taiwan for 10 years, married)

5.2.2. Married women have more autonomy and power in Taiwan

The second major contrast that VMMs observed was the social role of married women in Taiwan. Quyết described that

> Taiwanese women have more power within the marriage, this is not the case in Vietnam. Sometimes husbands and wives may discuss together in urban areas in Vietnam, but usually men makes the final decision. Especially in rural area, men have way more power within the marriage.

Similar to Ko and Chang's finding that Vietnamese families maintain traditional division of labour (Ko and Chang 2007), general social expectations toward married women in Vietnam are more conservative:

> Women like us in Vietnam, if we were married to Vietnamese, they would expect that you stay at home, give birth to babies, and take care of their parents. Those would be your duties. They are more conservative. My husband's family is traditional as they worship the ancestors regularly, but I don't have any problem with that. They encourage me to go out, earn some money, work, and learn ... (28 years old, in Taiwan for 10 years, married)

> I feel married women here in Taiwan have more autonomy. In Vietnam, once you are married, you belong to your husband. It might be because of the individual circumstances, or the economy, as soon as they (the Vietnamese women) reach a certain age, they have to marry. In Taiwan, you have more autonomy, people would think it makes little difference whether a woman is married or not, as long as she is capable of making her own living, right? So it's okay not to get married. Women can make decisions for themselves here. (32 years old, in Taiwan for 12 years, married)

Hương had worked to support her natal family before graduating from junior high school in Vietnam. I asked whether such 'married women have more autonomy' ideology applied to herself as well. 'I think so. My marital family was opposed of the idea that I attended adult schools at night, but after a while they noticed that it was a good thing for me, they let me make my own decision.'

Several interviewees proposed that differences in terms of household division of labour between Vietnam and Taiwan show that married women in Taiwan have more power. Even for those who have to do most of the housework at home because husbands and in-laws would not help, they acknowledge that men share more housework in Taiwan than in Vietnam, based on what they heard from neighbours, their observation from grocery stores, and discussions from TV programmes:

> Considering the husband-wife equality, I think in Taiwan husbands and wives are more equal. Vietnamese men are more chauvinistic. When I get busy, I'd do tons of laundry all at once and ask my husband to hang them for drying. He would do so and asked me, 'Which of your brothers-in-law would help hanging clothes? I have four sisters in my family, all married. Last time when my husband went back to Vietnam with me, he saw all my brothers-in-law crossing their legs, doing nothing while women were busy with household chores'. (Focus group, Kaohsiung)

5.2.3. Son preference is really serious here in Taiwan, especially among older women

The persisting 'valuing male more than female' ideology seemed to be more prevalent in Taiwan than in Vietnam. Many mothers-in-law constantly reminded the interviewees about the importance that a family should have at least a son, while some fathers-in-law implicitly expressed their joy when VMMs gave birth to a son after having a daughter:

> As what I see in my own family, Vietnamese families don't have that much of the 'valuing male more than female' idea as in Taiwan. My mother-in-law is not a very rigid person but when she pressured me a lot after I gave birth to a daughter, that I should try to get pregnant again soon so that the family may have a grandson. (Focus group, Kaohsiung)

Growing up in Ho Chi Minh City, Tram gave birth to two sons and was running a Taiwanese-style noodle soup breakfast shop in a town an hour away from Taipei. She constantly received compliments from senior Taiwanese women on her 'accomplishment' of giving births to two sons. 'In my own natal family girls were more appreciated than boys, I would like to have daughters, too. My mother-in-law treated me nicely and never pressured me. Once when I was chatting with a customer, she said that 'I did a good job' for giving birth to two sons, I told her that it must be nice to have three granddaughters and she was like, no, no, no, it is better to have sons than daughters.'

San used her natal family in Southern Vietnam as an example, to illustrate how son preferences persist in rural areas. She has 11 siblings and among these 12 children, only two were male. She felt that in Taiwan people generally hold more equitable gender attitudes than in Vietnam, except for some mother-in-law's. But such pressure would not fall on every daughter-in-law, San described her own experience: 'my brother-in-law had a son when I came to Taiwan, as long as there is one grandson in the family, my mother-in-law is satisfied, so I was not pressured by her for this matter'.

Figure 1 shows the differences by gender and country for different age groups who chose 'disagree' and 'strongly disagree' towards whether one must have at least a son.

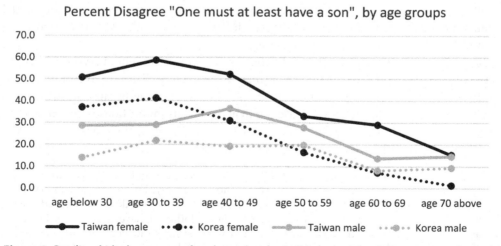

Figure 1. Patrilineal ideology among females and males in Taiwan and South Korea: proportions who chose 'disagree' by age groups, EASS 2006.

The highest percentage who chose 'disagree' were respondents aged between 30 and 39. For the younger generations below age 39, the most liberal were females in Taiwan, followed by females in Korea, males in Taiwan, and males in Korea. However, females in Korea aged 40–49 were more traditional than males in Taiwan, and those older than 50 were even more traditional than males in Korea. When considering that VMMs' mothers-in-law may actually fall into this age range (age 50 and above), one could imagine how such patrilineal ideology may affect VMMs' integration and wellbeing. Overall, the educational gradients were more visible for females in Taiwan, implying that those with less education may hold more rigid ideas on son preferences, followed by Korean females. Yet the differences between Taiwanese men who had secondary education and those who had university education were less than 5%; for Korean men, having received higher education do not necessarily mean they hold less rigid gender ideology (Figure 2).

5.3. Similarities across three societies: gendered expectations towards daughters

For VMMs who were not involved in civic organisations, most of them expressed that there appeared little differences in the pre-and post-migration gender systems. These interviewees share common experiences that their social worlds were confined in the private spheres: they did not have pre-migration work experiences, and have been housewives after migration. Indeed, there are some similarities in the gender systems across three societies. Using the Asia Barometer survey collected around the year of 2006, Table 4 provides empirical findings that urban Vietnam, Taiwan, and Korea share similar gendered expectations toward children especially to daughters.

For example, expectations that are related to marriage and family, 'Cares about family' and 'Find a good marriage partner' are more common wishes for daughters than for sons. Across three countries, these two marriage and family wishes ranked at top three for daughters. Fifty percent in Korea and fifty-five in Taiwan chose 'Find a good marriage partner' as their top wishes for daughters. On the other hand, these two wishes are not as important when it applied to sons. 'Finding a good marriage partner' actually ranked

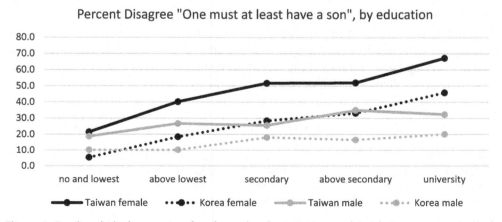

Figure 2. Patrilineal ideology among females and males in Taiwan and South Korea: proportions who chose 'disagree' by education levels, EASS 2006.

Table 4. Gendered expectations: Top five wishes for sons and daughters in Vietnam, Taiwan, and South Korea.

Rank	Wishes for sons		Wishes for daughters	
	South Korea			
1	Respected by the general public	46%	Find a good marriage partner	55%
2	Cares about family	32%	Loving and charitable	39%
3	Loving and charitable	31%	Cares about family	38%
4	Fulfilled spiritually	21%	Respected by the general public	24%
5	Find a good marriage partner	20%	Fulfilled spiritually	19%
Taiwan				
1	Loving and charitable	38%	Find a good marriage partner	57%
2	More proficient in profession	30%	Loving and charitable	40%
3	Respected by the general public	29%	Cares about family	29%
4	Cares about family	25%	Very wealthy	19%
5	Very wealthy	24%	Fulfilled spiritually	14%
Vietnam				
1	Loving and charitable	51%	Cares about family	52%
2	More proficient in profession	44%	Find a good marriage partner	45%
3	Cares about family	28%	Loving and charitable	41%
4	Respected by the general public	26%	More proficient in profession	23%
5	Find a good marriage partner	15%	Fulfilled spiritually	21%

Source: Asia Barometer Survey 2006.

seventh in Taiwan for sons (not shown in Table 4). Most interestingly, 'loving and charitable' appeared to be the second wish for Korea and Taiwan, and third for Vietnam for daughters. The gender systems may change as Taiwan and Korea progress socially, economically, and politically, yet the data showed rather traditional wishes for daughters across these three societies.

5.4. After so many years, I realise that it is a matter of confidence regardless of if you are migrant women or local women

In accordance with The Convention on the Elimination of all Forms of Discrimination Against Women (CEDAW) from the United Nations, the Taiwanese and Korean governments have been making continuous efforts in promoting and implementing gender mainstreaming policies at all sectors. Some VMMs had the chance to attend lectures and workshops on CEDAW that raised their awareness on gender. Through working with local feminist-minded officers, they socialise in a rather empowering way than others without such exposure, which were revelled from their gender-sensitive observations. For example, back in 2012, Hương who had just arrived for 2 and half years, expressed that while serving her co-ethnics in the community, she felt certain gender role ideologies and a more equal division of labour may only apply to Taiwanese women, not to those from Southeast Asia:

> Umm, speaking about gender equality, it's more equal in Taiwan than in Vietnam. But, females from abroad are treated with less equality. Taiwanese women are treated better than we who from abroad. If we were equal then such bad things wouldn't happen ... come on, now we are part of the four hundred thousand migrants living here. How many of us new immigrants can be like you (interviewer, the author) being treated equally? How many? (25 years old, in Taiwan for 2½ years, married)

When Hương served her co-ethnics in need of support in Southern Taiwan, she witnessed several cases of VMMs suffering from domestic abuse or receiving unequal treatment from the marital family members. She expressed anger towards such 'ethnicised' gender inequality. Chinh, who migrated to Taiwan as early as 1996 and has become quite active in supporting newcomers, has a different way of interpreting what shapes the social hierarchies.

> After so many years, I realized that be it local women or migrant women, what matters is whether a woman has confidence or not. I always encourage the newcomers to study and to show more confidence, so that you will win other people's respect.

In both Taiwan and Korea, VMMs' efforts in becoming a recognised daughter-in-law and social participation outside the private sphere had improved their social status in the marital family. Compared to our first meeting in 2011 in Korea, when Chí was doing some part-time interpretation work in a community migrant centre, I sensed that she gained more confidence in 2017. She reflected on how her very strict mother-in-law changed after a decade. 'My mother-in-law now trusts me that I am doing the best I could, her attitudes improved like 70% compared to the first four years when I had to rely on my husband and being a dependent of the family.' Meanwhile, she indicated that many VMMs' divorces took place because they could not stand the very rigid gendered family roles in Korea.

> There was a time that I thought I was about to give up the marriage for similar reasons, but I wanted to do better for my daughter, I wanted to be able to guide her in her life, so I went on to study in the university to fulfil the requirements to teach in elementary school.

6. Discussion

Using the case of intra-Asia marriage migration, this study demonstrates how various aspects of gender systems – at the micro, the interactional, and the macro levels – may influence migrants' integration processes into the marital family and the host society. The various forms and layers of patriarchal structures – both in the public and private spheres – in the migrant destination societies largely determine whether VMMs could meet the marital family's gendered expectations in the earlier post-migration stage, and whether they may become culturally integrated into the more equitable segment of the gender systems. Further, the perceived differences between the origin and destination contexts constitute the gendered 'contexts of exit and reception' that allow some VMMs experience upward mobility in terms of gender equity. Overall, I show that some VMMs experienced upward social mobility in the context of a more equitable gender system in Taiwan. For some VMMs in Korea, they had 'married up' to a richer country yet many experienced the processes of 'marrying down' to a more rigid gender system especially in the private sphere. Such results correspond to the global gender-related indices that ranked Taiwan as more equitable than Vietnam, followed by Korea (WEF 2015), reflecting that richer new immigrant destination societies do not necessarily guarantee more equitable gender systems, which may create integration challenges for female marriage migrants.

This study advances the scholarly understanding of the wide spectrum and heterogeneity of intra-Asia marriage migrants' integration experiences, from typical dimensions of language acculturation or adjustments of family roles, to the cultural dimension of gender equality and the political dimension of civic participation. Through a thoughtful selection of interviewees who were involved in civic organisations, I demonstrate the 'potential change in women's situation when the migration process increases their participation in the public sphere', which fills the knowledge gap of migration and gender proposed by Giorguli and Angoa (2016, 543). From a life course perspective, their integration experiences and empowered life reflections responded to the core research question of whether transnational marriage migration may empower women (Hugo 2000). Echoing the experiences of Thai marriage migrants entrepreneurs in Sweden (Webster and Haandrikman 2016), adapting more liberal gender ideologies may further expose marriage migrants to like-minded local networks in the civic sphere that facilitate their integration into the labour markets.

The contexts of destination matters. Narratives from VMMs highlighted the nuanced differences in the gender systems between Vietnam and Taiwan, and between Vietnam and Korea, which may seem similar and being lumped into the same category in the Western literature. As Taiwan and Korea transition from industrialised to post-industrialised societies, public attitudes towards gender equality and family traditions may fall on a wide liberal-conservative spectrum, depending on the individual's age cohort, education level, place of residence and other socio-cultural factors that may shape one's ideological inclinations (Raymo et al. 2015). A comparative study showed that the relative share of housework among Korean men is 19 percent, lower than Taiwanese man's 23 percent (Qian and Sayer 2016). Such evidence indicates that the division of household labour in both Taiwan and Korea remain traditional, yet Korea is considered worse than Taiwan, echoing Vietnamese migrants' observations in this current study.

There exist a few limitations of this current study. First, the gaps in gender systems that VMMs perceived may involve their understanding of Vietnam's situation in recent years or during their childhood before they migrate. Second, the contents of interviews did not contain sufficient information to contrast regional differences within Vietnam. Third, despite that VMMs who were involved in civic organisations include those who met their husbands through commercial brokers or with limited education experiences in Vietnam, averagely speaking, they received more education in Vietnam and a significant proportion of them met their husbands through personal encounters. Nevertheless, I meant to showcase their unique characteristics and emphasise the heterogeneous integration experiences among VMMs.

The research momentum on the gendered processes of transnational migration across the globe and within Asia are likely to continue in the decades to come (Yeoh 2014; Asis 2003; Hondagneu-Sotelo 2011; Yeung and Mu 2019). In addition to uncovering the gendered marital pattern of ethnic intermarriage across various migrant destinations (Qian and Qian 2020; Utomo 2020) and the gendered impact of residential choices (Chiu and Choi 2020), this current study acknowleges the voices of marriage migrants of lower social status both in the origin and the destinations, on how gender systems affect their integration processes and shape their life trajectories. Theory-informed and gender-sensitive integration policy are needed to provide marriage mirants early expousre to an equitable gender system that faciliate their adaptation into the labour markets as well as the ability to recognise and confront gender-related and ethnicised everyday discrimination, leading to healthier subsequent life and aging experiences.

Notes

1. VMMs' counts of first entry visa (as a spouse of Taiwanese) from year 1998 to 2003 issued by the Ministry of Foreign Affairs; 2004–2016: monthly report of marriage registration by country of origin. Ministry of Interior.
2. Data Source: Statistics Korea (http://www.index.go.kr/potal/main/EachDtlPageDetail.do?idx_cd=2430#quick_02)
3. The AsiaBarometer (AB) survey is a collaborative project across Asian societies based in University of Niigata Prefecture, Japan (www.asiabarometer.org). Survey institutions applied multi-stage-stratified random sampling and quota sampling, which targeted at respondents between age 20 and 59 through face-to-face interviews. With a sample size of 1000 per wave, I use aggregated data from Vietnam and Korea surveyed in 2003, 2004, and 2006; and the Taiwan data was surveyed in 2006.
4. The East Asian Social Survey (EASS) 2006 module focuses on family dynamics and thus includes in-depth questions on marriage and family relations, attitudes on marriage and family life, etc. Survey institutions applied stratified probability sampling strategy and recruited adult respondents in registered households. The fieldwork was conducted between June 2006 and December 2006 through face-to-face interviews. Response rates for China, Japan, South Korea, and Taiwan were 39%, 54%, 66% and 42%, respectively.

Acknowledgements

The author would like to wholeheartedly thank the Vietnamese interviewees, leaders and staff of migrant centers in Taiwan and South Korea, and Vietnamese interpreters in South Korea in making the multi-sited fieldwork and this research possible. Fundings for two waves of long term fieldwork were from the University of California Pacific Rim Research Program and the Taiwan Ministry of Science and Technology.

Disclosure statement

No potential conflict of interest was reported by the author.

References

Aboim, Sofia. 2010. "Gender Cultures and the Division of Labour in Contemporary Europe: A Cross-National Perspective." *The Sociological Review* 58 (2): 171–196.
Asis, M. M. B. 2003. "When Men and Women Migrate: Comparing Gendered Migration in Asia." United Nations Division for the Advancement of Women (DAW) Consultative Meeting "Migration and mobility and how this movement affects women", Malmö, Sweden, December 2–4.
Bélanger, D., and M. Barbieri. 2009. "Introduction: State, Families, and the Making of Transitions in Vietnam." In *Reconfiguring Families in Contemporary Vietnam*, edited by Danièle Bélanger, and Magali Barbieri, 1–44. CA: Stanford University Press.
Bélanger, D., H.-K. Lee, and H.-Z. Wang. 2010. "Ethnic Diversity and Statistics in East Asia: 'Foreign Brides' Surveys in Taiwan and South Korea." *Ethnic and Racial Studies* 33 (6): 1108–1130.
Bélanger, D., and T. G. Linh. 2011. "The Impact of Transnational Migration on Gender and Marriage in Sending Communities of Vietnam." *Current Sociology* 59 (1): 59–77.
Brinton, Mary C. 2001. *Women's Working Lives in East Asia*. Stanford, CA: Stanford University Press.
Chang, Hsin-Chieh. 2016. "Marital Power Dynamics and Wellbeing of Marriage Migrants." *Journal of Family Issues* 37 (14): 1994–2020.

Chang, Hsin-Chieh. 2017. "A Two-Step Social Integration Model Among Transnational Marriage Migrants: "Marital Family First, Host Society Second." In *International Marriages and Marital Citizenship: Southeast Asian Women on the Move*, edited by Asuncion Fresnoza-Flot, and Gwenola Ricordeau, 176–195. London: Routledge.

Chao, Elaine. 2005. "A Study in Social Change: The Domestic Violence Prevention Movement in Taiwan." *Critical Asian Studies* 37 (1): 29–50.

Charmaz, Kathy, and L. Belgrave. 2003. "Qualitative Interviewing and Grounded Theory Analysis." In *The Sage Handbook of Interview Research: The Complexity of the Craft*, edited by Jaber F. Gubrium, James A. Holstein, Amir B. Marvasti, and Karyn D. McKinney, 311–330. Thousand Oaks, CA: Sage Publications.

Chiu, Tuen Yi, and Susanne Y. P. Choi. 2020. "The Decoupling of Legal and Spatial Migration of Female Marriage Migrants." *Journal of Ethnic and Migration Studies* 46 (14): 2997–3013. doi:10.1080/1369183X.2019.1585018.

Croll, E. 2001. *Endangered Daughters: Discrimination and Development in Asia*. London: Routledge.

Donato, Katharine M, Joseph T Alexander, Donna R Gabaccia, and Johanna Leinonen. 2011. "Variations in the Gender Composition of Immigrant Populations: How They Matter." *International Migration Review* 45 (3): 495–526.

Giorguli, Silvia E, and Maria Adela Angoa. 2016. "International Migration, Gender and Family: A Miroir From Latin America." In *International Handbook of Migration and Population Distribution*, edited by Michael J White, 543–572. Berlin: Springer.

Hondagneu-Sotelo, Pierrette. 2003. *Gender and US Immigration: Contemporary Trends*. Los Angeles: Univ of California Press.

Hondagneu-Sotelo, Pierrette. 2011. "Gender and Migration Scholarship: An Overview From a 21st Century Perspective." *Migraciones Internacionales* 6 (1): 219–233.

Hsia, H. C. 2009. "Foreign Brides, Multiple Citizenship and the Immigrant Movement in Taiwan." *Asian and Pacific Migration Journal* 18 (1): 17–46.

Hugo, G. 2000. "Migration and Women's Empowerment." In *Women's Empowerment and Demographic Processes: Moving Beyond Cairo*, edited by Harriet Presser, and Gita Sen, 289–317. Oxford: Oxford University Press.

Itzigsohn, José, and Silvia Giorguli-Saucedo. 2005. "Incorporation, Transnationalism, and Gender: Immigrant Incorporation and Transnational Participation as Gendered Processes." *International Migration Review* 39 (4): 895–920.

Kim, M. 2010. "Gender and International Marriage Migration." *Sociology Compass* 4 (9): 718–731.

Kim, Hee-Kang. 2012. "Marriage Migration Between South Korea and Vietnam: A Gender Perspective." *Asian Perspective* 36 (3): 531–563.

Kim, Sang-Wook, Ying-Hwa Chang, Noriko Iwai, and Lulu Li. 2014. East Asian Social Survey (EASS), Cross-National Survey Data Sets: Families in East Asia, 2006. EASSDA [distributor], Inter-university Consortium for Political and Social Research [distributor].

Ko, Chyong-fang, and Han-Pi Chang. 2007. "A Comparative Study of the Social Values of Vietnam, Indonesia, and Taiwan." *Taiwan Journal of Southeast Asian Studies[In Chinese]* 4 (1): 91–112.

Maliepaard, Mieke, and Richard Alba. 2016. "Cultural Integration in the Muslim Second Generation in the Netherlands: The Case of Gender Ideology." *International Migration Review* 50 (1): 70–94.

Mason, Karen Oppenheim. 1997. "Gender and Demographic Change: What Do We Know?" In *The Continuing Demographic Transition*, edited by S. Amin, I. Diamond, F. Steele, G. W. Jones, R. M. Douglas, J. C. Caldwell, and R. M. D'Souza, 158–182. New York: Oxford University Press.

Min, Pyong Gap. 2001. "Changes in Korean Immigrants' Gender Role and Social Status, and Their Marital Conflicts." *Sociological Forum* 16 (2): 301–320.

Patton, Michael Quinn. 2002. "Two Decades of Developments in Qualitative Inquiry: A Personal, Experiential Oerspective." *Qualitative Social Work: Research and Practice* 1 (3): 261–283.

Pfau-Effinger, Birgit. 2004. "Socio-Historical Paths of the Male Breadwinner Model – An Explanation of Cross-National Differences." *The British Journal of Sociology* 55 (3): 377–399.

Qian, Zhenchao, and Yue Qian. 2020. "Generation, Education, and Intermarriage of Asian Americans." *Journal of Ethnic and Migration Studies* 46 (14): 2880–2895. doi:10.1080/1369183X.2019.1585006.

Qian, Yue, and Liana C Sayer. 2016. "Division of Labor, Gender Ideology, and Marital Satisfaction in East Asia." *Journal of Marriage and Family* 78 (2): 383–400.

Raymo, James M., Hyunjoon Park, Yu Xie, and Wei-jun Jean Yeung. 2015. "Marriage and Family in East Asia: Continuity and Change." *Annual Review of Sociology* 41: 471–492.

Ridgeway, Cecilia L., and Shelley J. Correll. 2004. "Unpacking the Gender System a Theoretical Perspective on Gender Beliefs and Social Relations." *Gender & Society* 18 (4): 510–531.

Ridgeway, Cecilia L., and Lynn Smith-Lovin. 1999. "The Gender System and Interaction." *Annual Review of Sociology* 25 (1): 191–216.

Röder, Antje, and Peter Mühlau. 2014. "Are They Acculturating? Europe's Immigrants and Gender Egalitarianism." *Social Forces* 92 (3): 899–928.

Rodríguez-García, Dan. 2015. "Intermarriage and Integration Revisited International Experiences and Cross-Disciplinary Approaches." *The ANNALS of the American Academy of Political and Social Science* 662 (1): 8–36.

Su, Dejun, Chad Richardson, and Guang-zhen Wang. 2010. "Assessing Cultural Assimilation of Mexican Americans: How Rapidly Do Their Gender-Role Attitudes Converge to the US Mainstream?" *Social Science Quarterly* 91 (3): 762–776.

Suzuki, T. 2008. "Korea's Strong Familism and Lowest low Fertility." *International Journal of Japanese Sociology* 17 (1): 30–41.

Teerawichitchainan, Bussarawan, John Knodel, Vu Manh Loi, and Vu Tuan Huy. 2010. "The Gender Division of Household Labor in Vietnam: Cohort Trends and Regional Variations." *Journal of Comparative Family Studies* 41 (1): 57–85.

Törngren, Sayaka Osanami, Nahikari Irastorza, and Miri Song. 2016. "Toward Building a Conceptual Framework on Intermarriage." *Ethnicities* 16 (4): 497–520.

Utomo, Ariane J. 2020. "Love in the Melting Pot: Ethnic Intermarriage in Jakarta." *Journal of Ethnic and Migration Studies* 46 (14): 2896–2913. doi:10.1080/1369183X.2019.1585008.

Walby, Sylvia. 1990. *Theorizing Patriarchy*. Oxford: Basil Blackwell.

Wang, H. Z. 2007. "Hidden Spaces of Resistance of the Subordinated: Case Studies From Vietnamese Female Migrant Partners in Taiwan." *International Migration Review* 41 (3): 706–727.

Wang, H. Z. 2011. "Gendered Transnationalism From Below: Capital, Women, and Family in Cross-Border Marriages Between Taiwan and Vietnam." In *International Marriages in the Time of Globalization*, edited by E. K. Heikkila, and B. S. A. Yeoh, 69–85. New York: Nova Science.

Wang, H. Z. 2019. "Gender, Family Reproduction, and Transnational Capital Accumulation (性別、家庭再生產與跨國資本積累)." In Global Production Pressures Chains and Taiwanese-invested factory regime in Vietnam (全球生產壓力鏈與越南台資工廠). Unpublished Manuscript.

Wang, H. Z., and D. Belanger. 2008. "Taiwanizing Female Immigrant Spouses and Materializing Differential Citizenship." *Citizenship Studies* 12 (1): 91–106.

Webster, Natasha A., and Karen Haandrikman. 2016. "Thai Women in Sweden: Victims or Participants?" *Social Science Asia* 2 (1): 13–29.

WEF. 2015. *The Global Gender Gap Report 2015*. The World Economic Forum.

Werner, Jayne Susan, and Daniele Belanger. 2002. "Introduction: Gender and Việt Nam Studies." In *Gender, Household, State: Đổi Mới in Việt Nam*, edited by Jayne Susan Werner, and Daniele Belanger, 13–28. New York: Cornell University Press.

Yeoh, Brenda SA. 2014. "Engendering International Migration: Perspectives from Within Asia." In *Global and Asian Perspectives on International Migration*, edited by Graziano Battistella, 139–152. New York: Springer.

Yeung, Wei-Jun Jean, and Zheng Mu. 2020. "Migration and Marriage in Asian Contexts." *Journal of Ethnic and Migration Studies* 46 (14): 2863–2879. doi:10.1080/1369183X.2019.1585005.

Happiness of female immigrants in cross-border marriages in Taiwan

Chun-Hao Li and Wenshan Yang

ABSTRACT
Drawing on data from the Survey of Foreign and Chinese Spouses' Living Requirements in 2013, we probe the effects of economic and acculturative factors on psychological well-being, particularly happiness, of female immigrants in cross-border marriages in Taiwan, while social demographic variables are controlled. In the economic aspect, while being employed negatively affects immigrant brides' happiness, family income, as expected, is positively associated with psychological well-being. However, during acculturation, immigrant brides who have stayed longer in Taiwan, especially for more than 10 years, report a lower level of happiness. Also, different types of social networks and resources may be available for them to cope with the difficulties encountered. Immigrant brides accessing professional organisations are more likely to report being 'very happy'. Finally, perceived friendliness is an important protective factor among female marriage immigrants. More interestingly, perceived friendliness plays a role in mediating the influence of economic and acculturative predictors on psychological well-being.

Introduction

Taiwan, Japan, South Korea, and Singapore have become increasingly diverse in their ethnic composition, especially through an increase of cross-border marriages (Yeung and Mu 2020), predominately involving female immigrants who are mainly from their neighbouring countries, and some Southeast Asian nations, including Vietnam, the Philippines, Cambodia, and Thailand. In general, leaving their motherland, immigrants start new lives in their destinations and begin the process of acculturation. In East Asia today, a great number of female immigrants are suffering acculturation difficulties. Numerous studies have discussed the consequences of acculturation of immigrants, especially on their psychological well-being and mental health.

The experiences of female marriage immigrants in East Asia are different from what we have learned from numerous studies on migration. Therefore, two arguments are worthy to be noted about these studies. First, these are based on the experiences of Hispanic (Rogler, Cortes, and Malgady 1991; Hovey and Magaña 2000), European

(Jasinskaja-Lahti et al. 2006), and Chinese (Ying 1988) immigrants in Western societies (Moon, Kim, and Kim 2014). Second, major theories informing conceptions of psychological well-being draw heavily from Western-centric perspectives (Hernandez et al. 2016). Few studies have focused on the phenomenon in Asia, especially marriage immigrants in host countries in Asia. Consequently, we have limited knowledge of the psychological well-being of marriage migrants within Asian societies. Additionally, the experiences of immigrant brides in these Asian countries are unique. They migrate to the host societies alone, marry husbands they hardly know, live with their husband's family right after their arrival, and are inevitably forced to assimilate into the mainstream culture in the host societies.

Starting new lives in host societies, the female immigrants in cross-border marriages face at least two types of issues. Encountering new social values and culture, immigrant brides face acculturative difficulties. Additionally, immigrant brides marrying into Taiwanese families may encounter issues that all people in the host societies deal with on a daily basis, such as economic difficulties. Thus, in this study, we would like to investigate how economic and acculturative factors are associated with the happiness of immigrant brides in the context of Taiwan.

Literature review

Happiness is a colloquial term that refers to people's affective and cognitive evaluations of their lives (Diener 2000), which can represent the outcomes of acculturation for immigrants. Ward (1996) suggested a conceptual framework that examines the roles played by factors such as length of residency, language fluency, acculturation difficulties, social support, etc., in the acculturation process. Taking a bottom-up approach, we extend Ward's framework by including economic factors to investigate the happiness of immigrant brides during their acculturation in Taiwan.

Acculturative perspective

Acculturation refers to a 'culture learning process experienced by individuals who are exposed to a new culture or ethnic group' (Organista, Marin, and Chun 2010, 102). During acculturation, individuals including both immigrants and natives may learn new norms, values, attitudes, and behaviours from each other and change their own. For immigrants, Gordon (1964) views acculturation as a process of adoption of the cultural norms and behavioural patterns of the natives or the majority.

Immigrants may experience acculturative stress arising from the acculturative process (Williams and Berry 1991). The acculturation results can be positive or negative adaptation, and may vary among individuals, as Berry (2006, 289) mentions: '[n]ot all groups and individuals undergo acculturation in the same way … .' If the acculturation stress is hard to overcome and the immigrant is unable to adjust, this may in turn impair psychological well-being and even lead to symptoms of mental illness (Organista, Marin, and Chun 2010). In the following, we outline the association of the acculturative factors, length of stay in the host society, access to social networks, perceived discrimination, and acculturative difficulties, with the psychological well-being of immigrants.

Length of stay in host society

Miglietta and Tartaglia (2009) suggest that a long-lasting stay in a host county makes it easier for immigrants to become familiar with the social context and then enhance their sociocultural competence and psychological well-being in the destinations. However, empirical research has shown that the relationship between the immigrant's length of residency in the host society and psychological well-being may be positive (Oh, Koeske, and Sales 2002; Yang, Wang, and Anderson 2010), negative (Aycan and Berry 1996), or not significant (Shin, Han, and Kim 2007).

Specifically, a positive association between length of residence and psychological well-being has been found among Korean women immigrants in the United States (Oh, Koeske, and Sales 2002) and among Vietnamese women in transnational marriages in Taiwan (Yang, Wang, and Anderson 2010). Both studies show that women immigrants with a longer stay in the host society are more likely to report better psychological well-being than those with shorter residency. In contrast, Aycan and Berry (1996) show a negative association between length of residence in the host society and psychological well-being. They explain that length of stay in the host country has an indirect effect on psychological well-being, as during acculturation, immigrants are more likely to encounter barriers and discrimination.

Shin, Han, and Kim (2007) indicate an insignificant association of length of residence in the host country with immigrants' happiness or depression. Similar results have been reported by Safi (2010), who categorises the length of residency in the host society into four ordered categories, 1–5 years, 6–10 years, 11–20 years, and over 20 years. She reports that immigrants' psychological well-being does not increase until after 20 years of stay in the new country.

Social networks

Studies have shown the importance of social networks and social support for coping with acculturation difficulties and other issues (Martínez, Ramírez, and Jariego 2002; Jasinskaja-Lahti et al. 2006; Negi et al. 2013; Fernández et al. 2015). Social networks comprise strong ties and weak ties (Granovetter 1973). Research has shown a direct positive effect of social support networks on an individual's well-being in general (e.g. Cohen and Wills 1985; Komproe et al. 1997) and on immigrants' adjustment in particular (Lin, Ye, and Ensel 1999; Hovey and Magaña 2000; Shen and Takeuchi 2001). Strong social network ties provide crucial social support to immigrants and maintain their psychological well-being (Vega et al. 1991; Jasinskaja-Lahti and Liebkind 2001; Martínez García et al. 2002; Finch and Vega 2003; Noh and Kaspar 2003). Weak ties which serve as secondary social networks for immigrants are also important. Negi et al. (2013) argue that by attending church, immigrants forge social ties and receive social support, which facilitate their economic and psychological well-being. In addition, the networks immigrants leave behind in their home countries are also important sources of support that promote their adjustment in the new host society (Schultz 2001).

Studies of social networks conventionally emphasise the support function of social networks to highlight their positive effects on the psychological well-being of immigrants. However, immigrants may access different social networks and resources to cope with different difficulties, or they may be in serious difficulties which require assistance from social networks or resources other than those usually available to them. When the social networks or resources are effectively meeting their demands, immigrants may report higher psychological well-being. At the same time, that they seek access to different social networks and resources at different times may also reflect the seriousness of the difficulties they face, which can directly affect their psychological well-being.

Perceived discrimination

Community atmosphere as well as social networks, which provide social support, can affect acculturation outcomes (Vega and Rumbaut 1991; Jayasuriya, Sang, and Fielding 1992; Fumhan and Sheikh 1993; Farrell, Aubry, and Coulombe 2004). Community atmosphere reflects general attitudes towards immigrants, whether negative or positive. An open attitude towards immigrants creates a friendly welcoming atmosphere for newcomers. In contrast, immigrants living in an unfriendly host society will perceive discrimination against them.

Research reveals that perceived discrimination has the power to destroy both self-esteem (Gil, Vega, and Dimas 1994; Gil and Vega 1996) and psychological well-being (Rumbaut 1994) of young immigrants. For immigrants, perceived discrimination is also one of the acculturative stressors which may affect psychological well-being and mental health. A study by Viruell-Fuentes (2007) reveals that Mexican Americans in the United States who perceive discrimination experience depression and poor general health. Davin (2007) additionally highlights discrimination as one of the potential barriers for marriage migrants that limit their ability to expand their social networks. Consequently, the lack of social networks and support may impair immigrants' psychological well-being and health (Vega et al. 1991; Thoits 1995; Berkman and Glass 2000; Cohen 2004).

Economic perspective

Although acculturative difficulties can cause a great deal of stress and impair the psychological well-being and mental health of immigrants, the effects of economic factors can be additionally important in determining the quality of the immigrant's life in the host society. Methodologically, without controlling for the economic effects, we are unable to explicitly illustrate the impact of acculturative difficulties on immigrants' psychological well-being. Thus, two indicators of economic conditions are emphasised: employment status and family income.

Employment status

In general, being employed is positively related to psychological well-being. However, do the findings from studies of the general population apply to immigrants? Bartram (2011) argues that having a paid job is one main characteristic contributing to the psychological well-being of immigrants. Immigrants' participation in the labour market in the host society is often viewed as an indication of their economic integration (Aycan and Berry 1996). Additionally, employment status has been found to be positively associated with the health of immigrant women (Iglesias et al. 2003; Yang, Wang, and Anderson 2010). Aroian (2001) and Aroian et al. (1998) have explained that paid employment of immigrant women supports their family financially, brings the women a sense of purpose and accomplishment, and helps them gain respect from the family.

Hurh and Kim's (1990) study reveals contradictory findings that for female immigrants, employment status is positively associated with their mental health, but high individual earnings impair mental well-being. They further point out that 'most of the employed wives carry a double burden of performing the household tasks and working outside the home due to the immigrant life conditions (financial needs and opportunity) and persistence of the traditional gender-role ideology (women as a homemaker)' (Hurh and Kim 1990, 709). For immigrant women, employment outside the home is additional work, which could impair their psychological well-being. A negative relationship between employment and psychological well-being is also reported by Ferree (1979), who argues that the negative impact of employment on the psychological well-being of immigrant women occurs because the division of labour within the family is not rearranged.

Family income
Research at the individual (Ferrer-i-Carbonell 2005; Caporale et al. 2009; Tsui 2014) and national level (Diener and Oishi 2000; Hagerty and Veenhoven 2003) has illustrated that increased income enhances happiness. Li and Tsai (2014) have revealed that family income is positively associated with happiness in the general Taiwan population. Scholars (e.g. Diener et al. 1993; Caporale et al. 2009; Tsui 2014) have evaluated the relationship between happiness and not only absolute income but also relative income. The relative income hypothesis argues that how individuals feel about their well-being depends on the distance between their actual income and a reference value, which is determined by the income of people around them and the level of income that the individuals themselves have. The effect of income on happiness is positive but non-linear and weak.

Easterlin (2001) illustrates that on both the macro and micro levels, the greater the increase in income, the smaller the happiness output. Scholars have argued that once basic needs are met, higher income is no longer associated with higher subjective well-being. In contrast, Stevenson and Wolfers (2013) report no weakening in the relationship between income and subjective well-being as income rises. Kahneman and Deaton (2010), analysing the Gallup-Healthways Well-Being Index (GHWBI), find that emotional well-being, referring to the emotional quality of an individual's experience (e.g. happiness and so on) reported for the previous day, and life evaluation, measured as a person's thoughts on his or her life, both rise steadily with *log* income. However, 'there [was] no further progress beyond an annual income of USD$75,000' (Kahneman and Deaton 2010, 16489). They further suggest that low income is associated with misfortune (e.g. divorce, ill health, and being alone) and impaired emotional well-being (Kahneman and Deaton 2010).

Although some scholars prefer to emphasise the association between relative income and happiness, and some have suggested that their relationship is non-linear and weak, most scholars in general agree that the relationship between income and happiness is positive. The authors agree that the association of family income with happiness is distorted by other factors. For example, poor immigrant brides may be confronted by unfortunate life events or social and economic difficulties. Once the effects of these events and difficulties are controlled for, the relationship between family income and happiness may be minimal.

Methods

Data

The present research draws on data from the Survey of Foreign and Chinese Spouses' Living Requirements in 2013, a national survey by Taiwan's National Immigration Agency (NIA).[1] It involved a stratified systematic sample comprising marriage immigrants living in Taiwan as of March 31, 2013 (NIA 2014).[2] In general, the survey research team followed the Taiwan Social Change Survey protocol to implement proportional sampling. The same fraction was used for all sub-populations to ensure proportionate representation, and the sample represented marriage immigrants residing in Taiwan during the survey period, September–December 2013.

Due to the predominance of women in marriage migration, the gender-disproportionate sample originally consisted of 13,688 marriage immigrants: 647 males and 13,041 females. The final dataset only includes 10,198 *female* marriage immigrants (see Table 1).[3] Most surveyed female marriage immigrants were residing in northern Taiwan (46.0%) and were from Mainland China (66.0%), currently married (95.2%), and between their late 20s and early 40s (82.2%), with a high school diploma or less education (86.8%). Please note that 27.9% of female marriage immigrants were from Southeast Asia, but due to the limitation of the digitised data, we were unable to further distinguish their countries of origin.

Variables

Dependent variable

The dependent variable in this study is 'happiness,' an indicator of subjective well-being. Following Lera-López, Ollo-López, and Sánchez-Santos (2016), 'happiness' is measured based on opinions and self-assessment of individuals. The extent of happiness is the outcome of immigrant brides' self-reporting of their agreement with the statement, 'Overall, I feel my life in Taiwan is happy.' The answers to the statement – 'strongly disagree' (0.7%), 'disagree' (7.5%), 'agree' (63.1%), and 'strongly agree' (28.7%) – show a distribution skewed more toward general agreement than toward disagreement. To account for small proportions, respondents answering 'strongly disagree' and 'agree' are combined for further analysis.

Key independent variables

The key independent variables are in two dimensions: economic and acculturative. Economic factors include employment status and family income. On the former, the survey asked respondents 'Were you employed during the period [week] of August 05–11?', and respondents chose one option from 13 categories. We identified the nature of each category and collapsed them into 'housewife' (37.8%), 'employed' (58.6%), 'unemployed' (2.4%), and 'retired' (1.3%). It is worth noting that the employed immigrant brides included those who were employed for payment and those who worked in family businesses. As shown in Table 1, 75.2% of immigrant brides' families made less than NT$ 60,000, equivalent to almost US$ 2000, per month. However, this figure was much less than the average monthly income of the national population which was NT$96,493 (equivalent to US$3216) in 2014.[4]

Table 1. Distributions of respondents' 'happiness' and characteristics, and their cross-tabulations.

	Very unhappy or unhappy N = 839 8.23% Very unhappy or unhappy	Happy N = 6430 63.05% Happy	Very happy N = 2929 28.72% Very happy	Total N = 10,198 100.00% Total N (%)	χ^2	Association
Region of residence					373.03***	0.135[a]
Northern Taiwan	6.63	70.00	23.37	4694 (46.03)		
Central Taiwan	9.03	66.03	24.94	2314 (22.69)		
Southern Taiwan	10.78	48.45	40.77	2747 (26.94)		
Eastern Taiwan	5.19	64.33	30.47	443 (4.34)		
Nation of origin					39.41***	0.044[a]
Mainland China	9.28	62.61	28.11	6727 (65.96)		
HK or Macau SAR	2.52	57.86	39.62	159 (1.56)		
Southeast Asia	6.29	64.45	29.26	2847 (27.92)		
Other	6.88	62.58	30.54	465 (4.56)		
Age group					90.53***	−0.117[b]
						−0.067[c]
15–24 years	2.21	62.83	34.96	226 (2.22)		
25–34	5.91	62.86	31.22	4077 (39.98)		
35–44	9.90	63.05	27.05	4303 (42.19)		
45–54	11.26	62.29	26.45	1119 (10.97)		
55–64	9.47	68.25	22.28	359 (3.52)		
65 years or above	6.14	61.40	32.46	114 (1.12)		
Educational level (completed)					46.87***	0.048[a]
						0.069[b]
						0.039[c]
Junior-high or below	7.71	65.71	26.58	5538 (54.30)		
High school	8.95	61.11	29.95	3309 (32.45)		
College	8.87	56.16	34.98	609 (5.97)		
University or higher	8.36	57.55	34.10	742 (7.28)		
Marital status					81.53***	0.063[a]
Married	7.79	62.82	29.38	9713 (95.24)		
Separated/divorced	18.36	64.25	17.39	207 (2.03)		
Widowed	15.83	70.14	14.03	278 (2.73)		
Employment					37.10***	0.043[a]
Housewife	6.36	62.94	30.70	3850 (37.75)		
Employed	9.40	63.22	27.38	5978 (58.62)		
Unemployed	7.50	63.33	29.17	240 (2.35)		
Retired	10.77	58.46	30.77	130 (1.27)		
Chinese speaking ability					8.47	−0.023[b]
Not good (low)	6.49	61.47	32.03	231 (2.27)		

(Continued)

Table 1. Continued.

	Very unhappy or unhappy N = 839 8.23% Very unhappy or unhappy	Happy N = 6430 63.05% Happy	Very happy N = 2929 28.72% Very happy	Total N = 10,198 100.00% Total N (%)	χ^2	Association
Good (medium)	7.02	64.67	28.31	2208 (21.65)		−0.014[c]
Very good (high)	8.62	62.64	28.74	7759 (76.08)		
Self-reported Health					27.98***	
Ill	17.09	61.97	20.94	234 (2.29)		0.052[a]
Healthy	8.02	63.08	28.90	9964 (97.71)		0.258[b]
						0.045[c]
Spouse's educational level					97.37***	
Junior-high or below	10.94	64.71	24.35	3281 (32.17)		0.069[a]
High school	7.25	63.31	29.45	4513 (44.25)		0.140[b]
College	6.71	62.97	30.32	1029 (10.09)		0.089[c]
University or more	6.11	58.33	35.64	1375 (13.48)		
Spouse's health					128.49***	
Ill	15.56	64.61	19.84	1215 (11.91)		0.112[a]
Healthy	7.24	62.84	29.92	8983 (88.09)		0.290[b]
						0.104[c]
Family income[d]					285.88***	
Less than NT$20K	16.74	62.69	20.56	1099 (10.78)		0.118[a]
NT$20K–29,999	10.76	65.02	24.22	1515 (14.86)		0.178[b]
NT$30K–39,999	9.30	62.95	27.74	1795 (17.60)		0.147[c]
NT$40K–49,999	7.08	64.17	28.75	1680 (16.47)		
NT$50K–59,999	6.84	65.89	27.28	1580 (15.49)		
NT$60K–69,999	3.93	60.58	35.48	992 (9.73)		
NT$70K–99,999	4.32	61.15	34.53	973 (9.54)		
NT$100 K or more	3.01	55.14	41.84	564 (5.53)		
Length of residency					68.72***	
Less than 2 years	3.61	58.63	37.76	527 (5.17)		−0.113[b]
2–3 years	5.79	61.32	32.99	967 (9.48)		−0.079[c]
3–5 years	7.32	62.34	30.33	956 (9.37)		
6–7 years	7.04	61.90	31.06	966 (9.47)		
8–9 years	8.26	64.15	27.59	1138 (11.16)		
10 years or more	9.43	63.87	26.70	5644 (55.34)		
Social network					325.24***	
Professional org. in TWN	14.49	43.25	42.26	904 (8.86)		0.126[a]
Primary NET in TWN	6.03	65.45	28.52	7647 (74.99)		

(Continued)

Table 1. Continued.

	Very unhappy or unhappy N = 839 8.23% Very unhappy or unhappy	Happy N = 6430 63.05% Happy	Very happy N = 2929 28.72% Very happy	Total N = 10,198 100.00% Total N (%)	χ^2	Association
Secondary NET in TWN	15.11	63.25	21.64	781 (7.66)		
Primary NET at origin	14.90	62.36	22.75	866 (8.49)		
Perceived friendliness					3320.24***	0.404[a]
Strongly disagree (low)	41.55	50.70	7.75	426 (4.18)		0.760[b]
Disagree (medium)	8.33	78.18	13.49	6641 (65.12)		0.481[c]
Agree/strongly agree (high)	3.48	32.64	63.88	3131 (30.70)		
Need for assistance					168.42***	0.091[a]
No needs	6.34	64.68	28.98	5379 (52.75)		
Acculturative needs	4.83	61.72	33.45	1408 (13.81)		
Economic needs	15.05	61.27	23.68	1229 (12.05)		
Child-care needs	12.15	61.06	26.79	1284 (12.59)		
Employment needs	9.91	60.69	29.40	898 (8.81)		

***$p < 0.001$.
**$p < 0.01$.
*$p < 0.05$.
Measures of association between happiness and the characteristics of the sample include: [a]Cramer's V; [b]Gamma; [c]Pearson's r; [d]US$1 is approximately equal to NT$30. Therefore, NT$10,000 is equivalent to US$333, and NT$30,000 is nearly equal to US$1000.

The other set of key predictors chosen measured the acculturative situations of immigrant brides, including length of residency in Taiwan, social networks available for consulting, and perceptions of people's friendliness. The variable of the length of stay in Taiwan was measured in seven categories, from 'less than 1 year' to '10 years or longer.' For analytical purposes, the first two categories were combined. The six ordinal categories of length of residency were 'less than 2 years' (5.2%), '2–3 years' (9.5%), '4–5 years' (9.4%), '6–7 years' (9.5%), '8–9 years' (11.2%), and '10 years or longer' (55.4%).

Ryan et al. (2008) stress that migrants access established and new networks, both in their country of origin and within the new host society. Immigrant brides rely on different social networks to face diverse acculturative and daily difficulties. Taking into account immigrant brides' unique cross-border marriage experience, we used the information collected by asking respondents, 'What resources would you use or who would you go to, when you encounter difficulties?' There were 22 optional categories, which were re-grouped into five options: 'professional organisations in Taiwan,' 'primary social networks in Taiwan,' 'secondary social networks in Taiwan,' and 'primary social networks at origin.' Respondents were asked to choose five categories and rank them by their importance. In this study, we were only concerned with the most important resources or social networks for dealing with acculturative or other difficulties. As shown in Table 1, most immigrant brides accessed primary social networks in Taiwan to consult them about their difficulties; they accounted for almost three-quarters of respondents. Some females in cross-border marriages in Taiwan depended on secondary social networks in Taiwan and primary social networks at origin; these accounted for 7.7% and 8.5% respectively. Additionally, 8.9% of immigrant brides primarily consulted professional organisations or personnel for their difficulties. These figures indicate that difficulties faced by immigrant brides were not necessarily acculturation relevant; some respondents faced difficulties that required them to consult professional organisations, such as legal institutes, governmental agents, religious organisations, etc. They also imply some immigrant brides may prefer to access professional organisations for help.

The survey additionally asked respondents to evaluate their agreement with the statement, 'People surrounding me are kind or friendly.' There were four ordered categories: (1) strongly disagree, (2) disagree, (3) agree, and (4) strongly agree. Because very few respondents chose 'strongly agree,' the last two categories were combined. In fact, 4.2% of immigrant brides strongly denied that people around them were friendly, while 30.7% of respondents felt accepted in Taiwanese society. However, almost two-thirds of immigrant brides felt unwelcome. Using the information collected, we were able to rate immigrant brides' perceptions of the kindness or friendliness of Taiwanese people around them. The evaluation of the 'friendliness' variable in this study also implied immigrant brides' perception of discrimination, with lower 'friendliness' scores reflecting a higher perception of being discriminated against.

Control variables
Among variables illustrating the characteristics of the sample, besides marital status and education, the control variables in the analytical model additionally included Chinese speaking ability, health, and need for assistance. The first two are ordinal and the last is nominal. Most respondents (76.1%) evaluated their Chinese speaking ability as very good (high), while 2.3% and 21.7% of immigrant brides reported 'not good (low)' and

'good (medium)' ability, respectively.[5] Most immigrant brides self-evaluated as healthy (accounting for 97.7%). Only 2.3% of respondents reported being 'ill.'

Furthermore, respondents were asked to indicate their five greatest needs for assistance from ten options, which we re-categorised into five options for further analysis, including (1) no needs (52.8%), (2) acculturative needs (13.8%), (3) economic needs (12.1%), (4) child-care needs (12.6%), and (5) employment needs (8.8%). We controlled for husband's health and education. Most (88.1%) immigrant brides reported their husbands were healthy. Similar to the educational levels of the immigrant brides, the majority (76.4%) of the husbands received a high school diploma or less education.

Methodology

In this research, we examined economic and acculturative factors associated with the ordinal response variable, the extent of *happiness* of immigrant brides, with three categories from level 1–3, which were ordered as (1) strongly disagree/disagree, (2) agree, and (3) strongly agree. Given the ordinal nature of 'happiness' with multiple categories, *ordered logistic regression analysis* is our main analytical technique. The authors first did a Brant test to examine the parallel regression assumption (proportional odds assumption, or PO assumption), which hypothesises that the effect of a particular predicting factor is constant across separate binary models fit to the cumulative cut points. However, the omnibus Brant test of the PO assumption for the overall model, $\chi^2_{(45)}$ = 664.10 ($p < 0.001$), indicated that the PO assumption for the full model was violated. We finally used the partial proportional odds (PPO) model to estimate the odds of being beyond a certain category relative to being at or below that category of *happiness*. In the PPO model, the effects of predictors violating the parallel regression assumption are allowed to vary across categories.

Statistical results

The PPO model was fitted to estimate the ordinal outcome variable, happiness, from a set of control variables, economic factors, and acculturative factors. Results of the Brant test show that some predictor variables, namely nation of origin, age group, health, length of residence, and spouse's education and health meet the PO assumption, while this assumption is untenable for other predictors, namely region of residence, education, marital status, employment status, family income, social networks, and need for assistance.

Note that to investigate the importance of perceived friendliness to immigrant brides' happiness, two models are included (see Table 2). Comparing the results of models 1 and 2, we are able to diagnose the significance of 'perceived friendliness' for enhancing the happiness of immigrant brides in Taiwan. As shown in Table 2, both models are significant; their log likelihood ratio chi-square test statistics are significantly different from zero (model 1: LR $\chi^2_{(43)}$ = 1266.54, $p < 0.001$; and model 2: LR $\chi^2_{(45)}$ = 3817.51, $p < 0.001$). The statistics show that both models are better than the null model with no independent variables in predicting the ordinal response variable, *happiness*.

Both models in Table 2 present the coefficients and the odds ratios (OR) of the predictor variables. A positive logit coefficient normally indicates that an individual is more likely to be in a higher category of *happiness* (1: very unhappy/unhappy; 2: happy;

Table 2. Partial proportional ratio models of happiness of immigrant brides in Taiwan.

	Model 1				Model 2			
	$Y>1$ vs $Y=1$		$Y>2$ vs $Y\leq2$		$Y>1$ vs $Y=1$		$Y>2$ vs $Y\leq2$	
	Coef.	OR	Coef.	OR	Coef.	OR	Coef.	OR
Control variables								
Nation of origin								
Ref: Mainland China								
HK or Macau SAR	0.29	1.33	0.29	1.33	0.04	1.04	0.04	1.04
Southeast Asia	0.24***	1.27	0.24***	1.27	0.29***	1.33	0.29***	1.33
Other	0.12	1.13	0.12	1.13	0.20	1.22	0.20	1.22
Region of residence								
Ref: Northern Taiwan								
Central Taiwan	−0.11	0.90	0.34***	1.41	−0.20	0.82	0.18*	1.20
Southern Taiwan	−0.21*	0.81	1.07***	2.92	−0.36***	0.70	0.72***	2.06
Eastern Taiwan	0.77***	2.15	0.77***	2.15	0.60***	1.83	0.60***	1.83
Age group								
Ref: 15–24 years								
25–34	0.00	1.00	0.00	1.00	−0.06	0.94	−0.06	0.94
35–44	−0.37*	0.69	−0.09	0.92	−0.41*	0.66	−0.17	0.84
45–54	−0.32	0.73	0.07	1.07	−0.38	0.68	−0.03	0.97
55–64	0.15	1.16	0.15	1.16	0.03	1.03	0.03	1.03
65 years or above	0.64*	1.89	0.64*	1.89	0.60*	1.82	0.60*	1.82
Educational level								
Ref: Junior-high or below								
High school	−0.27**	0.77	0.08	1.09	−0.24**	0.78	0.07	1.07
College	−0.40*	0.67	0.15	1.17	−0.37*	0.69	0.07	1.07
University or higher	−0.59***	0.56	0.05	1.05	−0.59***	0.55	0.08	1.08
Spouse's educational level								
Ref: Junior-high or below								
High school	0.14**	1.15	0.14**	1.15	0.17**	1.18	0.17**	1.18
College	0.20*	1.22	0.20*	1.22	0.28**	1.33	0.28**	1.33
University or more	0.26**	1.30	0.26**	1.30	0.24**	1.27	0.24**	1.27
Marital status								
Ref: Married								
Separated/divorced	−0.32*	0.72	−0.32*	0.72	−0.34*	0.71	−0.34*	0.71
Widowed	0.15	1.16	−0.43*	0.65	0.17	1.19	−0.48*	0.62
Self-reported health								
Ref: Ill								
Healthy	0.35*	1.41	0.35*	1.41	0.22	1.24	0.22	1.24
Spouse's health								
Ref: Ill								
Healthy	0.33***	1.39	0.33***	1.39	0.34***	1.40	0.34***	1.40
Needs for assistance								
Ref: No needs								
Acculturative needs	0.07	1.08	0.07	1.08	0.08	1.08	0.08	1.08
Economic needs	−0.83***	0.44	−0.31***	0.74	−0.75***	0.47	−0.30**	0.74
Child-caring needs	−0.78***	0.46	−0.31***	0.73	−0.77***	0.47	−0.36***	0.70
Employment needs	−0.50***	0.61	−0.19*	0.83	−0.31***	0.74	−0.31***	0.74
Economic predictors								
Employment status								
Ref: Housewife								
Employed	−0.19***	0.83	−0.19***	0.83	−0.30***	0.74	−0.12*	0.89
Unemployed	0.10	1.11	0.10	1.11	0.13	1.14	0.13	1.14
Retired	0.06	1.06	0.06	1.06	−0.53	0.59	0.32	1.37
Family income								
Ref: Less than NT$20K								
NT$20K-29,999	0.26**	1.30	0.26**	1.30	0.19*	1.21	0.19*	1.21
NT$30K-39,999	0.33***	1.39	0.33***	1.39	0.33***	1.39	0.33***	1.39
NT$40K-49,999	0.44***	1.56	0.44***	1.56	0.43***	1.54	0.43***	1.54
NT$50K-59,999	0.44***	1.56	0.44***	1.56	0.41***	1.50	0.41***	1.50
NT$60K-69,999	0.89***	2.43	0.89***	2.43	0.82***	2.27	0.82***	2.27
NT$70K-99,999	0.87***	2.39	0.87***	2.39	0.72***	2.05	0.72***	2.05

(Continued)

Table 2. Continued.

	Model 1				Model 2			
	Y > 1 vs Y = 1		Y > 2 vs Y ≤ 2		Y > 1 vs Y = 1		Y > 2 vs Y ≤ 2	
	Coef.	OR	Coef.	OR	Coef.	OR	Coef.	OR
NT$100 K or more	1.11***	3.03	1.11***	3.03	0.90***	2.47	0.90***	2.47
Acculturative predictors								
Length of residency								
Ref: Less than 2 years								
2–3 years	−0.13	0.88	−0.13	0.88	−0.14	0.87	−0.14	0.87
4–5 years	−0.23*	0.80	−0.23*	0.80	−0.13	0.87	−0.13	0.87
6–7 years	−0.16	0.86	−0.16	0.86	−0.11	0.90	−0.11	0.90
8–9 years	−0.30**	0.74	−0.30**	0.74	−0.19	0.83	−0.19	0.83
10 years or more	−0.31**	0.73	−0.31**	0.73	−0.27*	0.77	−0.27*	0.77
Social network								
Ref: Professional organisations								
Primary NET in Taiwan	0.94***	2.55	−0.63***	0.53	0.92***	2.52	−0.63***	0.53
Secondary NET in Taiwan	0.21	1.23	−0.70***	0.50	0.23	1.26	−0.82***	0.44
Primary NET at origin	0.11	1.12	−0.68***	0.51	0.14	1.15	−0.66***	0.52
Perceiving friendliness								
Ref: Strongly disagree (low)								
Disagree (medium)					1.87***	6.52	0.46***	1.59
Agree/strongly agree (high)					2.84***	17.07	2.84***	17.07
Constant	1.63***	5.11	−1.65***	0.19	−0.04	0.96	−2.74***	0.06
Number of cases	10,198				10,198			
LR χ²	1266.54***				3817.51***			
Pseudo R²	0.07				0.22			
Log likelihood	−8081.98				−6806.49			

***$p < 0.001$.
**$p < 0.01$.
*$p < 0.05$.

3: very happy). Therefore, in the column titled '$Y > 1$ vs $Y = 1$,' a positive coefficient shows immigrant brides were more likely to be *very happy* or *happy* than *very unhappy/unhappy*. A positive coefficient in the '$Y > 2$ vs $Y \leq 2$' column reveals that respondents were more likely to be *very happy* than *happy* or below.

Economic factors

For immigrant women, holding a paid job may make them contribute to the family economy and gain respect from family members, enhancing their psychological well-being. However, some scholars have pointed out that having a job can also decrease happiness, as it imposes a double burden on immigrant women, and also makes them often encounter discrimination. The Taiwanese data reveal a negative association between being employed and happiness. Compared to housewives, being unemployed did not necessarily lead to an increase or decrease in happiness (both ORs are not significant at $\alpha = 0.05$). However, being employed reduces the happiness of immigrant brides. Employed immigrant brides were less likely to report a high level of happiness than housewives.

The relationship between family income and happiness is complicated, because it can be mediated or moderated by other factors. For example, poor immigrant brides may be confronted by unfortunate life events or social and economic difficulties. Table 2 shows that while other factors are controlled for, the association of *family income* with the happiness of immigrant brides in Taiwan, in general, is positive. Interestingly, the statistical results reveal not only the positive effect of family income on immigrant brides' happiness but also that the relationship is linear. The logit coefficients gradually grow with a rise in family income levels in both models.

In sum, employment status did not improve the happiness of immigrant brides in Taiwan as family income did. Being employed for pay could undermine the psychological well-being of immigrant brides. Family income for immigrant brides, however, was as important as for the general population in Taiwan for enhancing psychological well-being. In addition, its effect on the happiness of immigrant brides could be linear.

Acculturative factors
As scholars have suggested, the effect of length of stay in the host country on the psychological well-being of immigrant brides may be both direct and indirect. On the one hand, length of residence is positively associated with psychological well-being, because a long-lasting stay in a host country makes it easier for immigrant brides to become familiar with the social context in the destinations. On the other hand, their association can be negative, because immigrant brides staying longer in a host nation are more likely to encounter discrimination and barriers, and then report lower psychological well-being.

In general, *length of residency* could impair the psychological well-being of immigrant brides in Taiwan; the longer immigrant brides stay in Taiwan, the lower their reported happiness. However, the effects of *length of residency* of less than 10 years on happiness were not significant when *perceived friendliness* was controlled for. This finding suggests perceived friendliness played an intermediating role between length of residency and psychological well-being, especially for the immigrant brides staying in Taiwan for less than 10 years.

Social networks for consulting regarding difficulties were important for immigrant brides' acculturation. Studies have shown social networks were helpful for coping with acculturation difficulties (Martínez García et al. 2002; Jasinskaja-Lahti et al. 2006; Negi et al. 2013; Fernández et al. 2015). However, the type of social networks can matter; some types may be more important than others in enhancing psychological well-being. In this research, we found that those who accessed primary social networks in Taiwan were happier than those who depended on professional organisations. Up until a certain level of happiness, the relationship between access to social networks and happiness was negative. This result reveals that immigrant brides seeking assistance from professional organisations in Taiwan were more likely to report being *very happy* than those accessing primary or secondary networks for help. It seems that immigrant brides with the ability to find resources from professional organisations were happier than those without.

Perceived discrimination is a risk factor, which can harm the psychological well-being of acculturating individuals. Empirical research (see Williams, Neighbors, and Jackson 2003; Paradies 2006) which reveals a negative relationship between perceived discrimination and well-being has confirmed the association between perceptions of discrimination and poor psychological well-being. Verkuyten (1998) points out that discrimination can create a sense of powerlessness. Individuals being discriminated against perceive a lack of control over important life outcomes. Acculturating individuals who perceived being discriminated against would, in general, be more likely to have negative outcomes in terms of their psychological well-being. In contrast, perceived friendliness would bring immigrant brides a positive acculturative outcome. In our study, the positive and significant association between the perception of the locals' friendliness and the psychological well-being of immigrant brides was obvious.

Also note that inclusion of perceived friendliness significantly changed the effects of high levels of *family income, employment status, length of residency*, and types of *social networks* accessed on the psychological well-being of immigrant brides. It is possible perceived friendliness mediated the effects of these predictors on immigrant brides' happiness.

Conclusion and discussion

Similar to South Korea and other East Asian countries, Taiwan has been experiencing increasingly diverse ethnic composition due to a rapid increase of cross-border marriages, predominantly involving female immigrants. The immigrant brides, especially those from Southeast Asia, usually migrate to the host society alone, marry husbands they hardly know, and live with their husband's family right after arrival, without any choice. Their experiences are different from voluntary immigrants who travel overseas to seek better opportunities. The former are forced to assimilate into the host culture.

Understanding the mechanism affecting the psychological well-being of female marriage immigrants in Taiwan is crucial. Marriage immigrants, accounting for about 2% of the national population, have given birth to over 380,000 children since 1998. The psychological well-being of immigrant brides also directly affects the well-being of their offspring and that of the national population indirectly.

The present study taking a bottom-up approach reveals that economic and acculturative factors are associated with the psychological well-being of immigrant brides in Taiwan. First, female marriage immigrants employed for pay or in a family business were unhappier than those being homemakers were. Based on the perspective of power dynamics within family, Hurh and Kim (1990) and Ferree (1979) explain that without the rearrangement of the within-family division of labour, employment outside the home for immigrant brides means additional work, which burdens them with a double load and impairs their psychological well-being. Second, *family income* is one of the most influential variables in the present research found to be a protective factor for immigrant brides. Family income not only represents the socioeconomic status of an individual but also is associated with his/her real consumption power. Although the families of immigrant brides in Taiwan were poorer than the general population, family income still significantly contributed to the happiness of female marriage immigrants. Meanwhile, the results illustrate that the positive effect of family income on the happiness of immigrant brides perhaps was linear. This perhaps is because that the family income of immigrant brides is generally lower than the national average family income in Taiwan.

This study additionally probes the effects of three acculturative factors, length of residency, social networks for dealing with difficulties, and perception of friendliness, on the happiness of female immigrants in cross-border marriages. Our results, showing that immigrant brides staying longer than 2 years reported worse psychological well-being than the newcomers arriving in Taiwan within the past two years. We argue that with a longer stay in Taiwan, the immigrant brides experienced more unexpected difficulties and hardships. Immigrant brides may have started their life in Taiwan as happy new brides with an expectation of a better and easier life than that in their homeland.

However, they gradually understood that the economic situation of their husbands' families was not as good as they had expected. Hopes of improving the economic status or life standards of their native families through the cross-border marriage were dashed. Meanwhile, they had to face economic hardships and other issues which local Taiwanese were also encountering and had to take more responsibilities to improve the economic status and conditions of their husbands' families.

In this study, we also examine whether the types of social networks or resources accessed by immigrant brides were associated with the extent of their happiness. Interestingly, immigrant brides accessing professional organisations were more likely to report 'very happy' than those who mainly accessed primary social networks in Taiwan. This finding implies that immigrants who accessed professional organisations had adapted socio-culturally. This group of immigrant brides already possessed certain abilities that enabled them to communicate and interact with the professional organisations. These abilities may have enhanced their confidence and self-esteem. This may also imply the efficiency of governmental policies for newcomers in empowering immigrant brides in Taiwan.

It is not surprising that we found the positive function of perceived friendliness in this study. When immigrant brides perceived local people around them as friendly, they felt accepted, rather than discriminated against. Studies on discrimination help us understand the positive contribution of perceived friendliness on happiness. It has been reported that perceived discrimination destroys personal self-esteem (Gil, Vega, and Dimas 1994; Gil and Vega 1996), prevents immigrants from expanding their social networks (Davin 2007), reduces psychological well-being (Rumbaut 1994), and leads to depression and poor general health (Viruell-Fuentes 2007).

Most interestingly, we found perceived friendliness plays an intermediating role that mediates the effects of some economic and acculturative factors on the happiness of immigrant brides. The changes in the logit coefficients of predictors when *perceived friendliness* was controlled for in model 2 show the evidence. First, that the logit coefficients for *being employed* change from −0.19 to −0.12 means being a paid employee is *positively* associated with perceived friendliness, which has a positive association with *happiness*. This finding reveals that immigrant brides working for pay perceived the community atmosphere positively, and felt accepted. Second, because immigrant brides with higher family income (e.g. NT$60,000 and more) were more likely to perceive a friendly community atmosphere, the positive effects of family income on their happiness became smaller. Third, the negative association between length of residency and psychological well-being became weaker or insignificant when *perceived friendliness* was controlled for. This evidence reveals that the longer immigrant brides stayed in Taiwan, the less they perceived a friendly community atmosphere. Finally, the negative effect of accessing secondary social networks in Taiwan on happiness became stronger (from −0.70 to −0.82), indicating that those depending on secondary social networks were less likely to have a positive perception of a community atmosphere.

In sum, in this research, we found that the Taiwanese government which has allocated large budgets to establish policies for newcomers plays. On the one hand, 52.8% of immigrant brides reported no need for assistance (see Table 1). On the other hand, the governmental policies may have empowered immigrant brides to be able to access professional organisations in Taiwan to consult for their problems and then to enhance their happiness. However, based on this research, we suggest the government is needed to make efforts to create a friendly atmosphere for immigrant brides, by reducing discrimination from the natives, to enhance the perceived friendliness of society. Female marriage immigrants in Taiwan may be jeopardised by both acculturative and economic issues. However, perceiving a friendly atmosphere reduces the negative effects of economic and acculturative difficulties. In the past decade, the central and local governments have allocated large budgets to initiate services to empower immigrant brides and their children, and to integrate this particular population. However, the hostile attitudes and behaviours of Taiwanese, and/or their misunderstanding of governmental policies and services can determine immigrant brides' perception of friendliness. Therefore, the future efforts of the governments should focus on increasing the mutual understanding between the majority population and immigrant brides, and on enhancing immigrant brides' understanding of and access to services that reduce economic and acculturative difficulties.

Limitations and suggestions for future research

Although our data are the only such data accessible in Taiwan, it is worth noting that relying on the currently *released* data may have some limitations. First, this is a cross-sectional study that can only infer the associations of predictors with the extent of happiness of immigrant brides, not their causal relationships. Second, the sampling frame does not cover all immigrant spouses. Around 40% of marriage immigrants with legal status resided outside of Taiwan during the survey period. We suspect the immigrant brides residing in Taiwan differed from those staying outside of Taiwan. The absent immigrant brides were probably wealthier and happier than those surveyed because they were able to travel overseas or return to their homelands and access social networks at their country of origin. Third, to protect the privacy of immigrants, in the released data, immigrants from Southeast Asian countries are viewed as one category. Generalising conclusions from such data may cause potential biases in the patterns of happiness. It may cause us to overlook different extents of happiness among the Southeast Asian immigrants. Additionally, although the sample design paid careful attention to the current residence, the released data do not provide a variable to distinguish immigrant brides residing in rural communities from their urban counterparts.

To overcome these limitations, we offer suggestions for further research. First, a panel study can provide opportunities to examine the causal relationships of predicting factors with the measures of immigrant brides' well-being. More importantly, researchers with longitudinal data can investigate the trajectory of immigrant brides' well-being and the association of happiness with their life course. Second, further research should incorporate a paper-based questionnaire survey with the interviews to include those who are unable to participate in the interviews. This method can alleviate sampling errors caused by deficient sample frame coverage. Third, researchers should negotiate with the relevant government agency to gather data distinguishing immigrant brides by their urban/rural residence and by their origins. Consequently, comparison studies can be done among immigrant brides residing in locations with different extents of urbanisation and with diverse Southeast Asian origins.

Notes

1. This is the only national survey available to study marriage immigrants in Taiwan and is quite current.
2. The total number of immigrants (about 289,430) in the sampling frame was far below that of documented immigrants (476,019). The former figure was calculated based on Tables 3-1 and 3-2 in the survey report. The population in the sampling frame was first stratified by current residential city or county and the four categories of origin including Southeast Asia, Mainland China, Hong Kong or Macau SARs, and others. The research team then implemented systematic sampling.

    Data were collected with face-to-face interviews; interviewers were mainly local Taiwanese who spoke Mandarin, the major language used for the interviews. The survey team prepared the questionnaires not only in Mandarin but also in foreign languages. When the interviewees were not able to communicate, the questionnaires in suitable languages were provided to them. The average interview duration was about 30 min.
3. Table 1 shows not only the distribution of surveyed immigrant brides' happiness and characteristics but also their associations. For the latter, we provide the cross-tabulations of happiness and the characteristics of respondents, as well as 1–3 appropriate indices of association measures including Cramer's V, Gamma, and Pearson's r, depending on the measurement levels of variables.

    Specifically, the top panel shows the distribution of the 'happiness' measurement, including three categories – very unhappy or unhappy (839; 8.2%), happy (6430; 63.1%), and very happy (2929; 28.7%). The large bottom panel reveals the distribution of respondents' characteristics and their associations with 'happiness.' Reviewing the extent of all the association indices, we find most of the characteristics of immigrant brides are weakly associated with reported happiness, with some exceptions. However, the values of Cramer's V (0.404), Gamma (0.760), and Pearson's r (0.481) show that the association between 'perceived friendliness' and 'happiness' is considerable.
4. The information was retrieved from http://win.dgbas.gov.tw/fies/, on July 10, 2016.
5. To investigate collinearity among independent variables, we created a correlation matrix, not presented here because of space limitations. National origin and Chinese speaking ability were significantly associated with each other. Chinese speaking ability was not significant in the ordinal logistic regression analysis, and was excluded from further analyses.

Disclosure statement

No potential conflict of interest was reported by the authors.

References

Aroian, Karen J. 2001. "Immigrant Women and Their Health." *Annual Review of Nursing Research* 19 (1): 179–226.

Aroian, Karen J., Anne E. Norris, Carol A. Patsdaughter, and Thanh V. Tran. 1998. "Predicting Psychological Distress Among Former Soviet Immigrants." *International Journal of Social Psychiatry* 44 (4): 284–294.

Aycan, Zeynep, and John W Berry. 1996. "Impact of Employment-Related Experiences on Immigrants' Psychological Well-being and Adaptation to Canada." *Canadian Journal of Behavioural Science/Revue Canadienne des Sciences du Comportement* 28 (3): 240.

Bartram, David. 2011. "Introduction to the Special Issue 'Migration and Happiness'." *Journal of Social Research & Policy* 2 (2): 5–8.

Berry, John W. 2006. "Acculturation Stress." In *Handbook of Multicultural Perspective on Stress and Coping*, edited by Paul T. P. Wong and Lilian C.J. Wong, 287–298. New York, NY: Springer.

Caporale, Guglielmo Maria, Yannis Georgellis, Nicholas Tsitsianis, and Ya Ping Yin. 2009. "Income and Happiness Across Europe: Do Reference Values Matter?" *Journal of Economic Psychology* 30 (1): 42–51.

Cohen, Sheldon. 2004. "Social Relationships and Health." *American Psychologist* 59 (8): 676–684.

Cohen, Sheldon, and Thomas A Wills. 1985. "Stress, Social Support, and the Buffering Hypothesis." *Psychological Bulletin* 98 (2): 310–357.

Davin, Delia. 2007. "Marriage Migration in China and East Asia." *Journal of Contemporary China* 16 (50): 83–95.

Diener, Ed. 2000. "Subjective Well-being: The Science of Happiness and a Proposal for a National Index." *American Psychologist* 55 (1): 34–43.

Diener, Ed, and Shigehiro Oishi. 2000. "Money and Happiness: Income and Subjective Well-being Across Nations." In *Culture and Subjective Well-being*, edited by Ed Diener and Eunkook M. Suh, 185–218. Cambridge, MA: MIT Press.

Diener, Ed, Ed Sandvik, Larry Seidlitz, and Marissa Diener. 1993. "The Relationship Between Income and Subjective Well-being: Relative or Absolute?" *Social Indicators Research* 28 (3): 195–223.

Easterlin, Richard A. 2001. "Income and Happiness: Towards a Unified Theory." *The Economic Journal* 111 (473): 465–484. doi:10.1111/1468-0297.00646.

Farrell, Susan J., Tim Aubry, and Daniel Coulombe. 2004. "Neighborhoods and Neighbors: Do They Contribute to Personal Well-being?" *Journal of Community Psychology* 32 (1): 9–25.

Fernández, Itziar, Prado Silván-Ferrero, Fernando Molero, Elena Gaviria, and Cristina García-Ael. 2015. "Perceived Discrimination and Well-being in Romanian Immigrants: The Role of Social Support." *Journal of Happiness Studies* 16 (4): 857–870.

Ferree, Myra Marx. 1979. "Employment Without Liberation: Cuban Women in the United States." *Social Science Quarterly* 60 (1): 35–50.

Ferrer-i-Carbonell, Ada. 2005. "Income and Well-being: An Empirical Analysis of the Comparison Income Effect." *Journal of Public Economics* 89 (5–6): 997–1019.

Finch, Brian Karl, and William A. Vega. 2003. "Acculturation Stress, Social Support, and Self-rated Health among Latinos in California." *Journal of Immigrant Health* 5 (3): 109–117.

Fumham, Andrian, and Shaheen Sheikh. 1993. "Gender, Generation, and Social Support Correlates of Mental Health in Asian Immigrants." *International Journal of Social Psychiatry* 39 (1): 22–33.

Gil, Andres G., and William A. Vega. 1996. "Two Different Worlds: Acculturation Stress and Adaptation among Cuban and Nicaraguan Families." *Journal of Social and Personal Relationships* 13 (3): 435–456.

Gil, Andres G., William A. Vega, and Juanita M. Dimas. 1994. "Acculturative Stress and Personal Adjustment among Hispanic Adolescent Boys." *Journal of Community Psychology* 22 (1): 43–54.

Gordon, Milton M. 1964. *Assimilation in American Life: The Role of Race, Religion, and Origins*. New York, NY: Oxford University Press.

Granovetter, Mark S. 1973. "The Strength of Weak Ties." *American Journal of Sociology* 78 (6): 1360–1380.

Hagerty, Michael R., and Ruut Veenhoven. 2003. "Wealth and Happiness Revisited – Growing National Income Does Go with Greater Happiness." *Social Indicators Research* 64 (1): 1–27.

Hernandez, Rosalba, Mercedes Carnethon, Frank J. Penedo, Lizet Martinez, Julia Boehm, and Stephen M. Schueller. 2016. "Exploring Well-being among US Hispanics/Latinos in A Church-based Institution: A Qualitative Study." *The Journal of Positive Psychology* 11 (5): 511–521.

Hovey, Joseph D., and Cristina Magaña. 2000. "Acculturative Stress, Anxiety, and Depression among Mexican Immigrant Farmworkers in the Midwest United States." *Journal of Immigrant Health* 2 (3): 119–131.

Hurh, Won Moo, and Kwang Chung Kim. 1990. "Correlates of Korean Immigrants' Mental Health." *The Journal of Nervous and Mental Disease* 178 (11): 703–711.

Iglesias, Edgar, Eva Robertson, Sven-Erik Johansson, Peter Engfeldt, and Jan Sundquist. 2003. "Women, International Migration and Self-reported Health. A Population-based Study of Women of Reproductive Age." *Social Science & Medicine* 56 (1): 111–124.

Jasinskaja-Lahti, Inga, and Karmela Liebkind. 2001. "Perceived Discrimination and Psychological Adjustment among Russian-Speaking Immigrant Adolescents in Finland." *International Journal of Psychology* 36 (3): 174–185.

Jasinskaja-Lahti, Inga, Karmela Liebkind, Magdalena Jaakkola, and Anni Reuter. 2006. "Perceived Discrimination, Social Support Networks, and Psychological Well-being Among Three Immigrant Groups." *Journal of Cross-Cultural Psychology* 37 (3): 293–311.

Jayasuriya, Dharmasoka L., David Sang, and Angela Fielding. 1992. *Ethnicity, Immigration and Mental Illness: A Critical Review of Australian Research*. Canberra: Bureau of Immigration Research.

Kahneman, Daniel, and Angus Deaton. 2010. "High Income Improves Evaluation of Life but Not Emotional Well-being." *PNAS* 107 (38): 16489–16493. doi: 10.1073/pnas.1011492107.

Komproe, Ivan H., Mieke Rijken, Wynand J. G. Ros, Jacques A. M. Winnubst, and Harm 'tHart. 1997. "Available Support and Received Support: Different Effects Under Stressful Circumstances." *Journal of Social and Personal Relationships* 14 (1): 59–77.

Lera-López, Fernando, Andrea Ollo-López, and José Manuel Sánchez-Santos. 2016. "How Does Physical Activity Make You Feel Better? The Mediational Role of Perceived Health." *Applied Research in Quality of Life* 12 (3): 511–531.

Li, Chun-Hao, and Ming-Chang Tsai. 2014. "Is the Easy Life Always the Happiest? Examining the Association of Convenience and Well-being in Taiwan." *Social Indicators Research* 117 (3): 673–688.

Lin, Nan, Xiaolan Ye, and Walter M. Ensel. 1999. "Social Support and Depressed Mood: A Structural Analysis." *Journal of Health and Social Behavior* 40 (4): 344–359.

Martínez García, Manuel F., Manuel García Ramírez, and Isidro Maya Jariego. 2002. "Social Support and Locus of Control as Predictors of Psychological Well-being in Moroccan and Peruvian Immigrant Women in Spain." *International Journal of Intercultural Relations* 26 (3): 287–310.

Miglietta, Anna, and Stefano Tartaglia. 2009. "The Influence of Length of Stay, Linguistic Competence, and Media Exposure in Immigrants' Adaptation." *Cross-Cultural Research* 43 (1): 46–61.

Moon, Seung-Jun, Chan Souk Kim, and Tae Woo Kim. 2014. "Chinese Immigrants in Korea: The Relationship Between Interpersonal Communication and Acculturation." *Asian and Pacific Migration Journal* 23 (3): 325–344.

National Immigration Agency. 2014. *The Report of the Survey of Foreign and Chinese Spouses' Living Requirements in 2013*. Taipei: Ministry of the Interior, Taiwan. (in Chinese).

Negi, Nalini Junko, Lynn Michalopoulos, Javier Boyas, and Adrianna Overdorff. 2013. "Social Networks That Promote Well-being Among Latino Migrant Day Laborers." *Advances in Social Work* 14 (1): 247–259.

Noh, Samuel, and Violet Kaspar. 2003. "Perceived Discrimination and Depression: Moderating Effects of Coping, Acculturation, and Ethnic Support." *American Journal of Public Health* 93 (2): 232–238.

Oh, Yunjin, Gary F. Koeske, and Esther Sales. 2002. "Acculturation, Stress, and Depressive Symptoms among Korean Immigrants in the United States." *The Journal of Social Psychology* 142 (4): 511–526.

Organista, Pamela Balls, Gerardo Marin, and Kevin M Chun. 2010. *The Psychology of Ethnic Groups in the United States.*. Thousand Oaks, CA: Sage Publications.

Paradies, Yin. 2006. "A Systematic Review of Empirical Research on Self-reported Racism and Health." *International Journal of Epidemiology* 35 (4): 888–901.

Rogler, Lloyd H., Dharma E. Cortes, and Robert G. Malgady. 1991. "Acculturation and Mental Health Status among Hispanics: Convergence and New Directions for Research." *American Psychologist* 46 (6): 585–597.

Rumbaut, Ruben G. 1994. "The Crucible Within: Ethnic Identity, Self-esteem, and Segmented Assimilation among Children of Immigrants." *International Migration Review* 28 (4): 748–794.

Ryan, Louise, Rosemary Sales, Mary Tilki, and Bernadetta Siara. 2008. "Social Networks, Social Support and Social Capital: The Experiences of Recent Polish Migrants in London." *Sociology* 42 (4): 672–690.

Safi, Mirna. 2010. "Immigrants' Life Satisfaction in Europe: Between Assimilation and Discrimination." *European Sociological Review* 26 (2): 159–176.

Schultz, O. 2001. "The Effect of Social Psychological Training on Personality Changes among Immigrants (The German Example)." In *Psychological Problems among Russian Immigrants in Germany*, edited by N. S. Hrustaleva, 38–45. St. Petersburg: St. Petersburg University Press.

Shen, Biing-Jiun, and David T. Takeuchi. 2001. "A Structural Model of Acculturation and Mental Health Status Among Chinese Americans." *American Journal of Community Psychology* 29 (3): 387–418.

Shin, Hye Sook, Hae-Ra Han, and Miyong T. Kim. 2007. "Predictors of Psychological Well-being Amongst Korean Immigrants to the United States: A Structured Interview Survey." *International Journal of Nursing Studies* 44 (3): 415–426.

Stevenson, Betsey, and Justin Wolfers. 2013. "Subjective Well-being and Income: Is There Any Evidence of Satiation?" *The American Economic Review* 103 (3): 598–604.

Thoits, Peggy A. 1995. "Stress, Coping, and Social Support Processes: Where Are We? What Next?" *Journal of Health and Social Behavior* 35: 53–79.

Tsui, Hsiao-Chien. 2014. "What Affects Happiness: Absolute Income, Relative Income or Expected Income?" *Journal of Policy Modeling* 36 (6): 994–1007.

Vega, William, Bohdan Kolody, Ramon Valle, and Judy Weir. 1991. "Social Networks, Social Support, and Their Relationship to Depression among Immigrant Mexican Women." *Human Organization* 50 (2): 154–162.

Vega, William, and Ruben Rumbaut. 1991. "Ethnic Minorities and Mental Health." *Annual Review of Sociology* 17 (1): 56–89.

Verkuyten, Maykel. 1998. "Perceived Discrimination and Self-esteem among Ethnic Minority Adolescents." *Journal of Social Psychology* 138 (4): 479–493.

Viruell-Fuentes, Edna A. 2007. "Beyond Acculturation: Immigration, Discrimination, and Health Research among Mexicans in the United States." *Social Science & Medicine* 65 (7): 1524–1535.

Ward, Colleen. 1996. "Acculturation." In *Handbook of Intercultural Training*, edited by D. Landis and R. S. Bhagat, 24–147. Thousand Oaks, CA: Sage Publications.

Williams, Carolyn L., and John W. Berry. 1991. "Primary Prevention of Acculturative Stress among Refugees: Application of Psychological Theory and Practice." *American Psychologist* 46 (6): 632–641.

Williams, David R., Harold W. Neighbors, and James S. Jackson. 2003. "Racial/Ethnic Discrimination and Health: Findings from Community Studies." *American Journal of Public Health* 93 (2): 200–208.

Yang, Yung-Mei, Hsiu-Hung Wang, and Debra Anderson. 2010. "Immigration Distress and Associated Factors Among Vietnamese Women in Transnational Marriages in Taiwan." *The Kaohsiung Journal of Medical Sciences* 26 (12): 647–657.

Yeung, Wei-Jun Jean, and Zheng Mu. 2020. "Migration and Marriage in Asian Contexts." *Journal of Ethnic and Migration Studies* 46 (14): 2863–2879. doi:10.1080/1369183X.2019.1585005.

Ying, Yu-Wen. 1988. "Depressive Symptomatology Among Chinese-Americans as Measured by the CES-D." *Journal of Clinical Psychology* 44 (5): 739–746.

Physical versus imagined communities: migration and women's autonomy in India

Esha Chatterjee and Sonalde Desai

ABSTRACT
India has seen a rise in the proportion of internal migrants between 1983 and 2007-08. Much of this increase is attributed to female marriage migrants. However, there is limited literature analysing the well-being of female marriage migrants in India. This paper seeks to examine whether women's autonomy in the public sphere is a function of: (a) the geographical community where the woman resides, or (b) imagined communities (the mindset of the communities to which the woman's family belongs), using multilevel mixed-effects logistic and ordered logistic regression. Analysing data from the India Human Development Survey (IHDS), 2012, for more than 34,000 ever-married women aged 15–49 years, the study finds that the communities in the mind (norms about marriage migration in the caste/sub-caste to which the woman's family belongs) are more important than the physical communities to which the women have migrated, in relation to certain aspects of women's physical autonomy and autonomy to participate in civic activities. In contrast, a woman's economic autonomy is a function of both 'imagined' and 'physical' communities. Thus, the opportunities available to women who migrate for marriage are shaped by both geographical communities, and more importantly, by the norms in her community about marriage migration.

Introduction

India, is home to an estimated 400 million internal migrants (UNESCO 2013) and about two-thirds of these are migrants for marriage. Marriage related migration forms an increasingly important phenomenon, with many articles in this issue also referring to high levels of migration for marriage (Li and Yang 2020; Mu and Yeung 2020; Yeung and Mu 2019). However, theoretical frameworks for understanding these migrations and their impact on individual well-being remain poorly developed. Literature on migration is informed by two diverse streams of literature. The first focuses on who migrates and does not migrate; the second focuses on the ways in which migrants assimilate in the destination communities. Neither of these two, pay adequate attention to gender (Hugo 2000; Pedraza 1991).

Studies of determinants of migration tend to start from the experience of men and often focus on labour migration or distress driven migration. Even when attempts are made to incorporate gender in the migration literature, this focus is often extended by examining the feminisation of labour migration or the manner in which male labour migration affects women, either by encouraging tied migration or by influencing their lives in the absence of their partners (Desai and Banerji 2008; Gulati 1993; Menjivar and Agadjanian 2007). Migration for marriage – a unique dimension of women's migration – has received attention only as a specialised phenomenon in the study of transnational migration (see Charsley and Shaw 2006) with a focus on mail order brides (Kojima 2001; Lu 2005; Wang and Chang 2002; Yeung and Mu 2019), or more recently, in studies of Internet brides.

Consequences of migration and their implications for individual well-being are often studied within the framework of immigrant assimilation and acculturation and tend to view migrants either as victims or agents (Yeung and Mu 2019) where integration is seen as the ultimate goal. This is particularly true in the literature on marriage migration where only one of the spouses is a migrant (Chen and Yip 2020; Chiu and Choi 2020). This Eurocentric approach to migrant assimilation fails to capture the cultural transformations that take place when marriage migration becomes normative, as we document for India. In this paper, we argue that once marriage migration becomes part of an established pattern, norms relating to appropriate behaviours develop, that have little to do with actual physical location of specific brides and grooms.

Magnitude of marriage migration in India

The magnitude of women's internal migration for marriage in India can be staggering. The National Sample Survey (NSS) data suggest that from 1983 to 2007–08, the proportion of permanent internal migrants as a percentage of the population of India had risen from 23% to 29% (Rao and Finoff 2015). About 87% of this rise was due to an increasing percentage of female permanent migrants, particularly marriage migrants. In the same time frame, however, it has been seen that the percentage of women who migrated for economic reasons was low and decreased further from 2.6% to 1.1%. Moreover, data from the NSS shows that between 1993 and 2007–08, there was an increase in the incidence of marriage migration from 24.7% to 43.5% of the rural female population. These trends are supported by the Census data for 1991 and 2001. In urban areas, on the other hand, marriage migration for females increased from 12.1% to 27.7% between 1993 and 2007–08 (Rao and Finnoff 2015). Rao and Finnoff (2015) posit that a rise in marriage migration is not necessarily a 'disguised economic migration of women'.

Figure 1 shows the reasons for migration for long-term female migrants using data from the India Human Development Survey (IHDS) (2004–05, 2011–12), where at least one member of the household was left behind to provide information about migration. It is important to note that these reasons for migration are fuzzy descriptions of the underlying processes. It can be seen that about 72% of the female migration in India can be attributed to marriage, with marriage migration being most prevalent among women aged 25 years and below.

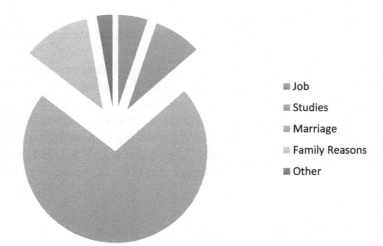

Figure 1. Reasons for long-term migration (rural females). Sources: Indian Human Development Survey IandII. India Human Development Survey II (2011–12).

While a few studies have examined female migration within India (Bhattacharya 2000; Fulford 2013; Premi 1980; Rosenzweig and Stark 1989), by and large, research on female migrants has been limited, mainly because most women report that they migrated because of marriage (Rao and Finnoff 2015). However, as Fulford (2013) notes, the phenomenon of marriage migration has generally received little attention. The lack of attention to women's migration patterns is mostly due to a poor understanding of the issue of marriage migration, a gap that this paper seeks to fill.

Marriage-related migration in India is distinct from simple geographic mobility. It is caused by two forces: (1) in some castes and communities, all men in the natal village are considered to be relatives and there are strict prohibitions against the marriage of a woman within the same village; and, (2) where such prohibitions do not exist, women may still marry outside the village if it is difficult to find an appropriate match within the same village. Where marriage migration is part and parcel of the accepted kinship system, a complex web of social norms emerges that defines the relationship of a woman with her marital family and community. These practices include veiling, communications with older male relatives and control over land and other resources.

These practices suggest that studies of marriage migration must distinguish between physical movement and the norms and social structures that evolve around the practice of marriage migration. In this paper, using data from the India Human Development Survey (IHDS) of 2011–12, for over 34,000 ever-married women aged 15–49 years, we examine the role of geographical movement vis-à-vis the social norms surrounding exogamous marriage practices in shaping indicators of women's autonomy in the public sphere.

We use the concepts of physical and imagined communities to distinguish between these two phenomena. The term 'physical communities' refers to the geographical locations of women, specifically whether they continue to live in the localities where they grew up. In contrast, the term 'imagined communities' refers to the behavioural and kinship norms that develop around the practice of exogamous marriages. The question that is addressed here is: How are different markers of women's physical, economic and civic autonomy affected by these two different dimensions of marriage migration?

We begin by discussing the concepts of physical and imagined communities, and explaining the gap filled by this paper by comparing the role of these types of communities in shaping certain dimensions of women's autonomy in the public sphere. The following section examines the existing literature on kinship patterns, marital choice, and women's agency. In the subsequent sections, we define our research questions, operationalise autonomy in the context of this study, describe the data and methods used, elaborate on the results, and conclude and place this study in the context of the existing literature.

Physical communities: shaped by women's migration

Although geographical location is the key concept around which migration studies are centred, the way in which physical location affects individuals covers a broad terrain while encompassing changes in resources, opportunities, social support networks, and social constraints. Even if gender is not taken into account, the impact of migration on individuals remains contested (Portes 1997; Yeung and Mu 2019). While in some cases, migration may be associated with higher income earning opportunities, opportunities to absorb new ideas and cultures, and the ability to reshape identities in a way that escapes traditional social control, in others, it may be associated with isolation, discrimination, and the continued adherence to traditional values.

The issue of whether migration empowers women is fraught with even greater challenges since it adds an additional layer of segmentation – that of gender (Hugo 2000). Boyd and Grieco (2003) emphasise the importance of understanding gender-specific migration experiences. An important question relates to examining how patriarchal norms are changed or renegotiated after migration. Another issue that emerges is how migration impacts interpersonal relations and power dynamics within the family. Literature on international migration indicates that migrants who go to advanced economies such as the US have access to better job opportunities in the destination country as compared to the country of their origin. However, it is observed that female migrants often work as low-skilled labourers and become the primary earners for their families (Luke and Munshi 2011). This process has sometimes been reported as empowering for women and increases their decision-making ability in their households (Boserup 1970; Grasmuck and Pessar 1991). In other instances, it has been found that even if women make large financial contributions to the household, migrant women continue to follow traditional beliefs and abide by their husbands' decisions (see, for example, Kibria 1993; Menjívar 1999; Parrado and Flippen 2005; Zhou 1992).

The high incidence of migration of women in India due to marriage results in an abrupt change in women's day-to-day lives. Nearly 95% of the female respondents in the IHDS started out their married lives by living with their husbands' parents. When women move from their own village or town to their husbands' hometowns, they are compelled to change both their residence and culture. While before marriage they are surrounded by uncles and cousins, post-marriage they are surrounded by strangers and may experience an even greater constraint in venturing out to unfamiliar places. Their social support networks are transformed from that of their childhood friends, sisters and aunts, to mothers-in-law and relatives of their husbands who subject the new brides to intense scrutiny, and are often critical of the latter's actions and behaviour even while expecting considerable deference from them (Raheja and Gold 1994). This brief review, therefore, suggests that migration, particularly for married women, may be associated with a substantial curtailment of their autonomy.

Imagined communities: rooted in kinship norms

Physical movement is distinct from social and behavioural norms that emerge in response to marriage patterns, which either prescribe or proscribe marriage within the natal community. Anthropologists have long recognised the subtle power dynamics embedded in marriage arrangements in India (Oberoi 1998). Arranged marriages remain common in the Indian context, with nearly 95% of the women reporting that their spousal choice was made solely by their parents or jointly by the parents and bride (Allendorf and Pandian 2016; Andrist, Banerji, and Desai 2013). Jejeebhoy et al. (2013) reported that while marriages arranged by the parents are still the norm, there is wide regional variation between the northern and southern states. These findings are consistent with earlier studies in other developing countries (Hamid, Stephenson, and Rubenson 2011; Heaton, Cammack, and Young 2001; Niraula and Morgan 1996; Pimentel 2000; Xu and Whyte 1990), in that women in marriages arranged by the family experienced less agency, and had a lower level of communication and interaction with their spouses as compared to their counterparts in self-arranged or semi-arranged marriages.

These marital choices are located within the well-defined norms of who is an acceptable marriage partner. Kinship patterns in India are bifurcated along the lines of who is considered an appropriate partner with the major distinction pertaining to communities in which marriages may be permitted within a village or those in which they are not (Karve 1965). The northern kinship pattern is built on the assumption that every family in a village is related to each other, and that this consanguinity prohibits marriage within the natal village of the bride. In fact, villages are often divided along the lines of bride-givers and bride-takers, with the families selecting brides from villages defined as bride-givers (for example, villages to the east) and marrying their daughters into villages defined as bride-takers (for example, villages to the west). In contrast, the southern kinship pattern is built around consanguineous marriages with women not only being permitted to marry within their own village but the preferred partner often being a maternal uncle or cross-cousin (Bittles 1994).

Curiously, village endogamy persists even when a family moves to an urban area. Families continue to identify with their place of origin and proscribe marriage with a partner whose family originates from their own village or set of villages. This suggests that the complex kinship rules embodied in who is an eligible partner have acquired symbolic meaning above and beyond where the bride and the groom physically reside.

This reification of the geographical location of permissible brides and grooms shares many characteristics with Benedict Anderson's description of an imagined community (Anderson 1983). When talking of the nation as a socially constructed community imagined by people who perceive themselves as a part of that community, Anderson notes:

It is imagined because the members of even the smallest nation will never know most of their fellow-members, meet them, or even hear of them, yet in the minds of each lives the image of their communion. (Anderson 1983, 49)

Ray Pahl makes a similar distinction between community on the ground and community in the mind (Pahl 2005). In traditional Indian society, a community is used to define a conglomerate of a particular caste or religious groups that are closely bounded and where belonging to that community confers both status and norms of appropriate behaviour (Srinivas 1996). The membership of these communities is shaped by rules defining appropriate marriage partners. This distinction in marriage and kinship patterns is not simply that of the acceptable geographical location of a potential bride and groom but spills over into an interrelated complex of how families define themselves vis-à-vis others, how inheritance patterns are shaped, and how the families of the bride and groom relate to each other (Bloch, Rao, and Desai 2004).

Kinship patterns, marital arrangements and women's agency

Dyson and Moore (1983) noted the difference between endogamous and exogamous marriage systems as the key difference that shapes diversity in gender systems and demographic outcomes across India. Their seminal paper on female autonomy notes:

In India, as in most other developing agrarian societies, kin relationships still constitute for the great majority of people the prime avenue of access to such scarce social resources as information, economic assistance, and political support. An individual's power, influence, and social ranking are often closely related to his or her ability to exploit kin linkages. Thus cultural practices – such as those of the north Indian system – that tend to constrain or erode the personal links between a married woman and her natal kin directly diminish the woman's autonomy. If, at the same time, norms of avoidance make it difficult for the woman to establish affective links within the household into which she marries, she is left socially almost powerless. (Dyson and Moore 1983, 46)

A number of studies also report the prevalence of regional differences in kinship norms that dictate the amount of support a woman can expect from her natal family after marriage. In the north where patrilineal and exogamous marriages are prevalent, once women go to their husbands' homes, they are no longer expected to contribute to their natal family (nor can they expect support from them). In contrast, in the southern states where endogamous marriages are more common, women get greater support from their natal families (Chakraborty and Kim 2010; Das Gupta 2010). However, the literature on the relationship between regional location and women's autonomy is not uniformly consistent. While Jejeebhoy and Sathar (2001) find a strong divide between women's autonomy in the northern state of Uttar Pradesh and the southern state of Tamil Nadu, Rahman and Rao (2004) do not see this divide between women living in Uttar Pradesh and Karnataka. Thus, the strength of the relationship between marriage patterns and women's autonomy, after controlling for regional effects, remains an empirical question.

Research questions

This brief review suggests that it is important to distinguish between the two aspects of marriage migration: the first shapes the woman's physical surroundings while the second shapes her normative framework. One of the challenges of studying the relationship between marriage migration, kinship patterns and women's autonomy lies in clearing the confusion between various levels of analysis. Migration and kinship patterns are not synonymous, nor are geographical locations and kinship patterns.

While there may be a normative preference for women to marry in the village or to marry a close relative in the southern kinship pattern, relatively few women seem to actually marry within the village even in South India; and even fewer actually marry close relatives. The preference for finding a groom within a closed community may be just that, a preference. This preference may be competing with the desire to find an educated groom, a groom closer to the bride's age, and perhaps one with a high income. For families that belong to communities that proscribe to village exogamy, residing in urban areas doesn't imply, not marrying daughters within the same city, but rather marrying them to grooms from a family, not originating from the same ancestral village(Grover 2017). Thus, a bride who grew up in Delhi may well marry a groom from Delhi as long as both their families do not originate from the same set of villages in Mathura district. Figure 2 maps the women's responses to the following two questions:

(1). In your community (caste), in a family like yours, is it permissible to marry a daughter within her natal village? (Yes/No)
(2). What was your childhood place of residence? (Same village or town as your current residence, another village, another town, a metro city)

The results show that about 12% of the ever-married women belonging to a community wherein it is not permissible to marry a bride who shares a natal village with the groom, continue to live post-marriage in their childhood place of residence, while only 24% of the couples belonging to communities in which within-village marriage is permissible actually grew up in the same village or town where they are currently living.

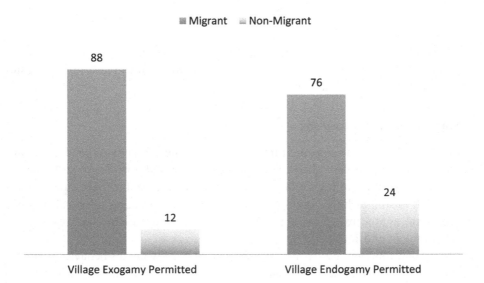

Figure 2. Distribution of migrant women by whether village endogamy is permitted in their caste/community. Source: India Human Development Survey II (2011–12).

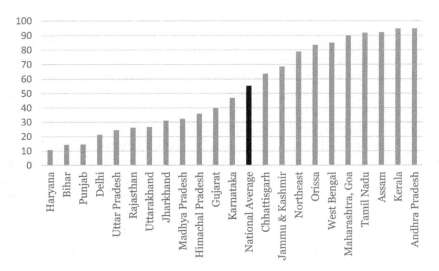

Figure 3. Percentage distribution of respondents whose communities permit endogamy by state. Source: India Human Development Survey II (2011–12).

If actual migration and kinship patterns are not perfectly aligned, geography and kinship patterns are even less correlated. For example, Muslims all around India are far more comfortable with consanguineous marriages, and hence, Muslim families in the North continue to practice endogamous marriages. Moreover, some of the areas at the junction of the North–South divide may belong either to castes or communities that follow exogamy or to those that do not (for example, in Gujarat and northern Karnataka) (see Figure 3).

Fortunately, this lack of perfect correlation also provides us with a handle to statistically examine the relationship between women's own migrant status, the kinship system in which they were raised, and their autonomy.

This paper seeks to examine whether women's autonomy in the public sphere is a function of:

(1). the geographical community where the woman resides; and
(2). imagined communities or the mindset of the communities (caste or sub-caste) to which the woman's family belongs

Defining women's autonomy

Research on women's empowerment notes the multidimensionality of gender (Desai and Andrist 2010; Desai and Temsah 2014; Malhotra, Schuler, and Boender 2002; Mason 1995; Narayan 2006; Presser and Sen 2000). A number of past studies have operationalised autonomy by distinguishing between household decision-making, physical autonomy, and economic autonomy (Jejeebhoy 2000; Jejeebhoy and Sathar 2001; Koenig et al. 2003; Rammohan and Johar 2009).

In this paper, however, our focus is on those aspects of women's behaviour that are in the public arena and that are most likely to be influenced by both the geographical and imagined communities. Hence, we focus on the following three aspects of women's autonomy that are measured in the IHDS survey:

(1). *Physical autonomy* – Women in India often do not go out of the house alone but tend to be escorted by the husband, a female family member, or sometimes adolescent boys (Jejeebhoy and Sathar 2001). In fact, in northern India, women are conspicuous by their absence in public areas. Families have various rationalizations for this such as the likelihood of assault or insult, lack of experience among the women in dealing with the external world, or preservation of family status. However, regardless of the reason, their inability to venture out to commonplace locations like the grocery store or a friend's home reduces women's physical autonomy.

(2). *Economic autonomy* – Women in India (and in South Asia, in general) have remarkably low labour force participation rates, and at least in India, these figures have either stagnated or declined a little instead of increasing over time (Desai 2013). Even when women work, they often do so only on the family farm or in the family business. While this work also augments the overall household income and increases women's access to resources, it does not provide economic independence to women (Luke and Munshi 2011). Here we focus on women's wage work as a marker of their economic autonomy.

(3). *Autonomy in civic participation* – Increasingly women's civic participation in India has been rising. In this context, Self-help Groups (SHGs) have emerged as a particularly important force. Many of these SHGs are set up by development organisations, while others are set up with help from the government. As has been observed in Bangladesh, some of them have also been established as a part of the micro-credit movement in that country (Sanyal 2014), wherein these have reportedly helped to empower women (Hashemi, Schuler, and Riley 1996). Here, we explore women's participation in SHGs as a marker of their political, or more specifically, civic-participation autonomy.

These indicators have been chosen because they are hypothesised to be affected by both migrations at an individual level and exogamous kinship patterns at a community level. Women who grow up in a locality may be comfortable traversing it, may have greater contacts to find wage work, and may have connections that lead them to participate in group activities. At the same time, the normative aspect of belonging to castes and religious communities that encourage within-village marriages may not have any direct effect on these variables via connections and knowledge but may have an ideational impact that may affect the families' willingness to allow women greater autonomy and women's own expectation of this autonomy. The North Indian kinship pattern of village exogamy rests on the notion that all women born and raised in a village are part of a common family while those raised outside are 'others', who may be treated differently. For example, while travelling through a village in the northern state of Haryana, when one sees two married women in their twenties walking through the village, one with her face covered with her sari and another whose face is not covered, it is quite reasonable to assume that the veiled woman is the wife of a local resident while the unveiled woman is a daughter in a village household, who is visiting her pre-marital home(Chowdhry 1993).

Data and methods

The present study uses data from the second round of the IHDS, a nationally representative panel data wherein the first round of the survey was conducted in 2004–05. The first round comprised a sample of 41,554 households spread across all the States and Union Territories of India (except for Andaman and Nicobar, and Lakshadweep Islands), covering 384 districts, 1503 villages, and 971 urban blocks. The second round of the survey, which was conducted in 2011–12, sought to re-interview each of the 41,554 households interviewed in 2004–05, as long as any of the members of the household lived in the same locality. In 2011–12, 83% of the households that had been interviewed in 2004–05, in addition to split households in the village or city, were re-interviewed. Thus, during the second round of the survey, a total of 42,152 households were interviewed.

While the questionnaire on income and social capital was answered by the head of the household, who had the necessary information about the income and expenditure, and related matters of the household (often a man), ever-married women aged 15–49 years answered questions on health beliefs, gender relations, and marital and fertility history. The IHDS has, therefore, collected data on income, social capital, employment, gender relations, and prevalent community norms.

In 2011–12, 35,335 ever-married women aged 15–49 years were interviewed. The survey also contains 4,242 women above the age of 50, but they have been excluded for the present analysis due to the select nature of this sample as part of a panel design. The final sample for each analysis differs slightly due to the missing data that differs across different outcome variables, but in each case, the sample comprises over 34,000 cases.

Dependent variables

We focus on the following three dependent variables:

(1). *Physical Autonomy*: In order to measure the physical autonomy of women, the present study poses questions on whether women can go out of the home without taking permission from senior members of the household or their husbands. Further, the women are asked questions on whether a woman can go alone to the local health centre, the homes of relatives/friends in the neighbourhood, and the *kirana* (grocery) shop, or travel a short distance alone by bus or train. An index for physical autonomy is created by adding these mobility variables. Each of these variables takes a value of 1 if a woman can go out alone and takes a value of 0 otherwise. The index takes a value between 0 and 4, where 4 indicates that a woman has full autonomy to go out alone, and 0 indicates that she cannot go out alone anywhere without permission.

(2). *Economic Autonomy*: Women's economic autonomy is measured by whether the respondent undertook casual or regular employment that generated cash income during the year prior to the survey. Here we exclude work on the family farm or in family businesses because our focus is on women's independent work. Only women who worked for wages for at least 240 h during the year preceding the survey are counted as being employed.

(3). *Civic Participation Autonomy*: The IHDS collected information on whether women participated in an SHG, a credit society, a women's association, or in a political organisation. We focus on SHGs because these are the most development-oriented institutions in India while both women's associations and women's credit groups (when devoid of self-help aspects) are often more social in nature.

Independent variables

We focus on the following two main independent variables associated with migration as discussed above:

(1). Whether women grew up in the same village/town where they are currently residing; and
(2). Whether women's community (caste or sub-caste) allows for marriage within the village.

Control variables

Some of the important control variables used in the present study are the woman's age, education[1], and marital status, the number of household assets owned as a proxy for household wealth, family size, caste and religion, and place of residence.

Statistical model

Our first outcome variable is the number of places that women can visit alone, reflecting that physical autonomy ranges from 0 to 4, and is estimated by using ordinal logistic regressions. The other two outcomes are binary variables, modelled via the logit function.

However, it is important to point out one caveat – all the outcomes that we are interested in are affected by the place of residence. It is not possible to join an SHG if one does not exist in the village or locality. Certain states have set up SHGs while others have not; some villages are close to urban areas and have more voluntary organisations than others (Desai et al. 2010). Similarly, some villages are located near industries like brick kilns or textile weaving centres that provide wage employment to women, while others offer few opportunities for work. This geographical clustering occurs at both the state and village levels. We model this clustering by locating individual women within the villages or urban blocks that are nestled within states and estimate hierarchical models using the Mixed Command in STATA, and include random intercepts for both the state of residence and the village/urban block of residence.

Table 1 presents descriptive statistics for the variables used in this paper.

Results

For each dependent variable, we estimate three models. Model 1 includes only the variable indicating whether the respondent grew up in the same village or town as the place of current residence. Model 2 excludes the migration status for the respondent herself, but includes a variable showing whether her caste and community allows for marriage within the village. Model 3 includes both these variables. We also control for age, education, marital status, number of children, household size, number of assets owned by the household, and caste/religion in each of the three models.

In general, all the control variables operate in the direction that one would expect, with more educated and older women having greater autonomy than their peers. Women in metropolitan cities have greater autonomy than those in the least developed villages.

Table 1. Descriptive statistics for variables used in analyses.

Variable	Obs	Mean	Std. Dev.
No. of places can go alone	34,527	2.661	1.461
Engaged in wage work	35,281	0.245	
Member of self-help group	35,246	0.136	
Grew up in the same village/town	35,032	0.187	
Belongs to caste/community that allows endogamy	35,129	0.553	
Age	35,281	34.079	8.521
Marital Status			
Married but husband absent (Omitted)	35,281	0.076	
Married	35,281	0.869	
Widowed	35,281	0.044	
Separated/divorced	35,281	0.011	
Respondent's Education			
None (Omitted)	35,279	0.457	
Class 1–4	35,279	0.072	
Class 5	35,279	0.090	
Class 6–9	35,279	0.229	
Class 10–11	35,279	0.101	
Class 12 and some college	35,279	0.068	
College graduate	35,279	0.037	
Post-graduate	35,279	0.018	
No. of children	35,267	2.428	1.519
No. of assets owned	35,269	15.163	6.444
Household size	35,281	5.744	2.730
Place of Residence			
Metro city (Omitted)	35,281	0.075	
Other urban	35,281	0.224	
Developed village	35,281	0.316	
Less developed village	35,281	0.384	
Caste/religion			
Forward castes (Omitted)	35,270	0.201	
Other Backward Classes	35,270	0.358	
Scheduled Caste/Dalit	35,270	0.221	
Scheduled Tribe/Adivasi	35,270	0.079	
Muslim	35,270	0.123	
Christian, Sikh, Jain, etc.	35,270	0.019	

Source: India Human Development Survey II (2011–12).

However, it is noteworthy that household wealth is associated with less rather than more autonomy, but even this is not surprising given that certain studies have noted that poorer women often have more autonomy than richer women since they cannot afford the luxury of seclusion (Sharma 1980). In each instance, the variance for the random intercept for state of residence and village/urban block are significantly different from zero, suggesting considerable heterogeneity in the outcomes across states and villages/blocks.

Physical Autonomy: Table 2 shows the results from the hierarchical ordinal logistic regression. The results show that the difference between migrants and non-migrants is not statistically significant. However, the addition of community acceptance of endogamous (within-village) marriage has the significant effect of increasing women's physical autonomy. Moreover, when both variables are included in the model (Model 3), the effect of community norms and individual migration status does not vary, suggesting that the correlation between each of these factors and women's physical autonomy stems from different sources.

Economic Autonomy: Table 3 shows results from the hierarchical logistic regressions for women's participation in wage work. Once again, random intercepts for both the state of residence and the village/urban block of residence are included. This table shows that both

Table 2. Determinants of women's physical autonomy; results from hierarchical ordinal logistic regressions.

Variables	Model 1 Odds.	Model 2 Odds.	Model 3 Odds
Grew up in the same village/town	0.997		0.986
Belongs to caste/community that allows endogamy		1.157**	1.157**
Age	1.044**	1.044**	1.044**
Married	0.601**	0.596**	0.595**
Widowed	1.602**	1.597**	1.590**
Separated/divorced	1.455**	1.436**	1.462**
Class 1–4	1.266**	1.269**	1.269**
Class 5	1.168**	1.172**	1.172**
Class 6–9	1.467**	1.465**	1.468**
Class 10–11	1.728**	1.728**	1.737**
Class 12 and some college	2.048**	2.056**	2.061**
College graduate	2.568**	2.573**	2.570**
Post-graduate	2.878**	2.886**	2.910**
No. of children	1.122**	1.123**	1.123**
No. of assets owned	0.987**	0.987**	0.986**
Household size	0.945**	0.945**	0.945**
Other urban	1.068	1.073	1.069
Developed village	0.882	0.895	0.890
Less developed village	0.739**	0.748*	0.748*
Other Backward Classes	0.977	0.972	0.975
Scheduled Caste/Dalit	1.076	1.073	1.076
Scheduled Tribe/Adivasi	1.064	1.054	1.059
Muslim	0.751**	0.710**	0.712**
Christian, Sikh, Jain, etc.	0.914	0.896	0.907
var(_cons[level 3 state of residence])	1.895**	1.912**	1.914**
var(_cons[village/block nested within state])	2.948**	2.907**	2.933**
Sample Size	34,255	34,341	34,110

Notes: Ancillary parameters that are cut points used to differentiate the adjacent categories of the index on women's physical mobility are not reported in the table, more detailed tables can be requested from authors.
Source: India Human Development Survey II (2011–12).
*$p < 0.05$.
**$p < 0.01$.

dimensions of migration – individual migration status and whether endogamy is permitted in the community – are statistically significant determinants of women's wage work. Once again, these appear to tap into very different dimensions of migration and controlling for one does not seem to substantially change the coefficient for the other.

Autonomy in Civic Participation: Results from the hierarchical logistic regressions for women's participation in SHGs are shown in Table 4. The impact of two migration variables in this table is similar to that observed in Table 2 for women's physical autonomy. While belonging to a caste that allows endogamous marriages increases women's participation in civic activities, the same is not the case for women's own migration status. The difference between migrant and non-migrant women is not statistically significant.

Discussion

In direct contrast to assimilation and acculturation literature, we focus on migration that is not exceptional or foreign but rather an integral part of the way in which cultures and social norms shape and are shaped by marriage migration. Whether an woman migrates for marriage or not, if she is raised in a kinship system where marriage migration is common, her life is governed by broader social norms developed around the dominant

Table 3. Determinants of women's economic autonomy; results from hierarchical logistic regressions.

Variables	Model 1 Odds	Model 2 Odds	Model 3 Odds
Grew up in the same village/town	1.140**		1.131**
Belongs to caste/community that allows endogamy		1.107*	1.103*
Age	1.027**	1.027**	1.027**
Married	1.133	1.113	1.129
Widowed	3.394**	3.380**	3.387**
Separated/divorced	3.497**	3.695**	3.525**
Class 1–4	0.992	0.992	0.990
Class 5	0.751**	0.751**	0.753**
Class 6–9	0.600**	0.597**	0.599**
Class 10–11	0.558**	0.567**	0.556**
Class 12 and some college	1.075	1.068	1.080
College graduate	2.537**	2.560**	2.540**
Post-graduate	7.486**	7.706**	7.606**
No. of children	1.142**	1.142**	1.145**
No. of assets owned	0.879**	0.878**	0.879**
Household size	0.908**	0.910**	0.908**
Other urban	1.551**	1.581**	1.594**
Developed village	1.917**	1.941**	1.978**
Less developed village	1.699**	1.706**	1.749**
Other Backward Classes	1.422**	1.399**	1.412**
Scheduled Caste/Dalit	2.596**	2.563**	2.599**
Scheduled Tribe/Adivasi	2.121**	2.067**	2.096**
Muslim	0.804**	0.774**	0.773**
Christian, Sikh, Jain, etc.	1.265	1.226	1.265
Constant	0.274**	0.272**	0.255**
var(_cons[level 3 state of residence])	1.868**	1.846**	1.846**
var(_cons[village/block nested within state])	2.184**	2.173**	2.184**
Sample Size			

Source: India Human Development Survey II (2011–12).
*$p < 0.05$.
**$p < 0.01$.

discourse which assumes that marriage migration is a fact of life. Our results show that whether the respondent is a migrant or whether she grew up in her current community is associated with her higher participation in wage labour but has no impact on women's physical autonomy or their autonomy to participate in civic activities. However, women who belong to communities which allow for marriage within their natal villages are far more likely to score higher on all the three dimensions of autonomy – physical autonomy, economic autonomy and civic participation.

These results take us directly to the question we began with: Is autonomy a function of women's own geographical community or is it defined by the communities of mind to which their families belong? Our results seem to suggest that the latter is far more important than the former. Long-time residence in a community may offer women greater knowledge about the community and the available infrastructure, and help them improve their social networks. Nonetheless, these are not sufficient to improve their autonomy. In contrast, marriage patterns that are oriented towards village endogamy develop norms and ideologies that permit far greater autonomy than those that are oriented towards village exogamy.

In communities where exogamy is pervasive, a social distance between young brides and their parents-in-law is developed, even encouraged, as a result of which women's autonomy is routinely curtailed. In contrast, in communities where village endogamy

Table 4. Determinants of women's civic participation autonomy; results from hierarchical logistic regressions.

Variables	Model 1 Odds	Model 2 Odds	Model 3 Odds
Grew up in the same village/town	1.067		1.048
Belongs to caste/community that allows endogamy		1.234**	1.228**
Age	1.031**	1.031**	1.031**
Married	1.134	1.142	1.135
Widowed	0.899	0.916	0.900
Separated/divorced	0.745	0.780	0.757
Class 1–4	1.416**	1.413**	1.413**
Class 5	1.303**	1.302**	1.310**
Class 6–9	1.449**	1.442**	1.448**
Class 10–11	1.430**	1.441**	1.428**
Class 12 and some college	1.229*	1.237*	1.235*
College graduate	0.726*	0.731*	0.741*
Post-graduate	0.434**	0.403**	0.416**
No. of children	1.150**	1.153**	1.151**
No. of assets owned	0.991	0.991	0.991
Household size	0.961**	0.961**	0.962**
Other urban	3.487**	3.414**	3.515**
Developed village	6.234**	6.209**	6.366**
Less developed village	6.760**	6.719**	6.896**
Other Backward Classes	1.111	1.106	1.106
Scheduled Caste/Dalit	1.373**	1.36**8	1.369**
Scheduled Tribe/Adivasi	1.076	1.064	1.060
Muslim	0.707**	0.684**	0.682**
Christian, Sikh, Jain, etc.	0.970	0.999	0.978
Constant	0.002**	0.002**	0.002**
var(_cons[level 3 state of residence])	10.034**	8.953**	8.873**
var(_cons[village/block nested within state])	4.406**	4.328**	4.341**
Sample Size			

Source: India Human Development Survey II (2011–12).
*$p < 0.05$.
**$p < 0.01$.

and close relative marriages are encouraged, young brides may be treated with greater latitude, and their freedom of movement may be taken for granted. These changes do not take place in a single generation but evolve over a long time and become entrenched as a part of gender norms in a community, thus affecting both migrant and non-migrant brides. These results parallel the observations by Alaka Basu in her work on migrants from North India and South India living in New Delhi. She found that in spite of both groups being migrants and both living in the same slum, women from South India (where kinship patterns are governed by endogamy) experienced far greater autonomy than their peers from North India (Basu 1992).

These results also make us reflect on, and explain to some extent, the conflicting results of existing studies on regional differences in women's autonomy in India. For example, we can reconcile to some extent, the divergent findings of Jejeebhoy and Sathar (2001) with those of Rahman and Rao (2004). The former study examines differences in women's autonomy and other aspects of gender empowerment between Uttar Pradesh and Tamil Nadu, and finds large differences; in contrast, the latter study examines the differences in similar outcomes between Uttar Pradesh and Karnataka, and finds relatively small differences. If village exogamy casts an overarching shadow over women's autonomy, the states with a lower degree of exogamy (and a greater degree of endogamy) may be more likely to have outcomes that are more favourable to women. Since only 46% of the women in Karnataka come from communities where endogamy is permitted, as compared to a corresponding figure of 92% in Tamil Nadu, it is not surprising that the contrast between Uttar Pradesh and Tamil Nadu is sharper than that between Uttar Pradesh and Karnataka.

It is also important to note that personal migration status is not totally irrelevant, particularly when we examine participation in wage labour. Non-migrant women are far more likely to be employed than migrant women, even when other factors including village endogamy are held constant. This may be due to differences in the cost and the benefits offered to the extended family by women's economic autonomy, on one hand, and women's physical autonomy and civic participation, on the other. In general, women's participation in the public sphere is seen to reflect negatively on their family's status. In fact, families often gain higher status by restricting women's participation in the external world, or what the noted Indian sociologist Srinivas has called 'women's immurement' and 'Sanskritization' (Srinivas 1977). However, economic autonomy in the form of wage employment also brings benefits to the whole family by increasing household income. Thus, there may be lower restrictions on this type of autonomy than autonomy in women's movement and civic participation. In this case, women's local knowledge and connections may help them in finding work.

While interpreting our results, it is important to recognise that we have focused only on a few indicators of the public behaviours of women. These results say nothing about private behaviours such as women's control over resources within the household, their relationship with their family members, and domestic violence within the household. These behaviours may well be shaped by the kinship system but they are not easily visible to the world, and may contain a greater element of individual heterogeneity than public behaviours which are easily seen and emulated. If some women are free to participate in an SHG, their neighbours can see and emulate these behaviours. In contrast, if some women in a village have a greater say in making decisions regarding household expenditures, others may not easily see these internal household dynamics and hence, emulation in this case may not be nearly as important.

A second limitation of this study is also noteworthy. Although this study uses data from 2011–12, a large proportion of the women in this sample got married in the twentieth century, before the occurrence of massive educational expansion along with tremendous economic growth and the explosion of cable television. As research on developmental idealism (Thornton 2001) and on globalisation (Appadurai 1996) suggests, it is reasonable to expect that these changes may dampen the impact of kinship patterns on women's autonomy. Thus, it is possible that Indian kinship patterns may be undergoing a process of transformation, a fact that has not been captured by our survey data.

Eugene Hammel, in an influential paper titled, Theory of Culture for Demography, noted, 'Without putting too fine a point on it, the use of 'culture' in demography seems mired in structural-functional concepts that are about 40 years old, hardening rapidly, and showing every sign of fossilisation' (Hammel 1990, 456). As the results presented above suggest, concepts of geography as they relate to culture are even more fossilised. This may be particularly true for a Eurocentric theory of acculturation and assimilation where communities to which individuals migrate are seen as static, it is the individuals who must change to accommodate dissonance between their origin and destination communities.

The results in this paper show that communities in the mind (norms about marriage migration in the caste/sub-caste to which the woman's family belongs) are more important than physical (or geographical) communities to which a woman has migrated in relation to certain aspects of women's physical and political autonomy in the public sphere. In contrast, a woman's economic autonomy is a function of both 'imagined' and 'physical' communities. Thus, the opportunities available to women who migrate for marriage are shaped by both geographical communities and more importantly, by the norms in their communities (caste/sub-caste) about marriage migration. Finally, while demographic research has tended to focus on the importance of geography, geography and culture are closely linked and can provide a more nuanced understanding of demographic processes.

Note

1. Education is divided into educational levels that are of relevance to Indian educational system and thereby reflect both non-linearity and threshold effects. The categories used are no education, incomplete primary (class 1–4), primary completed (class 5), incomplete secondary (class 6–9), completed secondary (class 10–11), completed higher secondary and/or some college (class 12+), college graduation and post graduation.

Acknowledgement

The India Human Development Survey fieldwork, data entry and analyses were funded through a variety of sources including the US National Institutes of Health (grant numbers R01HD041455 and R01HD061048), International Development Research Centre, Canada, and the Ford Foundation.

Disclosure statement

No potential conflict of interest was reported by the authors.

Funding

The India Human Development Survey fieldwork, data entry and analyses were funded through a variety of sources including the US National Institutes of Health (grant numbers R01HD041455 and R01HD061048), International Development Research Centre, Canada, and the Ford Foundation.

References

Allendorf, Keera, and Roshan K. Pandian. 2016. "The Decline of Arranged Marriage? Marital Change and Continuity in India." *Population and Development Review* 42 (3): 435–464. doi:10.1111/j.1728-4457.2016.00149.x.

Anderson, Benedict. 1983. *Imagined Communities: Reflections on the Origin and Spread of Nationalism*. New York: Verso.

Andrist, Lester, Manjistha Banerji, and Sonalde Desai. 2013. "Negotiating Marriage: Examining the Gap between Marriage and Cohabitation in India." In *Marrying in South Asia: Shifting Concepts, Changing Practices in a Globalising World*, edited by Ravinder Kaur and Rajni Palriwala, 116–140. New Delhi: Orient Blackswan. Chapter 5.

Appadurai, Arjun. 1996. *Modernity at Large: Cultural Dimensions of Globalization.* Minneapolis: University of Minnesota Press.
Basu, Alaka Malwade. 1992. *Culture, the Status of Women, and Demographic Behavior: Illustrated with the Case of India.* Oxford: Clarendon Press.
Bhattacharya, Prabir C. 2000. "An Analysis of Rural-to-Rural Migration in India." *Journal of International Development* 12 (5): 655–667.
Bittles, Alan H. 1994. "The Role and Significance of Consanguinity as a Demographic Variable." *Population and Development Review* 20 (3): 561–584.
Bloch, Francis, Vijayendra Rao, and Sonale Desai. 2004. "Wedding Celebrations as Conspicuous Consumption: Signaling Social Status in Rural India." *The Journal of Human Resources* 39 (3): 675–695.
Boserup, Ester. 1970. *Women's Role in Economic Development.* New York: St. Martin's Press.
Boyd, Monica, and Elizabeth M. Grieco. 2003. "Women and Migration: Incorporating Gender into International Migration Theory." *Migration Information Source* 1: 1–7.
Chakraborty, Tanika, and Sukkoo Kim. 2010. "Kinship Institutions and Sex Ratios in India." *Demography* 47 (4): 989–1012.
Charsley, Katharine, and Alison Shaw. 2006. "South Asian Transnational Marriages in Comparative Perspective." *Global Networks* 6 (4): 331–344.
Chen, Mengni, and Paul Yip. 2020. "Remarriages and Transnational Marriages in Hong Kong: Implications and Challenges." *Journal of Ethnic and Migration Studies* 46 (14): 3059–3077. doi:10.1080/1369183X.2019.1585026.
Chiu, Tuen Yi, and Susanne Y.P. Choi. 2020. "The Decoupling of Legal and Spatial Migration of Female Marriage Migrants." *Journal of Ethnic and Migration Studies* 46 (14): 2997–3013. doi:10.1080/1369183X.2019.1585018.
Chowdhry, Prem. 1993. "Persistence of a Custom: Cultural Centrality of Ghunghat." *Social Scientist* 21 (9/11): 91–112.
Das Gupta, Monica. 2010. "Family Systems, Political Systems and Asia's 'Missing Girls': The Construction of Son Preference and Its Unravelling." *Asian Population Studies* 6 (2): 123–152.
Desai, Sonalde. 2013. "Women in Workforce: Burden of Success, Decline in Participation." *Yojana* 57: 56–59.
Desai, Sonalde, and Lester Andrist. 2010. "Gender Scripts and Age at Marriage in India." *Demography* 47 (3): 667–687.
Desai, Sonalde, and Manjistha Banerji. 2008. "Negotiated Identities: Impact of Male Migration on Women." *Journal of Population Research* 25 (3): 337–355.
Desai, Sonalde, Amaresh Dubey, B. L. Joshi, Mitali Sen, Abusaleh Shariff, and Reeve Vanneman. 2010. *Human Development in India: Challenges for a Society in Transition.* New Delhi: Oxford University Press.
Desai, Sonalde, and Gheda Temsah. 2014. "Muslim and Hindu Women's Public and Private Behaviors: Gender, Family and Communalized Politics in India." *Demography* 51 (6): 2307–2332.
Dyson, Tim, and Mick Moore. 1983. "On Kinship Structure, Female Autonomy, and Demographic Behavior in India." *Population and Development Review* 9 (1): 35–60.
Fulford, Scott L. 2013. "Marriage Migration in India." *Boston College Working Paper 820.* Boston College Economics Department.
Grasmuck, Sherri, and Patricia R. Pessar. 1991. *Between Two Islands: Dominican International Migration.* Berkeley and Los Angeles, CA: University of California Press.
Grover, Shalini. 2017. *Marriage, Love, Caste and Kinship Support.* New Delhi: Routledge.
Gulati, Leela. 1993. *In the Absence of their Men: The Impact of Male Migration on Women.* New Delhi: Sage Publications.
Hamid, S., R. Stephenson, and B. Rubenson. 2011. "Marriage Decision Making, Spousal Communication, and Reproductive Health among Married Youth in Pakistan." *Global Health Action* 4 (1): 5079.
Hammel, E. A. 1990. "A Theory of Culture for Demography." *Population and Development Review* 16 (3): 455–485.

Hashemi, Syed M., Sidney Ruth Schuler, and Ann P. Riley. 1996. "Rural Credit Programs and Women's Empowerment in Bangladesh." *World Development* 24 (4): 635–653.

Heaton, Tim B., Mark Cammack, and Larry Young. 2001. "Why is the Divorce Rate Declining in Indonesia?" *Journal of Marriage and Family* 63 (2): 480–490.

Hugo, Graeme. 2000. "Migration and Women's Empowerment." In *Women's Empowerment and Demographic Processes: Moving Beyond Cairo*, edited by Harriet Presser, and Gita Sen, 287–317. New York: Oxford University Press.

Jejeebhoy, Shireen J. 2000. "Women's Autonomy in Rural India: Its Dimensions, Determinants, and the Influence of Context." In *Women's Empowerment and Demographic Processes: Moving Beyond Cairo*, edited by Harriet Presser and Gita Sen, 204–238. New York: Oxford University Press. Chapter 9.

Jejeebhoy, Shireen J., K. G. Santhya, Rajib Acharya, and Ravi Prakash. 2013. "Marriage-related Decision-Making and Young Women's Marital Relations and Agency: Evidence from India." *Asian Population Studies* 9 (1): 28–49.

Jejeebhoy, Shireen J., and A. Zeba Sathar. 2001. "Women's Autonomy in India and Pakistan: The Influence of Religion and Region." *Population and Development Review* 27 (4): 687–712.

Karve, Irawati Karmarkar. 1965. *Kinship Organisation in India*. Bombay: Asia Publishing House.

Kibria, Nazli. 1993. *Family Tightrope: The Changing Lives of Vietnamese Americans*. Princeton, NJ: Princeton University Press.

Koenig, Michael A., Saifuddin Ahmed, Mian B. Hossain, and A. K. A. Mozumder. 2003. "Women's Status and Domestic Violence in Rural Bangladesh: Individual-and Community-Level Effects." *Demography* 40 (2): 269–288.

Kojima, Yu. 2001. "In the Business of Cultural Reproduction." *Women's Studies International Forum* 24 (2): 199–210.

Li, Chun-Hao, and Wen-Shan Yang. 2020. "Happiness of Female Immigrants in Cross-Border Marriages in Taiwan." *Journal of Ethnic and Migration Studies* 46 (14): 2956–2976. doi:10.1080/1369183X.2019.1585015.

Lu, Melody C-W. 2005. "Commercially Arranged Marriage Migration." *Indian Journal of Gender Studies* 12 (2-3): 275–303.

Luke, Nancy, and Kaivan Munshi. 2011. "Women as Agents of Change: Female Income and Mobility in India." *Journal of Development Economics* 94 (1): 1–17.

Malhotra, Anju, Sydney Ruth Schuler, and Carol Boender. 2002. "Measuring Women's Empowerment as a Variable in International Development." Background paper prepared for the World Bank workshop in Poverty and Gender: New Perspectives. Washington, DC.

Mason, Karen O. 1995. *Gender and Demographic Change: What do We Know?* Liege: International Union for Scientific Study of Population.

Menjívar, Cecilia. 1999. "The Intersection of Work and Gender" *American Behavioral Scientist* 42: 601–627.

Menjivar, Cecilia, and Victor Agadjanian. 2007. "Men's Migration and Women's Lives: Views from Rural Armenia and Guatemala." *Social Science Quarterly* 88 (5): 1243–1262.

Mu, Zheng, and Wei-Jun Jean Yeung. 2020. "Internal Migration, Marriage Timing and Assortative Mating: A Mixed-Method Study in China." *Journal of Ethnic and Migration Studies* 46 (14): 2914–2936. doi:10.1080/1369183X.2019.1585009.

Narayan, Deepa, ed. 2006. *Measuring Empowerment: Cross-Disciplinary Perspectives*. New Delhi: Oxford University Press.

Niraula, Bhanu B., and S. Philip Morgan. 1996. "Marriage Formation, Post-Marital Contact with Natal Kin and Autonomy of Women: Evidence from Two Nepali Settings." *Population Studies* 50 (1): 35–50.

Oberoi, Patricia. 1998. *Family, Kinship and Marriage in India*. Delhi: Oxford India.

Pahl, Ray. 2005. "Are All Communities Communities in the Mind?" *The Sociological Review* 53 (4): 621–640.

Parrado, Emilio A., and Chenoa Flippen. 2005. "Migration and Gender among Mexican Women." *American Sociological Review* 70 (4): 606–632.

Pedraza, Silvia. 1991. "Women and Migration: The Social Consequences of Gender." *Annual Review of Sociology* 17: 303–325.

Pimentel, Ellen E. 2000. "Just How do I Love Thee?: Marital Relations in Urban China." *Journal of Marriage and Family* 62 (1): 32–47.

Portes, Alejandro. 1997. "Immigration Theory for a New Century: Some Problems and Opportunities." *International Migration Review* 31 (4): 799–825.

Premi, Mahendra K. 1980. "Aspects of Female Migration in India." *Economic and Political Weekly* XV (15): 714–720.

Presser, Harriet B., and Gita Sen. 2000. *Women's Empowerment and Demographic Processes: Moving Beyond Cairo*. New York: Oxford University Press.

Raheja, Gloria Goodwin, and Ann Grodzins Gold. 1994. *Listen to the Heron's Words: Reimagining Gender and Kinship in North India*. Berkeley: University of California Press.

Rahman, Lupin, and Vijayendra Rao. 2004. "The Determinants of Gender Equity in India: Examining Dyson and Moore's Thesis with New Data." *Population & Development Review* 30 (2): 239–268.

Rammohan, Anu, and Meliyanni Johar. 2009. "The Determinants of Married Women's Autonomy in Indonesia." *Feminist Economics* 15 (4): 31–55.

Rao, Smriti, and Kade Finnoff. 2015. "Marriage Migration and Inequality in India, 1983–2008." *Population and Development Review* 41 (3): 485–505. doi:10.1111/j.1728-4457.2015.00069.x.

Rosenzweig, Mark R., and Oded Stark. 1989. "Consumption Smoothing, Migration, and Marriage: Evidence from Rural India." *Journal of Political Economy* 97 (4): 905–926.

Sanyal, Paromita. 2014. *Credit to Capabilities: A Sociological Study of Microcredit Groups in India*. New York: Cambridge University Press.

Sharma, Ursula. 1980. *Women, Work and Property in North-West India*. New York: Tavistock.

Srinivas, M. N. 1977. "The Changing Position of Indian Women." *Man* 12 (2): 221–238.

Srinivas, M. N. 1996. *Caste: Its Twentieth Century Avatar*. New Delhi: Penguin Books.

Thornton, Arland. 2001. "The Developmental Paradigm, Reading History Sideways, and Family Change." *Demography* 38 (4): 449–465. doi:10.2307/3088311.

United Nations Educational, Scientific and Cultural Organization (UNESCO). 2013. *Social Inclusion of Internal Migrants in India*. Paris: UNESCO. http://unesdoc.unesco.org/images/0022/002237/223702e.pdf.

Wang, Hong-zen, and Shu-ming Chang. 2002. "The Commodification of International Marriages: Cross-Border Marriage Business in Taiwan and Viet Nam." *International Migration* 40 (6): 93–116.

Xu, Xiaohe, and Martin K. Whyte. 1990. "Love Matches and Arranged Marriages: A Chinese Replication." *Journal of Marriage and the Family* 52: 709–722.

Yeung, Jean Wei-Jun, and Zheng Mu. 2019. "Migration and Marriage in Asian Contexts."

Zhou, Min. 1992. *Chinatown*. Philadelphia, PA: Temple University Press.

The decoupling of legal and spatial migration of female marriage migrants

Tuen Yi Chiu and Susanne Y. P. Choi

ABSTRACT
The literature on cross-border marriages between women from the global south and men from the global north largely assumes patrilocality as a direct result of hypergamous marriage migration. There has been little research into the experiences of brides who relocate to their husband's country to fulfil the roles of wife and mother but are not given citizenship rights or brides who do not relocate even after obtaining residency or citizenship in their husband's country. Inconsistencies between the legal and residential status of foreign wives suggest that researchers should *decouple legal and spatial migration*. Using ethnographic data from Mainland China–Hong Kong cross-border couples, this article examines the causes and consequences of two forms of decoupling: (1) wife migrates spatially before her legal status changes and (2) wife's change in legal status is not accompanied by spatial migration. We argue that these two forms of decoupling have their origins in state policies, economic constraints and personal choices, and that their impact on the intimate and household dynamics of cross-border families is gendered. Unravelling these complex dynamics sheds light on the intricate relationships between gender, marriage, migration and the state, and highlights the increasingly heterogeneous circumstances of cross-border couples.

Introduction

The rapid expansion of globalisation and transnationalism has made cross-border marriage migration a pervasive phenomenon. Although previous research has examined how marriage migration empowers or disempowers women, most studies have focused on the spatial dimension (spatial hypergamy, immigration and relocation), the legal dimension (immigration and citizenship laws) or their intersection, and assumed that marriage migrants undergo legal and spatial migration simultaneously. Few have looked at cases where marriage migrants' legal and spatial migration do not coincide, as in the Mainland China–Hong Kong case that this paper addresses. The assumption that spatial and legal migration go hand in hand may be, on the one hand, obscuring recognition of complex policies that are intended to decouple marriage migrants' legal and spatial migration for the benefit of the state and, on the other, under-representing foreign wives' patriarchal bargain or resistance to patrilocal norms in the context of cross-border marriages. In this article we propose a conceptual framework that decouples marriage migrants' legal and spatial migration in order to capture the nuances and paradoxes that exist in the broader category of cross-border marriage migration. We argue that it is not only legal migration or spatial migration *per se* but more importantly the inconsistency between them that underscores the gendered power geometry of marriage migration. We show that a framework in which legal and spatial migration are decoupled offers a way of untangling the intricate nexus of relations between gender, power and space, as it illuminates the conditions under which marriage migration may bring about new forms of agency and empowerment or disempower women in cross-border marriages.

Marriages between Mainland Chinese women and Hong Kong men serve as an interesting case. Cross-border marriages between Hong Kong men and Mainland Chinese women are comparable to cross-border marriages in other countries at the structural level, but not at the interpersonal level. Owing to the border system and socio-economic disparity between Mainland China and Hong Kong, cross-border marriages between the two places have largely followed the mainstream gendered pattern of global hypergamy (Constable 2004) – a pattern in which women from less developed countries marry men from more developed countries in the hope of finding a more modern and comfortable life. However, unlike the often-studied case of "commodified" international marriages that are meditated by profit-oriented marriage brokers such as commercial matchmaking agencies and purpose-specific tour companies (see for example Constable 2009; Lu 2005), cross-border marriages between Mainland Chinese women and Hong Kong men seldom involve the mediation of commercial matchmaking; instead, most couples meet via personal networks and social gatherings. Although some cross-border marriages are facilitated by non-institutionalized intermediaries, such as individual entrepreneur matchmakers and international kinship networks, the involvement of monetary transactions in the form of fixed fees or *hongbao* (red packets with cash as a thank-you gift) payable to the matchmaker after the successful match still renders these marriages similar to commercially arranged marriages (Lu 2005). The conceptualised distinctions of commercially arranged vis-a-vis non-commercially arranged cross-border marriages do not rely solely on the monetary transaction involved but more on hasty matchmaking arrangements which leave very limited time for the prospective partners to "cultivate emotions and engage in meaningful communication" (Kim 2015, 36) before deciding on the marriage. Although the instrumental motivations behind the commercially arranged union formation do not exclude the possibility of developing emotional and intimate bonding between the spouses after marriage, the lack of courtship prior to marriage and the relatively passive role of women in the selection process reinforce the women's subordinate position in both conjugal and inter-generational relations (Lu 2005), and adds uncertainty to the quality and stability of the marriage (Choi, Kim, and Ryu 2020). Without such commercialised matchmaking operations, women who meet their husbands in a more natural courtship setting (such as at workplace or in social gatherings) may have relatively more autonomy and power in spousal dynamics, which may in turn give them more space and agency to resist patriarchal marital norms, including the norm of patrilocality.

Secondly and relatedly, previous research has typically focused on one cross-border marriage migration scenario, that where foreign brides follow a patrilocality norm – a patriarchal pattern in which, after marriage, the wife moves into her husband's home or community (Palriwala and Uberoi 2005) – and stays in his place of residence. Underlying this prototype of marriage migration is the assumption that female marriage migrants will undergo geographical movement (which we refer to as *spatial migration*) and a change of legal status (which we refer to as *legal migration*) when they marry a foreign man. As the system of cross-border marriage migration is underpinned by patriarchal logic female marriage migrants are typically considered vulnerable victims in the immigration context. However, the case of Mainland China and Hong Kong presents two alternatives to the typical cross-border marriage migration scenario. The first involves Mainland wives who use two-way permits (TWPs) to relocate and settle in Hong Kong (most of them reside in Hong Kong more than 300 days per year) in order to take care of their husband and children before they obtain Hong Kong residency, i.e. they undergo *spatial migration before legal migration*. The second involves Mainland Chinese wives who do not follow patrilocality norms and instead remain in Mainland China even after obtaining Hong Kong residency, i.e. they undergo *legal migration without spatial migration*. These two scenarios have important implications for our understanding of cross-border marriage migration, as they demonstrate that previous research has not adequately considered the heterogeneity of marriage migration and the possibilities that, first, government policies might act as barriers to female marriage migrants' simultaneous legal and spatial migration, thus inevitably reinforcing the patriarchal system of marriage migration and further disempowering female marriage migrants (alternative one above); and second, that some female marriage migrants might find advantage of making patriarchal bargains or even rebel against the patriarchal system by remaining in their original place of residence after marrying a foreign man (alternative two above).

We define *legal migration* as a change in legal status and *spatial migration* as the physical act of moving from one place to another. Our framework aligns with Williams's (2010, 5) observation that "cross-border marriage migrants may not physically move as a direct result of their marriage." It also builds on Massey's (1994) work on the power geometry of spatial movements in which she suggested (149) that "some initiate flows and movement, others don't; some are more on the receiving end of it than others". The differentiated mobility and the differences in the degree of control over mobility among different social groups both reflect and reinforce power structures. What really empowers people is not merely access to mobility but control over mobility; some may be "doing a lot of physical moving" yet not be "in charge" of the process, in fact they "are effectively imprisoned by it" (Massey 1994, 149). On this reading the first form of decoupling, i.e. *spatial migration before legal migration*, is illustrative of a similar paradoxical relationship between mobility and power. This decoupling happens when the husband's government facilitates the spatial movement of his foreign wife to enable her to perform her wifely and motherly duties in his country, but withholds or delays access to residency and citizenship, making her legally vulnerable. Previous studies have suggested that the state has continued to systematically subordinate immigrant women by enforcing a dependent visa status on trailing spouses and marriage migrants, and by limiting their right to work after immigration, which in effect has introduced "elements of forced dependency into [their] marital relationships" (Balgamwalla 2014, 29; Kofman 1999). In the same vein, through interrogating the regularisation of the first form of decoupling by the state, this article highlights the influence of restrictive migration and citizenship policies on the intimate and household dynamics of cross-border marriages, and the particular legal and social precariousness to which foreign brides are subject. Furthermore, our framework extends the inquiry into the intersection of power and mobility by capturing other paradoxes within the realm of marriage migration. We examine the second form of decoupling, i.e. *legal migration without spatial migration*, to show how, in contrast, some women may bargain for autonomy whilst declining to migrate spatially and how some deliberately refuse to embark on a spatial migration journey in order to gain power within the marriage. Although the two forms of decoupling may not necessarily be new patterns of movements, this article contributes to the literature by revealing the ways in which the decoupling of legal and spatial migration is regularised by the state and the effects that that regularisation has on the power and agency of female marriage migrants. The context of Mainland China–Hong Kong marriage migration offers a unique opportunity to examine these two forms of decoupling as they exist side by side, which helps clarify under what conditions women are empowered or disempowered by legal and/or spatial migration, or the decoupling of them.

If, as some earlier studies on the legality and citizenship rights of foreign brides have shown, legal migration is one of the keys to the empowerment of foreign brides, state policies that allow foreign brides to migrate spatially without giving them legal rights are repressive in that they mobilise migrant wives' unpaid reproductive labour whilst minimising the host state's responsibility towards them. If, on the other hand, as other studies have suggested, patrilocality is a major contributor to the gendered vulnerability of female marriage migrants, migrating legally but not spatially may allow foreign wives to avoid the social isolation that marriage migrants often face. By staying in their place of origin, female marriage migrants may maintain their social support network and continue to benefit from their knowledge of local systems, which may enhance their psychological well-being (Li and Yang 2020). For instance, Newendorp (2008) observed that Mainland wives who used to live separately from their Hong Kong husband on the Mainland exhibited a stronger sense of independence, which, on the one hand, made their adjustment to post-reunion family life in Hong Kong more difficult (especially when they have to co-reside with their in-laws), but on the other hand, also empowered them to make decisions to leave and return to their hometown should problems, such as wife abuse, arise when they visited Hong Kong. This is especially the case when the marriage migrants have acquired the legal right to "freely" cross the border. It is possible, nevertheless, that both forms of decoupling curtail female marriage migrants' access to social security services in their place of residence. In summary, examination of the decoupling of legal and spatial migration not only challenges the general assumption that patrilocality is a necessary consequence of a woman's marriage to a man from a more affluent country, it also opens up space to investigate new strategies of state governmentality for managing marriage migration and women's strategies for gendered resistance against patriarchal marriage migration arrangements. Our decoupling framework is intended to reveal the nuances of the "gendered geographies of power" (Mahler and Pessar 2001) in marriage migration.

Gendered power in marriage migration

Extensive research has demonstrated that cross-border marriage migration is a highly gendered phenomenon, not only because most marriage migrants are women, but also because cross-border marriage mobility follows a patriarchal logic. First, most cross-border marriages involve women from less developed countries in the global south marrying men from more developed countries in the global north, thus constituting a kind of "global hypergamy" (Constable 2004, 10). Under the patriarchal norms of hypergamy, a marriage gradient exists such that women are expected to 'marry up', i.e. to marry men who are older, better educated and earn more (West and Zimmerman 1987). It has been shown, however, that men marrying foreign brides tend to have fewer socio-economic resources and lower occupational status than their male national peers (Choi, Cheung, and Cheung 2012; Davin 2007), but the logic of hypergamy pairs these men with women who have even lower socio-economic status, at least in global terms. This lays the foundations for gender inequality between a husband and his foreign wife and sometimes contributes to foreign wives' vulnerability to abuse (Chiu 2017).

Second, some feminists contend that marriage rules inherent in the patriarchal kinship system, such as patrilocal residence, have adverse effects on female marriage migrants' autonomy, bargaining power and status in the marriage and in the family as a whole (Palriwala and Uberoi 2005). Unlike migrants in chain migration who can usually turn to their co-ethnics for various forms of support (Hagan 1998), marriage migrants usually migrate alone and tend to live and interact mainly with their husband's family (Chatterjee and Desai 2020). Social isolation, together with language barriers and discrimination, may deprive the bride of her agency and compel her to obey her husband and in-laws (Constable 2004; Menjívar and Salcido 2002).

Third, to relocate to the husband's place of residence, female marriage migrants have to navigate the host country's immigration system, which usually includes a restrictive spousal sponsorship and authenticity scheme (Friedman 2015). This gives husbands authority over their foreign wives, putting female marriage migrants at a disadvantage because they have to depend on their husband for their legal right to remain in the host country and their route to permanent residency (Coté, Kérisit, and Coté 2001). Government policies that restrict female marriage migrants' access to public welfare and services further exacerbate their social and economic disadvantages (Chiu 2017). These institutional measures and the various spousal citizenship regimes signify an "extension of state sovereignty" to foreign wives via their husband (Jongwilaiwan and Thompson 2013, 372), which contributes to the unequal power relations between foreign wives and their husbands.

Although the above mentioned research has drawn attention to how patriarchy intersects with marriage migration to disempower female marriage migrants legally, socially and economically, researchers have also acknowledged female marriage migrants' agency and the bargains they are able to make within the framework of patriarchal marriage migration. In particular, scholars have highlighted the agency of women who seek cross-border marriage in order to escape or transform local patriarchal constraints, attain upward geographic and social mobility, and improve the economic opportunities available to them and their family back home (Constable 2004; Palriwala and Uberoi 2005; Piper and Roces 2003; Robinson 2007). Some of these women find themselves in a paradoxical situation: they have 'married up' by marrying a man from a more developed country, yet 'married down' in the sense that he occupies the bottom stratum of his society (Freeman 2004). Nevertheless, the "patriarchal bargain" these women make illustrates their agency exercised within limits of the patriarchal system of marriage migration

(Chaudhuri, Morash, and Yingling 2014). In the few cases in which men migrate to join their wives overseas, norms of patrilocality and male dominance may be reconfigured (Charsley 2005; Friedman 2017; Gallo 2006).

Research site

Hong Kong's immigration policies are tightly linked to its political history. Hong Kong was a British colony for more than 150 years but was reunified with Mainland China in 1997. Under the 'one country, two systems' policy Hong Kong and Mainland China are separated by two physical borders and laws restrict the movement of people, goods and capital between the two regions. A quota system was introduced in 1950 to tackle the massive influx of immigrants from Mainland China. Since the 1980s Hong Kong has suffered a 'marriage squeeze' which has encouraged single men in Hong Kong to look for a spouse in Mainland China (Choi and Cheung 2016). The Mainland spouses of Hong Kong residents are not, however, granted residency immediately after their marriage. Instead, the immigration of Mainland spouses and dependent children is governed by the one-way permit (OWP) scheme, which set a daily limit of 150 on the number of mainland residents who can immigrate to Hong Kong. Under the quota system Mainland brides have to wait between four to ten years to obtain Hong Kong residency. Once a Mainland bride has obtained residency she needs to reside continuously in Hong Kong for seven years before becoming eligible for permanent residency. Mainland wives who have yet to obtain a OWP are allowed to visit Hong Kong using a renewable TWP, which enables them to stay in Hong Kong to perform their duties as wives and mothers, but as non-residents with no access to welfare benefits enjoyed by residents and citizens. This policy has created a group of marriage migrants who migrated spatially to their husband's region before they were legally entitled to settle there (spatial migration before legal migration).

Despite the restrictions on spatial migration, the geographical proximity of Hong Kong and Mainland China and the combination of persistent economic disparity[1] and increased economic and social interaction between the two regions, have resulted in a rapid rise in the number of Mainland China–Hong Kong cross-border marriages. Since 2013 almost 40% of all marriages registered in Hong Kong have involved a Hong Kong man marrying a Mainland Chinese woman (Hong Kong Census and Statistics Department 2018). The number of Hong Kong citizens residing in south China is also significant – in 2008 49.2% of Hong Kong people residing in Shenzhen, a city just north of Hong Kong, had a Mainland spouse (HKSAR Government Planning Department and Shenzhen Statistics Bureau 2008). The geographical proximity of Hong Kong and south China means that couples in cross-border marriages have unusual flexibility when it comes to negotiating post-marital residence arrangements. In most international marriages the distance between the countries of the bride and the groom tends to limit the options for post-marital residence, but south China and Hong Kong are separated by only a few kilometres. This reduces the time and cost of commuting between the two, making frequent border crossings more feasible and a split family arrangement potentially less destructive of family life. Thus the patrilocality norm for cross-border marriages involving spouses from the global north and south is subject to subtle yet substantial pressure. This has given rise to cases in which the legal migration of a Mainland wife to Hong Kong is not followed by spatial migration; she may remain resident in Mainland China and the couple may create a split family, or her husband may move to reside with her in south China.

Research methods

The data for this study were collected between 2013 and 2016 as part of a larger project that involved interviewing 50 women in Mainland China and Hong Kong cross-border marriages, 10 Hong Kong men who had married a Mainland Chinese wife, and 5 staff working in non-governmental organisations (NGOs) providing services to cross-border families. Only six of the 50 female respondents had experienced simultaneous legal and spatial migration, 22 had migrated to Hong Kong before they obtained Hong Kong residency (the first form of decoupling) and 12 had migrated legally but not spatially i.e. they had not settled in Hong Kong after obtaining Hong Kong residency (the second form of decoupling). In 7 of these 12 cases the husband had moved to Mainland China and the remaining 5 involved split families. In all five cases involving a split household the wife had remained in south China and her husband resided in Hong Kong but visited south China regularly at weekends for family reunions. Among the remaining 10 female respondents, three lived in Shenzhen and held TWPs while waiting for OWPs, two had chosen not to undergo legal and spatial migration[2] and five were ineligible to do so because they are cohabiters. This article deals with the reasons for, and impact of, the decoupling of legal and spatial migration, so we focus on the experiences of the 34 decoupled respondents, whilst drawing on the experiences of other respondents as a reference point.

Respondents were recruited through NGOs providing services to Mainland Chinese female marriage migrants. The spouses of respondents were invited for interview separately to collect couple data. All interviews were based on a semi-structured interview protocol and lasted between one and two hours. Questions around the union formation, post-marital residence decision-making, everyday family life, immigration experiences, future plans, and marital and life satisfaction were asked. No data revealed the involvement of commercial matchmaking agencies, which is in line with the observations of previous studies (e.g. Chiu 2017; Newendorp 2008; Pong et al. 2014). Data from NGO staff and social workers also confirmed this observation. Participant observation was conducted intermittently between 2013 and 2016 in the NGOs and in cross-border families in Shenzhen and Hong Kong. Pseudonyms are used throughout the article to protect the privacy of respondents. The research was approved by the research ethics committee of the second author's institution.

The majority of the respondents came from a similar socio-economic background. Most of the female respondents were full-time housewives, although three were working full-time and seven part-time. Their educational level ranged from junior to senior high school. All but nine of the Hong Kong husbands worked as blue-collar or skilled workers. Respondents' monthly family income ranged from HK$2,000 to HK$30,000 (US$256 – US$3846); the modal range was HK$10,000 – $20,000 (US$1282 – $2564). Almost all the families had one or two children at kindergartens or primary school. Male spouses were on average 12.8 years older than their wives. The profile of our respondents is broadly similar to the profile of the population of female marriage migrants in Hong Kong (Choi and Cheung 2016), which suggests that cross-border marriages between Hong Kong men and Mainland Chinese women are largely hypergamous in nature (Chen and Yip 2020). The socio-economic background of female respondents was similar in terms of employment status and number of children regardless of whether they had experienced migration decoupling or not and regardless of the form of decoupling.

Spatial migration before legal migration

Forty-four percent of the Mainland Chinese wives we interviewed had migrated spatially before they migrated legally. The main reason for this decoupling was that they wanted to give birth to their children in Hong Kong so that their children would have the right of abode (equivalent to citizenship rights) in Hong Kong and be able to take advantage of Hong Kong's superior educational opportunities. Their decision was also motivated by the desire to be physically present to care for their family and children, as Sze explained:

> My kid is attending a Hong Kong school, I need to stay here and take care of him every day … There are things that my husband could not do. If there isn't a woman at home, the home does not look like a home (*jia bu xiang jia*)! (*Sze, aged 42, a housewife with a child aged 8, a TWP holder who moved to Hong Kong in 2012*).

Previous studies have suggested that female marriage migrants with residency status encounter a series of challenges, including assimilation problems related to language barriers, difficulty adapting to regional differences in customs and living environments, ignorance of local educational and legal systems, lack of recognition of their educational and occupational qualifications and social discrimination (Erez, Adelman, and Gregory 2009). Female marriage migrants who migrate spatially before they migrate legally face similar challenges but encounter additional difficulties as a result of their peculiar and precarious legal situation and even greater social marginalisation.

The state has relaxed the restrictions on their spatial movements without providing any resources to support their life in Hong Kong and facilitate their assimilation into Hong Kong society. Officially, Mainland wives who live in Hong Kong using a TWP are visitors and therefore not entitled to state-funded medical care, education and training, public housing, assistance payments and other social welfare benefits provided by the Hong Kong government. Lacking these rights, these women encounter obstacles to social integration and cultural assimilation into Hong Kong society over and above those faced by migrants with legal residency. Jin's experience is a case in point:

> After coming here [Hong Kong], I wanted to learn and upgrade my skills. But I found that no matter what I wanted to do in Hong Kong, I needed to have a Hong Kong identity card [residency], even to access to some career training [courses sponsored by the government] … Living in Hong Kong [without residency] made me feel like a disabled person, I felt so useless. (*Jin, aged 28, university graduate, a TWP holder who had lived in Hong Kong since 2012*)

Not having access to the same rights and benefits as residents has compelled some female marriage migrants to go back to Mainland China for medical care because they could not afford the high costs charged to non-residents. Sze revealed:

> One time, I felt really sick and called 999 [the public emergency number] but they refused to help because I didn't have a Hong Kong identity card. Each medical consultation cost HK$570 (around US$72 for not residents). How was I supposed to afford that? [I] went to

see doctors in Shenzhen as it was cheaper there. (*Sze, aged 42, a housewife with a child aged 8, a TWP holder who moved to Hong Kong in 2012*)

Jin and Sze's experiences illustrate the way in which lack of a residency renders female marriage migrants living in Hong Kong under a TWP semi-objects of the state. They are subject to Hong Kong laws, but are denied access to many services and benefits provided by the state. Most importantly, as 'visitors' they cannot work legally, which makes them financially dependent on their husbands. When these husbands struggle to support the family and experience high financial stress some blame their Mainland wives for being economically unproductive and having imposed an additional burden on an already tight family budget by migrating spatially to Hong Kong. This puts a strain on the marriage and in some instances leads directly to marital conflict.

Migrating spatially before migrating legally also makes it more difficult for female marriage migrants to care for their children. A marriage migrant living in Hong Kong using a TWP has to return to China quarterly or annually to renew her permit. The renewal procedure typically takes two to three weeks to complete and sometimes may take longer. As well as costing them time and money, the permit renewal process conflicted with these marriage migrants' caregiver role. When a female marriage migrant is waiting for her TWP to be renewed she cannot cross the border, even in an emergency. Unless they could find someone trustworthy to take care of their children they had to take their children with them when they travelled to China to renew their TWP; however this would disrupt their children's schooling and thus affect their academic performance. Most of our respondents had little childcare support in Hong Kong, because their natal family had remained in Mainland China. Although Hong Kong in-laws provided care in a few cases this could cause conflict over parenting style.

In summary, the effect of the decoupling of spatial and legal migration on female marriage migrants' ability to parent their children is two-edged. Although decoupling has made it easier for them to care for their family and children, it also forces them to constantly organise their personal and family lives around restrictive government migration and border regulations. Given the low fertility rate in Hong Kong, the government has in recent years recognised that new arrivals from the Mainland – most of them are children with a Mainland mother and a Hong Kong father – are a major source of population growth for Hong Kong (Legislative Council Secretariat 2015). As the primary caregivers of many of these children, Mainland wives' reproductive labour is recognised as a contribution to society; yet they have remained semi-subjects of the state. As a result, when spatial migration precedes legal migration there is an extended period in which the Mainland spouse often feels trapped in a paradoxical situation that resembles Sassen's (2003) description of a form of exclusion in which migrants are "unauthorised [as full legal resident] yet recognised".

Legal migration without spatial migration

The three major factors responsible for the second form of decoupling, legal migration without spatial migration, are the structural constraints that limit cross-border families' ability to reunite and settle in Hong Kong, personal preference for a familiar lifestyle and fear of facing discrimination in Hong Kong.

The couple's inability to afford the housing for an expanded family may deter female marriage migrants from settling in Hong Kong even after obtaining Hong Kong residency. Census data indicate that Hong Kong men who marry Mainland Chinese women tend to come from the lower strata of the social hierarchy (Choi and Cheung 2016). The high price of accommodation in Hong Kong and the long waiting time for public rental accommodation mean that many of these men have difficulty providing adequate accommodation for their Mainland spouse and children should they join him and settle in Hong Kong. Because housing and living costs are considerably lower in south China than in Hong Kong some cross-border couples had opted to reside on the Mainland, with the husband moving to south China, or had split the household to create a 'weekend family', with the husband living in Hong Kong with his parents on weekdays and joining his wife and children in south China at weekends. Another factor which may push the couple into deciding not to live in Hong Kong is the husband's workplace being in south China; in such cases the husband may decide to live in Mainland China after marriage.

These structural and family barriers can mean that the hopes of Mainland wives who wanted to improve their status and living conditions by marrying a Hong Kong man are dashed. Some of our respondents felt confused about their identity and had difficulties in developing a sense of belonging to Hong Kong society. They were perplexed to find themselves still living in Mainland China despite their husband, children and themselves being legal Hong Kong residents or citizens. The disconnect between the reality of their everyday life (living in south China) and their legal status (a Hong Kong resident) had left them feeling trapped in a kind of limbo (Levitt and Schiller 2004), marginalised by the governments on both sides of the border. Mrs. Xia explained how she felt:

> Neither the Hong Kong government nor the Mainland Chinese government helps us. We are literally marginalised people ... [Because I still live in south China] I don't get the welfare benefits to which a resident of Hong Kong is entitled. Hong Kong people think that I am a Mainlander because my family resides in south China. But Mainlanders don't treat me as a Mainlander either, because I have obtained Hong Kong residency [this entails giving up household registration (*hukou*) in China]. They think that I have come back to the Mainland to take their resources. If we wanted to purchase a house in China, we would have to pay heavier taxes than a couple with a Mainland household registration and go through a lot of procedures and restrictions because legally we are not citizens of Mainland China. (*Mrs. Xia, aged 40, married with a child aged 8, obtained Hong Kong residency but remained in Shenzhen*)

Female marriage migrants' perception that they were doubly marginalised and rejected might eventually lead to resentment about having married a Hong Kong man. Mrs. Xia continued:

> If I had known earlier ... what it would be like to not really be a person on either side [of the border], not a Hong Konger, not a Mainlander ... If I had known earlier about the embarrassment, I would not have chosen to marry a Hong Kong man.

However, not all female marriage migrants who remained in China after obtaining Hong Kong residency were compelled to do so by external factors. Other reasons why the wife's legal migration might not be accompanied by spatial migration included the lifestyle preferences of the couple, the wife's fear of adaptation difficulties and discrimination and a desire to avoid the conflict that would result from sharing a residence with in-laws in Hong Kong. In other words, the patrilocality norm notwithstanding, decisions about post-marital residence were influenced by a range of pragmatic concerns related to the couple's socio-economic circumstances and personal preferences. In particular, although in some cases the decoupling of legal and spatial migration was due to the family's unfavourable circumstances, other couples deliberately used decoupling to maximise family wellbeing by compartmentalising individual family members' work, family and leisure lives. Some men in cross-border marriages had been working in Mainland China for a considerable time when they married and had got used to the leisurely and carefree lifestyle there. They therefore preferred to continue living in Shenzhen even after helping their Mainland Chinese wife obtain Hong Kong residency and arranging for their children to attend schools in Hong Kong.

The Mainland Chinese wife's preference was also an important factor, as Mrs. Liang explained:

> Living in Hong Kong is stressful. Whatever you do, you feel as if you are a new immigrant ... Sometimes our conversations became excited, we got loud and people at another table would complain. Then I realised that speaking loudly might bother other people. I am used to living here [south China] and talking loudly. It does not seem strange to people here. People in Hong Kong found it unacceptable and would think that you were weird and discriminate against you by saying 'Mainlanders are like this.' (*Mrs. Liang, aged 33, married with one child aged 7, resident in Shenzhen for more than 8 years after obtaining Hong Kong residency*)

Alongside their familiarity with south China, perceived discrimination against new immigrants in Hong Kong was another important factor in some Mainland wives' reluctance to move to Hong Kong. Although Mainland Chinese immigrants and Hong Kong residents share the same skin colour and cultural heritage, Mainland immigrants are nevertheless stereotyped as dirty, greedy and uncultivated by their Hong Kong counterparts (Newendorp 2008). Mainland immigrants are also stigmatised as unproductive freeloaders who take advantage of the Hong Kong government's welfare services (Kung 2013). Against this background lack of fluency in Cantonese or speaking Cantonese with a Mainland accent can elicit overt discrimination from some Hong Kong residents. Mrs. Liang told us that being a new immigrant in Hong Kong had destroyed her self-esteem and sense of autonomy to such an extent that she had "no self-confidence when [I] was living in Hong Kong" and had decided to settle in Shenzhen instead.

Furthermore, the habits and lifestyle of Mainland Chinese wives are usually different from those of their in-laws. Living in a small Hong Kong apartment with their in-laws thus easily leads to conflict and it was to avoid such conflict that some of our female respondents had decided to live in Shenzhen even though this entailed separation from their husband. It is notable that if the wife *chose* not to migrate physically following her legal migration, this was empowering for her. Most of our female respondents were internal migrant workers who had stayed in south China for an extended period of time during which they had established networks of friends and colleagues. Staying in the familiar south Chinese environment therefore boosted their sense of security.

The group of Mainland wives who had not migrated spatially after their legal migration and had maintained a split family reported that they had more autonomy in household management as a result of this arrangement. Living separately from their husband during the week meant that they had more freedom to manage their household and parent their children as they wished. Although this by no means meant that they had complete control over the household – because they still had to accommodate their husband's preferences when he visited – they seemed to value the additional autonomy provided by their husband's regular absences. Mrs. Wu reminisced:

> I'd never turn on the TV during the week. When he [her husband] turned on the TV, it disturbed me. I would ask my husband to turn down the volume but would not insist that he switched off the TV. But when he was away, I took charge of the home. I would not turn on the TV so that my children could study in a quiet envrionment. (*Mrs. Wu, aged 33, married with 3 children aged 4–9, obtained Hong Kong residency in 2008 but remained in Shenzhen until 2012*)

Mrs. Wu was satisfied with the split household arrangement as it meant she could avoid conflict with her in-laws and husband. Nevertheless, many female marriage migrants found that the extended separation and the lack of intimate time entailed in the split household arrangement weakened their intimacy with their spouse.

In short, even though some Mainland spouses might have had little choice about remaining on the Mainland, living in a split household with their husband had given them greater autonomy during the working week and this could be seen as a passive form of patriarchal bargain that they made to cope with the authority of the husband (as they still needed to submit to their husband at weekends, when he was with them). Mainland spouses who made an active choice to stay in their original place of residence were able to avoid the disadvantages that came with spatial migration and benefited from existing support networks and local knowledge. In this sense their active choice of post-marital residence could be seen as resistance against the patrilocality norm and the patriarchal system of marriage migration more broadly.

Discussions and conclusion

The existing literature on cross-border marriages has focused on *either* the spatial or the legal dimension of marriage migration, *or* their intersection, generating an assumption that all marriage migrants undergo legal and spatial migration simultaneously. Our analyses showed that whilst most female marriage migrants might eventually undergo both legal and spatial migration, some experience a disjunction between legal and spatial migration, in the form of *spatial migration before legal migration* or *legal migration without spatial migration*. The main reason for the former type of decoupling was the proliferation of government restrictions on migration and the granting of residency and citizenship, whereas the latter form was related to the economic and family circumstances of cross-border families and the personal preferences of female marriage migrants and/or their husbands. Our findings contribute to the literature in multiple ways. First, in proposing a framework which acknowledges the possible decoupling of legal and spatial migration we have also presented a more varied, nuanced approach to unfolding the multiple and sometimes inconsistent pathways of marriage migration and illustrated the associated variations in the impact of marriage migration on the power and agency of female marriage migrants. We argue that it is not only legal migration or spatial migration *per se* but more importantly the inconsistency between them that underscores the complex relationship between gender, power and space. Spatial migration alone can be sufficient to disempower women but migrating spatially without migrating legally may further exacerbate the vulnerabilities of female marriage migrants in both private and public spheres. By withholding or delaying the granting of residency and citizenship to marriage migrants the state traps women in a limbo in which their reproductive labour is exploited in the interests of the state but they are legally excluded from access to public and welfare benefits, which inevitably impeded their assimilation into the receiving society.

On the other hand, whilst legal migration provides marriage migrants with legal and social protections in the host society, spatial migration may disrupt their social support network and thus increase their vulnerability as immigrants. Legal migration without spatial migration can thus represent women's embodied (although limited) agency and a striving for freedom and autonomy, or even a rebellion against the oppressive patriarchal system. By voluntarily remaining in the region of origin, women may be empowered not only by their existing support networks but also by avoiding the potential difficulties of assimilation should they physically migrate to the society where they legally belong. This is important as it demonstrates that for some women voluntary spatial immobility is emancipatory. This contradicts the common belief that only those who are mobile are the agents of change and those who are immobile and/or left behind are lack of power. Nevertheless, there are women who would have liked to migrate spatially in order to benefit from spatial hypergamy but ended up trapped in their region of origin because of financial and family circumstances, often feeling resentful as a result. These women also encountered a distinct assimilation barrier as they felt confused about their identity when being trapped in a limbo between the sending and receiving societies. This indicates that spatial movement may not necessarily be disempowering for women; not having the chance to migrate spatially may instead drive some women to feel disempowered. In other words, it is not mobility *per se* that is empowering, but having control over one's mobility. This uneven contour of power geometry attests to the fact that heterogeneous assimilation patterns may exist among different subgroups of migrants (see also Chang 2020; Qian and Qian 2020).

Second, our decoupling concept also sheds light on the state's role in contouring the gendered geography of marriage migration. The existence of a cohort of female marriage migrants who relocate physically before migrating in the legal sense is a result of government policies designed to regulate the flow of migrants from Mainland China to Hong Kong. The TWP system allows the state to mobilise female marriage migrants' reproductive labour whilst minimising its responsibility towards them. The TWP system illustrates the paradox of an immigration system that is intended to control population growth and a marriage migration regime that supposedly recognises family reunification as a fundamental human right. The framework we have outlined also allows us to uncover the ways in which migration policy is used to uphold the interests of the state rather than those of citizens and their immigrant family members.

Third, turning to the implications of decoupling for family functioning in cross-border marriages, the existence of legal migration without spatial migration due to economic constraints on the wife settling in her husband's country is an illustration of the formidable structural obstacles that some female marriage migrants face to creating a normative family. These obstacles compel some of them to opt for long-term existence as a split family. We should, however, recognise that in some cases female marriage migrants and their spouses are exercising agency and choosing to compartmentalise their work, family and leisure lives in order to achieve personal goals. Our analysis of decoupling suggests that although lack of residency rights creates extra hassle for marriage migrants, it does not prevent them from fulfilling their familial roles. Similarly, legal residency nominally enables but does not guarantee female migrant migrants' ability to maintain familyhood, which requires concomitant material basis. In the spatial dimension, our analysis of decoupling shows that cross-border mobility could be results of repressive governmentality that uses granting access to mobility to withhold or delay residency or citizenship rights, but it also suggests that migrants take advantage of what flexibility they have – in this case spatial flexibility – to maximise their individual and familial interests within the framework of government and economic restrictions. In other words, while marriage migrants and their families struggle through the migratory transitional period, they are also actively strategising under the constraints (Yeung and Mu 2019) by creatively utilising their mobility resources.

To conclude, we illustrated how the framework of decoupling of legal and spatial migration is conducive to unravelling the non-normative and inconsistent migration and integration trajectories of female marriage migrants and to capturing the nuanced and complex power dynamics in cross-border marriage migration that would otherwise be overlooked. Given the heterogeneity existed among marriage migrants, future studies should go beyond the simplistic binary conceptualisation of marriage migrants as either victims or agents (Quah 2020) and to examine why marriage migration is empowering for some but disempowering for others.

However, our findings may be coloured by the idiosyncrasies of the Hong Kong context. Firstly, we note that the geographical proximity of Hong Kong and south China, and the freedom with which Hong Kong husbands can commute between Mainland China and Hong Kong, give cross-border couples unusual flexibility in devising their post-marital residence arrangements. The particularities of the spatial and legal context of Hong Kong have not only opened up space for Mainland wives to negotiate gendered power with their husbands, they also give husbands the freedom to transcend the patriarchal script and opt to live with their wives in Mainland China. Nevertheless, advances in transportation and the information communication technology and the opening up of economic opportunities in the global south may result in the residential arrangements for cross-border couples similar to those we have observed in Hong Kong becoming more widespread, perhaps driven by the increase in the number of men from the global north working and living in the global south. Secondly, the Hong Kong case is also peculiar in the sense that the Hong Kong government has set barriers not only to marriage migrants' gaining citizenship but also to their obtaining legal residency while waiting for naturalisation. Many Western countries have recognised family reunification as a human right and have already set up measures to reunification of citizens with foreign spouses and children, such as allowing the foreign spouses and children of citizens to enter the country on dependents' visas. Although it is common practice to delay the granting of citizenship to foreign spouses to combat sham marriages[3], the imposition of restrictions on residency for family reunification is less common. However, Taiwan[4] and Macau share similar historical and political contexts to Hong Kong and have also imposed similar restrictions on the mobility and residency of Mainland spouses (but not foreign spouses coming from countries other than Mainland China). The case of Singapore is also analogous to the Hong Kong case (Yeoh and Chee 2016). We believe further comparative case studies would help to illuminate how nation states act to reinforce or restructure the patriarchal system of marriage migration and how, in other contexts, decoupling of legal and spatial migration may open up or limit space for cross-border spouses to reconfigure the existing gendered power geometry of cross-border marriage migration.

Notes

1. Hong Kong is still generally considered more socio-economically developed than most areas of Mainland China despite China's rapid economic growth in recent decades.
2. Reasons include fear of difficulty adapting to Hong Kong life and feeling that legal migration was unnecessary as they had no plans to move to Hong Kong.
3. For examples, Germany and the United States require that international marriage migrants wait for 2 years before applying for permanent residency or naturalisation (Constable 2003; Mix and Piper 2003). Other countries that delay permanent residency and naturalisation include Japan and South Korea (Bélanger, Lee, and Wang 2010).
4. Taiwan removed the restrictions on Mainland spouses' residency and right to work in 2009 (Friedman 2015) and since then the rules for Chinese spouses have been the same as those for marriage migrants from other countries.

Acknowledgement

The first author gratefully acknowledge the support of the Asia Research Institute at the National University of Singapore, where part of the study was conducted.

Disclosure statement

No potential conflict of interest was reported by the authors.

Funding

This work was supported by Hong Kong Research Grant Council [grant number GRF2120461].

ORCID

Tuen Yi Chiu http://orcid.org/0000-0002-5901-236X
Susanne Y. P. Choi http://orcid.org/0000-0003-3879-2915

References

Balgamwalla, S. 2014. "Bride and Prejudice: How US Immigration Law Discriminates Against Spousal Visa Holders." *Berkeley Journal of Gender Law and Justice* 29 (1): 25–71.
Bélanger, D., H. K. Lee, and H. Z. Wang. 2010. "Ethnic Diversity and Statistics in East Asia: 'Foreign Brides' Surveys in Taiwan and South Korea." *Ethnic and Racial Studies* 33 (6): 1108–1130.
Chang, H-C. 2020. "Do Gender Systems in the Origin and Destination Societies affect Immigrant Integration? Vietnamese Marriage Migrants in Taiwan and South Korea." *Journal of Ethnic and Migration Studies* 46 (14): 2937–2955. doi:10.1080/1369183X.2019.1585014.
Charsley, K. 2005. "Unhappy Husbands: Masculinity and Migration in Transnational Pakistani Marriages." *Journal of the Royal Anthropological Institute* 11 (1): 85–105.

Chatterjee, E., and S. Desai. 2020. "Physical versus Imagined Communities: Migration and Women's Autonomy in India." *Journal of Ethnic and Migration Studies* 46 (14): 2977–2996. doi:10.1080/1369183X.2019.1585016.

Chaudhuri, S., M. Morash, and J. Yingling. 2014. "Marriage Migration, Patriarchal Bargains, and Wife Abuse." *Violence Against Women* 20 (2): 141–161.

Chen, M., and P. Yip. 2020. "Remarriages and Transnational Marriages in Hong Kong: Implications and Challenges." *Journal of Ethnic and Migration Studies* 46 (14): 3059–3077. doi:10.1080/1369183X.2019.1585026.

Chiu, T. Y. 2017. "Marriage Migration as a Multifaceted System: The Intersectionality of Intimate Partner Violence in Cross-Border Marriages." *Violence Against Women* 23 (11): 1293–1313.

Choi, S. Y. P., and A. K. L. Cheung. 2016. "Dissimilar and Disadvantaged: Age Discrepancy, Financial Stress, and Marital Conflict in Cross-Border Marriages." *Journal of Family Issues*. http://jfi.sagepub.com/content/early/2016/06/03/0192513X16653436.full.pdf+html.

Choi, S. Y. P., Y. W. Cheung, and A. K. L. Cheung. 2012. "Social Isolation and Spousal Violence: Comparing Female Marriage Migrants with Local Women." *Journal of Marriage and Family* 74 (3): 444–461.

Choi, Y., D.-S. Kim, and J. Ryu. 2020. "Marital Dissolution of Transnational Couples in South Korea." *Journal of Ethnic and Migration Studies* 46 (14): 3014–3039. doi:10.1080/1369183X.2019.1585021.

Constable, N. 2003. *Romance on a Global Stage: Pen Pals, Virtual Ethnography, and 'Mail Order' Marriages*. Berkeley, CA: University of California Press.

Constable, N. 2004. *Cross-border Marriages: Gender and Mobility in Transnational Asia*. Philadelphia: University of Pennsylvania Press.

Constable, N. 2009. "The Commodification of Intimacy: Marriage, Sex, and Reproductive Labor." *Annual Review of Anthropology* 38: 49–64.

Coté, A., M. Kérisit, and M. L. Coté. 2001. *Sponsorship–for Better or for Worse: The Impact of Sponsorship on the Equality Rights of Immigrant Women*. Ottawa: Status of Women Canada.

Davin, D. 2007. "Marriage Migration in China and East Asia." *Journal of Contemporary China* 16 (50): 83–95.

Erez, E., M. Adelman, and C. Gregory. 2009. "Intersections of Immigration and Domestic Violence." *Feminist Criminology* 4 (1): 32–56.

Freeman, C. 2004. "Marrying Up and Marrying Down: The Paradoxes of Marital Mobility for Chosonjok Brides in South Korea." In *Cross-border Marriages: Gender and Mobility in Transnational Asia*, edited by N. Constable, 80–100. Philadelphia: University of Pennsylvania Press.

Friedman, S. L. 2015. "Regulating Cross-Border Intimacy: Authenticity Paradigms and the Specter of Illegality among Chinese Marital Immigrants to Taiwan." In *Migrant Encounters: Intimate Labor, the State, and Mobility Across Asia*, edited by S. Friedman and P. Mahdavi, 206–230. Philadelphia, PA: University of Pennsylvania Press.

Friedman, S. L. 2017. "Men who 'Marry Out': Unsettling Masculinity, Kinship, and Nation through Migration Across the Taiwan Strait." *Gender, Place and Culture*. doi:10.1080/0966369X.2017.1372373.

Gallo, E. 2006. "Italy is not a Good Place for Men: Narratives of Places, Marriage and Masculinity Among Malayali Migrants." *Global Networks* 6 (4): 357–372.

Hagan, J. M. 1998. "Social Networks, Gender, and Immigrant Incorporation: Resources and Constraints." *American Sociological Review* 63 (1): 55–67.

HKSAR Government Planning Department and Shenzhen Statistics Bureau. 2008. *Survey of Hong Kong People Living in Shenzhen*. Hong Kong: Planning Department of HKSARG; Shenzhen Statistics Bureau.

Hong Kong Census and Statistics Department. 2018. *Marriage and Divorce Trends in Hong Kong, 1991 to 2016*. Hong Kong: Hong Kong Census and Statistics Department.

Jongwilaiwan, R., and E. C. Thompson. 2013. "Thai Wives in Singapore and Transnational Patriarchy." *Gender, Place and Culture* 20 (3): 363–381.

Kim, H. M. 2015. "Intimacies and Remittances: The Material Bases for Love and Intimate Labor between Korean Men and Their Foreign Spouses in South Korea." In *Migrant Encounters: Intimate Labor, the State, and Mobility Across Asia*, edited by S. Friedman and P. Mahdavi, 25–45. Philadelphia, PA: University of Pennsylvania Press.

Kofman, E. 1999. "Female 'Birds of Passage' a Decade Later: Gender and Immigration in the European Union." *International Migration Review* 33 (2): 269–299.

Kung, C. L. 2013. "The Prejudicial Portrayal of Immigrant Families From Mainland China in Hong Kong Media." In *International Handbook of Chinese Families*, edited by K. B. Chan, 211–227. New York: Springer-Verlag.

Legislative Council Secretariat. 2015. *Population Profile of Hong Kong*. Hong Kong: Author.

Levitt, P., and N. G. Schiller. 2004. "Conceptualizing Simultaneity: A Transnational Social Field Perspective on Society." *International Migration Review* 38 (3): 1002–1039.

Li, C.-H., and W. Yang. 2020. "Happiness of Female Immigrants in Cross-Border Marriages in Taiwan." *Journal of Ethnic and Migration Studies* 46 (14): 2956–2976. doi:10.1080/1369183X.2019.1585015.

Lu, M. C. W. 2005. "Commercially Arranged Marriage Migration: Case Studies of Cross-Border Marriages in Taiwan." *Indian Journal of Gender Studies* 12 (2 & 3): 275–303.

Mahler, S. J., and P. R. Pessar. 2001. "Gendered Geographies of Power: Analyzing Gender Across Transnational Spaces." *Identities: Global Studies in Culture and Power* 7 (4): 441–459.

Massey, D. 1994. *Place, Space and Gender*. Minneapolis: University of Minnesota Press.

Menjívar, C., and O. Salcido. 2002. "Immigrant Women and Domestic Violence." *Gender & Society* 16 (6): 898–920.

Mix, R., and N. Piper. 2003. "Does Marriage "Liberate" Women from sex Work? Thai Women in Germany." In *Wife or Worker? Asian Women and Migration*, edited by N. Piper, and M. Roces, 53–71. Lanham, MD: Rowman and Littlefield Publishers, Inc.

Newendorp, N. D. 2008. *Uneasy Reunions: Immigration, Citizenship, and Family Life in Post-1997 Hong Kong*. California: Stanford University Press.

Palriwala, R., and P. Uberoi. 2005. "Marriage and Migration in Asia." *Indian Journal of Gender Studies* 12 (2-3): 5–29.

Piper, N., and M. Roces, eds. 2003. *Wife or Worker?: Asian Women and Migration*. Lanham, MD, USA: Rowman and Littlefield Publishers.

Pong, S. L., D. Post, D. Ou, and M. S. Fok. 2014. "Blurring Boundaries? Immigration and Exogamous Marriages in Hong Kong." *Population and Development Review* 40 (4): 629–652.

Qian, Z., and Y. Qian. 2020. "Generation, Education, and Intermarriage of Asian Americans." *Journal of Ethnic and Migration Studies* 46 (14): 2880–2895. doi:10.1080/1369183X.2019.1585006.

Quah, S. E. L. 2020. "Transnational Divorces in Singapore: Experiences of Low-income Divorced Marriage Migrant Women." *Journal of Ethnic and Migration Studies* 46 (14): 3040–3058. doi:10.1080/1369183X.2019.1585023.

Robinson, K. 2007. "Marriage Migration, Gender Transformations, and Family Values in the 'Global Ecumene'." *Gender, Place and Culture* 14 (4): 483–497.

Sassen, S. 2003. "The Repositioning of Citizenship: Emergent Subjects and Spaces for Politics." *CR: The New Centennial Review* 3 (2): 41–66.

West, C., and D. H. Zimmerman. 1987. "Doing Gender." *Gender and Society* 1 (2): 125–151.

Williams, L. 2010. *Global Marriage: Cross-Border Marriage Migration in Global Context*. Basingstoke: Palgrave Macmillan.

Yeoh, B. S. A., and H. L. Chee. 2016. "Migrant Wives, Migrant Workers, and the Negotiation of (il)Legality in Singapore." In *Migrant Encounters: Intimate Labor, the State, and Mobility Across Asia*, edited by S. Friedman and P. Mahdavi, 184–205. Philadelphia, PA: University of Pennsylvania Press.

Yeung, W.-J. J., and Z. Mu. 2020. "Migration and Marriage in Asian Contexts." *Journal of Ethnic and Migration Studies* 46 (14): 2863–2879. doi:10.1080/1369183X.2019.1585005.

Marital dissolution of transnational couples in South Korea

Yool Choi, Doo-Sub Kim and Jungkyun Ryu

ABSTRACT
This study examines the risk of transnational divorce in Korea using marriage and divorce registration data between 2010 and 2014 from Statistics Korea. We raise two research questions. First, how does risk of marital dissolution differ by type of marriage? Second, how do the socio-demographic factors of a transnational couple affect the probability of divorce? We find that transnational marriage has an extremely high risk of divorce within the first 48 months of marriage. About 19% of marriages between a Korean husband and a foreign wife were dissolved, while only 6% of marriages between Korean nationals ended within 48 months. Both Chinese husbands and wives have the highest risk of divorce, and foreign women from Southeast Asian countries also have a substantially high risk of divorce. Another important finding is that less educated foreign wives have a significantly higher probability of divorce than foreign wives with higher education. Lastly, acquisition of citizenship lowers the risk of divorce for foreign spouses. Given the increasing number of transnational couples in Korea, this study presents the actual risk of divorce according to marriage duration for the first time and provides the most complete description of transnational marital dissolution thus far.

Introduction

The marital stability of transnational marriage has been well examined in Western countries (Jones 1994; Kalmijn, de Graaf, and Janssen 2005; Zhang and Van Hook 2009; Milewski and Kulu 2014). Such studies have examined the stability of transnational marriage and how it differs from that of marriage between two nationals or two immigrants. Despite some degree of contextual variation, most studies have pointed to weak marital stability among transnational couples. Surprisingly few studies, however, have examined the marital stability of transnational marriages in non-Western contexts. This could be attributed to the fact that transnational marriage has been a relatively rare phenomenon in many non-Western countries. Patterns of global migration have changed rapidly and several traditional sending countries are now receiving countries (Kim 2006, 2010; Jones 2012).

This study examines the stability of transnational marriages in South Korea (hereafter Korea). Korea has recently transformed from a sending to a receiving country and has become a multi-ethnic society. The number of transnational marriages in Korea has rapidly increased, and this emerging trend has called attention to various issues including marital stability, quality of married life, the social/educational environment of multi-ethnic children, and citizenship status. While many prior studies have examined these issues both qualitatively and quantitatively, the actual risk of transnational marital dissolution has not yet been explored (Lee 2005; Kim 2006, 2012).

Due to increasing rates of marriage-based immigration, Korea provides a particularly interesting context in which transnational marital dissolution can be examined. In Korea, the majority of transnational marriages are between a Korean husband and a foreign wife. This phenomenon can largely be attributed to a substantial squeeze in the marriage market in rural areas where Korean men with low socioeconomic status have had difficulty in finding a suitable spouse domestically (Kim 2006, 2010). Looking for wives overseas through matchmaking agencies, increasingly the preferred method of finding a wife since the early 1990s, has become one of the new features of marriage patterns in Korea (Wang and Chang 2002; Kim 2006, 2015; Jones and Shen 2008).

More broadly, female marriage migration from less developed Asian countries to wealthier East Asian countries has become increasingly prevalent in recent years, with Korea, Taiwan, Japan, and Singapore as major destinations (Hugo 2005; Kim 2006, 2010; Jones 2012; Li and Yang 2019; Yeung and Mu 2019). In addition to issues common to all transnational marriages such as cultural dissimilarities between spouses, prior studies have found that foreign wives who come to East Asia also face a commercialised marriage process, heterogeneous composition between spouses, and negative stereotypes about foreign wives in the destination countries (Wang and Chang 2002; Constable 2005; Kim 2010; Jones 2012; Yeung and Mu 2019). Based on these specific contexts of cross-border marriage in East Asia, prior studies have documented marriage immigrants' marginalised adaption process and their psychological wellbeing (Yu and Chen 2016; Li and Yang 2019). Institutional and cultural constraints that marriage immigrants experience such as gender dynamics or legal system have been also investigated (Röder and Mühlau 2014; Maliepaard and Alba 2016; Chang 2020; Chiu and Choi 2020). Many of these studies demonstrate that marriage immigrants' unstable marital life and marginalised experiences are often led to marital dissolution. Some studies, for example, qualitatively examine marriage immigrants' experiences on the divorce trajectories (Mand 2005; Liversage 2012; Quah 2019).

While these significant findings on cross-border marriage in East-Asia have generated considerable scholarly discussion, little has been explored on the empirical evidences of marriage immigrants' actual risk of marital dissolution. To fill the gap, this study aims to present a thorough empirical description of transnational marital dissolution by using a Korean registration data set. We raise two key research questions. First, how does risk of marital dissolution differ according to type of marriage, that is, marriage between two Korean nationals (type 1), between a Korean husband and a foreign wife (type 2), and between a Korean wife and a foreign husband (type 3)? Second, how do the socio-demographic factors of the transnational couple – country of origin and citizenship status of the foreign spouse, and age and education of the couple – affect the probability of divorce? We analyse these questions based on three theoretical perspectives – the heterogamy perspective, the selectivity perspective, and the cost of divorce perspective – and address whether these theoretical perspectives successfully explain the risk of transnational divorce in the Korean context.

The Korean context

Figure 1 shows the population trends of foreign residents and marriage immigrants and crude divorce rates in Korea from the mid-1990s to 2014. The number of registered foreign residents continuously increased during this time. Two major migration flows – temporary unskilled labour migration and marriage-based settlement migration – contributed to this rapid increase in foreign residents in Korea (Kim and Ryu 2016). Labour immigrants typically stay only temporarily, so they do not significantly affect family formation in Korean society. In contrast, the increasing number of marriage immigrants directly impacts Korea's demographic composition and family formation. Korea currently has about 150,000 residents with marriage migrant visas. The number of annual transnational marriages has increased at a rapid pace since the early 1990s and reached a peak in 2005. Since then, it has gradually decreased. For example, in 2005, about 42,400 transnational marriages were registered, which accounted for about 13.5% of all marriages registered in that year. In 2016, there were 20,600 transnational marriages, which accounted for 7.3% of all marriages registered in that year (Statistics Korea 2017).

Transnational marriage in Korea has several important characteristics. The first notable pattern is that marriage between a Korean husband and a foreign wife, and marriage between a Korean wife and a foreign husband typically differ. Transnational marriage in Korea after 1995 has thus far been primarily between a Korean husband and a foreign wife. In 2010, marriage between a Korean husband and a foreign wife constituted about 81% of total transnational marriages. For the 2010 marriage cohort, China and

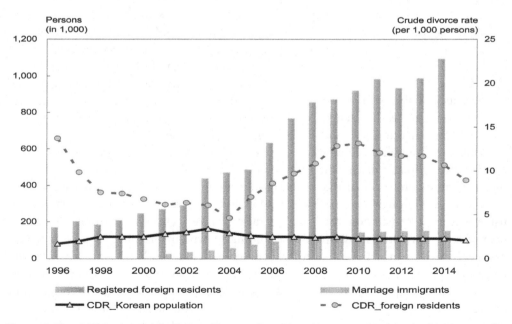

Figure 1. Trends in registered foreign residents and marriage immigrants and crude divorce rates for the entire Korean population and registered foreign residents, 1996–2015.

Japan were major sending countries for both foreign husbands and foreign wives. Excluding China and Japan, however, country of origin differed significantly among foreign spouses according to gender. Foreign wives were mostly from Southeast Asian countries such as Vietnam, the Philippines, and Cambodia, while foreign husbands were from mostly industrialised Western countries such as the United States, Canada, Australia and the UK (Kim 2015; Statistics Korea 2017).

Country of origin is a major factor in determining an immigrant's cultural dissimilarities and racial/ethnic differences from nationals at the place of destination, which is considered as one of the major determinants of transnational marital stability (Jones 1994; Kalmijn, de Graaf, and Janssen 2005; Zhang and Van Hook 2009; Milewski and Kulu 2014). Korea offers several additional complexities regarding country of origin such as the marriage process, visa status, and socio-demographic characteristics. For example, the majority of Chinese spouses are ethnic Koreans with Chinese citizenship.[1] As a result, they typically do not have strong language and ethnic differences from Korean nationals. They also have relatively stronger ethnic enclaves and social networks compared to other immigrant groups in Korea (Lee et al. 2006; Lee 2013).

Foreign wives from Southeast Asian countries also have a unique migration context. Many of them meet their Korean husbands through commercial matchmaking agencies (Wang and Chang 2002; Jones and Shen 2008; Kim 2010). Their marriages are decided in a very short time of two or three days. Therefore, these couples do not have enough time for developing a romantic relationship and understanding cultural differences. Previous studies have pointed out that this lack of mutual understanding causes critical problems such as racial prejudice, false information about the spouses, family abuse, and insecure legal status (Lee 2005; Kim 2010; Kim 2011). However, it is important to note that transnational couples have a clear motivation and seek transnational marriage through marriage agencies. While Korean men look for foreign women due to distorted local marriage markets, foreign women seek better economic opportunities by marrying Korean men (Wang and Chang 2002; Jones and Shen 2008; Kim 2010). The process and the underlying motivation of transnational marriage are factors that differentiate Southeast Asian women from other marriage immigrants.

The heterogeneous characteristics of Chinese spouses and Southeast Asian wives suggest that the migration context differs greatly by country of origin. In this study, we divide marriage immigrants broadly into four groups: wives from Southeast Asian countries, husbands from Western countries, spouses from Japan, and spouses from China. We discuss different migration contexts by country of origin in detail in the results section.

These factors unique to the Korean context impact our analysis in two ways. First, while many prior studies of transnational marriage in Western countries did not distinguish male and female foreign spouses, we conduct separate analyses for foreign husbands and foreign wives. This allows us to identify any (dis)similarities between these two types of marriages. Second, the heterogeneous migration contexts by country of origin prompt us to consider broader theoretical perspectives. Studies of transnational marriage have mainly focused on cultural dissimilarities and socio-demographic differences such as religion, age, and education among marriage immigrants (Kalmijn 1998; Kalmijn, de Graaf, and Janssen 2005; Zhang and Van Hook 2009). However, we note that there are several interesting dividing lines among marriage immigrants in Korea in terms of the marriage process, economic motivations, visa eligibility, and other factors. Rather than limit our analysis to cultural dissimilarities among transnational couples, we extend the theoretical background to include more general theories of divorce that examine the selectivity and cost of divorce.

Theoretical background

We use three theoretical frameworks to examine transnational marital stability. The first theoretical framework is the heterogamy perspective. This framework maintains that heterogamous marriages have a higher likelihood of separation than marriages between relatively homogamous partners (Kalmijn 1998; Zhang and Van Hook 2009). Factors such as age, education, religion, race/ethnicity, and nationality can impact spousal dissimilarity. Many studies have supported the validity of the heterogamy framework in various regional contexts (Bahr 1981; Jones 1996; Kalmijn, de Graaf, and Janssen 2005).

The reasoning underlying the heterogamy framework is that socio-cultural background plays a crucial role in establishing a person's preferences, values, and worldviews. Spouses with different socio-cultural backgrounds may experience a greater degree of misunderstanding and conflict than couples with the same or similar socio-cultural backgrounds (Kalmijn 1998; Milewski and Kulu 2014). Another difficulty of heterogamous marriage is that heterogamous couples often experience less social support than couples with a more homogamous marriage (Kalmijn, de Graaf, and Janssen 2005). Partnerships that cross strong social norms can face disapproval or receive less support from the spouses' kinship or social networks.

In terms of cross-border marriage, transnational couples are expected to have greater cultural dissimilarity between spouses than marriages between two nationals (Yeung and Mu 2019). The heterogamy perspective suggests that the risk of divorce increases as the 'cultural distance' between the national and the foreign spouse increases (Kalmijn, de Graaf, and Janssen 2005; Milewski and Kulu 2014). Limited social networks and the language problems of marriage immigrants are likely to further heighten the marital instability of transnational couples. In particular, if cross-border marriage is a relatively rare social phenomenon or if there exist negative stereotypes about marriage immigrants in the society, transnational couples have more difficulty in retaining social networks and supports. In sum, the heterogamy hypothesis emphasises the socio-cultural dissimilarity between transnational couples and the lack of social support from the receiving countries. Therefore, this perspective clearly predicts a higher likelihood of divorce for transnational marriages compared with marriages between two Korean nationals.

The second theoretical framework is the selectivity perspective. The selectivity perspective suggests that the high risk of divorce in transnational marriages can be attributed to spouses' compositional traits rather than to the characteristics of transnational marriage itself such as cultural differences or lack of social support (Milewski and Kulu 2014). This hypothesis emphasises that the socioeconomic and demographic characteristics of the spouses in transnational marriages may differ from those in marriages between two Korean nationals. For example, those who engage in transnational marriage may be less educated, married at very young ages, or belong to lower social strata, all of which heighten the risk of divorce.

Another important characteristic of transnational marriage is that spouses typically have larger gaps in age, education, and social strata compared to marriages between Korean nationals (Kim 2008, 2010). This different composition in socio-demographic characteristics between spouses is a key factor that potentially increases risk of divorce (Kalmijn 1998; Kalmijn, de Graaf, and Janssen 2005; Kim 2015). If the partner selection process of transnational marriage involves these additional dissimilarities between spouses, this could increase the marital instability of transnational couples. The selectivity hypothesis predicts that if we control for the spouses' socioeconomic and demographic characteristics, the high risk of divorce of transnational marriage may be reduced or even disappear.

The last theoretical perspective is the cost of divorce. The individual considers the costs and benefits of separation and calculates the net gains of the possible options. If the net gains from a marital union decrease, and if there is the presence of tension and conflict, individuals may be more inclined to consider marital dissolution as an option (Becker 1991; Blossfeld and Müller 2002). If the internal tension or external shocks are equal to all groups, we can expect that a group with a lower cost of divorce will be more likely to separate than a group with a higher cost of divorce.

Cost of divorce has not been explicitly considered when examining the marital stability of transnational couples. We adopt this framework because marriage immigrants in Korea face different costs of divorce, depending on a number of factors. The main focus is that marriage immigrants have diverse migration contexts in terms of the marriage process, such as visa eligibility, cultural background, education level, and economic motivation. This heterogeneity among marriage immigrants may differentiate their cost of divorce and result in different likelihoods of marital dissolution.

In sum, this study explores the marital stability of transnational couples based on three theoretical frameworks: the heterogamy perspective, the selectivity perspective, and the cost of divorce perspective. Based on these theoretical frameworks, our analysis proceeds in two steps. With marriage and divorce registration data from Statistics Korea, we first calculate the marriage duration specific risk of divorce and present the cumulative probabilities of divorce according to marriage duration. The key interests are how the cumulative divorce probabilities differ by type of marriage and by the foreign spouse's country of origin, education level, and citizenship status. These bivariate relationships would depict a clear empirical description of transnational marital dissolution with a focus on heterogamy perspective and cost of divorce perspective. Then, a series of logistic regression analyses with the key characteristics of the couples are conducted to test the selectivity hypothesis. These results show how the observed bivariate relationships change when controlling for the effects of a couple's socio-demographic backgrounds.

Hypotheses

Marital stability by type of marriage

(a) **Heterogamy hypothesis**: Transnational marriages tend to be less stable than marriages between Korean nationals due to greater cultural differences and less social support.

(b) **Selectivity hypothesis**: The high risk of transnational divorce is mainly due to a couple's low socio-demographic characteristics and spousal dissimilarities.
(c) **Cost of divorce hypothesis**: Assuming that the cost of divorce is greater for the foreign spouse than for the Korean spouse, transnational marriage is likely to have a lower risk of divorce than marriage between Korean nationals.

Based on our theoretical frameworks, heterogamy perspective and cost of divorce perspective suggest competing hypotheses. While the cost of divorce for foreign spouses is likely to be higher than for Korean nationals because marriage immigrants without Korean citizenship have to return to their country of origin when divorced, we assume that transnational couples are more likely to divorce than intra-national couples as suggested by the heterogamy perspective. Previous empirical studies have revealed that transnational couples experience an extremely lower quality of married life, particularly marriages between a Korean husband and a foreign wife (Chung and Lim 2011; Kim 2012a). Cultural differences and insufficient social support are one of the key reasons of the vulnerable marital life and this fact limits the impact of the cost of divorce hypothesis.

Marital stability by country of origin

(a) **Heterogamy hypothesis**: Foreign spouses whose countries of origin have greater cultural differences from Korea are more likely to divorce.
(b) **Selectivity hypothesis**: The different socio-demographic characteristics of foreign spouses by country of origin induce a gradient of risk in marital dissolution.
(c) **Cost of divorce hypothesis**: If the costs of divorce differ by country of origin, foreign spouses whose countries of origin have lesser costs of divorce are more likely to divorce.

If we consider cultural dissimilarity to be the main factor in risk of divorce, Chinese spouses would have the lowest risk of divorce since the majority of them are ethnic Koreans. In contrast to our hypothesis on marital stability by type of marriage, we predict that the cost of divorce is more consequential in determining the gradient of risk in marital dissolution by country of origin among the transnational couples who have similar quality of married life. Achieving upward social mobility by marrying a Korean husband is a significant motivating factor for many foreign women (Kim 2010; Jones 2012; Ryu and Kim 2013). This strong economic motivation could make foreign wives more amenable to cultural conflicts that may arise during the marriage (Kim 2012a). In addition, divorce would impact their legal status in Korea. However, the situation differs for ethnic Koreans, or *chosŏnjok*, as they are eligible for working visas that are unavailable to other immigrants. Therefore, the cost of divorce for *chosŏnjok* tends to be substantially lower than for other ethnicities for whom marriage migration is the only option to cross the border. Therefore, the foreign spouses whose countries of origin have lower costs of divorce in terms of the marriage process, visa eligibility, and legal status are more likely to divorce.

Marital stability by education

(a) **Cost of divorce hypothesis**: The relationship between education and marital dissolution reflects the cost of marital dissolution.

According to theories of family change, when the legal, social, and economic costs of divorce are high, highly educated people are more likely to divorce since they have the socioeconomic resources to manage the high costs of divorce. When the costs of divorce decline, however, the relationship between education and the risk of divorce becomes negative since financial strain plays a significant role in marital dissolution (Goode 1963; Raymo, Fukuda, and Iwasawa 2013). However, it has been argued that Korea, Taiwan, and Japan do not follow the prevailing theory. Though the social cost of divorce is considered to be high in these societies, a negative relationship between education and divorce has been found in previous empirical studies (Park and Raymo 2013; Raymo, Fukuda, and Iwasawa 2013; Cheng 2016).

For transnational couples, the migration context could potentially disrupt the relationship between the foreign spouse's educational attainment and socioeconomic resources. That is, immigrants' educational credentials acquired outside of Korea are not fully recognised in the Korean labour market. We assume that the regional context and the Korean spouse's characteristics are more consequential than the foreign spouse's characteristics and predict the negative association between education and divorce for transnational couples in Korea.

Marital stability by citizenship

(a) **Selectivity hypothesis**: Foreign spouses with Korean citizenship have a lower risk of divorce. They tend to be more adapted to Korean society as well as have a good relationship with their Korean spouses.
(b) **Cost of divorce hypothesis**: Foreign spouses who attain Korean citizenship are more likely to divorce than those who do not as their cost of divorce becomes much lower.

Based on the selectivity hypothesis, it is expected that foreign spouses who hold citizenship tend to have higher levels of integration with Korean society and culture. In order to attain Korean citizenship, marriage immigrants have to remain married for at least two years and have a good relationship with their spouse as the Korean spouse's agreement is required to apply for citizenship. We assume that those who hold citizenship have different characteristics regarding cultural adaptation and spousal relationship from those who do not. In accordance with the selectivity hypothesis, we expect that foreign spouses who hold citizenship are less likely to divorce compared to their non-citizen counterparts.

In contrast, the cost of divorce for foreign spouses with Korean citizenship is likely to be much lower than those who do not have citizenship as they would not have to return to their country of origin in the event of divorce. Another important point is that the Korean media frequently report on the problem of sham marriages between Korean nationals and marriage immigrants. This is one of the strongest negative stereotypes of marriage immigrants in Korea, especially for foreign wives from less developed countries (Hsia 2007; Kim 2011; Ahn 2013). If sham marriages really are prevalent, then citizenship would be positively associated with divorce. Among these two competing hypotheses, we predict that citizenship lowers the risk of divorce. The legal process for attaining citizenship requires strong bonds between spouses, which reflects a better quality of married life. Despite some occurrences of sham marriage, we expect the overall pattern to support the selectivity hypothesis.

Data, variables and methods

Data

This study analyses the marriage and divorce registration data collected by Statistics Korea. Statistics Korea has collected information on transnational marriage and divorce since 1991. Each dataset of marriage and divorce includes the year and month in which the event both occurred and was registered. These datasets also include key socio-demographic variables such as gender, education, region, and occupation. To calculate the marriage duration specific risk of divorce, it is necessary to identify the number of marriages (denominator) and the number of divorces (numerator) according to duration of marriage. Since the registration data do not include individual IDs, it is impossible to match the exact same person between the two datasets. Instead, we construct individual matched samples between the marriage and divorce datasets using marriage month, age, gender, country of origin, education level, and citizenship status as key variables. For the matching process between the two datasets, 42,525 types of couples are constructed based on combination of these information, and the probability of divorce is calculated for each type.

In this study, we restrict our data to marriages and divorces between 2010 and 2014 and use only six types of information: date, age, gender, country of origin, education, and citizenship status. First of all, it should be noted that naturalised foreign residents only began to be registered from 2010. For marriages and divorces occurring before 2010, foreign residents with Korean citizenship were registered as Koreans nationals. If someone married as a foreign resident, attained citizenship during the marriage, and then divorced prior to 2010, there would be a mismatch between the marriage and divorce data. The same person listed as a foreign resident in the marriage data would be identified as a Korean national in the divorce data. This leads to an underestimation of the risk of divorce for transnational marriages. Therefore, we follow individuals who married in 2010 ($n = 317,015$) and match them against the following four years of divorce records (48 months), which is the longest duration available for the 2010 marriage cohort.[2]

To construct a matched dataset between marriage and divorce records we need information that is *common* to both the marriage and divorce datasets and that is assumed to be *unchanged* during the observed period of 48 months. Although the data provide more than these six variables, these six are the *only* ones to meet these criteria, with education and citizenship as possible exceptions. Since the analysis of this study follows a relatively short period of 48 months and post-marital educational upgrading is not common in

Korea, we find it safe to assume that the educational level of our sample did not change during the observed period (Choi et al. 2007).

In terms of citizenship, three types of individuals are included in our datasets: foreign residents *without* Korean citizenship, foreign residents who married *with* Korean citizenship, and foreign residents who achieved citizenship *during* their marriage. Note that while the divorce data include all types of individuals, the marriage data do not include foreign residents who achieved citizenship *during* their marriage. This mismatch induces an overestimation of the association between citizenship status and risk of divorce. We address this issue in two ways. First, we examine the effects of citizenship on divorce within two years of marriage considering that foreign residents who marry Korean nationals without Korean citizenship are not eligible for citizenship within the first two years of marriage. Secondly, we calculate the proportion of naturalisation according to duration of marriage from the external data (*The 2012 Korean National Multi-culture Family Survey*) and impute the calculated numbers (individuals) into the marriage dataset.[3] Since we are fully reliant on this external dataset for estimating the number of naturalised foreign residents, the generalisability and the robustness of our results are limited. Our findings on the relationship between citizenship status and risk of divorce after 24 months should therefore be interpreted with caution. We exclude the citizenship variable in the final logistic regression analysis for the same reason.

Another limitation of the dataset is the issue of unobserved late registration for both marriage and divorce events. Our data do not include marriages that occurred in 2010 but were not registered until the end of 2014, nor do they include divorces that occurred between 2010 and 2014 but were not registered until the end of 2014. Our analytic strategy is to assume that all marriage and divorce registrations were completed within two years following the event. This is based on evidence that the vast majority of marriages in Korea are registered within the first two years of marriage (Park and Raymo 2013).[4]

Variables

The first question raised in this study is whether and to what extent marital stability differs according to type of marriage. To answer this question, a type of marriage variable that divides the sample into three sub-groups is created: type 1 marriage between two Korean nationals, type 2 marriage between a Korean husband and a foreign wife, and type 3 marriage between a Korean wife and a foreign husband.

The second research question is how the foreign spouse's country of origin, educational attainment, and citizenship status are associated with risk of divorce. We construct 12 categories for country of origin for the 2010 marriage cohort – six for foreign wives and six for foreign husbands. The top six countries of origin for foreign wives are China, Vietnam, the Philippines, Japan, Cambodia, and other. The primary countries of origin for husbands are China, Japan, the United States, Canada, Australia, and other. Education level has three categories: primary school or less, secondary education, and post-secondary education. Citizenship is a binary variable in which Korean citizens are coded as 1, and non-citizens are coded as 0.

Utilising information on couple's age and education, variables such as age at marriage and spousal dissimilarity in age and education are also created to be adopted in logistic regression analyses. The age at marriage variable has five categories (15–19, 20–29, 30–

39, 40–29, and 50+ years old). The age difference variable has three categories: the wife is older than the husband, the husband is older than or the same age as the wife (by 0–9 years), and the husband is older than the wife by 10 or more years. The educational difference variable is also recoded into three categories: the wife's education is higher than the husband's, the spouses have the same level of education, and the husband's education level is higher than the wife's (when the level of education is divided into three categories as described above).

Methods

In this study, we calculate the marriage duration specific risk of divorce for the first 48 months of marriage and present the cumulative probability of divorce according to marital duration. While most previous studies used crude divorce rates to compare marital stability between domestic and transnational marriages, this is the first study to show actual risk of divorce according to duration of marriage for transnational couples in Korea. The cumulative divorce probability by type of marriage, foreign spouse's country of origin, educational attainment, and citizenship status is analysed.

In this study, a series of logistic regression analyses are conducted to examine the risk of divorce after controlling for the effects of a couple's socio-demographic characteristics.[5] The logistic regression analysis proceeds in two steps. First, the probability of divorce within the first 48 months of marriage by type of marriage is estimated. Three models are established for this analysis. The first model includes only the type of marriage; the second model includes the type of marriage, husband's education and age, and wife's education and age; and the third model includes the type of marriage, wife's age and education, and spousal dissimilarity variables in terms of age and educational attainment. The main focus is to examine whether and to what extent risk of divorce by type of marriage changes when controlling for the effects of spouses' socio-demographic characteristics and spousal dissimilarities. We then estimate the probability of divorce within the first 48 months of marriage by country of origin using the same three models.

Results

Descriptive statistics of the 2010 marriage cohort

We first present the descriptive statistics of the 2010 marriage cohort by types of marriage in Table 1. There are several notable differences between the three types of marriage. First, foreign wives who married with Korean husbands (type 2 marriage) are much younger and less educated than Korean wives in type 1 marriage. Their Korean husbands are also less educated and much older than Korean husbands in type 1 marriage. Compared to foreign wives in type 2 marriage, foreign husbands in type 3 marriage do not have much difference from Korean husbands in type 1 marriage. Foreign husbands in type 3 marriage are slightly older than Korean husbands in type 1 marriage, but there is no great difference in educational level. In sum, the socioeconomic composition of type 2 marriage has a great difference from that of type 1 marriage. The characteristics of type 3 marriage are relatively similar to those of type 1 marriage.

Table 1. Descriptive statistics of the 2010 marriage cohort.

	Korean H + Korean W	Korean H + Foreign W	Foreign H + Korean W
Husband's age at marriage (%)			
15–19	0.2	0.0	0.2
20–29	34.9	7.9	27.8
30–39	52.9	42.2	35.4
40–49	7.5	35.7	19.3
50+	4.5	14.2	17.3
Wife's age at marriage (%)			
15–19	0.6	14.7	0.4
20–29	55.6	50.1	35.9
30–39	34.4	21.2	38.7
40–49	6.2	10.6	17.0
50+	3.2	3.4	8.1
Husband's education (%)			
Primary or less	1.0	4.0	1.5
Secondary	30.4	66.8	38.3
Post-secondary	68.7	29.1	60.2
Wife's education (%)			
Primary or less	1.1	3.4	1.1
Secondary	31.0	74.6	41.1
Post-secondary	67.9	22.0	57.8
N	285,355	25,790	5,870

Marital stability of transnational marriage in Korea

We compare marital stability between the three types of transnational marriage. The crude divorce rate (CDR) is the most conventional measure to represent rates of marital dissolution. It is calculated as the number of divorces per 1,000 persons. Figure 1 shows the CDR for Korean nationals and foreign residents. The CDR for Korean nationals remained pretty stable from 1996 to 2014. In contrast, the CDR for foreign residents increased rapidly from 2003 to 2009 and then decreased. It appears that the general trend of CDR for foreign residents is high. However, the CDR greatly depends on the age and gender structure of the population in question, and thus it is difficult to directly compare the risk of divorce between Korean nationals and foreign residents. As an alternative measure, the cumulative probability of divorce within the first 48 months of marriage is presented in Figure 2.

About 19% of marriages between a Korean husband and a foreign wife were dissolved within 48 months. About 13% of marriages between a Korean wife and a foreign husband ended within 48 months. However, only 6% of marriages between Korean nationals ended within 48 months. Transnational marriage, particularly marriage between a Korean husband and a foreign wife, experienced an extremely high risk of divorce. These findings corroborate previous studies that have pointed to foreign women's vulnerable position in the union and their lower quality of married life (Kim 2006; Chung and Lim 2011; Kim 2014).

Another significant finding is that, although marriages between a Korean wife and a foreign husband had a higher risk of divorce compared with marriages between Korean nationals, their divorce rate was substantively lower than marriages between a Korean husband and a foreign wife. This gap points to differences in the nature of marriage between these two types of transnational marriage.

This result seems to support the heterogamy hypothesis. It should be noted, however, that this is a bivariate relationship between type of marriage and risk of divorce. The

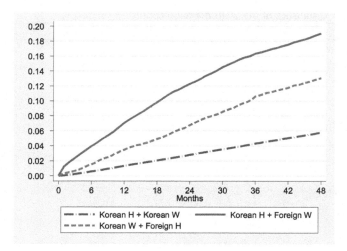

Figure 2. Cumulative probability of divorce by type of marriage.

differentials in the risk of divorce by type of marriage could be weakened or even disappear when the effects of spouses' socio-demographic characteristics are controlled for. The results of the logistic regression analysis are presented in the last part of the results section.

Country of origin

This study also examines whether and to what extent risk of divorce differs according to the foreign spouse's characteristics. The first characteristic is country of origin, which is a crucial factor in determining cultural and ethnic differences (Jones 1994; Kalmijn, de Graaf, and Janssen 2005; Zhang and Van Hook 2009). These differences are closely related to the heterogamy hypothesis. The background information by country of origin is summarised in Table 2.

It is expected that Chinese spouses have a lower risk of divorce than other foreign spouses as they have the lowest level of cultural and ethnic differences from their Korean spouse. Another important difference is that the majority of foreign wives from

Table 2. Differentials in the foreign spouse's background by country of origin.

Foreign wife	China	Vietnam	Philippines	Cambodia	Japan
Marriage process	Network/ Personal	Marriage agency	Marriage agency	Marriage agency	Religious institution
Cultural differences	Low	High	High	High	High
Ethnic differences	Low	High	High	High	Low
Foreign husband	China	Japan	US	Canada	Australia
Marriage process	Network/ Personal	Network/ Personal	Network/ Personal	Network/ Personal	Network/Personal
Cultural differences	Low	High	Middle	Middle	High
Ethnic differences	Low	Low	High	High	High

Note: Information about the marriage process and cultural differences are derived from *The 2012 Korean National Multi-culture Family Survey* (See Appendix 1 for more detail).

Southeast Asia meet their Korean husbands through marriage agencies, which are known to put foreign women in vulnerable marriage conditions (Jones and Shen 2008; Kim 2012a, 2015; Ahn 2013; Lee 2013). This different marriage process is expected to result in a lower risk of divorce among Chinese wives. In contrast, all foreign husbands meet their Korean wives through individual networks or personal connections, which suggests another important distinction between type 2 and type 3 transnational marriages.

Figure 3 shows the cumulative probability of divorce within 48 months by country of origin. Contrary to our expectations, both Chinese husbands and wives had the highest risk of divorce. About 23% of Chinese wives experienced divorce within 48 months of marriage, about 15% of wives from the three Southeast Asian countries witnessed marital dissolution, and 9% of Japanese wives got divorced. Chinese husbands also had the highest risk of divorce at 26%, and Japanese husbands at 18%. Less than 7% of foreign husbands from the three Western countries experienced divorce within four years of marriage. The cumulative probability of divorce among foreign husbands from Canada and Australia was less than that of divorce between Korean nationals (about 6%).

These results suggest that the heterogamy hypothesis does not fully explain the observed patterns of risk of divorce by country of origin. The higher risk of divorce among Chinese spouses may be due to socio-demographic characteristics that distinguish them from other foreign spouses. We test this selectivity hypothesis using a logistic regression analysis and present the results at the end of the results section.

The cost of divorce theory provides another alternative explanation to the heterogamy hypothesis. There is much qualitative evidence to indicate that Chinese spouses have the lowest cost of divorce among foreign spouses (Lee et al. 2006; Kim 2010; Lee 2013). Most Chinese spouses are ethnic Koreans and are eligible for work visas that are unavailable to other foreign spouses. This easy access to a visa means that a Chinese spouse who gets divorced would not have to return to China, while other foreign spouses without Korean citizenship would have to return to their country of origin. Chinese immigrants also have strong ethnic enclaves and compose the largest illegal immigrant population in Korea. This contextual background may lower the cost of divorce for Chinese spouses as they have both the option and resources to stay in Korea after a divorce.

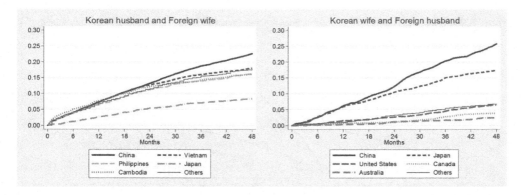

Figure 3. Cumulative probability of divorce by type of marriage and country of origin of the foreign spouse.

Education

The cumulative probability of divorce by educational attainment is provided in Figure 4 (wife's education) and Appendix 2 (husband's education).

Both foreign wives and husbands showed a negative relationship between education and divorce. Less educated wives and husbands are more likely to divorce. It is important to note that foreign wives with the lowest tier of education experienced an extremely high risk of divorce. More than 1 out of 2 foreign wives with primary education or less ended their marriage within 48 months. We further examine the educational gradient in divorce by country of origin, given that the cost of divorce may differ by country of origin (Figure 5 and Appendix 3). The relationship between education and divorce was found to be negative for all countries. However, there is some variation in the educational gradient in divorce among the five countries. For example, 70% of Vietnamese wives with primary or less education divorced within 48 months. Cambodian wives in the same category witnessed 60% divorce, and Chinese and Filipina wives, 50% divorce within 48 months.

Though the cost of divorce is extremely high for foreign spouses, the relationship between education and marital dissolution was found to be negative. The question we can raise from this pattern is why do less educated foreign wives who are assumed to have the least socioeconomic resources to manage the high cost of divorce have a higher probability of divorce? If we consider that education is a crucial resource in deciding the quality and nature of union formation, the internal tensions, conflicts, and satisfaction levels in marriage life could greatly differ according to the educational attainment of spouses. Unfortunately, the available variables in this dataset are limited, and we cannot excavate the exact mechanisms underlying educational differences in divorce any further. However, our findings clearly depict an educational gradient in transnational divorce and provide evidence for heterogeneity in the quality of married life by education.

Citizenship

Figure 6 shows the cumulative probability of divorce by citizenship status. As discussed in the data section, we calculate the duration specific risk of divorce separately for the time periods between 0–24 months and 25–48 months. The sample of marriages between 0–24

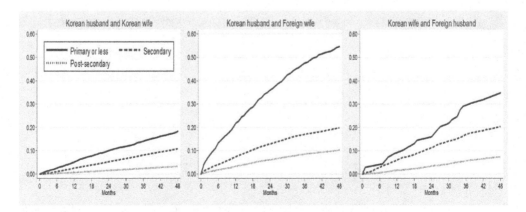

Figure 4. Cumulative probability of divorce by type of marriage and wife's education.

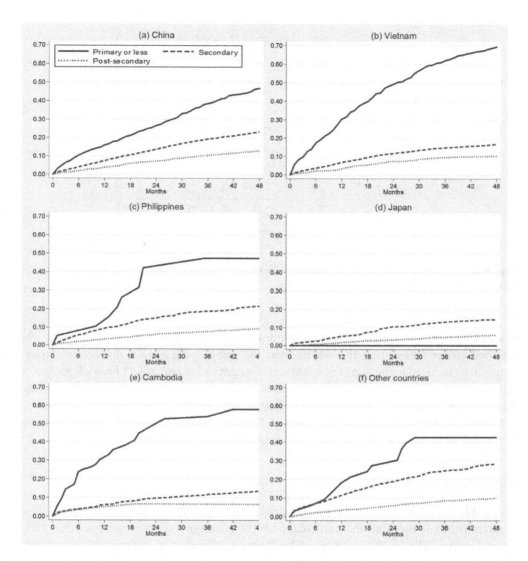

Figure 5. Cumulative probability of divorce for marriages between a Korean husband and a foreign wife by wife's education and country of origin.

months includes two groups of foreign wives: those who married *with* citizenship and those *without* citizenship. For 25–48 months, the data include foreign wives who married *with* citizenship, those who attained citizenship *during* marriage, and those who did not have citizenship.

In the first 24 months, foreign residents with Korean citizenship were less likely to divorce than those without citizenship. About 13% of non-citizen foreign residents divorced within 24 months, but only about 8% of foreign residents who held Korean citizenship ended their marriage. This result suggests that selectivity for divorce matters more than the cost of divorce hypothesis. It is expected that foreign residents who hold citizenship have a higher level of assimilation into Korean society and more social and institutional support.

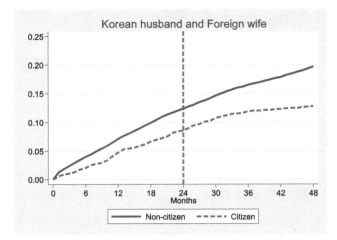

Figure 6. Cumulative probability of divorce for marriages between a Korean husband and a foreign wife by wife's citizenship status.

After 24 months, the cumulative probability of divorce of citizens and non-citizens has not risen in proportion to the marriage duration. When we include foreign wives who attained citizenship during the marriage in the sample, the risk of divorce of citizens seems to be reduced while that of non-citizens does not change notably. Those who achieved citizenship during marriage are likely to maintain a better relationship with their Korean husband and relatives. This result also indicates that the sham marriage stereotype is not supported. If sham marriages were prevalent, Korean citizenship would lead to an increase in the risk of divorce. However, our results show the opposite pattern.

Logistic regression analysis

This study also conducts a series of logistic regression analyses to predict the probability of divorce within 48 months after controlling for the effects of a couple's socio-demographic characteristics. The results are presented in Table 3. When we do not control for any covariates in model 1, those in type 2 marriages are over 200% more likely to divorce than those in type 1 marriages. Type 3 marriages reveal about 120% higher probability of divorce than type 1 marriages. When the effects of a couple's age and education are controlled for, the coefficient for type 2 marriages largely decreased to 1.604. The coefficients for type 3 marriages also decreased from 2.194–1.682.

The high divorce rates of transnational marriage couples are largely due to the different socio-demographic characteristics of transnational couples, in particular for those in type 2 marriages. Although the effects of type of marriage are not completely removed when controlling for the included covariates, a substantial decrease in the effects of transnational marriage on divorce is observed. These results are robust even when spousal dissimilarities in age and educational attainment are included in model 3.

Finally, logistic regression analyses were conducted to predict the probability of divorce by country of origin while controlling for a couple's socio-demographic characteristics and spousal dissimilarities. Table 4 shows the results for marriages between a Korean husband and a foreign wife (type 2), and Appendix 4 presents the results for marriages between a

Table 3. Logistic regression for the probability of divorce within 48 months by type of marriage and socio-demographic characteristics of the couple ($N = 317{,}015$).

	Model 1	Model 2	Model 3
Marriage combination (ref: Korean H + Korean W)			
Korean H + Foreign W (type 2)	3.071	1.604	1.625
Korean W + Foreign H (type 3)	2.194	1.682	1.729
Demographic characteristics			
H's age at marriage (ref: 50+)			
15–19		1.336	
20–29		.759	
30–39		.712	
40–49		1.033	
W's age at marriage (ref: 50+)			
15–19		1.460	1.056
20–29		.994	.769
30–39		1.076	.872
40–49		1.372	1.375
Socioeconomic characteristics			
Husband's education (ref: Primary or less)			
Secondary		.872	
Post-secondary		.486	
Wife's education (ref: Primary or less)			
Secondary		.717	.517
Post-secondary		.364	.145
Spousal dissimilarities			
Age differences (ref: H older than or same as W by 0–9 years)			
W older than H			.860
H older than W (10+)			1.259
Educational differences (ref: Same level of education)			
W higher than H			2.090
H higher than W			.682
Constant	.063	.240	.267

Note: The coefficients are the odds ratios. This analysis deals with the population, and thus standard errors are not reported in this table.

Korean wife and a foreign husband (type 3). Despite controlling for a couple's age and educational attainment, the effects of country of origin on divorce did not change substantially. These results suggest that the selectivity hypothesis does not explain well Chinese spouses' high risk of divorce. As mentioned above, their high risk of divorce may be explained by their lower cost of divorce. However, this speculation is still tentative and further research is needed to support this argument.

It is worth noting that the coefficient for Japanese wives increased markedly compared to other foreign wives after controlling for socio-demographic characteristics. This pattern is also observed with foreign husbands (see Appendix 4). The coefficients for Japan and the three Western countries increased as the covariates were included. These patterns imply that the high risk of divorce for foreign spouses from less developed countries is partly due to their socio-demographic composition. It should also be noted that a negative relationship between educational attainment and risk of divorce was still observed after controlling for other covariates.

Discussion

Given the increasing number of transnational couples and growing concern regarding the marital stability of marriage immigrants in Korea, this study presents the actual risk of

Table 4. Logistic regression for the probability of divorce within 48 months for marriages between a Korean husband and a foreign wife by country of origin of the foreign husband and socio-demographic characteristics of the couple (N = 25,790).

Korean husband + foreign wife	Model 1	Model 2	Model 3
Country of origin (ref: China)			
Vietnam	.786	.588	.599
Philippines	.704	.717	.719
Japan	.391	.726	.668
Cambodia	.699	.501	.513
Other countries	.777	.994	.983
Demographic characteristics			
H's age at marriage (ref: 50+)			
20–29		.463	
30–39		.648	
40–49		.785	
W's age at marriage (ref: 50+)			
15–19		2.471	1.339
20–29		1.938	1.251
30–39		1.505	1.165
40–49		1.247	1.149
Socioeconomic characteristics			
Husband's education (ref: Primary or less)			
Secondary		.879	
Post-secondary		.714	
Wife's education (ref: Primary or less)			
Secondary		.446	.393
Post-secondary		.246	.159
Spousal dissimilarity			
Age differences (ref: H older than or same as W by 0–9 years)			
W older than H			.621
H older than W (10+)			1.309
Educational differences (ref: Same level of education)			
W higher than H			1.597
H higher than W			.926
Constant	.232	.542	.492

Note: The coefficients are the odds ratios. This analysis deals with the population, and thus standard errors are not reported in this table.

divorce according to marriage duration for the first time and provides the most complete description of transnational marital dissolution thus far. It is found that transnational marriages, especially those between a Korean husband and a foreign wife, have an extremely high risk of divorce within the first 48 months. In terms of country of origin, both Chinese husbands and wives have the highest risk of divorce, and foreign wives from Southeast Asian countries also reveal a high risk of divorce. Another important finding is that less educated foreign wives have a significantly higher probability of divorce than foreign wives with more education. It also turns out that attaining Korean citizenship lowers the risk of divorce for foreign spouses. Finally, the idea that sham marriages make up a significant portion of transnational marriages, one of the strongest negative stereotypes about foreign wives, is not supported in this study.

This study also attempts to test the validity of three theoretical perspectives in the Korean migration context. The high risk of transnational divorce compared to intranational divorce seems to support the heterogamy hypothesis. After controlling for a couple's socio-demographic characteristics, however, the high risk of divorce of transnational marriage greatly decreases. It is possible that including other key variables related to marital dissolution such as previous marital experience, occupation, income, place of residence, and religion would further weaken the observed high risk of divorce. The sociodemographic characteristics of transnational couples seem to be more important factors than cultural differences in explaining the risk of divorce, which is the key argument of the selectivity hypothesis. Furthermore, the relationship between country of origin and risk of divorce does not support the heterogamy perspective. Although Chinese spouses had the lowest degree of cultural difference and the highest level of social support, they were found to have the highest risk of divorce compared to other foreign spouses.

It is important to note that the heterogamy hypothesis, the major theoretical perspective in transnational marriage scholarship, does not fully explain the observed patterns of transnational marital dissolution in Korea. This may be due to the different migration contexts between Korea and Western countries. The motivation and the process of transnational marriage are crucial factors that differentiate the migration contexts. Both Korean husbands and foreign wives have clear reasons and aims in looking overseas for spouses. Korean men look for foreign brides as they have difficulty in finding potential Korean spouses in the local marriage market whereas foreign women have strong economic motivations for marrying Korean men (Wang and Chang 2002; Jones and Shen 2008; Kim 2010; Jones 2012). The marriage process often takes a very short time and many of them make their final decision to commit to a transnational marriage based on rational calculations rather than a strong romantic bond (*The Economist*, November 12, 2011). When both Korean husbands and foreign wives decide on transnational marriage, they may take the risk of typical problems embedded in cross-border marriage such as language problems, ethnicity issues, socio-cultural differences, and social prejudices about transnational marriage in both the sending and receiving countries. This unique marriage migration context may weaken the validity of the heterogamy hypothesis in Korea.

The primary contribution of this study is that we provide an empirical basis for future research and suggest a contextual modification of current theories of transnational marriage. Our study is also the first to present the high risk of divorce faced by transnational couples in Korea. However, the findings from this study may not be easily generalisable to other East Asian countries with different socio-cultural contexts. Given that marriage immigration has become an increasingly prevalent social phenomenon in East Asian countries, subsequent research should examine the underlying mechanisms of the marital instability of marriage immigrants in the region.

Notes

1. Ethnic Koreans in China are known as *chosônjok* and are the result of massive Korean emigration to China from the mid-1920s to the mid-1940s when Korea was under Japanese colonial rule.
2. The number of the 2010 marriage cohort is 325,823. We excluded foreign residents who married with foreign spouses. We also excluded individuals whose report year is earlier than 2010 or later than 2012 based on our assumption that all marriage and divorce registrations were completed within two years following the event.
3. For example, number of naturalised foreign residents whose duration of marriage was between 25–36 months divided by the total number of foreign residents whose marriage duration was between 25–36 months. Then, we apply this proportion to those in the 2010 marriage cohort whose duration of marriage was between 25–36 months.
4. We need to impute the number of divorces that occurred in 2013 but were registered in 2015 as well as the number of divorces that occurred in 2014 but were registered in 2015 or 2016. It

is assumed that the 2013 and 2014 divorce cohorts have the same proportion of two-year late registrations as the 2012 divorce cohort, which is observed in our dataset. This estimation strategy is based on Park and Raymo (2013). We conduct separate analyses with the assumptions that every marriage and divorce was registered on time and that every marriage and divorce was registered within five years of the event. However, both results are found to be very similar to the assumption that marriages and divorces were registered within two years of the event.
5. The event history analysis could be a better option in terms of methodological consistency. However, constructing an event history data structure based on our variables in the model demands an extremely complex data constructing process and results in additional data loss due to the non-matching cases. We acknowledge that adoption of the logistic analysis rather than the event history analysis may be a potential limitation of the study.

Acknowledgement

This work was supported by a National Research Foundation of Korea Grant funded by the Korean Government (NRF-2017S1A3A2065967).

Disclosure statement

No potential conflict of interest was reported by the authors.

References

Ahn, Jean. 2013. "A Study on Marriage Migration-Related Laws: From the Standpoint of Human Rights of Marriage Immigrant Women." *Hanyang Law Review* 30 (1): 41–74.
Bahr, Howard M. 1981. "Religious Intermarriage and Divorce in Utah and the Mountain States." *Journal for the Scientific Study of Religion* 20 (3): 251–261.
Becker, Gary S. 1991. *A Treatise on the Family*. Enlarged edition. Cambridge, MA: Harvard University Press.
Blossfeld, Hans-Peter, and Rolf Müller. 2002. "Guest Editors' Introduction: Union Disruption in Comparative Perspective: The Role of Assortative Partner Choice and Careers of Couples." *International Journal of Sociology* 32 (4): 3–35.
Chang, Hsin-Chieh. 2020. "Do Gender Systems in the Origin and Destination Societies affect Immigrant Integration? Vietnamese Marriage Migrants in Taiwan and South Korea". *Journal of Ethnic and Migration Studies* 46 (14): 2937–2955. doi:10.1080/1369183X.2019.1585014.
Cheng, Yen-hsin Alice. 2016. "Better Education Has Become a Stabilizer of Marriages in Taiwan." *N-IUSSP Online News Magazine*, July 11.
Chiu, Tuen Yi, and Susanne Y.P. Choi. 2020. "The Decoupling of Legal and Spatial Migration of Female Marriage Migrants". *Journal of Ethnic and Migration Studies* 46 (14): 2997–3013. doi:10.1080/1369183X.2019.1585018.
Choi, Sang-Duk, Mee-Ran Kim, Jung-Mi Lee, Seung-Bo Kim, and Soo-Myung Chang. 2007. *Plans for Higher Education System Innovation and for the Realization of a Lifelong Learning Society*. Seoul: Korean Educational Development Institute.
Chung, Grace H., and Ji Young Lim. 2011. "Comparison of Marital Satisfaction Between Immigrant Wives and Korean Wives of Korean Men." *Family and Environment Research* 49 (5): 33–48.
Constable, Nicole, ed. 2005. *Cross-border Marriages: Gender and Mobility in Transnational Asia*. Philadelphia, PA: University of Pennsylvania Press.
Goode, William J. 1963. *World Revolution and Family Patterns*. New York: Free Press.
Hsia, Hsiao-Chuan. 2007. "Imaged and Imagined Threat to the Nation: The Media Construction of the Foreign Brides' Phenomenon as Social Problems in Taiwan." *Inter-Asia Cultural Studies* 8 (1): 55–85.

Hugo, Graeme. 2005. "The New International Migration in Asia: Challenges for Population Research." *Asian Population Studies* 1 (1): 93–120.
"International Marriage: Herr and Madame, Señor and Mrs". *The Economist*, November 12, 2011, 63–66.
Jones, Frank L. 1994. "Are Marriages That Cross Ethnic Boundaries More Likely to End in Divorce?" *Journal of the Australian Population Association* 11 (2): 115–132.
Jones, Frank L. 1996. "Convergence and Divergence in Ethnic Divorce Patterns: A Research Note." *Journal of Marriage and the Family* 58 (1): 213–218.
Jones, Gavin W. 2012. "International Marriage in Asia: What Do We Know, and What Do We Need to Know?" In *Cross-border Marriage: Global Trends and Diversity*, edited by Doo-Sub Kim, 13–49. Seoul: Korea Institute for Health and Social Affairs.
Jones, Gavin, and Hsiu-hua Shen. 2008. "International Marriage in East and Southeast Asia: Trends and Research Emphases." *Citizenship Studies* 12 (1): 9–25.
Kalmijn, Matthijs. 1998. "Intermarriage and Homogamy: Causes, Patterns, Trends." *Annual Review of Sociology* 24: 395–421.
Kalmijn, Matthijs, Paul M. de Graaf, and Jacques P. G. Janssen. 2005. "Intermarriage and the Risk of Divorce in the Netherlands: The Effects of Differences in Religion and in Nationality, 1974–94." *Population Studies* 59 (1): 71–85.
Kim, Doo-Sub. 2006. "A Conceptual Scheme of International Marriage of Koreans and Analyses of the Marriage and Divorce Registration Data." *Korea Journal of Population Studies* 29 (1): 25–56.
Kim, Doo-Sub, ed. 2008. *Cross-Border Marriage: Process and Dynamics*. Seoul: Institute of Population and Aging Research, Hanyang University.
Kim, Doo-Sub. 2010. "The Rise of Cross-Border Marriage and Divorce in Contemporary Korea." In *Asian Cross-Border Marriage Migration: Demographic Patterns and Social Issues*, edited by Wen-Shan Yang, and Melody Chia-Wen Lu, 128–153. IIAS Publication Series. Amsterdam: Amsterdam University Press.
Kim, Jae-Ryon. 2011. "The Reason Behind Marriage Migration in Korea: The Problems of International Brokerage and Measures to Promote Human Rights of Marriage Migrants." *Public Interest and Human Rights (Gong Ik Gwa In Kwon)* 9: 39–64.
Kim, Doo-Sub. 2012. "Spousal Dissimilarity in Age and Education and Marital Stability among Transnational Couples in Korea: A Test of the Transnational Openness Hypothesis." *Korea Journal of Population Studies* 35 (1): 1–30.
Kim, Hye-Soon. 2014. "Female Marriage Immigrants' Divorce and 'Damunhwa Policy': Immigration- and Gender-Blind Union of Family and Women Policies." *Korean Journal of Sociology* 48 (1): 299–344.
Kim, Doo-Sub. 2015. *International Marriage of Koreans and Adaptation of Foreign Spouses*. Seoul: Jipmoondang.
Kim, Doo-Sub, and Jungkyun Ryu. 2016. *Foreign Residents in Korea 2015: A Statistical Handbook in Graphs and Tables*. Seoul: The Commission for SSK Multi-cultural Research, Hanyang University.
Lee, Hye-Kyung. 2005. "Marriage Migration to South Korea: Issues, Problems, and Responses." *The Journal of Population Studies* 28 (1): 73–106.
Lee, Chang Ho. 2013. "Social Network of Migrants in Everyday Life: Focusing on the Cases of Philippine, Vietnamese and Korean-Chinese Migrants." *Journal of Diaspora Studies* 7 (2): 109–136.
Lee, Hye-Kyung, Kiseon Chung, Myungki Yoo, and Minjung Kim. 2006. "Feminization of Migration and Transnational Families of Korean-Chinese Migrants in South Korea." *The Journal of Asian Women* 40 (5): 258–298.
Li, Chun-Hao, and Wenshan Yang. 2020. "Happiness of Female Immigrants in Cross-border Marriages in Taiwan". *Journal of Ethnic and Migration Studies* 46 (14): 2956–2976. doi:10.1080/1369183X.2019.1585015.
Liversage, Anika. 2012. "Transnational Families Breaking Up: Divorce among Turkish Immigrants in Denmark." In *Transnational Marriage: New Perspectives From Europe and Beyond*, edited by Katharine Charsley, 145–160. New York, London: Routledge.

Maliepaard, Mieke, and Richard Alba. 2016. "Cultural Integration in the Muslim Second Generation in the Netherlands: The Case of Gender Ideology." *International Migration Review* 50 (1): 70–94.

Mand, Kanwal. 2005. "Marriage and Migration through the Life Course: Experiences of Widowhood, Separation and Divorce Amongst Transnational Sikh Women." *Indian Journal of Gender Studies* 12 (2&3): 407–425.

Milewski, Nadja, and Hill Kulu. 2014. "Mixed Marriages in Germany: A High Risk of Divorce for Immigrant-Native Couples." *European Journal of Population* 30 (1): 89–113.

Park, Hyunjoon, and James M. Raymo. 2013. "Divorce in Korea: Trends and Educational Differentials." *Journal of Marriage and Family* 75 (1): 110–126.

Quah, Sharon. 2019. "Transnational Divorces in Singapore: Experiences of Low-income Foreign Single Mothers".

Raymo, James M., Setsuya Fukuda, and Miho Iwasawa. 2013. "Educational Differences in Divorce in Japan." *Demographic Research* 28: 177–206.

Röder, Antje, and Peter Mühlau. 2014. "Are They Acculturating? Europe's Immigrants and Gender Egalitarianism." *Social Forces* 92 (3): 899–928.

Ryu, Jungkyun, and Doo-Sub Kim. 2013. "Effects of Perception for Upward Mobility on Fertility among Foreign Wives in Korea." *Korea Journal of Population Studies* 36 (2): 45–67.

Statistics Korea. 2017. Korean Statistical Information Service (KOSIS). Accessed July 23. http://kosis.kr/.

Wang, Hong-zen, and Shu-ming Chang. 2002. "The Commodification of International Marriages: Cross-Border Marriage Business in Taiwan and Viet Nam." *International Migration* 40 (6): 93–116.

Yeung, Jean Wei-Jun, and Zheng Mu. 2019. "Migration and Marriage in Asian Contexts".

Yu, Sojin, and Feinian Chen. 2016. "Life Satisfaction of Cross-Border Marriage Migrants in South Korea: Exploring the Social Network Effects." *International Migration Review* 52 (2): 597–634.

Zhang, Yuanting, and Jennifer Van Hook. 2009. "Marital Dissolution among Interracial Couples." *Journal of Marriage and Family* 71 (1): 95–107.

Appendices

Appendix 1. Marriage process and cultural differences by type of marriage and country of origin of the foreign spouse

Korean husband + foreign wife	China	Vietnam	Philippines	Cambodia	Japan
Marriage process					
Marriage agency	11.6	64.5	31.3	73.3	.8
Family, relatives, friend	62.1	31.4	40.0	23.6	15.8
Religious institution	1.3	0.8	18.0	0.9	50.1
Personal network	23.8	2.7	9.9	1.9	30.3
Others	1.3	0.5	0.9	0.4	3.0
Total	100 (%)	100(%)	100(%)	100(%)	100(%)
Cultural differences					
Yes	49.1	71.4	78.6	74.5	81.4
No	50.9	28.6	21.4	25.5	18.6
Total	100 (%)	100(%)	100(%)	100(%)	100(%)

Korean wife + foreign husband	China	Japan	U.S./Canada	Australia
Marriage process				
Marriage agency	4.3	2.5	1.0	0.0
Family, relatives, friend	57.9	35.0	42.4	39.5
Religious institution	1.1	18.8	4.9	3.6
Personal network	35.1	38.8	48.6	50.9
Others	1.7	5.0	3.2	6.0
Total	100 (%)	100(%)	100(%)	100(%)
Cultural differences				
Yes	12.9	63.3	49.4	61.5
No	87.1	36.7	50.6	38.5
Total	100 (%)	100(%)	100(%)	100(%)

Note: All information is derived from *The 2012 Korean National Multi-culture Family Survey*. For the marriage process, the respondents were asked 'How did you meet your spouse?' and for cultural differences they were asked 'Did you feel any cultural differences from your spouse?'.

Appendix 2. Cumulative probability of divorce by type of marriage and husband's education

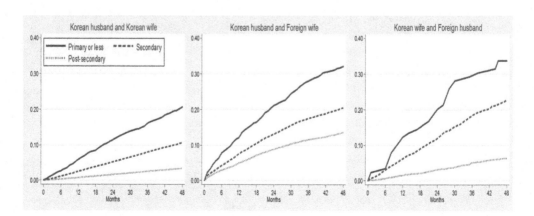

Appendix 3. Cumulative probability of divorce for marriages between a Korean wife and a foreign husband by husband's education and country of origin

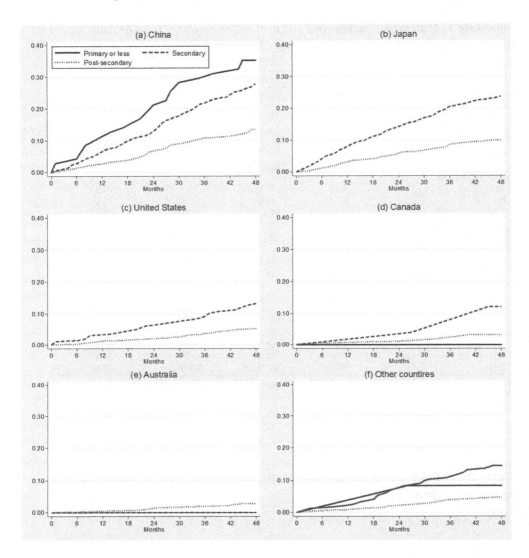

Appendix 4. Logistic regression for the probability of divorce within 48 months for marriages between a Korean wife and a foreign husband by country of origin of the foreign husband and socio-demographic characteristics of the couple (N = 5,870)

Korean wife + foreign husband	Model1	Model2	Model3
Country of origin (ref: China)			
Japan	.693	.839	.795
United States	.248	.510	.498
Canada	.154	.358	.358
Australia	.092	.195	.190
Other countries	.278	.536	.511
Demographic characteristics			
H's age of marriage (ref: 50+)			
20–29		.702	.945
30–39		.697	.927
40–49		.896	1.047
W's age of marriage (ref: 50+)			
15–19		1.202	
20–29		1.420	
30–39		1.363	
40–49		1.196	
Socioeconomic characteristics			
Husband's education (ref: Primary or less)			
Secondary		.894	.840
Post-secondary		.437	.292
Wife's education (ref: Primary or less)			
Secondary		.934	
Post-secondary		.669	
Spousal dissimilarity			
Age difference (ref: H older than or same as W by 0–9 years)			
W older than H			.979
H older than W (10+)			1.594
Educational difference (ref: Same level of education)			
W higher than H			.980
H higher than W			1.878
Constant	.263	.344	.325

Note: The coefficients are the odds ratios. This analysis deals with the population, and thus standard errors are not reported in this table.

Transnational divorces in Singapore: experiences of low-income divorced marriage migrant women

Sharon Ee Ling Quah

ABSTRACT
Global economic restructuring saw the dramatic expansion of feminised labour and extensive mobilisation of women from less wealthy to wealthier countries to supply reproductive labour. Some migrant women perform unpaid reproductive labour through marriage migration in their roles as wives, mothers and daughters-in-law. The paper seeks to understand the divorce experiences of low-income marriage migrant women in Singapore after their marriage with Singaporean husband has ended. By engaging theorisations on transnational families, the paper discusses the transnational aspects of the women's divorce biographies. Using empirical data collected through in-depth interviews, this article examines how the women work out their transnational divorce biographies in these three areas: one, coping with divorce proceedings and obtaining legal representation; two, working out the rights to remain in Singapore and other livelihood issues; and three, negotiate with ex-spouse over post-divorce co-parenting arrangements. To avoid framing the women's experiences in 'victim versus agent' binary terms, the paper examines both their struggles and strategies using a transnational, intersectional feminist framework. This analytical perspective allows the paper to discuss how unequal effects of globalisation and intersection of the women's social identities shape their divorce trajectories, in terms of the struggles they face and strategies they employ.

Introduction

While there has been a fecundity of research on the quality of transnational marriages (Constable 2005; Charsley 2006; Jones 2012; Yeoh et al. 2013; Yeung & Mu 2020), lesser attention has been paid to the dissolution of transnational marriages and the post-divorce lives of these families. It is only in recent years that there has been an emerging field of study on transnational divorce, mainly in the European contexts (Liversage 2012; Qureshi, Charsley, and Shaw 2014; Al-Sharmani 2017). Transnational divorce with its implications for changing migrant demographics and transnational family landscapes in Asia has not been sufficiently researched and understood. This paper together with another article in this special issue (Choi, Kim, and Ryu 2020), examines marital dissolution of transnational couples. While Choi, Kim, and Ryu (2020) uses quantitative methods to analyse the risk of divorce amongst transnational couples in South Korea, this paper adopts a qualitative approach to discuss the divorce biographies of low-income foreign marriage migrant women who had dissolved their mixed-nationality marriage with their Singaporean citizen ex-husband.

By 'divorce biography', I mean that divorce is conceptualised as a biographical process and understood as a non-linear trajectory through which divorcees simultaneously experience moments of hope and despair, undergo overlapping periods of distress and confusion as well as clarity and strength, and shift rapidly between chaos and stability (Quah 2015). Instead of going through 'expected' stages of the uncoupling process and emotional effects as commonly predicted and prescribed by self-help literature, I have argued that there is no single story of divorce but many divorce stories which reflect the intersection of multiple social identities divorcees hold, the different contexts they are located in and the complex events, interactions and processes they encounter (Quah 2015, 2018a, 2018b).

The project discusses the transnational aspects of divorce biographies of individuals who have dissolved their mixed-nationality marriage. Yeoh et al. posit that the transnational family 'derives its lived reality not only from material bonds of collective welfare among physically dispersed members but also a shared imaginary of "belonging" which transcends particular periods and places to encompass past trajectories and future continuities' (2005, 308). The paper takes Yeoh, Huang, and Lam (2005)'s theorisation of transnational family as a point of departure to conceptualise transnational divorced biography.

What is 'transnational' about the divorce biographies in this study is the border crossings that take place in their post-divorce familial lives. These divorced families construct their post-divorce familial arrangements and practices across nation-state borders and time zones. Even though the original frame of familial membership has been dissolved, it could be observed that there is a cross-border flow of financial, emotional and parental resources for the maintenance of physically dispersed members' welfare and familial intimacies. This transnational flow of resources is primarily for the welfare of children, less so for the collective welfare of the family as in the case of intact transnational families. There could also be a transnational flow of resources either between divorcees and their own family members or between divorcees and their former in-laws (Quah 2018a). The forms of resources could involve, for example, family members or former in-laws travelling overseas to assist with childcare responsibilities and/or providing financial assistance to the divorcee.

What is also 'transnational' about transnational divorced families' biographies is that their cross-border divorced family practices and relationships 'transgress' the national, normative construction of doing family (Tang 2018). In this case, these families transgress normative ways of doing transnational family, as well as doing divorced family. I argue that transnational divorced families are not like ordinary transnational families. Transnational divorced families certainly do not share a collective imaginary of belonging and reunion after the marital dissolution since the original frame of marital and familial membership is no longer intact. However, I argue that they construct a different, reconstituted form of imaginary of belonging and future continuities, lived out in unconventional, creative but workable ways. I suggest that they are another kind of 'Living Apart Together' (Martin, Cherlin, and Cross-Barnet 2011) family when children are in the picture and when uncoupled parents are willing to perform their parental responsibilities. Though living apart in divorced households and working out intimacy practices across borders, they are still 'together as a family' in a sense that they are compelled to work towards maintaining future continuities in a different kind of family narrative for the sake of their children (Quah 2018b). In addition, I argue that transnational divorced families are not exactly like ordinary divorced families. The former deals with particular issues that are unique to transnational divorced families. For example, the former would have to design a 'workable' divorced family narrative in cross-border spaces where members could be physically dispersed. Creative co-parenting and familial practices are often constructed in the cyber space to overcome physical distances and time differences (Quah 2018b). Even when divorced members are not physically dispersed across nations, transnational divorced families have to concern themselves with implications on their survival and co-parenting practices when a non-citizen divorced spouse struggles with the rights to remain, live and work in the host country (Quah 2018b). These unique challenges certainly make their post-divorce familial arrangements more complex than the case of ordinary divorced families.

Female marriage migrants: victim or agent?

Global economic restructuring in the 1970s saw the dramatic expansion of feminised labour supplied by women from developing countries. Women have been mobilised from poor to wealthy countries for the production of low-wage, disposable work either in manufacturing industries as factory workers or in private and intimate spheres as domestic helpers, healthcare workers, sex workers and marriage migrants (Sassen 2000; Ehrenreich and Hochschild 2003; Radhakrishnan and Solari 2015). A significant form of labour supplied by these migrant women is reproductive labour, which include 'activities conducted to achieve the reproduction of human beings intra- and inter-generationally' (Lan 2008, 1801). Reproductive labour performed by migrant women could be both paid and unpaid. Domestic helpers, healthcare workers, nannies, cleaners and sex workers carry out paid reproductive labour in private households and institutional settings while unpaid labour is performed by marriage migrants in their roles as wives, mothers and daughters-in-law (Lan 2008). The reproductive labour they produce encompasses intimate and emotional labour as well. Migrant women in the course of producing reproductive labour perform 'intimate labour' to develop, nurture and maintain interpersonal relationships in both home and host countries (Boris and Parrenas 2010) and 'emotional labour' to manage their emotions in accordance with expectations in various social settings and situations (Hochschild 2003).

Hochschild (2003) describes the love and care these women from poorer regions provide as the 'new gold' – a resource that is being excavated by wealthier countries to feed their demands for reproductive labour. She equates this 'new gold' to the colonial extraction of gold, ivory and rubber from the Third World during the nineteenth century (Hochschild 2003). She also draws attention to the large scale development of 'global care chains' where 'a series of personal links between people across the globe based on the paid or unpaid work of caring' has been established. In response to these unequal and uneven effects of globalisation on women's lives, transnational feminist scholars have argued that contrary to prominent development and feminist discourses, women are in fact not empowered by the global wave of feminisation of labour and migrant labour though it appears that their opportunities for mobility, workforce participation and economic opportunities have increased (see e.g. Grewal and Kaplan 1994; Mohanty 2003; Swarr and Nagar 2010; Radhakrishnan and Solari 2015; Mason 2017).

There has been a substantial body of literature theorising the experiences of migrant women from poor countries mobilised to supply paid and unpaid reproductive labour. On the one hand, there are scholarly works detailing the commodification and victimisation of migrant women, highlighting their vulnerability and powerlessness (Charsley 2006; Jackson 2007; Stephnitz 2009; Kim 2011). On the other hand, another group of scholars argue that such victimisation narratives are not an accurate and constructive portrayal of female labour migrants from developing countries (Cheng 2005; Kempadoo 2005; Parker 2005; Chong 2014). These scholars insist that far from being powerless victims, the women exercise agency and activism through the ways in which they resist exploitation and demonstrate resourcefulness, creativity and adaptability to assert their sense of selves in various ways under complex and trying conditions. By focusing on the narratives of agency, scholars like Chong (2014) claim that these female migrants would then be seen as individuals who have the potential of making productive contributions to society, and not as victims who require rescuing or as burdens that their host countries need to support.

I join scholars who have argued against the explanation of female marriage migrants' experiences within the strict confines of 'victim versus agent' binary (Faier 2007; Constable 2009). As also reiterated in the introductory paper of this special issue (Yeung & Mu 2020), we paint an incomplete picture of their experiences, disregard the complexity of each migrant's trajectory, overstate or understate the influence of broader political, economic and social forces that shape their biographies when we perceive female marriage migrants either as victims or agents. Instead of staying within the demarcation of 'victim versus agent' framing, this article discusses *both* the struggles and strategies of divorced female marriage migrants to disrupt their portrayal in such oppositional binary terms and reframe the analysis of their experiences in non-binary, non-linear, non-standardised and non-unidimensional ways.

As posited by Alba and Nee (2003) in their reconceptualisation of assimilation theory, migrants take on diverse paths of assimilating in their host society and do not achieve universal outcomes. Like other authors in this special issue (see e.g. Qian and Qian 2020), this paper shows how social categories such as country of origin, gender and class influence migrants' trajectories and outcomes. As compared with migrants from higher socio-economic background and countries ranked more highly in the global citizenship hierarchy, low-income divorced marriage migrant women from less wealthy countries certainly take on a different, perhaps more difficult path to navigate and adjust in their host society as they work out their transnational divorce biographies. While concurring with Alba and Nee (2003) in their position on the diversity of assimilation pathways migrants take on, the paper would like to take the discussion further and suggest that the adoption of a transnational, intersectional feminist lens to understand the complexity and multiplicity of the women's experiences is useful here.

Subscribing to transnational, intersectional feminist perspectives, the research is therefore concerned with examining inequalities and constraints brought about by global processes, regional hierarchy and local systems, and showing how these would impact the women's lives (Grewal and Kaplan 1994; Mohanty 2003; Swarr and Nagar 2010). To understand their experiences through the prism of intersectionality (Crenshaw 1989) is to recognise the heterogeneity of this group of women and demonstrate how the intersection of their social identities and locations would complicate their transnational divorce stories under the conditions of asymmetric global economic restructuring. In what follows, the paper investigates the struggles female marriage migrants encounter as a result of structural inequalities and the strategies they develop to resist these obstacles as they work out their transnational divorce biographies in these specific areas: one, coping with divorce proceedings and obtaining legal representation; two, working out the rights to remain in Singapore and other livelihood challenges; and three, negotiating with former spouse over post-divorce co-parenting arrangements. The discussions show how the women's biographies in some instances, move across borders and transgresses normative family arrangements due to the conditions they are situated in.

Transnational marriages and divorces in Singapore

To provide the context, Singapore has a sizeable proportion of transnational marriages with 36% of citizen marriages in 2015 comprising marriages between a Singapore citizen and a non-citizen, as compared to 32.8% in 1998 (Jones 2012; NPTD 2016). The majority of marriages between a Singapore citizen and a non-citizen are made up of marital unions between a Singaporean groom and a non-citizen bride. This particular coupling trend has been consistent since 1998 – 81% of transnational marriages were between Singaporean grooms and non-citizen brides, and in 2008, the proportion was 83% (NPS 2009a). The majority of non-citizen brides came from Asia; in 2008, 97% of non-citizen brides were from Asian countries (NPS 2009b). Though the 2009 government report by the National Population Secretariat does not indicate the countries in Asia these marriage migrant women were from, marriage solemnisers and counsellors have suggested that they were mainly from neighbouring developing countries like China, Malaysia, Indonesia, Thailand and Vietnam (*The Straits Times* 2016). This 'intra-Asian cross-nationality marriage' trend, as Toyota (2008, 1) calls it, is not unique in Singapore but articles in this special issue have also observed that it is part of a broader marriage pattern between East Asian males from Singapore, Hong Kong, Korea, Japan and Taiwan and foreign brides from China and Southeast Asian countries such as Vietnam, Thailand, Indonesia, The Philippines and Cambodia within the region (Chen and Yip 2020; Chiu and Choi 2020; Choi, Kim, and Ryu 2020; Yeung & Mu 2020).

Transnational divorce in Singapore accompanied the trend of increasing transnational marriages. According to official data specifically on marriages between a Singapore citizen and a non-resident (i.e. non-citizen and non-permanent resident),

> the number of marriages between a Singapore Citizen (SC) and a Non-Resident (NR) was around 6,000 to 7,000 annually for the three marriage cohorts from 2007 to 2009. Of these, around 400 to 500 marriages of each marriage cohort (7.1% to 7.9%) dissolved before the 5th anniversary. (MSF 2016)

In comparison, marital dissolution rates of total local resident marriages (i.e. marriages involving at least one Singapore citizen or permanent resident) appear to be lower. 'For couples who married in 2007 to 2009, the number of dissolved marriages before the 5th anniversary for resident marriages remained relatively stable at around 1500 to 1600 per year (dissolution rate of 6.4% to 6.8%)' (MSF 2016). With transnational divorce as an emerging family phenomenon with its implications on changing population demographics and family landscapes, I led an exploratory study during the period of 2014–2016 to understand transnational divorced individuals and their families in Singapore. The findings and discussions of the article are derived from this recently completed project.[1]

Research method

My epistemological position is shaped by transnational, intersectional feminism. As a migrant moving from a position of dominant ethnicity in my home country to being an ethnic minority in my host country, I am both insider and outsider to the experiences of marriage migrant women in the sample. The class dislocation I experienced as a result of transnational border crossings, and the intimate and emotional labour required of me to assimilate in my host society and adjust to a new minority status in my host country position me as an insider. However, my privileged position as a middle-class academic with secure, high-paying employment in my host country simultaneously places me outside of my respondents' migration experiences. Thus, my research approach is both inductive and interpretive; the investigation does not begin with a theory, but instead, inductively develop understandings from the data collected in the field, which I interpret with my partially insider, partially outsider positions.

The arguments of this article are supported by empirical findings of a broader project that set out to investigate the divorce and post-divorce experiences of Singapore Citizen (SC)-Non-Resident (NR) mixed nationality married couples in Singapore. Fieldwork research was carried in 2015 and 2016, which involved in-depth, one-on-one, once-off interviews with 47 transnational divorcees in Singapore. The respondents of the project were initially recruited through snowball sampling from personal networks and later through community organisations, which work closely with migrant communities in Singapore. Each interview lasted one to four hours. Most interviews were conducted in English. One obvious limitation of the study is that respondents with a low level of English speaking skills at times struggled with expressing themselves clearly in English. My research assistant and I tried to overcome the language barrier by repeating our questions and seeking clarification on their responses. We also took observation notes of their bodily and facial expressions during the interview. I conducted six interviews in Mandarin as requested by the respondents. My fluency in Mandarin put these six Mandarin-speaking respondents at ease and they could articulate their responses in a language they are proficient in. Furthermore, allowing respondents to speak in their mother tongue language means they were given the platform to project their voices without being subjected to the dominance of the English language. In this way, the study could gain insights into the cultural meanings and social worlds their mother tongue language carries. I translated these interviews into English for data analysis. Though it may be critiqued that the translation work might affect the consistency of data, what counts in translation work is meaning transfer, not a matter of synonym and syntax (Temple and Young 2004).

This article focuses on a subset of the larger sample of 47 transnational divorcees: divorced mothers of low-income backgrounds from countries positioned as lower ranked in a regional hierarchy with Singapore citizen children. Nine women in the larger sample fit this profile. These women, aged between 28 and 49 years old, are from neighbouring Southeast Asian countries, namely Malaysia, Indonesia, Vietnam and Thailand, and have earlier moved to Singapore as marriage migrants. They were non-residents at the point of transnational marriage. However, with marriage, some of these women's nationality and residence statuses shifted. Specifically in this sample, one gained Singaporean citizenship and three have become Singapore permanent residents (PRs) though they were all foreigners at the point of and during the marriage for a few years. The remaining five respondents are still on temporary residency permits such as Work Permit (WP), Short Term Visit Pass (STVP), Long Term Visit Pass (LTVP) or Long Term Visit Pass Plus (LTVP+) (see Table 1 for different categories of visit passes foreign spouses are eligible to apply). Holders of different types of visit passes have varying degrees of access to work, healthcare and housing entitlements and benefits.

Six out of the nine divorced mothers have one child; two have three children; and one has four children. Two female respondents are unemployed with no income. One of them has remarried another Singaporean man and is a homemaker. One respondent and her three children receive financial assistance from her employed mother and the government. The others earn an annual income of approximately SGD10,000 and SGD30,000, which is below the nation's medium income level of about SGD40,500.[2] Three out of the nine women are listed homeowners of the government-subsidised flats they live in. However, two of these three women would have to either sell or buy over their ex-husband's share as part of property settlement due to divorce. The other respondent is a homeowner of a government-subsidised three-bedroom flat and lives with her children. The respondent who has remarried another Singapore citizen man has moved into his government-subsidised three-bedroom flat. The remaining five women are in rental accommodation, renting either in the highly priced open market or from the government, which is typically a subsidised but small one-bedroom flat. The duration of marriage for these 9 respondents ranges between 3 and 10 years. All, except one, are plaintiffs who have filed for the petition to dissolve their marriages.

The data collected from the in-depth interviews was uploaded to NVivo qualitative data analysis software and an inductive coding method was adopted to analyse the material. Various distinct narrative patterns and themes emerged and would be discussed in the sections below. The narratives of the respondents are in no way meant to be representative of the experiences of transnational divorcees in Singapore, or transnational divorced population on the whole. They, however, provide a glimpse into the variety and complexity of uncoupling and post-divorce experiences of low-income non-resident divorced mothers in Singapore.

Coping with divorce proceedings and obtaining legal representation

Hwee Eng, a 47-year old divorced mother, was a Malaysian citizen when she met her Singaporean ex-husband; he was 16 years older than her and had been previously married. She became pregnant soon after, and that was when the beatings began. Refusing to let her baby born into an abusive environment, she travelled home to Malaysia to have her baby. Hwee Eng and her daughter remained in Malaysia for the next five years till Hwee Eng brought her daughter to Singapore for better education and future. The couple then got married in 2005 and applied for Hwee Eng's permanent residency three years into the marriage.

Table 1. Categories of visit passes foreign spouses are eligible to apply.

	Validity	Employment	Healthcare	Housing
STVP	Up to three months; can apply for extension of another three months, subject to approval (ICA 2016)	Not allowed to engage in any form of employment (paid or unpaid) or in any business (ICA 2016).	Not eligible for healthcare subsidies and health financing schemes of any sort (MOH 2013).	Under the Non-Citizen Spouse scheme, eligible to be listed as occupier not buyer. Eligible to buy new (only two-room type in non-mature estate) or resale flats if Singapore citizen spouse is 35 years old or above. Entitled to housing grants (SGD15,000 singles grant amount as Singapore citizen spouse regarded as single till foreign spouse obtains permanent residence or citizenship); can apply for top up grant when foreign spouse or child becomes Singapore citizen (HDB 2015a, 2015b).
LTVP	Ranges from three months to five years; typically one year (Chong 2014; eCitizen 2016). Must be sponsored by spouse (Chong 2014).	Full employment benefits with Letter of Consent issued by Ministry of Manpower to give approval to take up employment (MOM 2016a). Letter of Consent is awarded as long as the individual holds LTVP/LTVP+, is married to Singaporean and has found employment. *This benefit was extended to LTVP holders with effect from 1 Feb 2015.	Not eligible for healthcare subsidies and health financing schemes of any sort (MOH 2013).	Under the Non-Citizen Spouse scheme, eligible to be listed as occupier not buyer. Eligible to buy new (only two-room type in non-mature estate) if Singapore citizen spouse is 35 years old or above. Eligible to buy resale HDB flats if Singapore citizen spouse is 21 years old or above. Like STVP holders, entitled to singles housing grants and can apply for top up grant when foreign spouse or child becomes Singapore citizen (HDB 2015a, 2015b).
LTVP+ *Scheme was introduced in 2012 to allow foreign spouses of Singapore citizens longer duration of stay and accord them with healthcare and employment benefits (ICA 2016).	Three years in the first instance, up to five years for subsequent renewals (ICA 2016). Must be sponsored by spouse (Chong 2014).	Same entitlements as LTVP holders.	Eligible for partial healthcare subsidies for inpatient services at public hospitals, except for day surgery and at specialist outpatient clinics. Not eligible for outpatient services subsidies and health financing schemes (MOH 2013).	Same entitlements as LTVP holders.

(*Continued*)

Table 1. Continued.

	Validity	Employment	Healthcare	Housing
Permanent Residence (PR)	Permanent, with re-entry permit renewable for up to five years; must be sponsored by spouse if not an Employment or S Pass holder (Chong 2014).	Automatic right to work (Chong 2014)	Eligible for partial healthcare subsidies including inpatient and outpatient services, and partial health financing schemes such as Medishield Life (basic health insurance plan administered by the government) (MOH 2013).	Eligible to buy new (any flat type) or resale HDB flats with Singapore citizen spouse and apply for housing grants (a lower amount than Singapore citizen couples); can apply for top up grant when foreign spouse or child becomes Singapore citizen (HDB 2015a, 2015b).

After Hwee Eng became a Singapore permanent resident, she decided to sell her house in Malaysia with the intention of settling down in Singapore for good. This turned out to be a bad decision she later regretted. The violence at home worsened after she sold her house. Her daughter witnessed repeated violence against her mother and was also subjected to her father's beating. One would assume that Hwee Eng's permanent residency status should render her more bargaining power and allow her to walk away from the abusive marriage more easily. However, she stayed on for six years and explained her reasons for doing so:

> He would threaten me, ' ... I would cancel your PR. Where can you go now? You have no more place to go to!' ... I also never went to investigate if I could get my PR on my own. I think women are very vulnerable. We live under this kind of condition where we get threatened and beaten up like that because we are worried about the PR.

Though possessing permanent residency (PR) at this point, Hwee Eng lacked knowledge about her rights, and confidence in her ability to navigate local systems. Having only completed one year of secondary school education in Malaysia, being Mandarin-speaking in a country where English is the lingua franca, and as a poor, non-citizen woman with only a few hundred dollars of personal assets in a foreign land where she has no support network, the intersection of her class, gender, education and nationality over-determines her vulnerability and precarity. Marriage migrant women like Hwee Eng, as transnational feminist scholars (Radhakrishnan and Solari 2015) have sought to show, are seldom advantaged by social mobility, instead they often find themselves caught up in a multiplicity of oppressions and occupy a relatively weaker position and possess limited bargaining power in their transnational marriage (Mand 2005; Liversage 2012; Chiu and Choi 2020).

It took several police reports, her ex-husband's persistent breaching of personal protection orders, and the spiralling of her daughter's rule-bending ways when Hwee Eng finally snapped. She had a long and painful conversation with her daughter and collectively, they made the decision and formulated plans for Hwee Eng to file for divorce. Though her family in Malaysia did not provide financial assistance, the cross-border flow of emotional resources in terms of recognition and acceptance of her decision gave her confidence and courage to start plotting her exit. This marked the beginning of Hwee Eng's transnational divorce biography where she and her daughter would survive on their own while continuing to receive cross-border emotional support from her Malaysian family after the divorce.

When the decision to dissolve the marriage takes place, divorcees like Hwee Eng would have to navigate various institutions and systems to sort out matters concerning legal proceedings, financial matters, property settlement, living arrangements, child custody and childcare responsibilities as they construct their divorce biographies (Quah 2015). The process in working out different administrative systems, and staking one's claims can be confusing and stressful. It is especially more overwhelming for low-income, female marriage migrants from non-English speaking, developing countries who not only have inadequate knowledge of local policy environments, limited financial resources to cope with divorce costs such as legal fees and relocation expenses, and a lack of local community and social network to guide and support them through the ordeal, but also have to overcome language and cultural barriers. As a result, this group of women and their citizen children, already disadvantaged by their structural conditions, are further thrust deeper into greater turmoil, uncertainty and precariousness.

The study observes that low-income marriage migrant women, despite the odds stacked up against them, often demonstrate remarkable resourcefulness and strong will to employ different situational strategies for survival. As illustrated in this quote by Hwee Eng, she was fiercely determined in her attempts to find a way out for her and her daughter, and went to different sources to seek legal assistance:

> I went Legal Aid and they told me that I could not qualify for that $1,500 salary ... for two months over Chinese New Year, I worked OT [overtime] so my salary was $2,000 ... They said ... you have to go to Law Society. I went to Law Society and they also told me they could not help me ... I approached Willing Hearts[3] ... they recommend someone to you ... This is ACMI.

It is not uncommon for marriage migrant women to turn to local community organisations for information and support (see e.g. Sims 2012). Several women of the sample obtained legal aid at no or partial charge from the Archdiocesan Commission for the Pastoral Care of Migrants and Itinerant People (ACMI), a non-profit organisation that sets out to help with the needs of migrants in Singapore. With ACMI's assistance, these women could then have access to legal representation during the divorce proceedings. They could also then assert their rights and exert influence on the outcomes of divorce, which they otherwise would not have been able to achieve under typical abject circumstances with no financial means to engage a lawyer and not meeting the eligibility criteria to apply for legal aid from government organisations.

Working out the rights to remain in Singapore and other livelihood challenges

Besides working out divorce proceedings, most non-resident marriage migrant women in the sample would have to confront the issue of their temporary visa passes. While ordinary divorcees typically face problems relating to housing and finances at the outset of divorce, these foreign women are plunged right into visa chaos and overwhelmed by the uncertainty of their stay in Singapore. Their divorce biographies transgressing normative post-divorce practices and strategies would prove to be more complex than ordinary divorce biographies involving same-nationality couples. Unlike female marriage migrants who have managed to obtain PR or citizenship during the course of marriage like Hwee Eng, non-resident marriage migrant women face the imminent possibility of being sent back to their home country and be forcibly separated from their Singapore citizen children if their existing visa has expired or if their visa-sponsoring Singaporean husband chooses to terminate the sponsorship.[4] In other words, Singapore citizen husbands have at their disposal the rule of immigration law to exercise against their non-resident spouses. Such administrative systems (when used by Singapore citizen husbands) produce points of exclusion and disadvantage for non-resident marriage migrants (Jongwilaiwan and Thompson 2013) that deepen the vulnerabilities and precariousness of these mothers and their children. The unequal power relations within the transnational marriage and in transnational divorced families reflect broader structural inequalities. On a global scale, affluent and more highly ranked countries in global citizenship hierarchy enjoy greater power, privileges and benefits while less wealthy and lower ranked countries not only have lesser access to resources but also supply labour and materials to meet the needs and demands of wealthier countries. The global order when mapped onto the personal sphere shapes the relationship dynamics of individuals from different ends of the spectrum. There is certainly also a gendered dimension to this inequality in the case of transnational marriages and divorces. Gendered power dynamics in transnational marriages and divorces between low-income marriage migrant women from less wealthy countries and citizen husbands from wealthier countries is not uncommon (Jongwilaiwan and Thompson 2013; Quah 2018a; Chiu and Choi 2020).

Like many non-resident marriage migrant women on a temporary visa who have been reported to experience a high level of stress and anxiety over the uncertainty of their future in the host country (see e.g. Li and Yang 2020), several women whom I interviewed were distressed trying to fight against complex administrative systems to secure a longer period of stay in Singapore. Some had joint child custody with their Singaporean ex-husbands and were granted care and control of their children, but lacked the permit to stay. It is a catch-22 situation. The women would have chosen to bring their children back to their home countries so that they could find a job and receive family support in raising and caring for their children, especially when their Singaporean ex-husbands were shirking parental responsibilities in providing child support maintenance and raising their children. However, this was not an option for their Singaporean citizen children who were not citizens in their mothers' home countries. Since the women could not possibly abandon their children and leave them behind in Singapore, they had to find means to remain in Singapore. In the case of Chadapon, a Thai citizen whose Singaporean ex-husband had terminated his sponsorship of her visit pass, scrambled to find a low-waged job as a kitchen assistant so as to secure a work permit that would allow her to stay in Singapore for as long as her employers would renew her work license. In the shift from unpaid reproductive labour to paid work, uneducated, non-English speaking marriage migrant women often face limited employment opportunities; they qualify only for low-waged, low-skilled and labour-intensive work (Lan 2008) and remain vulnerable throughout. When I met Chadapon for the interview, her work permit was soon expiring and it was unclear if her employer still required her labour. Looking visibly troubled, she expressed her anguish in halting, broken English that she has picked up during her stay in Singapore:

> If I go back, I ok but what will happen to my kid? His father does not want him ... disappear ... He owe so much loan shark money. Who will look after my son if I go back? ... But Singapore make so hard for me to stay ... work permit expire soon, then what happen to my son and me after that?

Besides looking for a job and obtaining a work permit that would allow them to remain in Singapore, other women came up with survival strategies like approaching the immigration department and speaking with the immigration case officer, turning to their local member of parliament and ACMI for intervention, and looking for a Singaporean friend or colleague to act as their sponsor for their visa pass renewal application. In one particular case, the non-resident divorced mother had to return to her home country after the divorce but she took on the marriage migration route again by marrying another Singaporean man in order to make it back to Singapore and be close to her young son. The intersection of their location in the global and local order of hierarchy leaves them with no choice but to take on a certain trajectory in search of a good life.

As low-income, non-resident divorced mothers sort out their visit passes, they simultaneously have to deal with issues over their livelihoods, housing and childcare responsibilities as part of their divorce biographies (Quah 2015, 2018b). Often, their situations are made more challenging by their non-Singapore citizen status: the women are ineligible to apply for government rental flats and public assistance schemes. Rental prices even for a bedroom in a government-subsidised flat in the open market would typically wipe out up to half of their monthly paycheck. Often the women on a temporary visa pass (STVP or LTVP) had to settle for undesirable housing as their temporary visit status rendered them unstable, hence undesirable tenants. Many respondents also worked long shifts of up to 12 h, with little bargaining power over their working conditions and hours.

Under such abject circumstances, the women in the sample tapped on their resourcefulness and will to survive, developing different strategies to counteract the structural inequalities they were subject to. Their strategies to weave a situational, flexible and pragmatic divorce biography often involve a transnational flow of resources between their home country and the host country they are located in. The case of Ly Anh, a 32-year old Vietnamese divorced mother is a good example. Ly Anh's Singaporean ex-husband, after having found a new love, physically assaulted her so as to intimidate her into agreeing to the divorce and moving out of his house with their three-year son. With her child under her care and control and her ex-husband's irregular and inconsistent child support maintenance payments, Ly Anh decided to bring her young son to Vietnam and placed him under the temporary care of her mother so that she could return to Singapore to work. Similar to several other non-resident divorced mothers in the sample, Ly Anh's transnational divorce biography stretches from her host country to home country in order for her to carry out childrearing responsibilities. After she found a more stable job as a restaurant waitress and rented a room in the open market, she brought her son back to Singapore. The flow of childrearing resources continued to be cross-border when she arranged for her mother and aunt to take turns to travel from Vietnam to Singapore and help look after her son so that she could continue working. These extensive transnational childcare arrangements no doubt added strain on her finances. Her rental amount of SGD700 would double whenever her mother or aunt came to live with her and her son in a small rental room. She would also need to pay for their airfares and living expenses. Despite the financial stress, this was a strategy that allowed her to continue to care for her son. Though she managed to get her Singaporean colleague to agree to sponsor her visit pass renewal when her three-year LTVP+ was about to expire, she unfortunately did not secure a renewal of LTVP+ but was instead given a one-year LTVP. She later contacted me to express anguish over not being granted a longer visit pass and able to look to having improved work and living arrangements and a more certain future for her and her son. Her divorce biography remained turbulent but she remained determined in staying hopeful and working hard to have a better life with her son: ' … single mother not easy Singapore … anything I do … I work, stay and look after my son'. While such narrative of hope becomes the coping script these poor women use to deal with the structural inequalities they live with, and reflects their agency, the conditions they are situated in nevertheless present many obstacles to their existence.

Negotiating with ex-spouse over post-divorce co-parenting arrangements

> My ex-husband told me if he wanted the child, he would definitely get the custody … So he said give him the child … It is also good because the child is better off following him …

Lan, a 28-year old, non-resident mother filed for divorce after her husband ordered her mother and her out of his flat. Lan's mother had earlier travelled from Vietnam to Singapore upon Lan's request for childcare support so that Lan could work. Though Lan was the one to initiate the divorce, she found herself with little bargaining power during the divorce proceedings and was coerced into giving up custody of her child. Being on a one-year LTVP at the point of divorce, she was not only unfamiliar with local systems and her parental rights but also unconfident of her ability to be a single mother raising her son in Singapore or in Vietnam:

> In the beginning, I wanted baby to follow me. But will the Singapore government let me do that? If I get the child, I will definitely bring him back to Vietnam. Will Singapore government allow that? When I bring the child back, how will I look after him? He is not Vietnamese citizen … So I agreed to let him have baby.

As a poor, non-English speaking Vietnamese woman with an incomplete primary school education, the intersection of Lan's positions shaped her self-evaluation and explained the difficulties she would face as a divorced migrant. Unable to ascertain or counter her ex-husband's intimidations, she believed she had neither parental rights nor the ability to care for her son, and that her ex-husband would be far a more qualified candidate to be the custodial and resident parent.

One would expect divorce to disrupt the unequal gendered power relations between low-income marriage migrant women and their citizen husband. As observed, gendered asymmetric relations persist through the divorce proceedings and into the women's post-divorce interactions with their ex-spouses (Quah 2018a, 2018b). Singaporean ex-husbands, for instance, have the power to exclude non-resident mothers from staking child custody and other divorce claims by withdrawing sponsorship of their ex-wives' visit pass. Women in transnational marriages of under three years are particularly vulnerable. Under local jurisdiction, marital dissolution in the first three years of marriage is disallowed unless the family courts have provided permission to do so (Family Justice Courts Singapore 2015). Thus, a loophole that the Singapore citizen husband could exploit is to cancel his sponsorship of his foreign wife's visit pass, send her back to her home country within the three-year period, then file for divorce when the marriage has reached its three-year mark. Banished from Singapore, non-resident migrant wives would be entirely excluded and unable to contest any divorce claims made by ex-husbands (Chong 2014). Even for women whose marriages have passed the three-year mark and who technically have the right to participate in the divorce process, the women would often find themselves having lesser bargaining power than their Singaporean husband who, by virtue of familiarity and citizenship, would have a clearer understanding of local ways of getting things done, possess greater financial and social capital, and gain easier access to community resources and assistance schemes as a citizen. For example, Singaporean husbands would typically have the economic means to hire a lawyer or be eligible to apply for legal aid if he could not afford the legal costs, while the low-income marriage migrant women who have no money to get legal representation would not be eligible to seek legal aid as a non-Singapore citizen (Chong 2014).

After ending the marriage and losing her son's custody, Lan returned to her home country, Vietnam. Her LTVP had subsequently expired. Lan's family especially her mother encouraged her to stay on in Vietnam. However, Lan was never going to give up her son. She hung on to the imaginary of reunification with her son and laboured over this goal. Eventually, she went on the marriage migration route again and married another Singaporean man to gain geographical mobility. According to her, her current Singaporean husband treated her well and accepted her divorced and parental status.

Once back in Singapore, she started getting in touch with her ex-husband, demanding to see her son. Working out a functional post-divorce co-parenting arrangement is never easy for many divorced couples and the process would at times involve hostility, vengeance and lack of cooperation from the ex-spouse (Moore 2017). During the initial months, Lan would turn up at her ex-husband's flat on Saturdays to visit her son (a weekly access right accorded to Lan as stipulated in the court ruling) only to find that her ex-husband had deliberately brought her son out. She, therefore, did not manage to see her son for a few months. Through her social network comprising other marriage migrant women from Southeast Asian countries, she came to know about ACMI and turned to the organisation for legal aid. It was only after a volunteer lawyer at ACMI helped her lodge a complaint with the family court that she was able to see her son on Saturdays. However, she continued to encounter tremendous challenges in negotiating with her ex-husband over access matters from time to time. At the end of the interview, Lan expressed her aspiration to obtain permanent residency so that she could one day fight for the custody of her son and be reunited with him. She said she would be working with her ACMI lawyer on this matter.

Even though a number of female respondents like Lan are lucky beneficiaries of ACMI services, there are some in this study who had no knowledge of the existence of ACMI and other support services in Singapore that they could turn to. These women often turned to family members and relatives back in their home country for financial assistance, loans and childcare support. Among those who have stayed long enough in Singapore, they have forged relationships with other marriage migrant women and developed a local supportive network of diasporas from similar background; these women could gather more resources and come up with better strategies to survive and care for their citizen children, countering the challenges arising from their transnational divorces.

Discussion

This article has foregrounded the transnational divorce biographies of low-income, marriage migrant women from lower-ranked countries in the regional hierarchy, adding to the substantial literature on marriage migration, foreign bride phenomenon and transnational families. It has specifically looked at the ways in which the women coped with divorce proceedings, navigated local systems to obtain legal representation, fought for their rights to remain in Singapore, maintained livelihoods, provided care to their citizen children, and worked out post-divorce co-parenting arrangements with their citizen ex-husband.

The empirical material demonstrates the transnational aspects of the women's divorce biographies, thus extending Yeoh, Huang, and Lam's (2005) conceptualisation of transnational families. Though transnational divorced families do not share a collective imaginary of belonging like other intact transnational families, the findings show that transnational divorced families constitute a form of 'living apart together' familial arrangement. Their family practices, while transgressing normative familial frameworks of transnational families and divorced families, nevertheless work and make sense under the conditions they are located in. While living apart in separate households and in some cases, different countries, transnational divorced families reconfigure a particular family narrative through cross-border, creative and workable practices. The flow of financial, emotional and parenting resources at various points of their divorce biographies across borders go into the making of transnational divorced families. Even when the ex-husband was uncooperative in some cases, the women in this study nonetheless organised parenting and childcare arrangements with their ex-husbands, either on their own, or if the divorce proved too acrimonious, through a lawyer or community organisation.

Adopting a transnational, intersectional feminist perspective to understand the women's transnational divorce biographies, this article reveals the unequal effects of globalisation in Asia where poor women from less wealthy, neighbouring countries like Thailand, Vietnam and Malaysia take on the marriage migration route to supply reproductive labour to men from wealthier countries like Singapore. The regional hierarchy within which Singapore assumes a higher economic, political and social status in Asia while other less wealthy, developing countries occupy more lowly ranked positions are mapped onto and reproduced in marital and familial relations, as empirical findings of this study have shown. There is also a gender and class dimension to the unequal power relations within transnational marriages where local men from wealthier countries possess greater power than their poor foreign brides from less wealthy and lower ranked countries. As my respondents' accounts show, the unequal gender relations frequently persist into their divorce biographies. The intersection of the women's nationality, class, education level, language and gender complicates their trajectories, presents them with complex challenges and deepens their vulnerability.

Although the article foregrounds the women's struggles arising from the structural inequalities and constraints they are subjected to, what is salient in the study is also their multiple strategies in surviving their complex transnational divorce trajectories. The women demonstrated strong will, determination and ingenuity to seek different avenues of help, such as tapping on familial resources in their home country for childcare and financial assistance, consulting their diasporic network of friends for advice and recommendations, making appeals to their local member of parliament or the immigration department for resolution of visa and livelihood issues, reporting to local authorities to protect themselves from abuse, and approaching local community organisations for legal aid and welfare support.

As shown in the paper, the women's transnational divorce biographies are not unilinear and standardised. Transgressing the borders of nation-states and normative imaginaries of transnational and divorced families, the women's biographies shift between crisis and resolution, disorder and stability, social isolation and connectedness, vulnerability and resistance. The discussion of their divorce biographies has revealed the women's struggles and vulnerabilities, as well as their ingenuity and survival capabilities against the backdrop of broader structural inequalities. The article has therefore departed from the 'victim versus agent' binary discourse to highlight the complexity and multiplicity of their trajectories and expose the conditions that shape their experiences.

Notes

1. The research project, 'An exploratory study on Singaporean divorcees from transnational marriages' received research funding from Singapore Ministry of Social and Family

Development's Social and Family Research Fund during the period of 2014–2016. The Author of this chapter acknowledges that the Ministry does not endorse the project findings, methods or results in any way, and that any views, findings or results arising from the Research Project in this article are strictly the Author's own.
2. According to official statistics, the median gross monthly income from work, including Employer Central Provident Fund (CPF) contribution of full-time employed Singaporean residents in 2015 is SGD3,949 (MOM 2016b). Employer CPF contribution is at 17% of wage. Therefore, the median gross monthly income from work, excluding Employer CPF contribution in 2015 is estimated to be approximately SGD3375 (annual income at an approximate amount of SGD40,500).
3. Willing Hearts is a non-profit organisation in Singapore that operates a soup kitchen and distributes daily meals to low-income families and migrant workers.
4. Singapore citizen husbands could withdraw sponsorship of their foreign spouse's LTVP. Short extensions of their current visit passes, if they are undergoing divorce proceedings, may be given on a case by case basis and based on individual merit. According to government sources, for those who are divorced and have sole custody of young Singaporean children, Immigration and Checkpoints Authority of Singapore would generally facilitate their continuing stay in Singapore through a renewable LTVP so as to enable them to care for and raise their Singapore citizen children here. However, it is unclear what specific qualifications divorcing foreign spouses would need to warrant short extensions or renewals of their visit passes. The criteria for assessing the length of extensions granted is also unclear.

Disclosure statement

No potential conflict of interest was reported by the author.

References

Alba, R. D., and V. Nee. 2003. *Remaking the American Mainstream: Assimilation and Contemporary Immigration*. Cambridge: Harvard University Press.
Al-Sharmani, M. 2017. "Divorce Among Transnational Finnish Somalis: Gender, Religion, and Agency." *Religion and Gender* 7 (1): 70–87.
Boris, E., and R. Parrenas. 2010. *Intimate Labours: Technologies, Cultures and the Politics of Care*. Stanford, CA: Stanford University Press.
Charsley, K. 2006. "Risk and Ritual: The Protection of British Pakistani Women in Transnational Marriage." *Journal of Ethnic and Migration Studies* 32 (7): 1169–1187.
Chen, M., and P. Yip. 2020. "Remarriages and Transnational Marriages in Hong Kong: Implications and Challenges." *Journal of Ethnic and Migration Studies* 46 (14): 3059–3077. doi:10.1080/1369183X.2019.1585026.
Cheng, S. 2005. "The 'Success' of Anti-trafficking Policy: Women's Human Rights and Women's Sexuality in South Korea. Presented at Ethnography and Policy: What Do We Know About Trafficking?" CS Vance, Organiser Santa Fe, NM: Sch. Adv. R.
Chiu, T. Y., and S. Y. P. Choi. 2020. "The Decoupling of Legal and Spatial Migration of Female Marriage Migrants." *Journal of Ethnic and Migration Studies* 46 (14): 2997–3013. doi:10.1080/1369183X.2019.1585018.
Choi, Y., D.-S. Kim, and J. Ryu. 2020. "Marital Dissolution of Transnational Couples in South Korea." *Journal of Ethnic and Migration Studies* 46 (14): 3014–3039. doi:10.1080/1369183X.2019.1585021.
Chong, A. W. 2014. "Migrant Brides in Singapore: Women Strategizing Within Family, Market and State." *Harvard Journal of Law and Gender* 37: 331–405.
Constable, N. 2005. "Introduction: Cross-Border Marriages, Gendered Mobility, and Global Hypergamy." In *Cross-Border Marriages: Gender and Mobility in Transnational Asia*, edited by N. Constable, 1–16. Philadelphia: University of Pennsylvania Press.
Constable, N. 2009. "The Commodification of Intimacy: Marriage, Sex, and Reproductive Labor." *Annual Review of Anthropology* 38: 49–64.

Crenshaw, K. 1989. "Demarginalising the Intersection of Race and Sex: A Black Feminist Critique of Antidiscrimination Doctrine, Feminist Theory and Antiracist Politics." In the University of Chicago Legal Forum Volume: Feminism in the Law: Theory, Practice and Criticism, pp. 139–167.

eCitizen. 2016. "Visit Pass for Your Family Members." http://www.ecitizen.gov.sg/Topics/Pages/Visit-pass-for-your-family-members.aspx.

Ehrenreich, B., and A. R. Hochschild. 2003. *Global Woman: Nannies, Maids, and Sex Workers in the New Economy*. New York: Metropolitan Books.

Faier, L. 2007. "Filipina Migrants in Rural Japan and Their Professions of Love." *American Ethnologist* 34: 148–162.

Family Justice Courts Singapore. 2015. "FAQs on Divorce." https://www.familyjusticecourts.gov.sg/Common/Pages/FAQs-on-Divorce.aspx.

Grewal, I., and C. Kaplan. 1994. "Introduction: Transnational Feminist Practices and Questions of Postmodernity." In *Scattered Hegemonies: Postmodernity and Transnational Feminist Practices*, edited by I. Grewal and C. Kaplan, 1–33. Minneapolis: University of Minnesota Press.

Hochschild, A. R. 2003. "Love and Gold." In *Global Woman: Nannies, Maids and Sex Workers in the New Economy*, edited by B. Ehrenreich and A. R. Hochschild, 15–30. New York: Holt/Metropolitan Books.

Housing and Development Board (HDB). 2015a. "Schemes and Grants (New)." http://www.hdb.gov.sg/cs/infoweb/residential/buying-a-flat/new/schemes-and-grants.

Housing and Development Board (HDB). 2015b. "Schemes and Grants (Resale)." http://www.hdb.gov.sg/cs/infoweb/residential/buying-a-flat/resale/schemes-and-grants.

http://www.straitstimes.com/singapore/fewer-men-finding-love-with-foreign-wives.

Immigration and Checkpoints Authority (ICA). 2016. "Frequently Asked Questions: Visitor Services." http://www.ifaq.gov.sg/ICA/apps/fcd_faqmain.aspx#FAQ_30403.

Jackson, S. H. 2007. "Marriages of Convenience: International Marriage Brokers, 'Mail-Order Brides' and Domestic Servitude." *University of Toledo Law Review* 38: 894–922.

Jones, G. 2012. "International Marriage in Asia: What Do We Know, and What Do We Need to Know?" Asia Research Institute Working Paper Series No. 174. Singapore: National University of Singapore.

Jongwilaiwan, R., and E. C. Thompson. 2013. "Thai Wives in Singapore and Transnational Patriarchy." *Gender, Place and Culture* 20 (3): 363–381.

Kempadoo, K. 2005. *Trafficking and Prostitution Reconsidered: New Perspectives on Migration, Sex Work and Human Rights*. Boulder, CO: Paradigm.

Kim, J. 2011. "Trafficked: Domestic Violence, Exploitation in Marriage and the Foreign-Bride Industry." *Virginia Journal of International Law* 51 (2): 443–506.

Lan, P.-C. 2008. "New Global Politics of Reproductive Labor: Gendered Labor and Marriage Migration." *Sociology Compass* 2 (6): 1801–1815.

Li, C.-H., and W. Yang. 2020. "Happiness of Female Immigrants in Cross-Border Marriages in Taiwan." *Journal of Ethnic and Migration Studies* 46 (14): 2956–2976. doi:10.1080/1369183X.2019.1585015.

Liversage, A. 2012. "Transnational Families Breaking Up: Divorce among Turkish Immigrants in Denmark." In *Transnational Marriage: New Perspectives from Europe and Beyond*, edited by K. Charsley, 145–160. New York: Routledge.

Mand, K. 2005. "Marriage and Migration Through the Life Course." *Indian Journal of Gender Studies* 12 (2&3): 407–425.

Martin, C., A. Cherlin, and C. Cross-Barnet. 2011. "Living Together Apart in France and the United States." *Population (English Edition)* 66 (3–4): 561–582.

Mason, C. L. 2017. "Transnational Feminism." In *Feminist Issues: Race, Class and Sexuality*, edited by N. Mandell and J. Johnson, 62–89. Toronto: Pearson.

Ministry of Health. 2013. "Frequently Asked Questions: What Are the Healthcare Subsidies that LTVP+ Holders Are Eligible For?". https://crms.moh.gov.sg/FAQ.aspx.

Ministry of Manpower (MOM). 2016a. "Work Passes and Permits: Letter of Consent." http://www.mom.gov.sg/passes-and-permits/letter-of-consent.

Ministry of Manpower (MOM). 2016b. "Gross Monthly Income from Work." http://stats.mom.gov.sg/Pages/Income-Summary-Table.aspx.

Ministry of Social and Family Development (MSF). 2016. "Statistics on Marital Dissolutions." https://app.msf.gov.sg/Press-Room/Statistics-on-marriage-dissolutions.

Mohanty, C. T. 2003. *Feminism Without Borders: Decolonising Theory, Practising Solidarity*. Durham, NC: Duke University Press.

Moore, E. 2017. *Divorce, Families and Emotion Work: 'Only Death Will Make Us Part'*. London: Palgrave Macmillan.

National Population and Talent Division (NPTD). 2016. "Population in Brief 2016." https://www.nptd.gov.sg/PORTALS/0/HOMEPAGE/HIGHLIGHTS/population-in-brief-2016.pdf.

National Population Secretariat (NPS). 2009a. *Population in Brief*. Singapore Government Report. https://www.nptd.gov.sg/PORTALS/0/HOMEPAGE/HIGHLIGHTS/population-in-brief-2009.pdf.

National Population Secretariat (NPS). 2009b. *Marriages Between Singapore Citizens and Non-Singapore Citizens 1998-2008*. Singapore Government Report. https://www.nptd.gov.sg/PORTALS/0/HOMEPAGE/HIGHLIGHTS/20090617-media-release-occasional-paper-marriages-between-citizens-and-non-citizens-1998-to-2008.pdf.

Parker, L. 2005. *The Agency of Women in Asia*. Singapore: Marshall Cavendish.

Qian, Z., and Y. Qian. 2020. "Generation, Education, and Intermarriage of Asian Americans." *Journal of Ethnic and Migration Studies* 46 (14): 2880–2895. doi:10.1080/1369183X.2019.1585006.

Quah, S. E. L. 2015. *Perspectives on Marital Dissolution: Divorce Biographies in Singapore*. Singapore: Springer.

Quah, S. E. L. 2018a. "Cross-cultural Families in Singapore: Transnational Marriages and Divorces." In *Family and Population Changes in Singapore: A Unique Case in the Global Family Change*, edited by W. J. Yeung and S. Hu, 163–179. Abingdon, NY: Routledge.

Quah, S. E. L. 2018b. "Emotional Reflexivity and Emotion Work in Transnational Divorce Biographies." *Emotion, Space and Society* 29: 48–54. doi:10.1016/j.emospa.2018.09.001.

Qureshi, K., K. Charsley, and A. Shaw. 2014. "Marital Instability Among British-Pakistanis: Transnationality, Conjugalities and Islam." *Ethnic and Racial Studies* 37 (2): 261–279.

Radhakrishnan, S., and C. Solari. 2015. "Empowered Women, Failed Patriarchs: Neoliberalism and Global Gender Anxieties." *Sociology Compass* 9 (9): 784–802.

Sassen, S. 2000. "Countergeographies of Globalisation: The Feminisation of Survival." *Journal of International Affairs* 53 (2): 503–524.

Sims, J. M. 2012. "Beyond the Stereotype of the 'Thai-Bride': Visibility and Invisibility and Community." In *Transnational Marriage: New Perspectives from Europe and Beyond*, edited by K. Charsley, 161–174. New York: Routledge.

Stephnitz, A. 2009. *Male-Ordered: The Mail-Order Bride Industry and Trafficking Un Women for Sexual and Labor Exploitation*. The Poppy Project Report.

The Straits Times. 2016. *Fewer Singaporean Men Finding Love with Foreign Wives*. http://www.straitstimes.com/singapore/fewer-men-finding-love-with-foreign-wives.

Swarr, A. L., and R. Nagar. 2010. *Critical Transnational Feminist Praxis*. New York: Suny Press.

Tang, S. 2018. "Sexuality in Cultural Studies Doing Queer Research in Asia." Conference paper presented at the Australian Academy of the Humanities, Cultural and Communication Studies Section, Twentieth Anniversary Colloquium. November 14th 2018, University of Sydney.

Temple, B., and A. Young. 2004. "Qualitative Research and Translation Dilemmas." *Qualitative Research* 4 (2): 161–178.

Toyota, M. 2008. "Editorial Introduction: International Marriage, Rights and the State in East and Southeast Asia." *Citizenship Studies* 12 (1): 1–7.

Yeoh, B. S. A., H. L. Chee, T. K. D. Vu, and Y. E. Cheng. 2013. "Between Two Families: the Social Meaning of Remittances for Vietnamese Marriage Migrants in Singapore." *Global Networks* 13 (4): 441–458.

Yeoh, B. S. A., S. Huang, and T. Lam. 2005. "Transnationalising the 'Asian' Family: Imaginaries, Intimacies and Strategic Intents." *Global Networks* 5 (4): 307–315.

Yeung, W.-J. J., and Z. Mu. 2020. "Migration and Marriage in Asian Contexts." *Journal of Ethnic and Migration Studies* 46 (14): 2863–2879. doi:10.1080/1369183X.2019.1585005.

Remarriages and transnational marriages in Hong Kong: implications and challenges

Mengni Chen and Paul Yip

ABSTRACT
Marriage, divorce, and remarriage have undergone significant changes in the past two decades in Hong Kong. Types of marriages have become more diverse, with increasing number of cross-border marriages between Hongkongers and Mainland Chinese as well as cross-national marriages with non-local-and-non-Chinese ethnic groups. Meanwhile, divorces and remarriages are surging, with disproportionate increase of remarriages among those in transnational marriages. Particularly, the proportion of remarriages among marriages between Hong Kong men and Mainland women, and Hong Kong women and Mainland men increased to 40% and 27%, respectively in 2012. This study investigates assortative mating in marriages by separating remarriages from first marriages, to uncover the real patterns and uniqueness in Hong Kong. The results show that assortative mating in first marriages and remarriages appear across local marriages and six types of transnational marriages. And it also shows that remarriages between Hong Kong men and Mainland women have become more hypergamous, and more welfare support is needed to assist socially deprived cross-border couples to reside in Hong Kong.

Introduction

Over the past decades, the institution of marriage in Hong Kong has undergone significant changes. Singlehood and divorce are rising, and remarriage is surging. In 2014, cross-border marriages between Hong Kongers and Mainland Chinese accounted for about one-third of all marriages (HKCSD 2015). There are also a significant number of cross-national marriages among non-local-and-non-Chinese ethnic groups. Currently, the marriage market and marriage patterns in Hong Kong have become much more complex, both structurally and geographically compared to earlier years.

In the last 30 years, gender imbalance among those at marriageable ages has been reversed, from a male surplus in the 1970s to a female surplus in the 1990s, creating a marriage squeeze on local women in Hong Kong. In the 1970s, due to labour shortage in Hong Kong, a large influx of Chinese male workers were absorbed into the manufacturing sector, and under the 'touch-base policy', these men were allowed to become Hong Kong permanent residents even when they had illegally entered Hong Kong (So 2003). As a result of the male surplus, marriage with women from Mainland China became a more acceptable and affordable choice for these new migrants who were unable to compete well in the local marriage market. However, at that time, due to restrictions imposed by the Hong Kong Government to regulate the inflow of migrants into Hong Kong, it was very difficult for cross-border spouses and their children to obtain the right of abode in Hong Kong. Afterwards, due to the inflow of Mainland Chinese women who came to reunite with their Hong Kong husbands through the One-way Permit Scheme (OWP), and the increasing number of female foreign domestic helpers working in Hong Kong, a decline of the sex ratio took place between 1981 and 2011 (HKCSD 2012). After the change of sovereignty in 1997, Hong Kong, the former British colony, became a special administrative region of Mainland China. The restrictions on movements between Mainland China and Hong Kong have been relaxed, and due to the increase in cross-border marriages, the quota of the OWP has increased from 75 to 150 persons per day to facilitate family reunions (Weiss, Yi, and Zhang 2013). Furthermore, the number of students from Mainland China studying in tertiary education in Hong Kong has been increasing, and they are allowed to stay here on visa free for one year after graduation. Graduates who find jobs in Hong Kong are also allowed to stay on (Population Policy Strategies and Initiatives 2015). All these changes in the immigration policies have impacted demographic development in Hong Kong, and subsequently notably shaped the local marriage market.

This study explores assortative mating patterns in such a dynamic marriage market in Hong Kong, in view of rising rates of divorce, remarriage, and cross-border marriage, as well as growing concerns on the wellbeing of cross-border families, divorced families and stepfamilies (So 2003; Yip et al. 2014). Unfortunately, till now very limited information is available on divorces, remarriages and cross-border marriages in Hong Kong (Yip et al. 2014). Unlike previous studies, this study observes assortative mating in marriages by separating remarriages from first marriages, to uncover the real patterns and uniqueness in Hong Kong. To some extent, assortative mating reflects social boundary and distance, influences inter – and intra- generational mobility, and is also closely related to the quality and stability of marriage (Burr 1973; Kalmijn 1998; Nye and Berardo 1973). Zhang, Ho, and Yip (2012) have further noted that homogamy in terms of age, employment and education significantly affects marital and sexual satisfaction of first-married couples in Hong Kong.

Previous studies on assortative mating in Hong Kong have made comparisons between cross-border and local marriages in the selection patterns for age, education and occupation (Pong et al. 2014; Zhou 2016), but without separating remarriages from first marriages. In South Korea, Kim (2010) has observed a peculiar phenomenon that transnational marriages between Koreans and Mainland Chinese result in a very high proportion of remarriages. Actually, such a phenomenon has also appeared in Hong Kong. Lin and Ma (2008) have found that about 30% of transnational marriages between Hong Kong men and non-Hong-Kong women were remarriages; in contrast, only 10% of marriages among the locals (i.e. marriages between Hong Kong men and Hong Kong women) were remarriages. Comparing first and second marriages in the United States, Shafer (2013) has argued that unlike first marriages, assortative mating in remarriages is very unique in terms of education and gender. Compared to first marriages, remarriages are often heterogamous rather than homogamous (Dean and Gurak 1978; Gelissen 2004; Shafer 2013; Shafer and James 2013; Theunis, Pasteels, and Van Bavel 2015). Such differences cast doubts on the results of previous studies on assortative mating patterns in Hong Kong which did not differentiate between first marriages and remarriages.

Besides, second marriages have been found to be more unstable, with higher risk of divorce than first marriages (Becker, Landes, and Michael 1977; Bramlett and Mosher 2002; Martin and Bumpass 1989; McCarthy 1978). Also, the preference of spouse could have changed after the first marriage experience. Bearing in mind the prevalence of transnational remarriages as well as the uniqueness and instability of remarriages, this study seeks to explore assortative mating in remarriages in Hong Kong, which still remains under-researched. Based on the yearly marriage registration data in 1995–2012 provided by the Census and Statistics Department of Hong Kong, assortative mating in remarriages and in first marriages are first compared, and then how homogamy in remarriages varies between local couples and transnational couples are further investigated. Such comparisons demonstrate the complexity of marriage patterns in Hong Kong and provide some insights on the nature of remarriage.

Theoretical explanations of assortative mating

In the context of rising remarriages and cross-border marriages, there is a lack of established and integrated theories to explain mating patterns in these new types of marriages in Asia (Yeung and Mu 2020) . Demographic changes such as increasing cohabitation, rising divorce and remarriage may influence comparisons of spousal resemblance across time and place (Schwartz and Mare 2012). Some findings suggest that increases in cohabitation have not substantially altered trends in assortative mating, at least in the United States. Remarriage, however, which is similar to cohabitation and divorce, has small effects on the resemblance between spouses in the United States (Schwartz and Mare 2012).

In the context of western societies, Kalmijn (1998) explains why people marry within the group (endogamy) and why people marry someone who is similar to them (homogamy) by highlighting the interactions among three forces: (1) the individual's preferences for a spouse; (2) the influence of the social groups one belongs to; and (3) the marriage market where one seeks a spouse (Kalmijn 1998). Under this framework, mate selection in Hong Kong may be affected in three ways. First, individuals' preference for their marriage candidates may be influenced by the rising socioeconomic role of women. On one hand, highly educated and employed women may have become more attractive to highly educated men than before, as wives' earnings nowadays could contribute to the household income (Kalmijn 1998; Smits and Park 2009), thus increasing homogamy. On the other hand, women with higher education and high income would be less dependent on their partners and may prioritise other non-economic criteria when selecting spouses (Smits and Park 2009), thus decreasing homogamy.

Second, it has been anticipated that Hong Kong's return to China in 1997 would eventually blur boundaries between Hongkongers and Mainlanders, and facilitate cross-border marriages (Pong et al. 2014). Nevertheless, this may not necessarily lead to higher social integration, as Pong et al. (2014) has also mentioned the possibility of Mainlanders turning into 'another ethnicity' in Hong Kong, which on the contrary, may aggravate social stratification. Third, the changing marriage market, with an emerging female surplus and the deep-rooted tradition of hypergamous marriage, would create a marriage squeeze for both men of lower socioeconomic status and women of higher socioeconomic status. This structural mismatch would act as a push factor for them to seek non-local spouses who meet their criteria, and more often, they would end up in hypergamous transnational marriages (Yeung and Mu 2020). This is often labelled as 'global hypergamy' (Constable 2010), referring to the phenomenon of men of higher income marrying local women of lower income.

Though Kalmijin's theoretical work sheds some light on assortative mating and the surge of cross-border marriages, it provides very limited insights on the rapid increase of remarriages and mating patterns among remarried couples. Similar to the trend in Hong Kong, cross-border marriages and divorces are also increasing in Korea. Choi and the colleagues (Choi, Kim and Ryu, 2020) have found that compared to local marriage, transnational marriages in Korea has a much higher risk of divorce within the first two years of marriage. Kim (2010) has explained that apart from changes in the age-sex composition of the marriageable population, the value transformation driven by the expansion of the gender-equity orientation and globalisation has also made cross-border marriages and divorces more socially acceptable. Remarriage and cross-border remarriages have thus gradually become common choices after divorces. Boyle et al. (2008) have examined the influence of residential mobility and migration on union dissolution and found that moving twice or more for long and short distances both raise the risk of separation. Hannemann and Kulu (2015), have focused on union formation among immigrants and ethnic minorities in the UK setting, and observed specific patterns which support the idea that both 'mainstream society' and 'minority subculture' have their effects on union formation and dissolution, though hard to conclude which one has a greater impact. Particularly, those divorced or widowed and of low-socioeconomic status may find themselves in a disadvantageous position in the local marriage market, and are more likely to find a non-local partner for remarriage.

There are two classic hypotheses regarding mate selection in remarriage (Dean and Gurak 1978; Gelissen 2004): (1) the learning hypothesis suggests that from the experience of their first marriages, remarried people would learn about what kinds of persons are more suitable to be their spouse and are more likely to remarry those similar to themselves; and (2) the marriage market hypothesis suggests that the second marriage market is smaller and more heterogeneous than the first. Therefore, remarried people are more likely to end up in more heterogamous marriages. Besides, Qian and Lichter (2018) also support this view by arguing that marriage order is a valued trait for exchange in the marriage market, and thus previously married individuals are likely to 'cast a wider net' and make tradeoffs by lowering the requirement for other traits of their future spouse, such as education, income, racial status, or nationality. Through this mechanism, spousal pairing among remarriage is likely to be more diverse and complex than first marriages.

However, at present, the large proportion of cross-border and transnational marriages in Hong Kong indicates that the mate pool nowadays is much larger than before and no longer geographically limited to Hong Kong residents due to the reunification with China since 1997, and cultural openness to the non-Chinese groups in a globalised Hong Kong. However, whether the increasing openness of the marriage market in Hong Kong helps to maintain or reduce homogamy of remarriage is still unknown.

Data and method

The data are obtained from the Hong Kong Marriage Registry, and include all marriages registered in Hong Kong in the period 1995–2012. The available information from this dataset includes age, educational attainment, occupation, country of previous residence, length of stay in Hong Kong, marital status before the current marriage, number of previous marriages, years since dissolution of last marriage, and the duration of last marriage for both bride and bridegroom.

In Hong Kong, cross-border marriages are often referred to as marriages registered in Hong Kong between a Hong Konger and a Mainland Chinese. Besides, Hong Kong residents can also marry a Mainlander by applying for a Certificate of Absence of Marriage Record (CAMR) for the purpose of marrying in the Mainland. In the late 1980s and early 1990s, due to the restrictions in commuting between Hong Kong and the Mainland, most cross-border marriages were in this form. However, from the late 1990s till now, the annual number of CAMR applications has decreased greatly from 15,000 at its peak in the early 1990s to just a few hundred, while the number of cross-border marriages registered in Hong Kong has increased substantially, becoming a major trend. Commuting between the Mainland and Hong Kong has greatly improved since 1997, thus leading to an increase in marriages between Hong Kongers and Mainland Chinese. In this study, only the data of marriages registered in Hong Kong are used for cross-border marriages. Those not registered in Hong Kong are small in number, and their impact on the results would be minimal.

Unlike previous studies which mainly focused on cross-border marriages between Hong Kong men and Mainland Chinese women (Lin and Ma 2008; Ma, Lin, and Zhang 2010; Zhou 2016), six types of transnational marriages are considered here – Hong Kong bridegrooms with brides from Mainland China, from other Asian countries, and from western countries, and Hong Kong brides with bridegrooms from Mainland China, from other Asian countries, and from western countries. Such classifications would help to reveal the diversity of the marriage market and the marriage squeeze in Hong Kong. A broader term 'transnational marriage' rather than 'cross-border marriage' is used to include all types of marriages between Hongkongers and non-Hongkongers. The term 'local marriages' is used to refer to marriages between Hong Kong bridegrooms and Hong Kong brides.

Over the period of 1995–2012, there were a total of 759,664 marriages registered in Hong Kong. Previous residence and the length of stay for both brides and bridegrooms are used to identify marriages involving Hongkongers. For marriages of Hong Kong men, the data have been filtered to select marriages with the bridegrooms' previous residence being Hong Kong and living in Hong Kong since birth. Such criteria are also applied to identify marriages of Hong Kong women. Then marriages of Hong Kong men are classified into four types by their spouses' previous residence – Hong Kong men marrying Hong Kong women, Hong Kong men marrying Mainland Chinese women, Hong Kong men marrying women from other Asian countries, Hong Kong men marrying women from western countries (which include the U.S., Canada, Australia, New Zealand, and European countries). Marriages of Hong Kong women are similarly classified into four types. The classification is in accordance with the residential information and place of birth rather than ethnicity. Non-ethnic Chinese who were born in Hong Kong and have stayed in Hong Kong since birth would be classified as Hong Kong residents.

Apart from the above, the variable, the number of previous marriages, is used to identify first marriages and remarriages involving Hongkongers. If the number of previous marriages of a Hong Kong man is 0, then the current marriage is considered to be his first marriage, regardless of the previous marital status of his spouse. If the number of previous marriages of a Hong Kong man is larger than 0, then the current marriage is considered to be a remarriage, regardless of the previous marital status of his spouse. The same classification is applied to marriages of Hong Kong women. As the focus of this study is on mate selection of Hong Kong men and women, the current marriage is identified as first marriage or remarriage from the perspective of the Hongkongers. However, later in the modelling, previous marital status of spouses is also taken into account.

First, a descriptive analysis is given to show the latest trend and diversity of marriages and remarriages in Hong Kong, and to compare assortative mating patterns in remarriages and first marriages. We generate two variables to measure assortative mating by age and education. Age is a common indicator that demonstrates the marrying up and down phenomenon in a marriage, and education is a good indicator of social economic status. The age gap is constructed by taking the difference between the bridegroom's and bride's ages. A positive age gap means that the bridegroom is older than the bride, and a negative age gap means the reverse. Education in the marriage registration dataset has five categories – no schooling/kindergarten, primary, secondary, tertiary (non-degree), and tertiary (degree). As the number of people with no schooling/kindergarten is very small, this group is combined with those with primary education. Based on the educational attainment of bridegrooms and brides and their educational selection, the variable is constructed into three categories: homogamy, referring to bridegrooms and brides attaining the same level of education; hypergamy, referring to bridegrooms attaining higher education than their brides; hypogamy, referring to bridegrooms attaining lower education than their brides. To investigate how mate selection in remarriages varies between local couples and transnational couples, multinomial logistic regressions for remarriages of Hong Kong men and Hong Kong women respectively are performed. Remarriages between local men and local women are considered as the baseline group. The statistical analysis is carried out using STATA 13.

Results

Descriptive analysis

Table 1 shows that the median age at first marriage has gone up rapidly for both men and women: the age for men increased from 27.0 years in 1981 to 31.2 years in 2011, while that for women increased from 23.9 to 28.9. In 1981, 15.2% of men aged 35–39 were never married and about half of them had primary education or below, while only 4.5% of women in this age group were never married. In 2011, however, the proportion of never married had risen to 28.8% for men and 22.0% for women. Such increase was mainly driven by those with secondary or post-secondary education. Retreat from marriage, to some extent, reflects changes in marital and family relationships, in the role of women, as well as in the attitudes toward marriage and sexuality (Jones 2007). The sex ratio of both the 25–34 and 35–44 age groups had declined continuously and rapidly, and since 2001, women have outnumbered men in these age groups. This reversal is

Table 1. Key demographic indicators, 1981–2011.

	1981	1991	2001	2011
Sex ratio (No. of men per 100 women)				
Age 25–34	110.2	107.2	97.4	94.0
Age 35–44	120.1	114.6	99.6	83.6
Age at first marriage (years)				
Male	27.0	29.1	30.2	31.2
Female	23.9	26.2	27.5	28.9
% of never married population (age 35–39)				
Male: Total	15.2	16.0	23.2	28.8
Primary & below	8.4	5.8	2.4	0.8
Secondary	5.8	8.1	14.5	16.9
Post-secondary	1.1	2.0	6.3	11.1
Female: Total	4.5	10.4	18.8	22.0
Primary & below	1.1	2.5	1.5	0.5
Secondary	2.4	5.9	11.0	10.9
Post-secondary	1.0	2.0	6.3	10.5

Note: Figures include foreign domestic helpers.
Source: Demographic Trends in Hong Kong 1981–2011.

closely related to the changing composition of immigrants in Hong Kong during this period.

Apart from the changes in non-marriage, the profile of marriage itself has become much more complex. Figure 1 shows that the number of marriages declined from about 50,000 in 1981 to about 30,000 in 2000, and started to increase afterwards, reaching the peak at about 60,000 in 2012 and levelling off recently. However, this rebound was mainly due to the increasing number of cross-border marriages between Hong Kong residents (either men or women) and Mainland residents. As shown, the number of marriages would decrease to 40,000 if cross-border marriages were excluded, causing the magnitude of marriage rebound much weaker. Besides, the number of divorces increased dramatically from 2060 cases in 1981 to about 20,000 cases in 2014, while the number of remarriages (at

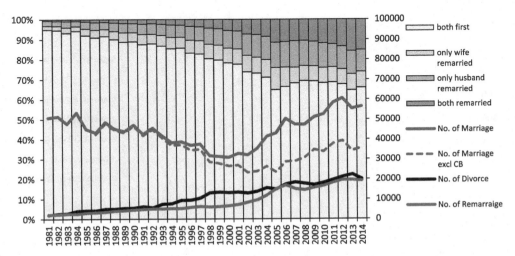

Figure 1. Trends of marriages, remarriages, and divorces, 1981–2014. *Source*: Demographic Trends in Hong Kong 1981–2011; Women and Men in Hong Kong Key Statistics 2015.

Note: CB stands for cross-border marriages registered in Hong Kong, including Hong Kong bridegrooms marrying Mainland brides as well as Hong Kong brides marrying Mainland bridegrooms.

least one party being remarried) followed a similar trend. Breaking down all marriages by previous marital status (see Figure 1), the distribution percent of marriages (by marriage order) became very diverse, with rising proportions of only husband, only wife, and both-parties remarriages. Altogether, remarriages accounted for about one-third of the total registered marriages in 2014, in contrast to only 5% in 1981.

Figure 2 shows the distribution of local marriages and transnational marriages of Hongkongers for the period 1995–2012 and Figure 3 shows the proportion of remarriages in each type of marriage. As shown in Figure 2, in 1995, 70% of marriages involved Hong Kong men marrying Hong Kong women, and in 2005, this proportion dropped to 49% and rebounded a little afterwards, but still at less than 60% in 2012. Among all types of transnational marriages, marriages between Hong Kong men and Mainland Chinese women have increased and currently account for about 37%. Other types of transnational marriages however, appeared to have decreased in the last 15 years. In Figure 3, the proportion of remarriages is calculated by using the number of remarriages in each type as the numerator and the total number of the respective type of marriages as the denominator. Among local marriages, the proportion of remarriages increased slightly in the past two decades, but still remained less than 10% in 2012. In contrast, amongst marriages of Hong Kong men with Mainland women and Hong Kong women with Mainland men, the proportion of remarriages increased dramatically – the proportion of the former increased from about 10% in 1995 to about 40% in 2012 and the proportion of the latter also reached 27% in 2012. The increasing trend of remarriages can also be observed in the marriages of Hong Kong men with other Asian women and Hong Kong women with Asian men. Although the proportion of remarriages involving westerners seemed to be fluctuating, it still remained at a higher level than that in local marriages.

Figures 2 and 3 imply that marriages in Hong Kong are getting more complex and diverse, with rapid rise of transnational marriages and disproportionate increase of

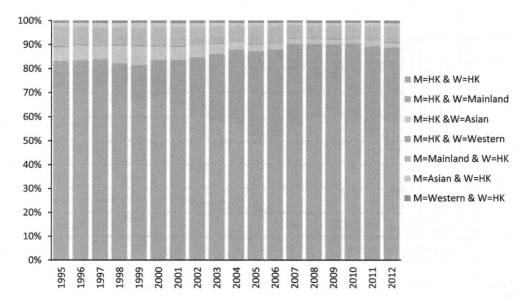

Figure 2. The distribution of different types of marriages among Hongkongers for the period 1995–2012. *Source*: Hong Kong marriage registration data, 1995–2012.

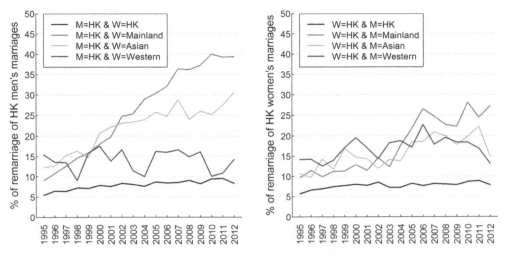

Figure 3. The proportion of remarriages in local and transnational marriages by gender, 1995–2012. *Source*: Hong Kong marriage registration data, 1995–2012.

remarriages among transnational marriages, particularly between Hongkongers and Mainlanders. On one hand, these indicate that the availability of non-local men and women have widened the window of opportunities for local people to enter into marriage or remarriage directly. On the other hand, there is also a possibility that an expanding pool of marriageable candidates could have indirectly contributed to the increase of divorces and remarriages, because couples in bad relationships may more easily give up on the present relationship and look for new relationships due to the ready availability of prospective mates. Both the direct and indirect effects may have played a role in the surge of transnational marriages and remarriages.

Table 2 compares the average age gap and educational selection for first marriage and remarriage across different types of marriages. As for the age gap in first marriages, marriages between Hong Kong men and western women (2.3 years), Hong Kong women and Mainland men (2.5 years), and Hong Kong women and Asian men (2.6 years), were very similar to the age gap in local marriages (2.2–2.5 years). The age gap in marriages between Hong Kong men and Mainland women (6.2 years), Hong Kong men and Asian women (5.2 years), and Hong Kong women and western men (3.7 years) were much larger than that between local couples. It is interesting to point out that for Hong Kong men, the age gap in remarriage was notably larger than that in first marriage, while for women, the age gap was smaller than that in first marriage. As for transnational remarriages, Hong Kong men tended to remarry much younger women, especially when brides came from the Mainland (14.1 years) or other Asian countries (11.2 years), whereas Hong Kong women remarried younger men from the Mainland (−0.8 years) or from other Asian countries (−0.1 years). Such differences between first marriage and remarriage suggest that when Hong Kong men remarried so with Mainland or other Asian women, they usually chose younger wives, following the tradition of age hypergamy. However, when Hong Kong women remarried, the age gaps narrowed greatly, indicating that they tended to be more open minded and not bounded by the norm of 'marrying up' to their male counterparts.

Table 2. Mate selection for age and education in first marriages and remarriages.

Types of marriages	Age gap (years) First marriage	Age gap (years) Remarriage	% of educational hypogamy First marriage	% of educational hypogamy Remarriage	% of educational homogamy First marriage	% of educational homogamy Remarriage	% of educational hypergamy First marriage	% of educational hypergamy Remarriage
HK men marrying								
HK women	2.2	5.9	4.8	6.1	85.8	85.5	9.5	8.3
Mainland women	6.2	14.1	4.2	5.9	78.6	77.7	17.3	16.4
Asian women	5.2	11.2	8.6	10.1	74.2	73.6	17.2	16.3
Western women	2.3	8.1	12.9	16.6	76.1	72.4	10.9	11.0
HK women marrying								
HK men	2.5	1.9	4.9	4.4	85.8	85.6	9.3	10.1
Mainland men	2.5	−0.8	10.4	10.6	81.6	81.9	8.0	7.5
Asian men	2.6	−0.1	9.2	9.4	75.8	74.7	15.1	16.0
Western men	3.7	3.4	6.6	6.1	65.6	60.8	27.8	33.2

Source: Hong Kong marriage registration data, 1995–2012.

Homogamy in educational selection was higher in local marriages than in transnational marriages. It is noteworthy that differences between first marriage and remarriage (i.e. differences observed across the columns in Table 2) were very slight, and homogamy was predominant. Marriages between Hongkongers and westerners deserve special attention. The proportion of hypogamy in remarriages between Hong Kong men and western women was 16.6% compared to 12.9% in first marriages; for remarriages between Hong Kong women and western men, the proportion of hypergamy increased from 27.8% for first marriage to 33.2% for remarriage. It is interesting that the differences across different types of marriage (i.e. differences observed across the rows in Table 2) were relatively larger, in both first marriage and remarriage: homogamy ranged from 65.6% to 85.8% in first marriage, and from 60.8% to 85.5% in remarriage. The persistence of homogamy in educational selection between first marriage and remarriage, and the variations of homogamy across different types of marriages indicate that transnational marriages, whether first marriages or remarriages, have contributed to the heterogamy in Hongkongers' marriages.

Multinomial logistic regression

In the first set of models for Hong Kong men, the mating patterns in transnational remarriages and those of local remarriages are compared. Table 3 shows the coefficients from the multinomial logistic regression. Compared to local remarriages, Hong Kong men involved in all types of transnational remarriages were more likely to be in the older age groups (i.e. the age groups of 45–54 and 55 and above). It is worth noting that the educational attainment and occupation of Hong Kong men showed different associations with the three types of remarriages: Hong Kong men who had low education or were in low skilled occupations were more likely to remarry Mainland or Asian women. In contrast, Hong Kong men who were highly educated or in managerial/professional occupations were more likely to remarry western women. Moreover, widowed Hong Kong men were more likely to remarry women from other Asian countries. Both husband and wife being in remarriage was more likely to occur in transnational remarriages than in local remarriages. Another noteworthy finding is that when compared with local remarriages, increase in the number of years since the dissolution of last marriage decreased the odds of entry into transnational remarriages. Besides, for Hong Kong men, the longer the duration of their last marriage, the less likely they were to remarry Mainland or Asian women.

In terms of age selection, age gap patterns varied across the three types of transnational remarriages. In remarriages of Hong Kong men and Mainland women, Hong Kong men were more likely to remarry much younger wives but less likely to remarry Mainland women who were older than them. In the remarriages of Hong Kong men and Asian women and Hong Kong men and western women, there were both remarrying down (i.e. bridegrooms older than brides) and remarrying up (i.e. bridegrooms younger than brides). In terms of educational assortative mating, hypergamy was more likely to occur in the remarriages of Hong Kong men and Mainland women, and hypogamy less likely to occur. In contrast, hypogamy was more likely to occur in remarriages with western brides. Moreover, remarriages with Asian brides were very heterogamous (brides and bridegrooms at different levels of education).

Table 3. Coefficients of multinomial logistic regression for Hong Kong men's remarriages (with remarriages of HK men with HK women as the reference group).

Variables	M = HK & W = Mainland	M = HK & W = Asian	M = HK & W = Western
Husband's age			
Ref. = Age 25–34			
Age 15–24	0.101	0.547	−11.09
Age 35–44	0.0182	0.132*	0.260
Age 45–54	0.415**	0.555**	0.634**
Age 55 and above	0.651**	0.796**	0.578
Husband's education			
Ref. = Secondary			
Primary or below	1.149**	0.653**	−0.0872
Tertiary (non-degree)	−1.584**	−1.135**	0.534*
Tertiary (degree)	−1.872**	−1.407**	0.835**
Husband's occupation			
Ref. = Associate professional/ Clerks/Service workers			
Managerial/professional	−0.167**	−0.103*	0.590**
Semi-skilled/unskilled	0.731**	0.579**	−0.00763
Economically Inactive	0.235**	0.155*	0.789**
Whether widowed			
Ref. = Divorced			
widowed	0.0328	0.243**	−0.268
Parties Remarried			
Ref. = only wife remarried			
Both remarried	0.438**	0.144**	0.668**
Years since last dissolution	−0.0541**	−0.0552**	−0.0361*
Duration of last marriage	−0.0234**	−0.0285**	0.00281
Time trends	0.143**	−0.0452**	−0.0853**
Age Gap: Husband–Wife			
Ref. = 0–5 years			
6–9 years	0.782**	0.465**	0.148
10+ years	2.188**	1.541**	0.754**
Younger 1–5 years	−0.167**	0.0790	0.233
Younger 6–9 years	0.0313	0.283	0.945*
Younger 10+	−0.0115	0.675*	1.714**
Educational selection			
Ref. = homogamy			
Hypogamy	−0.681**	0.220**	1.215**
Hypergamy	1.765**	1.537**	−0.299
Constant	−2.374**	−2.231**	−5.182**
Observations	72,083	72,083	72,083

Note: ** $p < .01$, * $p < .05$.

Table 4 shows the coefficients for Hong Kong women's remarriages. Compared to the prime age of marriage (i.e. age 25–34), both younger and older women were more likely to remarry Mainland men. However, remarriages with Asian or western bridegrooms were more likely to occur among Hong Kong women aged 35 and above, but less likely among much younger women (i.e. aged 15–24). Hong Kong women with lower education or in low skill occupations were more likely to remarry Mainlanders. In contrast, those with higher education or in managerial/professional occupations were more likely to remarry western men. In addition, widowed Hong Kong women were more likely to remarry Mainland or Asian men. Compared to local remarriages, both spouses being in remarriage was more likely to happen when Hong Kong women remarried Mainland or western men. Also, increase in the number of years since the dissolution of last marriage decreased the chances of remarrying non-local men, which is very similar to the findings on Hong Kong men. Moreover, the longer the duration of local women's last marriage, the lower the odds of remarrying Mainland or western men.

Table 4. Coefficients of multinomial logistic regression for Hong Kong women's remarriages (with remarriages of HK men with HK women as the reference group).

Variables	W = HK & M = Mainland	W = HK & M = Asian	W = HK & M = Western
Wife's age			
Ref. = Age 25–34			
Age 15–24	0.319**	0.347	−2.496*
Age 35–44	0.137**	0.234**	0.793**
Age 45–54	0.424**	0.293*	1.345**
Age 55 and above	0.810**	0.146	1.670**
Wife's education			
Ref. = Secondary			
Primary or below	0.961**	0.157	−1.778**
Tertiary (non-degree)	−0.992**	−0.138	0.988**
Tertiary (degree)	−1.276**	−0.0356	1.723**
Wife's occupation			
Ref. = Associate professional/ Clerks/Service workers			
Managerial/Professional	−0.117*	0.273**	0.683**
Semi-skilled/unskilled	0.668**	0.385*	−0.343
Economically Inactive	0.396**	0.00114	0.398**
Whether widowed			
Ref. = Divorced			
Widowed	0.672**	0.530**	−0.0475
Parties Remarried			
Ref. = only wife remarried			
Both remarried	1.014**	0.102	0.499**
Years since last dissolution	−0.0275**	−0.0273**	−0.0282**
Duration of last marriage	−0.0102**	−0.00737	−0.0261**
Time trends	0.0440**	0.000856	−0.0123
Age Gap: Husband-Wife			
Ref. = 0–5 years			
6–9 years	−0.00973	0.196	0.486**
10+ years	0.167**	0.269*	1.035**
Younger 1–5 years	0.632**	0.208*	0.208*
Younger 6–9 years	1.307**	0.782**	0.382*
Younger 10+	2.256**	2.070**	0.959**
Educational-selection			
Ref. = homogamy			
Hypogamy	1.339**	0.914**	−0.139
Hypergamy	−0.543**	0.556**	1.783**
Constant	−2.898**	−3.617**	−4.710**
Observations	33,495	33,495	33,495

Note: **$p < .01$, *$p < .05$.

Regarding age selection of Hong Kong women, all three types of transnational remarriages were relatively more heterogeneous, compared to local remarriages. Mate selection in terms of education demonstrates very different patterns from that observed in the models for Hong Kong men. First, unlike the very hypergamous remarriages of Hong Kong men and Mainland women, the remarriages of Hong Kong women and Mainland men turned out to be very hypogamous (i.e. local women marrying down). Second, unlike the very hypogamous remarriages of Hong Kong men and western women, the remarriages of Hong Kong women and western men were more likely to be hypergamous (i.e. local women marrying up).

Further, the trends of age and educational assortative mating over the period 1995–2012 were investigated by adding the interaction of age gaps and time trends as well as the interaction of educational selection and time trends in the multinomial logistic regression models. The coefficients of the interactions in the model for Hong Kong men and women are shown in Tables 5 and 6 respectively. Table 5 shows that there

Table 5. Coefficients of interactions with time trends in multinomial logistic regression for Hong Kong men's remarriages (with remarriages of HK men with HK women as the reference group).

Variables	M = HK & W = Mainland	M = HK & W = Asian	M = HK & W = Western
Age Gap: Husband–Wife			
Ref. = 0–5 years			
6–9 years	0.694**	0.434**	0.139
10+ years	1.624**	1.393**	0.746**
Younger 1–5 years	−0.0802	0.0840	0.195
Younger 6–9 years	0.399	0.403	1.849**
Younger 10+	0.811	1.758**	5.178**
*Age-selection * time trends*			
6–9 years * time trends	0.00748	0.00387	0.00248
10+ years * time trends	0.0543**	0.0141	−0.000646
Younger 1–5 years * time trends	−0.00799	−0.000171	0.00488
Younger 6–9 years * time trends	−0.0370	−0.0124	−0.153
Younger 10+ * time trends	−0.0788	−0.130	−1.703
Educational selection			
Ref. = homogamy			
Hypogamy	−0.660**	0.00369	1.553**
Hypergamy	1.577**	1.525**	−0.540
*Educational-selection * time trends*			
Hypogamy * time trends	−0.000458	0.0285*	−0.0485
Hypergamy * time trends	0.0190**	−.0000392	0.0327

Note: ** *p* < .01, * *p* < .05; other variables in Table 2 are controlled.

was an ever-increasing trend of Hong Kong men remarrying Mainland women with age 10 years and more younger than them or with lower education. Meanwhile, there was also an increasing trend of educational hypogamy in the remarriages of Hong Kong men and Asian women. In Table 6, it can be seen that there was a decreasing trend of Hong Kong women remarrying non-local men of 10 or more years older than them (whether from Mainland or other Asian countries or western countries). Over the period of 1995–2012, Hong Kong women were more likely to remarry Mainland men who were

Table 6. Coefficients of interactions with time trends in multinomial logistic regression for Hong Kong women's remarriages (with remarriages of HK men with HK women as the reference group).

Variables	W = HK & M = Mainland	W = HK & M = Asian	W = HK & M = Western
Age Gap: Husband–Wife			
Ref. = 0–5 years			
6–9 years	0.215*	0.0610	0.733**
10+ years	1.025**	0.824**	1.470**
Younger 1–5 years	0.468**	−0.0498	0.405*
Younger 6–9 years	0.793**	0.512*	0.507
Younger 10+	1.541**	1.645**	1.522**
*Age-selection * time trends*			
6–9 years * time trends	−0.0240*	0.0161	−0.0270
10+ years * time trends	−0.0926**	−0.0659**	−0.0471*
Younger 1–5 years * time trends	0.0164*	0.0295	−0.0212
Younger 6–9 years * time trends	0.0501**	0.0300	−0.0128
Younger 10+ * time trends	0.0677**	0.0445	−0.0582
Educational selection			
Ref. = homogamy			
Hypogamy	1.068**	0.955**	0.213
Hypergamy	−0.443**	0.466**	2.087**
*Educational selection * time trends*			
Hypogamy * time trends	0.0283**	−0.00583	−0.0369
Hypergamy * time trends	−0.0125	0.0101	−0.0346*

Note: ** *p* < .01, * *p* < .05; other variables in Table 3 are controlled.

Table 7. Summary of mating patterns and trends, 1995–2012.

	Hong Kong men			Hong Kong women		
	W = Mainland	W = Asian	W = Western	M = Mainland	M = Asian	M = Western
Age selection (time trends)						
Reference: normal age gap (0-5 years)						
Age hypergamy (men 5+ years older than women)	+ (↑)	+ (NS)	+ (NS)	+ (↓)	+ (↓)	+ (↓)
Age hypogamy (men younger than women)	− (NS)	+ (NS)	+ (NS)	+ (↑)	+ (NS)	+ (NS)
Educational selection (time trends)						
Reference: bridegroom = bride						
Educational hypergamy (men > women)	+ (↑)	+ (NS)	NS (NS)	− (NS)	+ (NS)	+ (↓)
Educational hypogamy (men < women)	− (↓)	+ (↑)	+ (NS)	+ (↑)	+ (NS)	NS (NS)

Note: '+' and '−' refer to positive or negative associations with the odds of remarrying non-locals against remarrying locals; '↑' or '↓' refers to the related trend increasing or decreasing; 'NS' refers to being non-significant.

younger or with lower educational attainment than them. At the same time, although marrying up is often practised in remarriages of Hong Kong women and western men, such educational hypergamy is actually declining in recent years.

Based on the results in Tables 2–5, Table 7 summarises mate selection patterns for age and education and related trends. It shows that hypergamy in remarriages of Hong Kong men and Mainland women was on the rise during the relevant 17 years, both in terms of age or educational selection. In contrast, age hypogamy and educational hypogamy were on the rise in remarriages of Hong Kong women and Mainland men, and age and educational hypergamy in remarriages between Hong Kong women and western men were in decline.

Conclusions and discussions

The institution of marriage in Hong Kong has been changing rapidly. By making comparisons, it is shown that assortative mating in first marriages and remarriages can be found across local marriages and transnational marriages (there are six types of transnational marriages, covering marriages with brides or bridegrooms from Mainland China, other Asian countries, and western countries). In terms of age selection, the findings are very consistent with western literature in that first marriage is more homogamous, while remarriages are more heterogamous (de Graaf and Kalmijn 2003; England and McClintock 2009; Gelissen 2004; Shafer 2009). However, for educational selection, a persistence of homogamy between first marriage and remarriage is observed, but with notable variations of homogamy across different types of marriages (i.e. local vs transnational marriages).

Further comparison of the characteristics and mating patterns in transnational remarriages and local remarriages, and examining the related trends in recent years, the logistic regression analyses have shown some interesting findings. Hongkongers (both Hong Kong men and women) of low socioeconomic status (SES) with low education and in low skill occupations are more likely to remarry Mainland women as the choice of spouse is limited for them due to their low SES, and Hongkongers of high socioeconomic status are more likely to remarry spouses from western countries. Nevertheless, there are also some gender differences. For Hong Kong men, remarriage with Mainland brides tends to be more age and education hypergamous, while remarriage with western brides tends to be more age and education hypogamous. In contrast, hypogamy is more likely to be practised by Hong Kong women who remarry Mainland men, while hypergamy is more likely to be practised by Hong Kong women who remarry western men.

Our findings further demonstrate that in the local marriage market where men marrying down and women marrying up are widely desired and practised, the marriage squeeze on Hong Kong men of lower SES and women of higher social class is somehow relieved by the availability of Mainlanders and westerners respectively. Instead of trying to find someone in the local marriage market, Hong Kong men with lower education and income look for Mainland brides, while Hong Kong women with higher education and income tend to marry western men. Existing literature focusing on cross-border marriages of Hong Kong men (Lin and Ma 2008; Zhou 2016) has, however, only shown one side of the marriage squeeze in Hong Kong. The squeeze on men as well as on women is somehow related to the continuous advancement of women's socioeconomic roles and financial independence.

Our analyses on the trends in mate selection show that in recent years, Hong Kong women have become more likely to remarry non-local men of younger age (whether bridegrooms from Mainland, other Asian countries or western countries). This may reflect the weakening of social norms on assortative selection for age and ethnic groups (Kershaw 2009). Apart from Hong Kong, a rise in age hypogamy has also been observed in Taiwan (Cheng 2015). Another interesting finding is that there is a declining trend of educational hypergamy in remarriages between Hong Kong women and western men. Such decline may be driven by the overall increase of local women's educational attainment. Due to the expansion of tertiary education opportunities, women have caught up very fast and even overtaken men in educational attainment. Currently, in Hong Kong, women already outnumber men in government-funded tertiary institutions in the first year intake (HKCSD 2015). Thus, the educational gap between men and women is gradually closing up.

The rapid rise of marriages between Hongkongers (including Hong Kong men and women) and Mainlanders is, however, characterised by a disproportionate increase in remarriages. Our findings show that in recent years, remarriages between Hong Kong men and Mainland women have become more hypergamous, while remarriages between Hong Kong women and Mainland men have become more hypogamous. The increasing social and economic interactions after the return of sovereignty to China in 1997 have facilitated cross-border marriages, widened choices for local residents to marry and remarry, and provided more opportunities to meet aspirations of family formation. Also, maintaining a stable marriage in Hong Kong has become difficult due to the hectic and long working hours which is not conducive to promoting a healthy marital relationship. At the same time, this provides opportunities to develop out of wedlock relationships in the workplace. Some have suggested that an increase in divorces can be related to the availability of mistresses across the border (Yip et al. 2014). Also, more attention should be paid to cross-border families and stepfamilies, as well as the quality and stability of these remarriages. A friendly welcoming social atmosphere is a very important protector to these families, as it is shown to be a crucial factor to the welling-being and mental health of these marriage immigrants (Li and Yang 2020).

Besides, the findings also show that those cross-border marriages are more likely to involve local men and women with lower education and income. Thus, more social and welfare support is needed to help these couples and families to settle in Hong Kong, especially for those with housing and job retraining needs. Domestic violence has also been reported among cross-border marriages, especially in those involving older husbands and younger wives. Support for these couples need also to be enhanced. Apart from the impact on the local marriage market, cross-border marriages and remarriages would also shape the population dynamics in Hong Kong. Through marriage migration, the arrival of migrants in Hong Kong can be a good source of a young population with relatively higher fertility rate (Basten and Verropoulou 2013; Leung 2011; Yip et al. 2014). Thus, the inflow of these marriage migrants will help slow down population ageing and the shrinking of the workforce.

Hence, it is important to be able to effectively tap into this human capital. In addition, the educational and professional qualifications of non-locals, especially those from the Mainland, are not recognised in Hong Kong. And there are many barriers to obtain accreditation, especially in the education and health care sectors for medical doctors, teachers and nurses. Therefore, it is important to make the social system more inclusive without compromising on standards. At the same time, some of the social and welfare policies need to be revised to be able to provide more timely support for those in need.

Hong Kong is a city where the East meets the West. Although non-Chinese residents constitute only 6.4% of the total population in Hong Kong (HKCSD 2011), this group has a significant influence on the local marriage market. A better and deeper understanding of transnational marriages could help generate timely and focused policies that remove obstacles to successful assimilation into Hong Kong society. This study that uncovers the increasing complexity of marriages in Hong Kong from the perspective of spousal pairing, could also provide some insights on mate selection in the ever-changing marriage market in the East Asian region as well.

Acknowledgements

This study is supported by the Strategic Public Policy Research Funding Scheme of Research Grant Council in Hong Kong (HKU-SPPR-12).

Disclosure statement

No potential conflict of interest was reported by the authors.

ORCID

Paul Yip http://orcid.org/0000-0003-1596-4120

References

Basten, Stuart, and Georgia Verropoulou. 2013. "'Maternity Migration' and the Increased Sex Ratio at Birth in Hong Kong SAR." *Population Studies* 67 (3): 323–334. doi:10.1080/00324728.2013.826372.

Becker, Gary S., Elisabeth S. Landes, and Robert T. Michael. 1977. "An Economic Analysis of Marital Instability." *Journal of Political Economy* 85 (6): 1141–1187.

Boyle, Paul J., Hill Kulu, Thomas Cooke, Vernon Gayle, and Clarah Mulder. 2008. "Moving and Union Dissolution." *Demography* 45 (1): 209–222.

Bramlett, Matthew D., and William D. Mosher. 2002. "Cohabitation, Marriage, Divorce, and Remarriage in the United States." *Vital Health Statistics* 23 (22): 1–32.

Burr, Wesley R. 1973. *Theory Construction and the Sociology of the Family*. New York: John Wiley & Sons.

Cheng, Yen-Hsin A. 2015. "Social Change and Age Hypergamy: The Shift in Spousal Age Preferences in Taiwan, 1976-2012." Paper presented at the Population Association of America 2015, San Diego, CA. http://paa2015.princeton.edu/abstracts/151223.

Choi, Yool, Doo-Sub Kim, and Jungkyun Ryu. 2020. "Marital Dissolution of Transnational Couples in South Korea." *Journal of Ethnic and Migration Studies* 46 (14): 3014–3039. doi:10.1080/1369183X.2019.1585021.

Constable, Nicole. 2010. *Cross-border Marriages: Gender and Mobility in Transnational Asia*. Philadelphia: University of Pennsylvania Press.

Dean, Gillian, and Douglas T. Gurak. 1978. "Marital Homogamy the Second Time Around." *Journal of Marriage and the Family* 40 (3): 559–570.

de Graaf, Paul M., and Matthijs Kalmijn. 2003. "Alternative Routes in the Remarriage Market: Competing-risk Analyses of Union Formation After Divorce." *Social Forces* 81 (4): 1459–1498.

England, Paula, and Elizabeth A. McClintock. 2009. "The Gendered Double Standard of Aging in US Marriage Markets." *Population and Development Review* 35 (4): 797–816.

Gelissen, John. 2004. "Assortative Mating After Divorce: A Test of Two Competing Hypotheses Using Marginal Models." *Social Science Research* 33 (3): 361–384.

Hannemann, Tina, and Hill Kulu. 2015. "Union Formation and Dissolution among Immigrants and Their Descendants in the United Kingdom." *Demographic Research* 33: 273–312.

Hong Kong Census and Statistics Department (HKCSD). 2012. "Demographic trends in Hong Kong – 1981-2011." Demographic Statistics Section, Census and Statistics Department. http://www.statistics.gov.hk/pub/B1120017032012XXXXB0100.pdf.

Hong Kong Census and Statistics Department (HKCSD). 2015. "Women and Men in Hong Kong - Key Statistics (2015 Edition)." Hong Kong Census and Statistics Department. http://www.statistics.gov.hk/pub/B11303032015AN15B0100.pdf.

Jones, Gavin W. 2007. "Delayed Marriage and Very Low Fertility in Pacific Asia." *Population and Development Review* 33 (3): 453–478. doi:10.1111/j.1728-4457.2007.00180.x.

Kalmijn, Matthijs. 1998. "Intermarriage and Homogamy: Causes, Patterns, Trends." *Annual Review of Sociology* 24: 395–421.

Kershaw, Sarah. 2009. "Rethinking the Older Woman-Younger Man Relationship." *The New York Times*, October 14.

Kim, Doo-Sub. 2010. "The Rise of Cross-border Marriage and Divorce in Contemporary Korea." In *Asian Cross-border Marriage Migration: Demographic Patterns and Social Issues*, edited by Wen-Shan Yang and Melody Chia-Wen Lu, 128–153. Amsterdam: Amsterdam University Press. IIAS Publication Series.

Leung, Ling. 2011. "The Low-fertility Problem in Hong Kong: Do Mainlanders' Births Help to Rejuvenate Low-fertility Problem." *World Academy of Science, Engineering and Technology* 5 (5): 789–795.

Li, Chun-Hao, and Wenshan Yang. 2020. "Happiness of Female Immigrants in Cross-border Marriages in Taiwan." *Journal of Ethnic and Migration Studies* 46 (14): 2956–2976. doi:10.1080/1369183X.2019.1585015.

Lin, Ge, and Zhongdong Ma. 2008. "Examining Cross-border Marriages in Hong Kong Since its Return to China in 1997." *Population, Space and Place* 14 (5): 407–418.

Ma, Zhongdong, Ge Lin, and Lei Zhang. 2010. "Examining Cross-border Marriage in Hong Kong: 1998-2005." In *Asian Cross-border Marriage Migration: Demographic Patterns and Social Issues*, edited by Wen-Shan Yang and Melody Chia-Wen Lu, 87–102. Amsterdam: Amsterdam University Press. IIAS Publication Series.

Martin, Teresa C., and Larry L. Bumpass. 1989. "Recent Trends in Marital Disruption." *Demography* 26 (1): 37–51.

McCarthy, James. 1978. "A Comparison of the Probability of the Dissolution of First and Second Marriages." *Demography* 15 (3): 345–359.

Nye, Francis I., and Felix M. Berardo. 1973. *The Family: Its Structure and Interaction*. New York: Macmillan.

Pong, Suet-long, David Post, Dongshu Ou, and Maggie S. Y. Fok. 2014. "Blurring Boundaries? Immigration and Exogamous Marriages in Hong Kong." *Population and Development Review* 40 (4): 629–652.

Population Policy Starategies and Initiatives. 2015. The Hong Kong Government of Special Administration Region. http://www.hkpopulation.gov.hk/public_engagement/pdf/PPbooklet2015_ENG.pdf.

Qian, Zhenchao, and Daniel T. Lichter. 2018. "Marriage Markets and Intermarriage: Exchange in First Marriages and Remarriages." *Demography* 55 (3): 1–27.

Schwartz, Christine R., and Robert D. Mare. 2012. "The Proximate Determinants of Educational Homogamy: The Effects of First Marriage, Marital Dissolution, Remarriage, and Educational Upgrading." *Demography* 49: 629–650.

Shafer, Kevin M. 2009. *Gender Differences in Remarriage: Marriage Formation and Assortative Mating After Divorce*. Columbus, Ohio: The Ohio State University.

Shafer, Kevin. 2013. "Unique Matching Patterns in Remarriage Educational Assortative Mating among Divorced Men and Women." *Journal of Family Issues* 34 (11): 1500–1535.

Shafer, Kevin, and Spencer L. James. 2013. "Gender and Socioeconomic Status Differences in First and Second Marriage Formation." *Journal of Marriage and Family* 75 (3): 544–564.

Smits, Jeroen, and Hyunjoon Park. 2009. "Five Decades of Educational Assortative Mating in 10 East Asian Societies." *Social Forces* 88 (1): 227–255.

So, Alvin Y. 2003. "Cross-border Families in Hong Kong: The Role of Social Class and Politics." *Critical Asian Studies* 35 (4): 515–534.

Theunis, Lindsay, Inge Pasteels, and Jan Van Bavel. 2015. "Educational Assortative Mating After Divorce: Persistence or Divergence from First Marriages?" *Zeitschrift für Familienforschung* 27: 183–202.

Weiss, Yoram, Junjian Yi, and Junsen Zhang. 2013. "Hypergamy, Cross-Boundary Marriages, and Family Behavior." IDEAS Working Paper Series, RePEc.

Yeung, Wei-Jun Jean, and Zheng Mu. 2020. "Migration and Marriage in Asian Contexts." *Journal of Ethnic and Migration Studies* 46 (14): 2863–2879. doi:10.1080/1369183X.2019.1585005.

Yip, Paul, Shu-Sen Chang, Frances Yik Wa Law, Lianne Tai, Sandra Tsang, and Melissa Chan. 2014. *A Study on the Phenomenon of Divorce in Hong Kong*. Hong Kong: The University of Hong Kong.

Zhang, Huiping, Petula S. Y. Ho, and Paul S. F. Yip. 2012. "Does Similarity Breed Marital and Sexual Satisfaction?" *Journal of Sex Research* 49 (6): 583–593.

Zhou, M. 2016. "Educational Assortative Mating in Hong Kong: 1981–2011." *Chinese Sociological Review* 48 (1): 33–63.

Index

Note: Endnotes are indicated by the page number followed by 'n' and the endnote number e.g., 20n1 refers to endnote 1 on page 20.

acculturation 10, 89, 94, 95; eurocentric theory of 130
Alba, Richard D. 20, 181
Ananta, Aris 35
Anderson, Benedict 119–120
Arifin, Evi Nurvidya 35
Aroian, Karen J. 97
Asia; immigrants in United States 6, 7; international and internal migration 2; marriage immigrants in 95; migrants' skills qualifications 3; migration and marriage in 3; mixed-method analysis 3; qualitative analysis 3; quantitative analysis 3
AsiaBarometer (AB) Survey 81, 91n3
Asian Americans 22; assimilation and intermarriage 19–20; current study 22; data and methods 22–4; discussion 29–31; education 18; generation and education 18, 20–2; intermarriage of 18; interracial marriage 19; results 24–9
assimilation 147; and intermarriage 19–20
assortative mating 6, 7, 52, 57; in China 52; ethnic perspectives 8; by family origins 66–7; in Hong Kong 198; in Indonesia 40; in Jakarta 40
Australia 76, 161, 201; migration-marriage link 53
Aycan, Zeynep 96

Bartram, David 97
Bayesian information criterion (BIC) statistics 25, 26
Beijing 8, 53, 54, 59, 65, 70, 72
Bélanger, D. 77
Berry, John W. 95, 96
Boyle, Paul J. 200
Britain; migration-marriage link 53

Cambodia 94, 155, 161, 182
Canada 161, 201
Carmalt, Julie H. 21, 30
caste/sub-caste; in Indian marriages 131
Certificate of Absence of Marriage Record (CAMR) 201

Chang, Hsin-Chieh 5, 9, 77
Chatterjee, Esha 5, 10
Chen, Mengni 12
China 2, 5, 7, 9, 161, 182; analytic strategy 57–9; assortative mating by family origins 66–71; data and methods 56; economic reforms 54; entry into first marriage 60–6; ethnic intermarriage in 37; fast-growing migrant population in 54; floating population 54; foreign investment 54; high-skilled migrants in 53; housing prices 8; hypotheses 55; improvement in education 54; internal migration 2; low-skilled migrants in 53; minority-majority type intermarriage 36–7; mixed-method study in 52; official language in 59; qualitative study 59; quantitative study 56–7; results 60; rural-to-urban migration 52; semi-skilled migrants in 53; theoretical issues and Chinese context 53–5
Chinese Family Panel Studies (CFPS) 8
Chinese immigrants 20, 95, 165
Chiu, Tuen Yi 5, 10
Choi, Susanne Y. P. 5, 10
Choi, Yool 11, 178, 200
chosônjok (Ethnic Koreans in China) 158, 171n1
civic participation autonomy 124, 129
classical assimilation theory 19–20
community atmosphere 97, 109
Constable, Nicole 2, 4
Convention on the Elimination of all Forms of Discrimination Against Women (CEDAW) 88
Correll, Shelley J. 78
cross-border marriage 2; female immigrants in Taiwan 94, 103; gendered power in marriage migration 138–9; intra-Asia 79; rising rates, in Hong Kong 10, 198, 201
cultural assimilation 3

Davin, Delia 97
Deaton, Angus 98
decoupling of legal and spatial migration; discussions 146–9; of female marriage

migrants 135; gendered power in marriage migration 138–140; legal migration without spatial migration 143–6; research methods 141–2; research site 140–1; spatial migration before legal migration 142–3
Dedoose 80–1
Desai, Sonalde 5, 10
descriptive analysis 202–7
divorce; cost of 157; country of origin 165; education and 166; between Korean wife and foreign husband 177; rate in Korea 6, 167, 175, 176; rising rates in Hong Kong 198; in Singapore 178, 182–3; by type of marriage 165
Domestic Violence Prevention and Treatment Act (DVPTA) 84
Dyson, Tim 120

East Asia 76, 94, 108, 153; cross-border marriage in 153; female marriage immigrants in 94
East Asian Social Survey (EASS) 91n4
Easterlin, Richard A. 98
economic autonomy, of women 10, 123, 124, 126, 128, 130
educational homogamy 8, 47
employment status 97, 104, 108
endogamy 8, 36, 199; in India 130; in Jakarta 42
ethnic assortative mating 7, 8; in Indonesia 36; in Jakarta 34, 40, 42
ethnic *kampungs* (urban settlements) 39, 49n4
Eugene Hammel 130
Europe 2
European countries 76, 77, 201
exogamy 10, 36, 42, 48, 128, 129

family income 106, 108
female immigrants in cross-border marriages 95
Ferree, Myra Marx 98, 108
first-generation Asians 19, 22, 23, 30, 31
foreign-born Asians 23
Fulford, Scott L. 117

Gallup-Healthways Well-Being Index (GHWBI) 98
gender systems 9; affect intra-Asia marriage migrants 75; affect Vietnamese marriage migrants (VMMs) 76; in origin and destination societies 76; in South Korea 78–9; in Taiwan 78–9, 84; in Vietnam 78–9
gendered geographies of power" 138
generational endogamy 7, 24, 30
Germany, international marriage migrants 149n3
Global gender gap index (GGI) 79, 89
global hypergamy 4, 136, 139, 200
global marriage-scapes 4
global north 4, 135, 139, 140, 148
global south 4, 135, 139, 148
globalisation 13, 130, 193, 200; and transnationalism 135
Gordon, Milton M. 19, 95

Han, Hae-Ra 96
happiness of female immigrants; acculturative perspective 95–7; control variables 103–4; in cross-border marriages in Taiwan 94; dependent variable 99; economic perspective 97–8; key independent variables 99–103; literature review 95; methodology 104; methods 99; statistical results 104–8; variables 99
heterogamy hypothesis 11, 156, 157, 158, 165, 170, 171
hierarchical logistic regressions 126, 127
high-skilled migrants, in China 52, 53, 71
hispanic immigrants 94–5
Ho, Petula S. Y. 198
Hochschild, A. R. 180
homogamy 12, 199, 202, 207
Hong Kong 3, 5, 6, 7, 9, 12, 13, 141, 149n1, 182, 212, 213; assortative mating in 198; cross-border marriage, rising rates of 198, 201; data and method 201–2; descriptive analysis 202–7; divorce, rising rates of 198; immigration policies 140; and Mainland China 201; marriage types of Hong Kong women 201; multinomial logistic regression 207–211; one-way Permit Scheme (OWP) 140, 198; quota system 140; remarriage, rising rates of 198; remarriages and transnational marriages in 197; results 202; theoretical explanations of assortative mating 199–200; types of transnational marriages 201; women, marriage types of 201
hongbao 136
hukou system 2, 54, 71
Hurh, Won Moo 98, 108
hypergamy 4, 11, 135, 136, 139, 200, 202, 211
hypogamy 12, 202, 207, 211

imagined communities; versus physical communities 117; rooted in kinship norms 119–120, 122
in-between marriage 37, 48
India Human Development Survey (IHDS) 10, 116, 117
India 3, 7; control variables 125; data and methods 123–4; dependent variables 124; discussion 127–131; imagined communities 119–120; independent variables 125; internal migration 2; kinship patterns 120; marital arrangements 120; marriage migration in 10, 116–18; migration and women's autonomy in 115; physical communities 118–19; research questions 120–2; results 5, 127; statistical model 125; women's agency 120; women's autonomy, defining 122–3
Indonesia 2, 3, 7, 8, 13, 35, 182; archipelago 34; ethnic assortative mating in 34; ethnic endogamy in 37; ethnicity in city 39–40; internal migration 2
Indonesian Marriage Law 38

Integrated Public Use Microdata Series March Current Population Survey (IPUMS-CPS) 22
intergenerational marriage 7, 22, 25, 28, 30
internal migration 52; in China 56
interracial marriage 7, 19, 22, 30
intra-Asia marriage migration 13, 76, 89

Jakarta 8; ethnic assortative mating norms 42; ethnic intermarriage in 7, 34; ethnicity and in-between marriage 36–8; exogamy among young adults 42–3; parents and kinship networks in marriage decisions 35–6; racial-based assortative mating 35; religious authorities in marriage decisions 36; research context 38–42; results 42–9; sample statistics 41; theoretical framework 36–8
Japan 21, 94, 153, 155, 161, 182; international marriage migrants 149n3
Jejeebhoy, Shireen J. 119, 120, 129

Kahneman, Daniel 98
Kalmijn, Matthijs 8, 48, 199
Kim, Doo-Sub 3, 11, 178, 198, 200
Kim, Kwang Chung 98, 108
Kim, Miyong T. 96
Korea 3, 6, 7, 9, 13, 82, 90, 182; citizenship, marital stability by 159–160; country of origin, marital stability by 158; cross-border marriages 200; divorce rates in 154, 200; education, marital stability by 159; transnational marriages in 11, 200; type of marriage, marital stability by 157–8; Vietnamese marriage migrants in 75; women immigrants in United States 96; *see also* South Korea
Kulu, Hill 200

legal and spatial migration, decoupling of; discussions 146–9; of female marriage migrants 135; gendered power in marriage migration 138–140; legal migration without spatial migration 143–6; research methods 141–2; research site 140–1; spatial migration before legal migration 142–3
legal migration 10, 136, 137, 138; spatial migration before 142–3; without spatial migration 143–6
legal systems, for cross-border marriage migrants 10
length of residency 95, 96, 107, 108
Li, Chun-Hao 9, 98
Lichter, Daniel T. 21, 30, 200
Lin, Ge 198
Linh, T. G. 77
living costs, in cities 53, 54, 144
logistic regression analyses 41, 161, 168
low-skilled migrants, in China 53

Ma, Zhongdong 198
Macau 9, 11, 148

Mainland China 3, 5, 99, 111n2, 140, 148, 198, 201, 211
Mainland China–Hong Kong 135, 138, 140, 198; cross-border marriage migration 136
Malaysia 182, 184, 187, 193
Mandarin, mastery of 59, 67, 80, 111n2, 183, 187
marital dissolution of transnational couples in South Korea 152; citizenship 166–8; country of origin 164–5; data 160–1; discussion 169–171; education 166; hypotheses 157–160; Korean context 154–6; logistic regression analysis 168–9; marital stability of transnational marriage in korea 163–4; methods 162; results 162–9; theoretical background 156–7; variables 161–2; *see also* divorce
marital instabilities 10
marriage immigrants 9, 94, 99, 108, 110, 153, 155, 156, 212
marriage timing 8, 13, 52, 66, 71
marriage-related migration in India 117
Mazzucato, Valentina 6
McDonald, Peter 37, 40
Mexico; migration-marriage link 53
Miglietta, Anna 96
migrant-receiving cities 54, 72
migrants' family formation behaviour, of Asian 1
migrants' social lives 1
migration and marriage experience in Asia 4
migration impact on; men and women 55
mixed-method analysis 3, 6, 8, 13; in China 52–4
Moore, Mick 120
Mu, Zheng 6, 8
multiculturalism 3
multinomial logistic regression 207–211
multivariate analysis 12, 40–1, 48, 60, 67

National Sample Survey (NSS) 116
native-born Asians 23
Nee, Victor 20, 181
neo-assimilation models 13
new assimilation theory 7, 20, 30, 181
New Zealand 201
Newendorp, N. D. 138
Nilan, Pam 38
non-ethnic Chinese 201
non-Hispanic whites 22, 23
North America 2, 3, 7, 76, 77
North India 120, 123, 129; kinship pattern 123

One-way Permit Scheme (OWP), in Hong Kong 198
online dating sites, in Jakarta 41; for specific ethnic groups/religions 44
ordered logistic regression analysis 104
ordinal logistic regressions 125, 126

Pahl, Ray 120
Park, Hyunjoon 172n4
partial proportional odds (PPO) model 104

patrilocality 136-7, 145, 146; for cross-border marriages 140
perceived discrimination 97, 107, 109, 145
perceived friendliness 9, 94, 107, 109, 111n3
Pew Report 18
Philippines 12, 20, 94, 155, 161, 182
physical autonomy 10, 122, 123, 124, 126, 130
physical communities 117, 118
physical versus imagined communities; data and methods 123-5; imagined communities 119-120; kinship patterns 120; marriage migration in India 116-18; migration and women's autonomy in India 115; research questions 120-2; results 125-7; women's autonomy 122-3; women's migration 118-19
Pong, Suet-long 199
population size 19, 21
Portes, Alejandro 4
post migration gender ideology 75
pribumi (natives/sons of the soil) 35
profit-oriented marriage brokers 136

Qian, Yue 6, 7
Qian, Zhenchao 6, 7, 21, 30, 200
Quah, Sharon Ee Ling 5, 12

race-generation assortative marriage 23
Rahman, Lupin 120, 129
Rao, Vijayendra 120, 129
Raymo, James M. 37, 172n4
Reformasi period 35
remarriage; rising rates in Hong Kong 198, 199, 200, 207, 212; and transnational marriages 197
residential registration system *see hukou* system
Ridgeway, Cecilia L. 78
Rodríguez-García, Dan 77
rural migrants 57, 60, 68
rural-to-urban migrants in China 8
Ryan, Louise 103
Ryu, Jungkyun 11, 178

Sassen, S. 143
Sathar, A. Zeba 119, 120, 129
Schans, Djamila 6
second-generation Asians 19, 21, 23, 27, 30, 31
semi-skilled migrants, in China 53
Shafer, Kevin 198, 199
Shanghai 54, 72
Shenzhen 72, 140
Shin, Hye Sook 96
Singapore 2, 3, 7, 11, 12, 13, 94, 182, 194n4; cross-national marriages 2; discussion 192-3; divorce proceedings and obtaining legal representation 184-8; ex-spouse over post-divorce co-parenting arrangements 190-2; female marriage migrants 180-2; Long Term Visit Pass (LTVP) 184, 185; Long Term Visit Pass Plus (LTVP+) 184, 185; permanent residents (PRs) 186; post-divorce practices and strategies 188-190; research method 183-4; Short Term Visit Pass (STVP) 184, 185; transnational divorces in 178; transnational marriages and divorces in 182-3; Work Permit (WP) 184
social isolation 138, 139, 193
social networks 9, 10, 23, 46, 96, 107, 108, 156, 192; immigrant brides rely on 103; strong ties and weak ties 96
South India 121, 129
South Korea 2, 94; citizenship 166-8; country of origin 164-5; data 160-1; discussion 169-171; education 166; gender systems compared 78-9; global gender-related indices 79; hypotheses 157-160; international marriage migrants 149n3; Korean context 154-6; logistic regression analysis 168-9; marital dissolution of transnational couples in 152; marital stability of transnational marriage in Korea 163-4; methods 162; results 162-9; theoretical background 156-7; variables 161-2; Vietnamese marriage migrants in 75; *see also* Korea
Southeast Asia 47, 88, 94, 110, 111n2, 155, 205; countries, marital dissolution in 165; new types of marriages in 199; women in 123
Southeast Asian countries 9, 11, 110, 155, 165, 182, 184, 192
southern kinship pattern, in India 119, 121
spatial and legal migration, decoupling of; discussions 146-9; of female marriage migrants 135; gendered power in marriage migration 138-140; legal migration without spatial migration 143-6; research methods 141-2; research site 140-1; spatial migration before legal migration 142-3
spatial migration 5, 10, 137; of female marriage migrants 135; legal and 142, 143-6
Srinivas, M. N. 130
Stevenson, Betsey 98
subjective well-being 6, 9, 99
Suharto rule 35
Suryadinata, Leo 35
Sweden; Thai marriage migrants entrepreneurs in 90

Taiwan 2, 3, 6, 7, 9, 11, 13, 90, 94, 103, 149n4, 182; autonomy and power in 85; domestic violence law 84; equitable gender system in 84; gender systems compared 78-9; gendered expectations towards daughters 87-8; global gender-related indices 79; migrant women or local women 88-9; partial proportional ratio models of happiness 105-106; social role of married women in 85; son preference in 86; Vietnamese marriage migrants in 75
Taiwanese 103, 106; spoke Mandarin 111n2
Tartaglia, Stefano 96
Thailand 182, 193; internal migration 2

third-plus generations Asians 21, 23
touch-base policy 197
Toyota, M. 182
transnational marriages 3; in Asia 2; in Hong Kong 197, 200; in Singapore 2, 182, 193n1; in South Korea 2, 152, 163, 200; in Taiwan 2
Tsai, Ming-Chang 98
two-step social integration model, of VMM 77
two-way permits (TWPs) 137, 140, 141, 147

United States 7, 82, 161, 201; Asian immigrants in 7, 18; born Asians 19, 21; immigrants to 21; intercultural dating 38; international marriage migrants 149n3; Korean women immigrants in 96; migration-marriage link 53; second marriages in 198
urban migrants 8, 56, 62, 67, 68
Utomo, Ariane J. 6, 7, 37, 40

Vertovec, Steven 2
Vietnam 2, 9, 12, 90, 161, 182; domestic violence law 84; family meals 82; gender systems compared 78–9; global gender-related indices 79; internal migration 2
Vietnamese marriage migrants (VMMs) 9; analytic strategy 80–1; discussion 89–90; fieldwork 80–1; gender and immigrant integration 77–8; gender systems compared 78–9; methods 79–89; nationally-representative social surveys 81; results 81–9; rigid gendered expectations 82; sample 80–1; in South Korea 75; in Taiwan 75; two-step social integration model of 77
village endogamy, in India 10, 119, 121, 130
Viruell-Fuentes, Edna A. 97

white endogamy 30
Willing Hearts 194n3
Wolfers, Justin 98

Yang, Wen-Shan 9
Yeung, Wei-Jun Jean 6, 8
Yip, Paul S. F. 12, 198

Zhang, Huiping 198